British Romanticism and Prison Reform

TRANSITS
LITERATURE, THOUGHT & CULTURE, 1650–1850

A landmark series in long-eighteenth-century studies, *Transits* publishes monographs and edited volumes that are timely, transformative in their approach, and global in their engagement with arts, literature, culture, and history. Books in the series have engaged with visual arts, environment, politics, material culture, travel, theater and performance, embodiment, connections between the natural sciences and medical humanities, writing and book history, sexuality, gender, disability, race, and colonialism from Britain and Europe to the Americas, the Far East, the Middle/Near East, Africa, and Oceania. Works that make provocative connections across time, space, geography, or intellectual history, or that develop new modes of critical imagining are particularly welcome.

Recent titles in the series:

British Romanticism and Prison Reform
Jonas Cope

Prolific Ground: Landscape and British Women's Writing, 1690–1790
Nicolle Jordan

Consuming Anxieties: Alcohol, Tobacco, and Trade in British Satire, 1660–1751
Dayne C. Riley

The Part and the Whole in Early American Literature, Print Culture, and Art
Matthew Pethers and Daniel Diez Couch, eds.

Teaching the Eighteenth Century Now: Pedagogy as Ethical Engagement
Kate Parker and Miriam L. Wallace, eds.

Women and Music in the Age of Austen
Linda Zionkowski with Miriam F. Hart, eds.

Louis Sébastien Mercier: Revolution and Reform in Eighteenth-Century Paris
Michael J. Mulryan

Alimentary Orientalism: Britain's Literary Imagination and the Edible East
Yin Yuan

For more information about the series, please visit www.bucknelluniversitypress.org.

British Romanticism and Prison Reform

JONAS COPE

LEWISBURG, PENNSYLVANIA

Library of Congress Cataloging-in-Publication Data

Names: Cope, Jonas, author.
Title: British romanticism and prison reform / Jonas Cope.
Description: Lewisburg : Bucknell University Press, 2024. | Series: Transits: literature, thought & culture, 1650–1850 | Includes bibliographical references and index.
Identifiers: LCCN 2024015303 | ISBN 9781684485352 (paperback) | ISBN 9781684485369 (hardcover) | ISBN 9781684485376 (epub) | ISBN 9781684485383 (pdf)
Subjects: LCSH: Romanticism—Great Britain. | Prison reform in literature. | Prisons in literature. | English literature—18th century—History and criticism. | English literature—19th century—History and criticism. | LCGFT: Literary criticism.
Classification: LCC PR448.P685 C67 2024 | DDC 820.9/145—dc23/eng/20240528
LC record available at https://lccn.loc.gov/2024015303

A British Cataloging-in-Publication record for this book is available from the British Library.

∞ The paper used in this publication meets the requirements of the American National Standard for Information Sciences—Permanence of Paper for Printed Library Materials, ANSI Z39.48-1992.

bucknelluniversitypress.org

Distributed worldwide by Rutgers University Press

For Mary

CONTENTS

ABBREVIATIONS

In citing works short titles have generally been used. Works frequently cited have been identified by the following abbreviations:

CNM	William Godwin, *Collected Novels and Memoirs of William Godwin*, ed. Mark Philp, 8 vols. (London: William Pickering, 1992)
CW	William Godwin, *Caleb Williams*, ed. Pamela Clemit, vol. 3 of *Collected Novels and Memoirs of William Godwin*, ed. Mark Philp (London: William Pickering, 1992)
DE	William Godwin, *Deloraine*, ed. Maurice Hindle, vol. 8 of *Collected Novels and Memoirs of William Godwin*, ed. Mark Philp (London: William Pickering, 1992)
MP	Jane Austen, *Mansfield Park*, ed. John Wiltshire (Cambridge: Cambridge University Press, 2005)
NA	Jane Austen, *Northanger Abbey*, ed. Barbara M. Benedict and Deirdre Le Faye (Cambridge: Cambridge University Press, 2006)
P	Jane Austen, *Persuasion*, ed. Janet Todd and Antje Blank (Cambridge: Cambridge University Press, 2006)
PJ	William Godwin, *An Enquiry concerning Political Justice*, ed. Mark Philp and Austin Gee, vol. 3 of *Political and Philosophical Writings of William Godwin*, ed. Mark Philp (London: William Pickering, 1993)
PPW	William Godwin, *Political and Philosophical Writings of William Godwin*, ed. Mark Philp, 7 vols. (London: William Pickering, 1993)
R	Leigh Hunt, *The Story of Rimini*, ed. Greg Kucich and Jeffrey N. Cox, vol. 1 of *The Selected Writings of Leigh Hunt*, ed. Robert Morrison and Michael Eberle-Sinatra, 6 vols. (London: Pickering and Chatto, 2003)
SL	William Godwin, *St. Leon*, ed. Pamela Clemit, vol. 4 of *Collected Novels and Memoirs of William Godwin*, ed. Mark Philp (London: William Pickering, 1992)

SS	Jane Austen, *Sense and Sensibility*, ed. Edward Copeland (Cambridge: Cambridge University Press, 2006)
SWLH	Leigh Hunt, *The Selected Writings of Leigh Hunt*, ed. Robert Morrison and Michael Eberle-Sinatra, 6 vols. (London: Pickering and Chatto, 2003)

British Romanticism and Prison Reform

INTRODUCTION

FOR MOST OF THE EIGHTEENTH-CENTURY in Britain, lawbreakers were whipped, branded, hanged, or transported to America. It was only in the last quarter of the century that the state of criminal justice in Britain changed relatively quickly. The onset of the War of American Independence in 1775 halted the practice of transporting criminals to the American colonies. Bodily and capital punishment in Britain were coming increasingly under attack by lawyers, philanthropists, the clergy, politicians, and others. These and other factors meant that a new solution to the growing problem of crime was needed. That solution came in the form of the reformed prison, or penitentiary, an institution designed to educate, discipline, rehabilitate, and spiritualize even the most hardened felons. The first British penitentiaries, such as the New Bayley Prison in Manchester and the new Gaol and Penitentiary House in Gloucester (forerunners of modern prisons), appeared in the English provinces in the 1790s. They were the product of a total revolution in penal thought and practice, rooted in the early eighteenth century and coterminous with the literary movement in Britain we call Romantic.

This book maps a connection between these two cultural phenomena. It bridges a substantial gap between historical accounts of the birth of the modern prison in the West, on the one hand, and historicist criticism of late eighteenth- and early nineteenth-century British literature, on the other. No full-length study to date has explored this particular connection, despite critically demonstrated need. Most literary critics interested in penal reform tend to pass by the Romantic period (c. 1776–1837) and proceed straight to the literature of the Victorians. One explanation of this practice is that Romantic writers, especially Romantic poets, have always been so readily identified with all things antiauthoritarian and anti-coercion[1] that it has been easy to overlook their interest in the historically important distinction between *un*-reformed imprisonment, a practice almost universally criticized in the early nineteenth century, and *reformed* imprisonment, a then largely unprecedented idea that received considerable support from philanthropists, clerics, lawyers, politicians, magistrates, and, as I emphasize, writers of various kinds.[2]

Although there has been no full-length treatment of the relation between a survey of Romantic literary texts and reformed imprisonment as theorized and practiced in late eighteenth- and early nineteenth-century Britain, nonetheless the past fifty years or so have witnessed several critical articles, a few book chapters and the occasional monograph entirely or in part on the relation between literary Romanticism and punishment in the British Isles. Judith Thompson, John Bugg, and Jon Mee, for instance, have explored connections between political imprisonment and poetic production in the late 1790s. Each has read one or more lyrics by Samuel Taylor Coleridge as inspired in part by the trial and imprisonment of his friend John Thelwall, in 1794, on a charge of treason. Thompson has said that, in his "This Lime-Tree Bower My Prison," Coleridge "discovers and dramatizes the resources for restoration and empowerment to be found in . . . confined and repressive circumstances"; Bugg, not only that the poetry written by political prisoners may have helped shape what M. H. Abrams has called the Greater Romantic Lyric, but also that the "birth of 'prison literature'" in the 1790s "is twin to the birth of British Romanticism"; and Mee, that the figurative imprisonment featured in the same poem both domesticates and compensates for the actual imprisonment of Thelwall and other fin de siècle political radicals.[3] In 1988, furthermore, Judith Scheffler argued for the importance of "women prison authors" to Romantic literary culture; and in 2016 and 2021, Gabriel Cervantes and Dahlia Porter traced the influence of the famous prison reformer John Howard (1726–1790) on the work of a variety of Romantic and pre-Romantic poets, novelists, and playwrights, such as William Cowper, John Thelwall, Elizabeth Inchbald, and William Wordsworth.[4] A subset of critical studies centered specifically on Newgate Prison as the locus of a radical print culture developed between approximately 1996 and 2010 including, most notably, the work of Iain McCalman.[5]

A few of the more recent studies on the subject of literature and punishment explore the relation between state power and marginalized demographics. In *Vagrant Figures: Law, Literature, and the Origins of the Police* (2020), for instance, Sal Nicolazzo argues that a variety of literary texts by British and American authors, including picaresque novels, gothic novels, slave narratives, memoirs, and Romantic lyrics, helped shape prevailing understandings of vagrancy and vagrants in the long eighteenth century, reinforcing the capaciousness of vagrancy as a juridical category that included not only the poor, but also the homeless, the "unemployed, sex workers, itinerant performers," "strangers," and racialized others. For Nicolazzo, the shared rhetoric of these texts insists on vagrancy as an increasing cultural threat in need of containment, a rhetoric ultimately useful to the consolidation of the police as a modern institutional power. Underlying the argument of *Vagrant Figures* is the basic theoretical assumption, shared by the present work, that "legal practices" and "institutions," such as policing and police, are "forged" and "enacted through the circulation of writing," both legal and literary.[6] In 2022, Carrie Shanafelt reexamined the largely unpublished writings of Jeremy Bentham on sexuality, maintaining that, for Bentham, any sort of sexual pleasure, whether procreative or nonprocreative, heterosexual or homosexual, normative or nonnormative, is healthy and legitimate, so long as it takes place between consenting adults; and that any desire on the part of authorities to punish nonnormative sexual acts may be aesthetically, rather than morally, motivated. Thus, according to Shanafelt, "in every aspect of his work, Bentham rigorously foregrounded the experiences and desires of nonnormative, nonconforming, disenfranchised, marginalized, and oppressed groups as deserving of liberty and custodianship of their own bodies—including not only women, enslaved persons, and people who seek same-sex intimacy but also necrophiles, suicidal people, and nonhuman animals."[7]

Two monographs in particular have helped create a firm basis for studies of British Romanticism and imprisonment in the twenty-first century: *The Shadow of Death: Literature, Romanticism, and the Subject of Punishment* (2007), by Mark Canuel, and *Wordsworth's Vagrants: Police, Prisons and Poetry in the 1790s* (2011), by Quentin Bailey. Canuel suggests that the opposition to the death penalty prevalent in the early nineteenth century led to a radical revision of the very meaning of punishment. Punishment became increasingly understood not "as a philosophy or doctrine but rather as a troubling conjunction of contending rationales, recommending a sense of lenience and economy on the one hand, and a sense of severity and rigor on the other."[8] Bailey, limiting his study to the early poetry of Wordsworth—particularly *Adventures on Salisbury Plain* (1793–1794), *The Borderers* (1795–1797), "The Ruined Cottage" (1797), and *Lyrical Ballads* (1798)—argues that these early poems participate in contemporary "discussions of . . . penal reform about the value of punishment, the relative importance of economic and psychological factors in the commission of crime, and the possibility of reformation and rehabilitation." One of his central points is that these texts all tend to "critique . . . the techniques and practices of the penal law" and "the model of remorse deployed by writers and reformers like Hanway, Howard, and Bentham."[9] For Bailey, that is, the fictional criminals in the early poems never repent or reform in conditions of seclusion and meditation, as contemporary penal reformers hoped that real criminals would; on the contrary, their antisocial attitudes only become more entrenched.

While these and other studies provide a strong foundation for a body of interdisciplinary scholarship on literary Romanticism and punishment, more essential work in this area remains to be done. David Philips has made the striking claim that "in the period from the late eighteenth to the mid-nineteenth century . . . the whole apparatus of the state dealing with the criminal law, police and punishment underwent a revolution as substantial as the Industrial Revolution that Britain was experiencing at the same time."[10] If we accept this statement as valid, we may wonder, in turn, why most literary anthologies used in college classrooms continue to make the Industrial Revolution unquestionably central to the genesis and development of British Romanticism, yet say virtually nothing about what Philips finds to be an equally important revolution in punishment.

A fairly common explanation for this discrepancy is that Romantic writers, on average, were either unaware of or mostly uninterested in imprisonment as a contemporary institution. Aileen Ward, for one, argues that "as Blake's prophetic expectations of regeneration on earth faded, his metaphors of bondage and freedom underwent a significant change. Prison came to seem not an instrument of class oppression but the very nature of earthly life: the manacles that bind humanity are mind-forged, 'chains of the mind' . . . not to be struck off by any act of political or social liberation."[11] Ward goes on to say that Blake, beginning in the 1790s, uses the prison image in an increasingly universal and metaphorical sense, overlooking imprisonment in Britain as a material and historical reality. She concludes that "with the passing of the historical crisis of the [French] Revolution the imagery of . . . prison was depoliticized in both Wordsworth . . . and Blake, to change into a wider symbolism of the human condition."[12] Uwe Böker makes the related but more extreme claim that "the new methods of incarceration . . . went unnoticed by the English Romantic poets," who were "more interested in poetic 'dungeons' of absolutist European descent than in the actual debates on prison reform" in and out of Parliament and across the British Isles.[13] Ulrich Broich likewise argues that "after the French Revolution . . . the prison discourse in England moves in new and diverse directions. . . . Writers are no longer primarily interested in specific abuses of the contemporary prison system and in specific concepts of reform but much more in prisons as products of a legal and social system that has to be questioned."[14] All three claims tend to exaggerate the truth. Of course Romantic poets used the language of imprisonment metaphorically and symbolically, and often. That is to be expected. Yet poets such as Wordsworth, Coleridge, and Leigh Hunt were all well aware of the rise of penitential imprisonment in Britain and the debates that fueled it. Their literary and nonliterary writings testify to this awareness, tentatively supporting reformed imprisonment even while acknowledging the fundamental inhumanity of the legal deprivation of liberty.

Thus a full-length, interdisciplinary study of literary Romanticism and the rise of reformative imprisonment in Britain is overdue. Broich noted in 2007 that "the literary discourse on prisons in the 1790s and after . . . has been neglected in previous studies" of Romanticism and punishment.[15] Gary Kelly likewise argued, a year later, that

> treatments of crime and punishment have tended to be divided into, and studied separately as, the literary and social representations on the one hand and the theoretical, statistical, documentary, legislative and similar kinds of representations on the other. Cultural studies and "new historicist" approaches to crime and punishment in the past few decades have been more inclined to bring these separate disciplinary and discursive spheres closer together. Nevertheless, there remains a need for, and a usefulness to, enabling that convergence.[16]

Enabling that convergence is a large part of the scholarly work that remains to be done. What Kelly calls the literary and the social representations of crime and punishment may, indeed, be studied side by side. Late eighteenth-century theoretical essays on the merits of solitary confinement in prisons, for instance, may be read alongside contemporary lyric poems on the virtues of solitary reflection in a narrow space. Poems and novels may be examined that simultaneously reinforce and resist the values explicit in the 1779 Penitentiary Act, as well as in numerous cultural documents influenced wholly or partly by this act—surveys of English prisons, political pamphlets, newspaper articles, reports of parliamentary committees, theoretical essays on punishment, and so on. These and related studies will clarify and strengthen awareness of what Cervantes and Porter, in 2016, called the "sustained cultural engagement with prison reform" that "cuts across genres, media, and social divisions" in late eighteenth- and early nineteenth-century Britain.[17]

To trace the nature and extent of this "cultural engagement," across authors of varying social stations, across media and genres, across the British Isles, across a period of roughly sixty years, is the work of a vast and emergent critical subfield. A single full-length study of this engagement cannot possibly aim to be exhaustive or representative. Nor does the present study have any pretensions to be either. The following chapters examine a specific set of literary and nonliterary texts that address the advent of prison reform in Britain via a shared and clearly defined set of rhetorical strategies, and it is clear that a very different set of authors, or genres, or rhetorical strategies, or media, may have been chosen for a related study within the same critical subfield. The intersectional relation between gender or race and the advent of contemporary reformative confinement, for instance, with which the recent work of Nicolazzo and Shanafelt is concerned, is an important and relatively new area of interest within this critical subfield. The explosion of gothic novels in the 1790s also deserves further consideration in light of the advent of penitential confinement. Gothic novels famously made "confinement, particularly of an innocent female character, . . . a major motif."[18] Mary Ellen Snodgrass notes, furthermore, that "after the formation of Gothic conventions in the late 18th century, authors used cells, murder holes, and oubliettes to accentuate claustrophobia, mental torment, and terror," "settings [that] typically produced a living death in some forgotten cell."[19] This one fact opens several possible critical investigations. How and to what extent is this motific trend in gothic literature a response to the cultural aftermath of the 1779 Penitentiary Act, for example, which proposed regulated solitary confinement, religious instruction, a labor regime, and a sparse diet as a means to the reformation and salvation of criminals; or to the forty-two new gaols and bridewells built in Britain between 1779 and 1787 in accordance with the principles of this act; or to the fact that a number of political prisoners in the mid-1790s awaited trial or served time within one of the new prisons, such as, most infamously, Coldbath Fields? These and numerous related avenues of inquiry remain to be explored in more detail.

This book connects the form and historicity of literary texts imaginatively organized around themes of imprisonment—a set of lyric and narrative poems and several novels—to the rise of penal reform and the birth of the modern prison in late eighteenth- and early nineteenth-century Britain. The texts I examine treat the prison image as essentially ambiguous. On the one hand, images of or associated with imprisonment suggest oppression, the arbitrary power of legal structures; on the other, they are allied to heightened meditation, intensified imagination, an awakened conscience, or sincere emotions. Thus Coleridge uses metaphors of imprisonment to describe a state of contentment, enlightenment, and freedom. Leigh Hunt capitalizes on his actual confinement in a London prison for two years to produce a poem—his most famous—whose imaginative heights he suggests are inversely proportionate to his physical limitations, as though he were actualizing the comment by Joseph Addison, that "a Man in a Dungeon is capable of entertaining himself with Scenes and Landskips more beautiful than any that can be found in the whole Compass of Nature"; or of J. G. Zimmermann (1728–1795), that "it is certainly true that a person possessed of a fine imagination may be much happier in prison, than he could possibly be without imagination amidst the most magnificent scenery"; or of Jean-Jacques Rousseau, that "if I want to depict the Spring I must be in the winter . . . if I want to describe a beautiful countryside I must be inside walls, and I have said a hundred times that if I were ever put in the Bastille, I would paint the tableau of freedom there."[20] John Keats uses images of immurement in his verse to describe a variety of moral and emotional trials, whose rewards are ultimately worth the pains of confinement; Lord Byron portrays imprisonment simultaneously as a source of anguish and a source of intellectual freedom; and several novels by William Godwin and Jane Austen associate conditions of seclusion and restraint with acute moral insight.

Another relevant class of (usually noncanonical) literary texts prevalent in the late eighteenth and early nineteenth centuries portrays actual, historical penal reform in Britain in ways that are unambiguously approving. In *The Prison: A Poem* (1790), for instance, Thomas Fowler urges Britons to

> Construct with speed the solitary cell;
> Each individual there humanely place
> And all improper intercourse expell.
>
> It surely far surpasses punishment
> If aught th' internal monitor can wake;
> Can prompt the real pang for time mis-spent,
> And firm resolve each error to forsake.[21]

The meaning of these lines is clear: imprisonment is hardly punishment if the prisoner is placed "humanely" in a "solitary cell" where he or she can be safe from "improper intercourse" and reflect on his or her past sins. Or there is the play *Such Things Are* (1788), by Elizabeth Inchbald, a play performed at Covent Garden and most likely read by Godwin. The father of prison reform himself, John Howard, appears in *Such Things Are* under the name of "Haswell," a character who dreams of a time when all men and women "sentenced . . . to confinement" will have their "hearts . . . bent down with penitence to Heaven."[22]

This book demonstrates how and to what extent these and related texts do important ideological work. The traditionally canonical poems by Coleridge, Hunt, Keats, Byron, John Clare, and others, for example, tend to elaborate, strengthen, and valorize an association between the deprivation of the body and the elevation of the imagination, with the elevation of the imagination often accompanying or facilitating moral reform. The less canonical poems are more or less straightforward propaganda for the new prisons. All such texts serve ultimately to reconcile a culture proverbially in love with civil freedom to the apparent inevitability of reformed imprisonment as the hegemonic, and ideally rehabilitative, form of punishment in the years to come. They represent the unsolicited cooperation of certain literary and private documents in enabling the penal revolution of the late eighteenth and early nineteenth centuries.

A SKETCH OF EARLY PENAL REFORM IN BRITAIN

There were comparatively few city gaols in Britain prior to the eighteenth century.[23] At that time, imprisonment was reserved mainly for persons of distinction awaiting trial, whereas felons were primarily whipped, branded, or hanged. The first bridewell, or house of correction, appeared in London in 1556. Bridewells were originally meant to address vagrancy, idleness, moral offenses, and other petty criminality by employing inmates in various trades and teaching them industrious habits. They were thus the "first experiment in corrective incarceration" in

Britain.[24] By the eighteenth century, however, bridewells in general had lost their institutional distinctiveness and become conflated with gaols, which were primarily custodial institutions.[25] The first transportation of serious criminals from the British Isles to the American colonies occurred in 1614–1615, though the regular use of transportation as an "intermediary punishment that fell between branding and the gallows" was not established until 1718.[26]

The first three-quarters of the eighteenth century in Britain saw a number of minor but important reforms in penal law and practice. Legislation was passed in 1670 to ensure that debtors and felons were kept separate in gaols, who beforehand were indiscriminately mixed;[27] in 1751, a law was passed to prohibit the sale of liquor in prisons (a practice that continued nonetheless);[28] Newgate Prison in London was razed in 1767 and rebuilt over the next several decades;[29] the practice of *peine forte et dure*, or the placing of weights on a person refusing to plead guilty until he or she either relented or died, ended in 1772;[30] Parliament authorized the appointment of clerics in prisons in 1773;[31] an act ordering prisons to be periodically cleaned, to include sick rooms, and to appoint a prison physician was passed in 1774;[32] and in the same year gaolers were forbidden by law to extract fees for themselves from acquitted or discharged prisoners prior to releasing them.[33]

These and other legislative reforms in Britain occurred in the context of a European-wide reevaluation of the meaning, aims, and justifications of punishment. In his *L'Esprit des lois* (*The Spirit of the Laws*) (1748), the French judge and political philosopher Montesquieu discouraged the use of extreme punishments, such as death, so as to limit the number of cases in which either victims of crimes were too afraid to prosecute, or juries were too afraid to convict (problems that resonated strongly in England). According to Leon Radzinowicz, Montesquieu "denounced the concept of punishment based on extreme intimidation and by so doing paved the way for more enlightened and humane doctrines to come."[34] The Italian philosopher and criminologist Cesare Beccaria followed suit in 1764 with the publication of *Dei delitti e delle pene*, first translated in English in 1767 under the title *Of Crimes and Punishments*. Beccaria argued that it is always better to prevent crimes by deterrence than to convict and punish criminals, since deterrence was likely to be effective in a society in which "the evil . . . [a punishment] inflicts on the offender exceeds the advantage he derived from his crime"; that a punishment should be proportionate in severity to its offense; that it should be applied uniformly and inevitably by all courts; and that torture should be eliminated.[35] The year 1771 saw the publication of *Principles of Penal Law*, by the British politician William Eden. Eden "laid the theoretical foundation for the reform of the penal code by contending that every wanton, unnecessary suffering inflicted by the legislature was tyrannical and unjustified."[36] He was for retaining the use of capital punishment, but only within a very narrow compass.

The year 1776 was an immense turning point in the history of British penal reform. The War of American Independence forced the British government to begin using old sea vessels, called hulks, as places of temporary confinement, since authorities could no longer transport felons to the American colonies (the transportation of British felons to Australia would begin in 1787). Hulks were meant as a temporary solution to the disruption of transportation, but lasted well into the nineteenth century. In 1776, the British evangelical philanthropist Jonas Hanway (1712–1786) published *Solitude in Imprisonment*, one of his many pamphlets on penal reform, and in the following year John Howard released his groundbreaking, magisterial *The State of the Prisons in England and Wales.* In *Solitude in Imprisonment*, Hanway emphasized the importance of individual reformation in penitential prisons; in his case, "reformation" meant religious conversion or redemption within the Church of England. Hanway argued that the suffering of offenders should no longer amount to "physical pain exploited in a drama intended for an audience"—as was the case at public hangings—but that suffering should become "a spiritual ordeal provoked for the prisoner's own good. The prison was simply the passive setting for such a struggle; the prisoner's own conscience inflicted the suffering. Hanway saw the prison as a more suitable emblem of divine justice, displacing the gallows, which had for centuries been considered an appropriate representation of the human predicament before an omnipotent judge."[37]

Arguably the strongest motivator both for the reform of prisons and for the establishment of imprisonment as *the* alternative to capital punishment was John Howard. By 1777, Howard had made well over 200 visits to prisons in the British Isles and abroad. Between 1773 and 1783 he is said to have traveled 42,033 miles in the process of compiling his data.[38] His *State of the Prisons* effectively made "the prison the center of focus, shifting all other forms of punishment to the margins" and "creat[ing] the impression that the prison was the natural and inevitable shape of punishment" for the foreseeable future.[39] Howard impressed the minds of his contemporaries in a way almost hard for us to imagine. One contemporary of his, an Anglican priest, called *State of the Prisons* both an "immortal Work" and "the strongest Exhibition of Philanthropy since the Foundation . . . of our Religion."[40] A British lawyer noted in 1785 that recent legislative acts of penal reform, inspired primarily by Howard, "constitute one of the happiest characteristics of the Age in which they have been adopted."[41] Countless artists paid tribute to Howard and his tireless pursuit of the reformation of prisons and prison administration across Europe. They respected his core beliefs; namely, that "each criminal . . . was a rational and immortal being, [that] reformation must be the primary end of punishment, and [that] reformation meant that a man should accept the salvation of God. These beliefs underlay the whole of his penal theory."[42]

In the wake of *State of the Prisons* in 1777, penal legislation was passed and prisons and bridewells were built or rebuilt in Britain at an astonishing rate. The first penitentiary opened at Horsham in Sussex in 1778. Its prisoners slept in separate cells at night (but could associate by day), the environment was clean and healthy, and all felons wore a uniform and drank only water.[43] The famous Penitentiary Act of 1779—"the most forward-looking English penal measure of its time"—proposed to erect two national penitentiaries in London (never built, though realized in 1816 in the form of the first national penitentiary in Britain, located at Millbank), whose purpose was to reform offenders through periodic solitary confinement, religious instruction and regular industry.[44] Numerous related acts of penal reform were passed in its wake. The Penitentiary Act also set the penological standard for scores of local gaols, bridewells, gaol-bridwell hybrids, and penitentiaries erected or reconstructed over the next two decades, including "forty-two new gaols and houses of correction . . . built in the years between 1779 and 1787," and a number of important institutions constructed thereafter, such as Gloucester Penitentiary in 1792 and Coldbath Fields House of Correction, in London, in 1794.[45]

The importance of the decline of capital punishment to the rise of the modern prison, moreover, cannot be underestimated. Not only capital punishment per se, but the nature and extent of its application in Britain, were a strong incentive to penal reform in the eighteenth and early nineteenth centuries. The issue was the so-called Bloody Code. In 1769, the jurist and judge William Blackstone noted that "It is a melancholy truth, that among the variety of actions which men are daily liable to commit, no less than an hundred and sixty have been declared by act of Parliament to be felonies without the benefit of clergy; or, in other words, to be worthy of instant death."[46] (Benefit of clergy was essentially a literacy test whose passing spared a first-time offender from execution, originally applied to clergy, but extended over time to any person convicted of a capital offense from which this benefit had not yet been removed.) The number of capital offenses in Britain eventually rose from a 160 to 200.[47] The main issue for penal reformers was that, in spite of these large figures, a relatively small and arbitrary number of capital offenders were actually killed by the Bloody Code. It was never applied uniformly, consistently, or fairly. Thus the Bloody Code

> made virtually every felony capital, but felons were in fact rarely executed. Many convicted felons received royal pardons, usually on the advice of the sentencing judge. Many others were accorded the "benefit of clergy," branded on the thumb (so that they could not again claim "benefit") and spared. Many of those pardoned, and many who received the benefit of clergy, were "transported" to one of the American colonies. Still, an occa-

sional "wretch" (the term commentators invariably used) was executed, usually after a public procession to the gallows. Minor felons were often whipped.[48]

The Bloody Code was significantly relaxed by the early nineteenth century,[49] and, conveniently, the new ideology of reformative confinement in penitential prisons was available to take its place.

The Bloody Code had its supporters as well as its detractors. The lawyer-turned-minister Martin Madan, in his *Thoughts on Executive Justice* (1785), argued that "the frequency of pardons . . . vitiated the terrors of the capital statutes," and he "proposed that no capital convicts should be reprieved from execution."[50] Madan saw the "frequent failure to carry out capital sentences" as "undoing all the good produced by the judicial drama" at the assizes.[51] The philosopher and clergyman William Paley, likewise, defended the death penalty in his *Principles of Moral and Political Philosophy* (1785). Paley supported the "doctrine of maximum severity" that was popular throughout the eighteenth century and that held that only "terrifying" and "barbaric" modes of execution would effectively deter crime and, thereby, reduce the amount of persons executed.[52] (Paley even wanted to "increase the horrors of execution in private by, for instance, casting murderers into a den of wild beasts."[53]) Both Madan and Paley came under attack in 1786 by the lawyer and legal reformer Samuel Romilly. Romilly "voiced more gentle and humane sentiments" than either of his two predecessors. He suggested that "crime was a product of a flawed society and that all members of it were comprehended in the guilt"; argued to reduce the number of capital offenses; denounced the use of the hulks; and pleaded for the systemic use of an institution, both charitable and penal, whose primary end was the reformation of offenders.[54]

THE CONTENT OF THIS BOOK

Twentieth- and twenty-first-century histories of imprisonment tend to fall under one of two classes: traditionalist and revisionist. Traditionalist histories "largely accepted the case argued by eighteenth- and nineteenth-century reformers that the 'Bloody Code' was arbitrary and savage, and considered that the reformers' stance was morally and rationally unassailable" as an alternative. Then, in 1975, the French historian Michel Foucault published *Discipline and Punish*, initiating a wave of so-called revisionist histories. The revisionists agreed with the traditionalists that the Bloody Code was gratuitously violent, erratically enforced, and clearly ineffective, but warned us not to accept reformed imprisonment uncritically. They found unsettling "parallels," in fact, "between the new prisons and other emerging institutions," such as factories and workhouses, and saw the penitentiary as yet "another institution concerned with discipline and social control"—a more efficient and ultimately more insidious way to punish living souls, rather than a humane or rational alternative to physical punishment and legalized murder.[55]

This book errs on the side of the traditionalist perspective, insofar as it takes the professed motivations of evangelical reformers seriously. Foucault, for his part, tends to dismiss these motivations as virtually nonexistent or inconsequential. He mostly tells us what he thinks penitentiaries *did* as though the religious and humanitarian debates that brought them into existence never happened. And yet, the fact is that a number of evangelical reformers in the late eighteenth and early nineteenth centuries saw penitential imprisonment as a humane alternative to disfigurement or death, an alternative meant not simply to hold or punish the body, but to regenerate and ultimately save human souls. Foucault understands the modern prison essentially as a mechanistic, bureaucratic, and ruthlessly efficient means of normalization, part of the widescale production of docile bodies and passive minds subject to the meddling interventions (and inventions) of psychologists and other extralegal specialists. None of this is to say that penitentiaries never became institutions designed, to varying extents, to shape the subjectivities of their inmates. They did. It is rather to give due emphasis to the importance of the motivations that lay behind such designs, motivations that the postmodernist narrative of the birth of the modern prison, particularly as Foucault tells it, downplays considerably.

A few relatively recent critics, contra Foucault and the revisionists, have, in fact, emphasized the role of religion in the advancement of penal reform in Britain. Laurie Throness convincingly argues, for instance, that secular justice in the form of the penitentiary was modeled explicitly on contemporary understandings of divine justice.[56] Lissa Paul reminds us that reform in punishment was coexistent with the rise of Methodism, and that "at the heart of the early Methodist mission was the constant reaffirmation that the sinful would be forgiven and redeemed."[57] Follett observes that evangelical MPs "cast the key votes that committed the House of Commons to criminal law reforms over Government objections," engaged in activism that "helped bring others around to the reformers' view" and "shaped the options for reform."[58] In 2019, Hilary Carey "challenge[d] the historical stereotypes which equate religious intervention with malevolent social control," "tak[ing] a lead from the 'religious turn' in historical writing about the penitentiary, including the rediscovery of the religious foundations of early prison reform."[59] All of the following chapters engage, to varying extents, with the religious origins of penitential imprisonment in Britain and the implications of these origins in literary and nonliterary writing.

The first chapter of this book explores how and to what extent "This Lime-Tree Bower My Prison" sympathizes with the values of Howardian penal reform as Coleridge understood it. In his insistence on the need to evangelize the poor and the unfortunate; in his belief, between 1795 and 1801, both in the doctrine of Necessity and in the association of ideas—doctrines held by "all the penologists" at the time;[60] in his glorification of John Howard; in his pleas, in prose and verse, for salutary conditions in British gaols; and in his faith in human perfectibility through introspection and penance; in all these respects Coleridge supported reformed imprisonment as the most viable alternative to capital punishment in the long run. His support is especially evident in "This Lime-Tree Bower My Prison" and in his more overtly pro-prison-reform poem, "The Dungeon" (as prepared for *Lyrical Ballads*). In the former, conditions of restraint, deprivation, and solitude induce in the speaker a spirit of moral and imaginative wakefulness; in the latter, the unreformed qualities of the dungeon are precisely what prevent its inmate from experiencing this wakefulness.

Chapter 2 studies the essays and novels of the husband of Mary Wollstonecraft, the father of Mary Shelley, and the philosophical anarchist, William Godwin. Godwin visited his politically radical friends in British prisons and established a philosophy stressing the fundamental evils of coercion in his major philosophical treatise, *An Enquiry concerning Political Justice* (1793). The first half of the chapter demonstrates that his statements on the evils of all coercion need to be balanced against his eventual concessions to the need for "mild" coercion in a vicious society, his comments on the virtues of monastic solitude, and his tendency to associate confined space—an association dramatized in his novel *Fleetwood* (1805)—with enlightened introspection, imagination, and piety. The second half of chapter 2 examines numerous scenes of imprisonment in three Godwinian novels: *Caleb Williams* (1794), *St. Leon* (1799), and *Deloraine* (1833). Critics such as Marilyn Butler, Pamela Clemit, and Peter Marshall have argued that one or more of these novels portray prisons as hopeless and unequivocal evils. Yet this view needs qualification. In all three texts the protagonist is forcefully placed in at least one prison (sometimes several) for an extended period of time, during which the narrative usually stays with the hero and explores the psychological effects of prolonged confinement. Many of these effects are not what one would expect from a writer of such anti-coercion politics as Godwin. Caleb Williams, Reginald St. Leon, and William Deloraine, that is, are all compensated for their respective confinements in dramatic ways. Caleb Williams learns in prison the value of a life of retirement, philosophy, and benevolence. Reginald St. Leon, while held in a number of prisons, engages in metaphysical speculation, forms a plan for the economic liberation of Hungary, and learns to value all human lives, especially the lives of his enemies. William Deloraine comes to love a castle-prison, in which he and his daughter are confined, as their own Miltonic paradise. Deloraine even receives intimations of his own immortality during this confinement, as the world of death and flux beyond the castle walls fades into meaninglessness.

The third chapter shifts from Godwin, a radical who visited his friends in metropolitan prisons, to the poet, journalist, literary critic, and essayist Leigh Hunt, a radical who lived in a prison himself for two years. Hunt was sentenced to two years in Horsemonger Lane Gaol in South London (1813–1815) for publishing a libel of the prince regent in his weekly paper the *Examiner*. His experience of confinement was sui generis. Throughout his sentence, he learned to balance his public identity as a political radical with his public identity as a man of letters, his health improved, his stock of literary and philosophical knowledge increased, he forged new relationships and strengthened existing ones, he established a new and lasting work ethic that he reported joyfully to his wife, he produced some of his best literary criticism, and he composed (most of) his most celebrated poem, *The Story of Rimini* (1816). In all these ways, Hunt effectively depoliticized his punishment, treating it less as the consequence of a political offense and more as a moral and imaginative retreat. Most critics who have examined *Rimini* in light of the circumstances of its composition say that Hunt wrote it as a way to escape a wretched and tedious confinement; they view the imagined world of the poem as utterly fantastic in contradistinction to the grim reality of life at Horsemonger Lane Gaol. I argue instead that Hunt wrote *Rimini* both to allegorize his experience of confinement and to immortalize it. *Rimini* dramatizes the long and gradual process by which Hunt was forced to refine his perceptual faculties, so as to be able to exhaust the aesthetic potential of a very limited set of sensory phenomena.

Chapter 4 is a joint study of (mainly) *Endymion* (1818), by John Keats, and *The Prisoner of Chillon* (1816), by George Gordon, Lord Byron, two artists fascinated with the psychological effects of imprisonment in general, and with the imprisonment of their friend, fellow poet, and early mentor, Leigh Hunt, in particular.

Keats took the imprisonment of Hunt and depoliticized it even more than Hunt did. He inaugurated his own poetic career with a sonnet called "Written on the Day That Mr. Leigh Hunt Left Prison" (1817), in which the power of the sonnet to achieve more in less space coalesces rhetorically with the power of Hunt to do the same in Horsemonger Lane Gaol. In his letters and in his verse, moreover, Keats routinely images both artistic power and perfect intimacy in terms of imprisonment. Often where there is an image of the creative imagination, or eroticism, or devotion, an image of confinement is nearby and somehow related. I argue that what Nicholas Roe calls "the aura of idealism and romance surrounding Hunt in prison" helped to motivate this practice.[61] Hunt lived in an actual prison for two years that he exploited as his sanctuary of imagination and love. Keats romanticizes and expands this Huntean narrative in "Ode to Psyche," *Lamia*, *Endymion*, and other poems, which tell us that in isolation, in seclusion, in and through a sort of sacred pain, the mind and heart may be purified and exalted. This practice offers a new way to understand certain crucial scenes in Keats's poetry that involve ambiguous enclosures, enclosures that critics such as Helen Vendler, Jacqueline Labbe, and Rachel Crawford have said suggest paradise as well as death, inspiration as well as sterility.[62]

Both Keats's *Endymion* and Byron's *The Prisoner of Chillon* dramatize states of vacuity and deprivation that ultimately lead to a kind of transcendence. *The Prisoner of Chillon* is a dramatic monologue voiced by an unnamed individual, known as the Prisoner, who is loosely based on a sixteenth-century Savoyard aristocrat, François Bonivard. In the poem, the Prisoner tells the story of his six long years held in confinement in Chillon Castle in Switzerland. Most critical responses to *The Prisoner of Chillon* amount to a psychological or moral appraisal of its speaker. The majority of readers insist that we find the Prisoner outright pathetic, since he shows no remorse in prison, creates nothing, gains no moral insight, undergoes no spiritual conversion, and leaves Chillon Castle unprepared to live sociably in the world. A few critics, on the other hand, admire the fact that the Prisoner adapts to life at Chillon Castle as though it were the real world, and as though the world outside of it were a prison. Although such readings are fair, the poem itself, it seems to me, mostly invites confusion over the integrity of its speaker—moral or otherwise. First of all, he may not be entirely reliable as a narrator. Second, there are solid reasons to admire him and solid reasons to pity or condemn him, but these are ultimately left in a state of unresolved tension. Rather than assess his character, therefore, I examine the poem historically as a response to contemporary interest in and enthusiasm for the practice of reformative solitude, especially as that interest and enthusiasm were generated via the wildly popular and sensational poem *Thoughts in Prison* (1777), written by the Anglican priest William Dodd in Newgate after he was tried and found guilty of forgery in February 1777. Dodd finished the poem in around two months, still in Newgate. Despite much popular protest, he received his (delayed) death sentence in May and was hanged in June.

The English Romantic poet John Clare, the subject of chapter 5, lived in two mental institutions between 1837 (age 44) and his death in 1864. The critical consensus on his illness is that he had bipolar disorder. This chapter is less interested in guessing at the state of his mental health, however, than in the way Clare acclimated to the asylums in a series of interrelated poems that read as a literary romance, a romance, as it happens, that conforms relatively consistently to the theory of romance advanced by Northrop Frye in his *Anatomy of Criticism* (1957) and *Secular Scripture* (1976), and that would not have taken the shape it did had not Clare increasingly imagined himself as homeless, and on and off as a captive, after 1836. The poems in question are collected under the title *Child Harold* (1840–1841). Further study of *Child Harold* is necessary because many critics of the poem to date hardly know what to do with it, reading it, if they read it at all, as emotionally volatile, as fragmented, as an awkward blend of literary forms and styles. Yet the obscurity of *Child Harold* is undeserved. The poem can be read as a unified or total text modeled after a literary form with a long and rich history, the romance, as well as an aesthetic inroad into what life in an early Victorian asylum was like for a poet who imaginatively responded to it. Clare created a lyrical romance out of his life at the asylums as a means of achieving a sort of mythological independence over space and time.

The sixth and final chapter begins by describing, with the assistance of archival evidence, how, between 1804 and 1808, Edward Austen Knight, the third eldest brother of Jane Austen, helped conceive, design, and oversee a reformed gaol and house of correction in the city of Canterbury, East Kent.[63] The new Canterbury Gaol and House of Correction, as it was called, was a progressive penal institution. Austen herself accompanied her brother on a periodical inspection of the new prison at least one time that we know of. I argue that several of her novels reflect this visit and, more broadly, the legal and political contexts that enabled it. The mature novels feature what I call penitential spaces, enclosed domestic spaces that share characteristics associated with the ideology and practice of contemporary reformative confinement. These spaces foreground and authenticate the moral growth or psychological development of characters who spend any considerable amount of time in them. I first describe the personal exposure Austen had to the administration of criminal justice at the local level through her acquaintances, friends, family, and especially her brother Edward Austen Knight. Afterward, I explain how her novels assimilate conditions linked to the new penitential confinement, such as enclosure, seclusion, piety, solitary reflection, routine, discipline, and sobriety, in ways that address contemporary social conflicts associated with the rise of corrective punishment. The time for this study is opportune. Recent historicist scholarship on Austen, crime, Evangelicalism, and the efforts of local government to relieve the unfortunate has facilitated an increasing body of work on Austen and punishment.[64]

1

SOLITARY CONFINEMENT

"This Lime-Tree Bower My Prison"

THE FAMOUS ANCIENT MARINER and his ill-fated crew are sailing northward on the Pacific, when their ship reaches the equator and suddenly halts. The winds die and the sails drop. The crew grow parched and despairing, as the sea around their frozen ship crawls with legged "slimy things." Things look bleak. Then at once a mysterious vessel made of bones—the Mariner calls it a "naked Hulk"—appears on the horizon, its sails torn to shreds. The hulk moves toward the Mariner and his crew without wind or sail. Soon the crew can make out its "naked ribs, which fleck'd / The sun that did behind them peer."[1] The Mariner describes the phenomenon with an arresting simile.

> And strait the Sun was fleck'd with bars
> (Heaven's mother send us grace)
> As if thro' a dungeon grate he peer'd
> With broad and burning face.[2]

Here the sun is personified. It is gendered male, and it has a "broad and burning face" that can "peer" through the "bars," earlier called "ribs," of the skeletal ship, "as if thro' a dungeon grate." The prison simile in these lines is one of the most striking images in the poem. The Mariner compares the bonelike frame of the skeletal ship to a grate fixed in the door of a prison, used to permit communication with an inmate while denying the inmate physical access to the communicator. One wonders where, exactly, the prison space is meant to be located, according to the spatial situation implied by this simile. Is the entire interior of the skeletal vessel the prison? Is it everything around that vessel, or on one or another side of it? Does it move as the ship moves? More, why is this simile here and what are its effects? Michael O'Neill reads the stanza less as a diegetic scene we are meant to visualize, and more as a grim symbol of earthly existence in general. O'Neill suggests that the word "'Sun' here puns on the 'Son' whose Mother is invoked in the next line; but this Son peers 'through a dungeon-grate,' a ferocious gaoler gazing at those imprisoned in this life."[3]

The stanza in question is also connected to the historical reality of imprisonment in the late eighteenth century. It seems likely, for instance, that the lines allude to the gaol fever epidemic in Britain. Gaol fever had been ravaging prisoners across the British Isles from the earliest times up to 1797, when Samuel Taylor Coleridge began "The Rime of the Ancyent Marinere." Only in the 1780s did conditions in prisons begin to improve. John Howard made the shocking observation in 1777 that goal fever had killed far more lawbreakers in Britain than the gallows ever did.[4] One of its most renowned victims, Lord George Gordon, died in Newgate Prison in 1793, a few years before "The Rime of the Ancyent Marinere" was composed. We now know that gaol fever, or typhus fever, is transferred by a microorganism called *Rickettsia prowazekii*, which is carried by body lice. As Margaret DeLacy points out, the microorganism requires "dirt (to support the lice) and malnutrition or stress (to lower resistance). Since lice do not fly and since they die rapidly once infected with typhus, they cannot carry the disease very far; close contact, therefore, is necessary to spread the disease and overcrowding is necessary to support a large epidemic."[5] The phrase "burning face" also makes sense in light of the fact that those infected with typhus are subject to high fevers.

It may also be no coincidence that the Mariner calls the ghostly skeletal ship a "Hulk." The actual hulks—decommissioned sea vessels used as prisons and harbored along the Thames and in southern seaports—were flourishing in 1797. Since their establishment in 1776, about 8,000 convicts had been sent to them by the time Coleridge was writing his poem.[6] If we think of the supernatural "naked Hulk" as inspired by the real British prison hulks, which, it should be noted, also needed no rigging and no sails, we can read the sickliness of its two-person crew as sly social commentary on the notoriously inhumane conditions on board the British prison ships. The skeleton ship advancing on the Mariner contains only two figures, Death and Death-in-Life. Death is portrayed as a skeleton with "jet-black and bare" bones, "patch'd" here and there "with purple and green" owing to the "rust / Of mouldy damps." His female companion, Death-in-Life, has flesh "as white as leprosy."[7] As the "Spectre-ship" veers close, the Mariner sees the grisly pair playing a game of dice. He learns that they are playing for human lives—the lives of himself and of his crew.[8] Soon the game is up; Death wins the crew. The Mariner sees two-hundred of his own men instantly fall dead aboard his ship. He recalls that

> Their souls did from their bodies fly,—
> They fled to bliss or woe;
> And every soul it pass'd me by,
> Like the whiz of my Cross-bow.[9]

The crew go either to "bliss or woe." In Protestant terms, this means that some of the crew are immediately relocated to paradise ("bliss")—that portion of Hades where Protestants believed souls destined for heaven wait out the time between their deaths and the Last Judgment—whereas others fly to Gehenna ("woe")—that portion of Hades where souls bound for hell wait out *their* time. Not Death, but Death-in-Life, wins the Mariner. He remains alive.

All lines from "The Rime of the Ancyent Marinere" cited so far refer to events that occur in part III of the poem. It is in part IV that the Mariner undergoes what Coleridge, in an 1834 note to the poem, calls his "penance."[10] With his crew dead at his feet, the Mariner finds himself alive and "alone, alone, all all alone / Alone on the wide wide Sea." He tries to pray, but finds that "Christ would take no pity" on him: "or ever a prayer had gusht, / A wicked whisper came and made / My heart as dry as dust." So the Mariner closes his eyes and over the next seven days he continues to try to pray. It is only when he both apprehends and "declare[s]" the "beauty" of all "living things," and when he blesses, in particular, the water snakes, that his curse is lifted: "the self-same moment I could pray; / And from my neck so free / The Albatross fell off, and sank / Like lead into the sea."[11]

An interesting juxtaposition is at work in parts III and IV of the poem. The skeletal ship may be read as an image of unreformed imprisonment. It is called a "Hulk," it moves without rigging or sails, it is described as a "dungeon," its crewmember Death is afflicted with mold and damp, and, last, Death and Death-in-Life cast dice for the lives of the Mariner and his crew, an event that "could have come to Coleridge via Thelwall's accounts of Newgate Goal, where dice gaming was rife and the living conditions were squalid and infested with vermin."[12] All this contrasts with the austere penal environment of the Mariner's ship. In the latter, after his crew fall dead, the Mariner repents his murder of the albatross in solitude. His "soul" is "in agony" as he tries to pray and win the pity of Christ, but finds that he is cursed with muteness.[13] It is only at the end of part IV of the poem that his curse is lifted. Suddenly, a "spring of love gusht" from his "heart" that enables him to speak again. His first speech act is to bless divine creation.[14] The pair of images is thus of a deathly hulk and a vessel of awakening conscience.

"This Lime-Tree Bower My Prison" also pairs images suggestive of reformed and unreformed imprisonment. Its speaker gains theological and imaginative insight when confined alone in the bower, a space dramatically offset by a degraded version of itself in the form of a "dell." A dell is a "deep natural hollow or vale of no great extent, the sides usually clothed with trees or foliage."[15] In the first verse paragraph of "This Lime-Tree Bower My Prison," the speaker imagines his friends descending a hill into an "o'erwooded" dell.[16] Critics have long viewed the dell as emblematic of a descent into a hellish world. Reeve Parker compares the wooded dell both to a "grave" and to an "underworld." Lucy Newlyn calls the dell sequence "essentially allegorical. Lamb and his companions are seen descending into a dark underworld, emerging into a wider prospect, and climbing to a height from which all can be viewed." For Charles J. Rzepka, the dell represents a momentary "bondage of the soul."[17] Without discounting the imagined descent into the dell as an allegorical descent into hell, an underworld, the grave, or bondage, we can also read the dell in terms of a prison space that is the physical and tonal opposite of the bower. If the lime-tree bower suggests qualities associated with the reformed prison, the dell suggests qualities associated with the unreformed prison. It is of course dark and dank. The friends "wind down" into an "usunn'd and damp" space where the main attraction is a line of "long lank Weeds" that seem to drip from a stone, which itself seems to drip (we will see that Coleridge often associates dampness with unreformed British prisons). The bower, by way of contrast, is a "prison" dramatically sunlit. It is a place of solitude and reflection and religious meditation. The group leaving the dell, for their part, are simply "glad" to be out of it, happy at the pleasant change of scene.[18] Thus in both "The Ancyent Marinere" and "This Lime-Tree Bower My Prison," two prisonlike spaces are contrasted, one associated with light, enlightenment, solitude, prayer, and repentance; the other with dampness, darkness, and death.

In many ways, "This Lime-Tree Bower My Prison" is a very different poem from "The Ancyent Marinere." The former is a seventy-seven-line lyric in verse paragraphs set in a garden; the latter is a 628-line lyrical ballad in ballad stanzas, with gothic overtones, set mostly across the Pacific Ocean. Yet for all these differences, the two share a similar moral arc. Each poem involves a kind of sin or crime and a penance meant to atone for it. Each poem dramatizes an experience of confinement and redemption in a relatively isolated environment. The Mariner shoots an albatross at sea in the middle of nowhere, all his crewmen die at his feet, he feels remorse, he apprehends the beauty and harmony of "happy living things," and last, in a fit of love, he "bless[es]" the "water-snakes" surrounding his ship.[19] The speaker of "This Lime-Tree Bower My Prison" pities himself, loses his sense of the beauty of divine creation, envies his absent friends, starts to imagine them happy on their walk, suddenly apprehends the beauty in and around his bower, and then "bles[ses]" a flying rook.[20]

"This Lime-Tree Bower My Prison," in fact, is a text whose explicit and implicit values harmonize with the values of penitential imprisonment extant around the time the poem was composed. It is a poem that wants to be reconciled to these values in their best conceivable form, to imprisonment that, if it has to exclude some or all access to the natural world, is at least humane and educative and teaches humility and redemption. My secondary aim is to situate "This Lime-Tree Bower My Prison" in what W. B. Carnochan calls the literature of confinement. In the literature of confinement, as Carnochan defines it, "imprisonment means being imprisoned by someone or by some force, whether external or internal; hence prison literature concerns the workings of power and resistance to power, whether represented by Zeus, by the state, or by compulsions and needs within." Among the kinds of prison dramatized in the literature of confinement, according to Carnochan, are "prisons of the self and mind," which "may be called imaginary in that imagination forms them."[21] The precise nature of the confinement represented in "This Lime-Tree Bower My Prison" is complex. On the one hand, the lime-tree bower in the poem is clearly not a prison; it is a metaphor, a mental construct, a prison "of the self and mind" actuated by an "internal" "force" in the form of "compulsions and needs" within the poet-speaker. On the other hand, the bower is, in fact, an actual constrictive spot. It confines the speaker indefinitely owing to an "external" accident that has mostly immobilized him (his wife having spilled hot milk on his foot). Thus the nature of the imprisonment in the poem is a hybrid of internal and external forces. Its speaker processes these forces, moreover, by adapting literary and rhetorical strategies used by writers as old as Boethius, who wrote from inside actual prisons.

COLERIDGE, POLITICS, AND PENAL REFORM

It is very likely that Coleridge approved of the regular use of religious education in the new British penitentiaries, as promoted by the reformers and ratified in the 1779 Penitentiary Act. His lifelong devotion to the spread of Christianity was far more consistent than his politics. At the onset of his public career, in his 1795 Bristol lectures and in his 1796 essays in the *Watchman*, Coleridge tried to reconcile his identity as an English political and religious dissenter with the new French revolutionary politics. Yet after the revolution failed and France expanded militarily, invading Switzerland in 1798, he realized that he had been misled in his eagerness for France. Eventually, between 1809 and 1830, he cultivated the view (as did an older John Milton) that individuals on average were incapable of rationally educating themselves and accommodating themselves to political and social reform. A "nationally endowed permanent class," in the form of what Coleridge called the clerisy, was needed to assist the populace in its moral and spiritual education.[22] Part of that moral and spiritual education, according to Coleridge, had to rest in the hands of highly educated Christians. His "enthusiastic faith in the educational role of the Church of England," in fact, only increased over time. John Colmer notes that

> Coleridge's message in his early political lectures, "Go, preach the Gospel to the poor," his insistence to the radical orator John Thelwall that Christianity was "a religion for Democrats," that it "certainly teaches in the most explicit terms the Rights of Man," that "it commands it's [*sic*] disciples to go everywhere, and every where to preach these rights" . . . his reference to the Bible as "The Statesman's Manual"

in 1816, and the argument of his last work *On the Constitution of the Church and State* all point to the fact that his Christian commitment to politics was fundamentally consistent throughout his life.[23]

Coleridge also shared with contemporary prison reformers a firm belief in the shaping power of environment. Between 1795 and 1801, the "association of ideas" and the "doctrine of Necessity," "formulated most completely by David Hartley and explicated and reinforced by Joseph Priestley, dominated every branch of Coleridge's thought until . . . 1801."[24] According to Peter Kitson, the doctrine of the association of ideas held that "knowledge is created by the external world and its action on our senses. Ideas are thus no more than mental copies of physical sensation; the order to which they are presented to the mind is governed by the order in which the sensations that caused them occurred. Knowledge and thought are entirely governed by the association of ideas according to their spatial and temporal contiguity." Kitson adds that "from this associationist premise, Hartley and Priestley developed the doctrine of Necessity; that is, that all our actions are determined by the environments in which we are placed. As such environments were arranged by God, then all actions and events were part of a predetermined and benevolent purpose."[25] These two doctrines are crucial in the context of late eighteenth-century penal reform. U.R.Q. Henriques reminds us that "all the penologists were influenced by the . . . Hartleian psychology of impression and association."[26] Moreover, if Hartleian psychology were true, "if all ideas, including moral ones, were derived from external sensation, it followed that people could be socialized by taking control over their sources of sensation. The attraction of the 'total institution' [i.e., the incipient penitentiary] then was that it afforded such a complete measure of control over the criminal's 'associations.'"[27]

The enforced intervals of solitude in penitentiaries, which occurred during sleeping hours and, depending on the institution, during certain portions of the day, were meant to limit the sources of sensation available to inmates and thereby to regulate their associations. Coleridge, for his part, advocated a similar practice in his conversation poems, written between 1795 and 1797, only with respect to elective as opposed to forced solitude. In fact, we can read the advocacy of forced solitude in penitentiaries and the advocacy of self-imposed solitude in the outside world as part of the same ideological and cultural matrix, insofar as, in both cases, regular solitude is specified as a crucial element in the moral and spiritual reform of all individuals. All the conversation poems describe the "moment of fullest being . . . as [a] sense of absolute solitude."[28] "This Lime-Tree Bower My Prison" even dramatizes the good that can come of nonvolitional solitude. Jeffrey Robinson views "This Lime-Tree Bower My Prison" as a poetic response to the political imprisonment of the radical British orator, journalist, poet, and elocutionist John Thelwall. Thelwall came to visit Coleridge at Nether Stowey in the summer of 1797, after he had served time in Newgate and was forced to exile himself from the political scene. Robinson claims that the poem, with Thelwall in mind, "transform[s] separation from a condition of political persecution to a newly preferred condition of being—the solitary 'liberty' of contemplation and the feeling of love." He adds: "Thelwall's actual imprisonment or enforced separation becomes rationalized metaphorically into 'the happy prison.'"[29] John Bugg, agreeing with Robinson that the thematic arc of "This Lime-Tree Bower My Prison" culminates in the topos of the happy prison, suggests that Coleridge "may have meant to comfort either of the Lambs, or Charles Lloyd, or even Thelwall." "Perhaps," Bugg adds, "in addition to offering solace, Coleridge was attempting to sympathize . . . with his friends' more dire bouts of confinement."[30] I agree with Robinson that the poem serves to transform and to rationalize the imprisonment of political radicals in the 1790s. Yet it does more than this. The same poem serves also to rationalize the legal confinement of a certain class of men and women whom Coleridge considered amenable to needed moral reform.[31]

The fate of Thelwall and other middle-class radicals imprisoned during the First Pitt ministry (1783–1801) may help explain why Romantic writers, such as William Wordsworth and Coleridge, supported Howardian penal reform in poetry rather than in polemical essays, indirectly rather than straightforwardly, tentatively rather than firmly. I question the view, common among literary historians and critics, that "the new methods of incarceration . . . went unnoticed by the English Romantics," who were "more interested in poetic 'dungeons' of absolutist European descent than in the actual debates on prison reform."[32] I grant the truth of one phrase in this quotation: "more interested." But a pervasive interest in the dungeon as a symbol of European absolutism does not mean that "the new methods of incarceration . . . went unnoticed" by English Romantic poets. The new methods were certainly noticed. The scores of poetic paeans to John Howard (to which Coleridge contributed) tell us that. It is more accurate to say that a segment of literary Romanticism in Britain responded steadily yet cautiously to contemporary advances in penal reform. And it may be no mystery why: between 1793 and 1832, but especially in the mid- to late 1790s and in the aftermath of the Napoleonic Wars, political radicals like Thelwall were being thrown into British prisons left and right. To condone reformed imprisonment during such periods may have been felt to suggest complicity in the imprisonment of political as well as nonpolitical offenders.

Coleridge was both aware of and sympathetic to the theoretical and practical advances in prison reform in late eighteenth-century Britain. Between 1795 and 1797—the years of the conversation poems—he expressed in writing his disapproval of capital punishment, penal transportation, and visible punishment such as the stocks and public hangings. He was also one of thousands of Britons who admired if not glorified John Howard. Howard died of swamp fever while visiting military hospitals in Russia in 1790. A monument to him was subsequently raised in the Cathedral of St. Paul in London, and several English poets, including William Cowper and William Lisle Bowles, wrote epitaphs for him. Coleridge wrote his own epitaph for Howard in Greek in 1792. In it he calls Howard "a star of salvation" to the "hopeless and heart-devoured"—a man who "stole from prisoners' minds their sleepless woe."[33] In 1796, Coleridge composed "Reflections on Having Left a Place of Retirement," a conversation poem that makes the name of John Howard a stand-in for the ideal humanitarian: "Sweet is the Tear that from some Howard's eye / Drops on the cheek of One, he lifts from Earth."[34] Coleridge praised Howard in prose too; in 1796, he wrote an article in the *Watchman* placing Howard in the company of Alfred the Great, John Milton, and the Puritan republican Algernon Sidney as a British hero "in honour among the nations of the world."[35]

One key aspect of Howardian prison reform that especially appealed to Coleridge was the need for proper ventilation in British gaols and houses of correction. His poem "The Dungeon" (1798) complains of "steams and vapour" in British gaols, which, according to the miasmatic theory at the time, possibly carried gaol fever.[36] In a lecture in 1795, Coleridge mentions the "sickly and tainted gales of a prison," and in an essay in 1818 he refers disparagingly to "the cold and damp of a prison."[37] At one point he also voiced his respect for the prison reformer John Jebb.[38] In 1785, Jebb wrote a Howardian pamphlet called *Thoughts on the Construction and Polity of Prisons*, advocating raising prisons on arcades to keep them away from moist soil, separate confinement of inmates, good lighting, exercise, and fresh air. In one important comment about prison construction, Jebb writes: "Let us imitate Nature. She effects her purposes by the simplest Means." In context Jebb is saying that the impossibly thick walls of prisons, although designed to prevent escapes, do less good in the long run than "*Lights* properly dispersed over the whole enclosed District," "Permission to the Prisoners to enjoy the Benefit of the Air," and the absence of chains and irons.[39] These modifications to prison architecture and administration suggest how it is that a prison can "imitate Nature." Nor was Jebb alone in suggesting that prisoners should occasionally enjoy "the Benefit of the Air." Jonas Hanway recommended in *Solitude in Imprisonment* that part of the grounds of a prison should be made into a forty-acre garden, "subdivided by walls into fifty or sixty parts," so that prisoners can "occasionally work in gardening, still suffering *solitude*." Hanway also proposed that each inmate should have access to his or her private area of the "garden-ground by subterraneous passages."[40]

We can read the Howardian prison as Jebb and Hanway imagine it as a practical version of what Coleridge recommends for inmates in his poem "The Dungeon." "The Dungeon" envisions its own way to rehabilitate lawbreakers, not in prisons, but through some sort of methodical exposure to sunlight, fresh air, and rustic sounds. An offender, the poem claims, needs a vigorously rural cure; he or she should be placed amid "sunny hues, fair forms, and breathing sweets / . . . melodies of woods, and winds, and waters."[41] This is essentially an aestheticized and ideal version of the access to nature that Jebb and Hanway advocated. All three writers suggest that the basic amenities of an outdoor environment—light, air, exercise, gardening—are vital to the moral reformation of offenders. "The Dungeon," importantly, no less than *Thoughts on the Construction and Polity of Prisons* and *Solitude in Imprisonment*, teaches us that it is better to reform criminals than to condemn them. It does not teach us that punishment or imprisonment per se is inhumane.[42] The poem is rather a critique of conditions in contemporary British prisons: idleness, unsanitariness, mixed clientele, poor ventilation, unregulated darkness.

I want to make a short aside here that pertains to Coleridge and one particular contemporary prison: the reformed bridewell (but really a gaol-bridewell hybrid) at Coldbath Fields, built in London in 1794.[43] Below is a well-known stanza from a poem provocatively called "The Devil's Thoughts." It was written collaboratively by Robert Southey and Coleridge and first published in the London *Morning Post* on September 6, 1799. The stanza reads:

> As he went thro'——fields he look'd
> At a solitary cell—
> And the Devil was pleas'd, for it gave him a hint,
> For improving the prisons of Hell.[44]

The meaning of the stanza is straightforward enough. Later editions of the poem insert "Cold Bath" where the blanks are. I mention the stanza because it often crops up in books on the history of imprisonment without much comment, leaving readers to assume that Coleridge viewed solitary cells in reformed prisons as punishments worse than anything the Devil could invent. But this is in all likelihood not the case. First, there is the fact that the stanza was not written by Coleridge, but by Southey.[45] Then there is the fact that Coleridge actually visited Coldbath Fields in 1811 with his friend Daniel Stuart, and left with a much different impression than the above lines suggest. He and Stuart went to see the politician John Gale Jones, who in 1810 had been sentenced to a year in Coldbath Fields for a political libel. Stuart mentions the visit in an article he wrote for the *Courier* in March 1811. He quotes Coleridge as having told Jones to his face that the facts of his treatment were "in direct opposition to the statement of the Newspapers" on the subject.[46] Jones was embarrassingly silent. He knew he was being treated far more leniently in Coldbath Fields than popular report had made out. Sara Coleridge, moreover, confirms the story at a later date: she recalls Stuart and her father as having found the imprisoned Jones in a room gleaming with sunshine and flowerpots. Sara concludes that the *Courier* article was "a most satisfactory vindication of the much calumniated Cold Bath Fields Prison, both as a House of

Correction, and as a place for the detention of depraved criminals."[47] David Erdman seems to agree with Sara on this last point. Erdman says that the *Courier* article "quite flew in the face of evidence on record in the assertion (on the mere word of the warden apparently) that the mutineers of '97 (whose mistreatment had been notorious when Coleridge was of the devil's party) had really been as gently treated as Jones was now."[48] The point here is not to validate or invalidate the uneven reports of the cruelties practiced in Coldbath Fields in the 1790s. The point is that we should not take the above-quoted stanza as representative of how Coleridge viewed the use of solitary confinement in prisons in his day.

REFORMATIVE CONFINEMENT DRAMATIZED: "THIS LIME-TREE BOWER MY PRISON"

On July 11, 1797, the poet Robert Southey, then in his twenties, wrote a letter to his friend John May. In the letter, Southey says that he feels "contempt" for the "oppressed." He goes on: "mental anguish can punish but a very small part of the wicked because that acuteness of feeling which is the best preservative of virtue, is blunted in them. . . . These men have no consciences. . . . The lower classes have indeed the terrors of religion . . . but the annals of Tyburn rarely record contrition. In general they either astonish us at the obdurate wickedness of the criminal, or the dreadful effects of our laws."[49] Southey composed this letter to John May on July 11. He had also written a letter to Coleridge on July 10, which has not survived, and which Linda Pratt suspects contains the same opinions as the July 11 letter to May. Here is Pratt:

> The day before writing this [July 11 letter] to May . . . Southey had written to Coleridge asking him to contribute something to his planned subscription edition of Chatterton. Although this letter has not survived, it is extremely likely that it contained remarkably similar opinions to those sent to May one day later. Certainly Coleridge's reply, the letter containing the earliest surviving version of "This Lime-tree Bower" [July 17, 1797], suggests that this was the case and that Southey had given full vent to his disgust at all mankind. In response, Coleridge set forth his own, very different views: "I am as much a Pangloss as ever—only less *contemptuous,* than I used to be, when I argue how unwise it is to feel contempt for any thing—." This message was given immediate reinforcement in the poem that formed an integral part of the letter, "This Lime-tree Bower."[50]

Thus according to Pratt, the letter Coleridge wrote to Southey on July 17, with its optimistic "message . . . given immediate reinforcement in the poem," reflects "Coleridge's preoccupation with correcting . . . [Southey's] misanthropy." She claims that "This Lime-Tree Bower My Prison" was meant as an "antidote to 'contempt.'"[51] But we can be more specific. The "contempt" Southey expressed in his July 11 letter to May had an explicit target. It was directed at the "oppressed," the "lower classes"; i.e., the demographic that filled British prisons. It was directed at convicted felons hanged at Tyburn, allegedly void of moral sensibility ("acuteness of feeling"), "consciences," and "contrition" due to their "obdurate wickedness." Let us say that Pratt is right; that the letter Southey wrote to Coleridge on July 10 "contained remarkably similar opinions" to the ones he expressed to John May on July 11. If this is true, then Coleridge wrote his response to Southey—his July 17 letter and the poem inserted in it—to and for a young man and fellow poet who assumed that lawbreakers had weak or no consciences and were unlikely or unable to experience "contrition."

That the rhetoric of "This Lime-Tree Bower My Prison" serves, at least in part, to correct a misanthropic view of criminals as congenitally insensitive, unvirtuous, amoral, and unrepentant is strengthened by its symbolic use of the rook image. It is to this image that I now want to turn.

Recall that the speaker of "This Lime-Tree Bower My Prison" mysteriously blesses a flying rook at a moment of emotional climax near the close of the poem. This is an act that has puzzled readers. Jacqueline Labbe, for instance, asks, "why a rook? Why not a linnet, a skylark, a nightingale? If Coleridge's project was to annex for himself the vision and freedom represented by a bird in flight . . . any bird would have done. That he chooses a rook, a bird not only a portent of doom but traditionally thought to be near-sighted as well, suggests that although he has succeeded in transforming the bower, it may well be temporary."[52] Labbe sees the use of the rook as contradictory. The rook is a conventional symbol of death, yet it is used in this poem as a powerful affirmation of the value of life. As such, the image "emphasizes the shaky nature of [Coleridge's] whole venture." I take Labbe to mean that an awkward attempt to turn a bird symbolic of death into a bird symbolic of life reflects the similarly awkward attempt, in the same poem, to reinvent a "feminine, womb-like space"—her view of the lime-tree bower—as a masculine "site of creative strength."[53] I agree that the rook is a symbol with dark associations. But so are the creepy, slimy, tiny-legged water snakes in "The Ancyent Marinere." The water snakes, being snakes, are associated with sin and temptation, yet as soon as the Mariner blesses them he is able to pray again; the albatross falls from his neck. The Mariner thus perceives a traditionally sinister creature as good and, as a result, is rewarded. The blessed rook in "This Lime-Tree Bower My Prison" is a close parallel to the blessed water snakes in "The Ancyent Marinere."

Furthermore, the lines in "This Lime-Tree Bower My Prison" on the rook (69–77) imply that criminals, in particular, should be spared what Southey felt for them—"contempt."[54] Consider the sound the rook makes in the poem and how that sound is heard. The speaker says:

> My gentle-hearted Charles! when the last Rook
> Beat its straight path along the dusky air
> Homewards, I blest it! deeming its black wing
> (Now a dim speck, now vanishing in light)
> Had cross'd the mighty Orb's dilated glory,
> While thou stood'st gazing; or, when all was still,
> Flew creeking o'er thy head, and had a charm
> For thee, my gentle-hearted Charles, to whom
> No sound is *dissonant* which tells of Life.[55]

To *creek* (or creak) is to "utter a harsh cry: said of crows, rooks, etc."[56] Yet Charles, or the version of Charles whom the speaker imagines walking on the Quantock Hills, hears nothing "harsh" when the rook flies over his head. In the language of the poem, he hears nothing "dissonant." Instead he is simply "charm[ed]" by a sound "which tells of life." That Charles specifically hears nothing *dissonant* here is important in light of a different poem by Coleridge, mentioned earlier and written around the same time as "This Lime-Tree Bower My Prison"—"The Dungeon." The speaker of "The Dungeon" uses the same word, *dissonant*, to describe "each poor brother who offends against us" and who is consequently put in a gaol. As noted above, "The Dungeon" recommends that we rehabilitate criminals in carefully selected rural environments in lieu of gaols. In time, the poem says, the criminal placed in such a haven will "relent," finding that he

> can no more endure
> To be a jarring and a *dissonant* thing,
> Amid this general dance and minstrelsy;
> But, bursting into tears, wins back his way,
> His angry spirit healed and harmonized
> By the benignant touch of love and beauty.[57]

These lines offer an analogy between moral correction and musical harmony. Moral correction is seen here as a matter of restoring the mental or emotional balance once held by a person and since lost. Earlier in the poem, the average offender is described as "distempered," or, in other words, "disordered, deranged, distracted, out of joint."[58] In a moral sense, this means that the offender is temporarily alienated from the "love and beauty" infused in all creation. It also means that his or her moral correction is not a matter of adding what he or she lacks, so much as restoring him or her to his or her rightful, natural state of harmony and balance. To tune an instrument is not the same thing as to break and rebuild it. The criminal has unfortunately chosen to do what it is impossible for the rook to do: to break the law of nature—i.e., human nature, the moral law—and so render him- or herself out of tune with nature. In so doing he or she has become less of a person and more of a "dissonant thing." But his or her humanity is not altogether dead. He or she can be retuned, be rehumanized; and therefore he or she is not to be unfeelingly condemned. The point is that the creed professed in "This Lime-Tree Bower My Prison," that "No sound is dissonant which tells of Life," includes, in particular, the cries of "dissonant" criminals whose very humanity and chance of rehabilitation is under threat. They too tell of life.

The speaker of "This Lime-Tree Bower My Prison," in addition to the criminals for whose humanity he indirectly pleads, is himself amenable to moral reform. His moral correction has already happened behind the scenes by the time he speaks the opening verse. We are meant to understand at the onset that he is humbler and less selfish now than he was before the events he narrates in the poem occurred. We see immediately that he has quieted his "appetitive desire for immediate self-satisfaction" (the sort of desire that, in other circumstances, may not unreasonably be said to inspire a criminal act) and replaced it with a sense of divine providence and a love of all living things.[59] More, he has done all this while alone and confined in a bower he calls his prison. Solitude, of course, has been instrumental to his reflection.

The new penitentiaries likewise stressed the importance of regular solitude as an aid to reflection and the examination of conscience. To this end they were aided by the efforts of English clergymen. The Anglican priest John Brewster, for instance, wrote a pamphlet in 1790 called *Sermons for Prisons*. The sermons in the pamphlet were designed to be read by salaried chaplains employed in penal institutions that practiced the separate confinement of prisoners. Brewster meant for his homilies to "afford some useful reflections in solitary confinement, to give hope to the afflicted heart, and to confirm the penitent in his resolutions of amendment." Here is a passage from Sermon Two:

> You may now enter into the secret recesses of your breast. . . . To secure this ["sincere"] repentance . . . should be the Use of your present solitary Life. You should call reflection to your Aid, who, in this hour of your distress, will not hide herself from your View. This reflection must be seconded by a diligent perusal of the word of God. . . . If this method were pursued . . . these walls, and heavy fetters, which confine the body, might, in many a happy Instance, disengage and set free the Soul.[60]

Now here is Coleridge in "This Lime-Tree Bower My Prison": "sometimes / 'Tis well to be bereft of promised good, / That we may lift the Soul."[61] It is indeed accurate to call this poem a kind of poetic homily that functions similarly to this prose sermon. The two are analogous. Granted that a poem about a sensitive, highly educated middle-class man alone in a prison of lime trees who learns to apprehend

God in nature is not the same thing as a sermon written by an Anglican priest for the average prisoner in a solitary cell. Yet both texts stress the importance of solitary religious reflection as a means to moral amendment for one temporarily deprived of liberties.[62] As Brewster puts it, if and as the solitary prisoner "reads and meditates on serious things, there is every reason to hope, that his heart will be corrected."[63]

A number of late eighteenth-century pamphlets on the use of solitude in prisons stress not the horror of solitary repentance, but its consolation. Thus Brewster says that prisoners, "of all men," "certainly have the greatest leisure for devotion" and may "dwell so long upon a train of religious reflections, as to acquire a relish for prayer." Moreover, when "the prisoner becomes sensible of his Situation he will consider the length of his devotions as a comfort to him."[64] One prayer Brewster recommends for prisoners is: "Grant that this Solitude and Confinement may recall my Soul from Vanity, bring me to a true Sense of my present Situation, and . . . promote the work of my Salvation." Another is: "make me sensible, that this bodily constraint is well calculated to bring me to a knowledge of myself."[65] An anonymous pamphlet called *The Prisoner's Companion* (1785) asks inmates, likewise, to "view . . . [their] solitary imprisonment" "not as an additional hardship and severity to punish or distress," but as a means to "recall to . . . [their] heart[s] the love of honesty."[66] The point is an old one: material adversity paradoxically yields religious and philosophical consolation. Punishment is no punishment if it mends what is broken. This is the essential process that "This Lime-Tree Bower My Prison" dramatizes.

The poem, in fact, may be read as a *consolatio* à la Boethius and Thomas More, who both wrote *consolationes* from actual prisons, as opposed to lime-tree bowers. The *consolatio* was a literary tradition that began in ancient Greece and Rome and persisted into the Middle Ages. It came in several different forms:

> Philosophers wrote treatises on death and the alleviation of grief. Letters of consolation were written to comfort those who had suffered bereavement or some other loss-experience, such as exile or illness; these might be highly personal, or possess the more detached character of an essay. . . . Extant specimens of ancient consolatory writing tend to draw on a relatively narrow repertoire of arguments and approaches. . . . Arguments typically employed include the following: all are born mortal; death brings release from the miseries of life; time heals all griefs; future ills should be prepared for; the deceased was only "lent"—be grateful for having possessed him. Normally grief is regarded as natural and legitimate, though not to be indulged in.[67]

If anyone reads a *consolatio* in the twenty-first century, it is probably the one that has remained the most famous: *On the Consolation of Philosophy*, written in an

Italian prison by the sixth-century Neoplatonic philosopher Boethius, while awaiting his execution. "This Lime-Tree Bower My Prison" has actually been compared to *On the Consolation of Philosophy* as a text that attempts to lift its author out of a depressing loneliness and hyper-self-consciousness.[68] It tends to adapt the familiar points of that mode—e.g., that men are mortal, that time heals all, that death is release, and so on—to a relatively unique late eighteenth-century setting and set of themes. If the poem maintains any sentiment customary in the classical and medieval *consolatio*, it is the idea that "grief" is "natural and legitimate, though not to be indulged in."

If we class "This Lime-Tree Bower My Prison" as a *consolatio*, moreover, we notice—borrowing the words of J. H. D. Scourfield—that it is both a "personal" and a "detached" *consolatio*. It is personal to the extent that its speaker apostrophizes and tries to console an actual friend of Coleridge, Charles Lamb.[69] Coleridge knew what had recently happened in the Lamb family (Charles's sister, Mary Lamb, had murdered their mother), and Lamb, to whom the poem is formally addressed, knew that Coleridge knew it. But at the same time, of course, the poem addresses a wider audience and has broader interests, including the interests of political radicals in Britain who were persecuted, exiled, or imprisoned in the 1790s.

Whether or not we class "This Lime-Tree Bower My Prison" itself as a *consolatio*, the poem may have been a trial run for a more traditional *consolatio*, in prose, which Coleridge was planning to write possibly as early as 1797, the preparatory work for which he had finished by 1804. As he told George Beaumont in 1804:

> I have now completed my materials . . . for a work, the contents of which you will conjecture from the Title—"Consolations & Comforts from the exercise & right application of the Reason, the Imagination, and the Moral Feelings." The "Consolations" are addressed to all in adversity, sickness, or distress of mind / the first part entirely practical—the second in which I consider distress of mind from gloomy Speculation will, of course, be speculative, & will contain a new Theodicee.[70]

It is interesting to recall that Thomas More arranged his own, three-book prison *consolatio*, *A Dialogue of Comfort against Tribulation*, similarly. Book II of *A Dialogue* is homely and "practical." Book III is a "speculative" treatise on the art of meditation and is more densely theological. As a whole, *A Dialogue* is more or less one long "Theodicee." Hence Coleridge may have written "This Lime-Tree Bower My Prison," which takes place in a figurative prison and certainly contains a theodicy, as a kind of poetic experiment en route to his planned prose *consolatio*.

Another feature of the poem that puts it in the tradition of prison writing more generally is its dramatic use of paradox. Rivkah Zim has noted that prison writers as diverse as Boethius, Madame Roland, Thomas More, and Oscar Wilde all rely heavily on "a series of paradoxes (such as light in darkness) that reconcile conceptual oppositions in constructed modes and create gain by loss."[71] All of this applies plainly to "This Lime-Tree Bower My Prison." The poem is a blend of "constructed modes"—the conversation poem, the *consolation*, the guide to picturesque scenery, the sublime meditation, the theodicy—that attempt to "reconcile conceptual oppositions" and "create gain by loss." Critics have said much along these lines. For K. M. Wheeler, the poem "expresses . . . the *synthesis* of expansion and contraction"; for Michael Raiger, it features the "paradox . . . that through suffering and loss, there is ultimately liberation"; for Rachel Crawford, the "lime-tree bower is both prison and sanctuary"; and for Felicity James, the bower is "at once a fixed prison and a place of growth, movement, and creativity."[72] Thus we have contraction and expansion, deprivation and liberation, stasis and dynamism. All such contraries are said to harmonize in the poem, as disparate notes in a chord.

Jacqueline Labbe may be the only critic who doubts that "This Lime-Tree Bower My Prison" actually "reconcile[s] conceptual oppositions." Labbe says that the bower "acts to shut down the imaginative activity of the poet," owing to its resemblance to the explicitly "feminine, womb-like space" of the garden. In her view, the bower does not creatively inspire the male speaker. It restricts him. It is so full of "feminine, domestic and low associations," in fact, that the speaker has to reinvent it as a more masculine and visionary space to get anything out of it.[73] In other words, he has to impose a nonexistent, masculine energy on a femininely textured bower in order to profit from it. I am inclined to disagree with Labbe on this point, seeing no convincing evidence in the poem that the speaker perceives the bower as an inherently feminized space, and, accordingly, feels he has to turn it into a more masculine one.

What ultimately matters is that the speaker "acknowledge[s], at the end of the poem, that the prison is no prison, and the loss no loss."[74] Why? For starters because there are ample resources available to the active mind while the body is in straitened circumstances. In the words of Stuart Curran: "the bower is a charged, a compressed chamber for imaginative play."[75] Or James Engell: for the poet-speaker, "Nature is everywhere equally full to our eye," whether we are stuck at home or scrambling over hills and mountains.[76] Another reason that the prison is no prison is that the poem insists that human perception and cognition not only adapt to confinement, but can thrive in it. Wheeler observes that "what seemed bad, ugly, or imprisoning, becomes good, beautiful, and releasing, not because the nature of the thing changes, but because the perception of it or the perceiver's perspective upon it changes."[77] The bower thus "produc[es] a way of seeing [rather] than a sight to be seen."[78]

Ultimately, the bower expands the mind as it restricts the body; it sharpens physical and imaginative perception; it promotes a relish for life; it replaces selfish preoccupations with a love of creator and creation. It is also important to recall that both Coleridge and Wordsworth started out in 1798 with poems bemoaning the use of unreformed prisons, not imprisonment per se. Wordsworth included his poem "The Convict" in the 1798 *Lyrical Ballads* and Coleridge included his poem "The Dungeon" in the same volume. Both poems are explicitly about state-sanctioned punishment and recommend obscure rural cures for offenders in lieu of traditional eighteenth-century penalties like whipping, branding, short-term imprisonment in unreformed gaols, transportation to the American colonies, and hanging. But Coleridge and Wordsworth, even before the publication of *Lyrical Ballads*, were entertaining the idea of humane correction in penitential prisons. "This Lime-Tree Bower My Prison" is a dramatic enactment of solitary reflection in a confined space, one with a solid, visible moral outcome. It insists that a just measure of privation, restraint, and discipline can redirect an erring spirit back on the path to some perceived moral good.

2

WILLIAM GODWIN, "MILD COERCION," AND THE HAPPY PRISON TRADITION

IMAGINE INTRODUCING THE POLITICAL VIEWS of William Godwin to a roomful of undergraduates in a course on British Romanticism. Most of these undergraduates probably never heard of Godwin, and so the first thing to do is to get them interested. So after mentioning that Godwin was the father of the author of *Frankenstein*, the husband of the first major radical feminist in history, and the father-in-law of one of the greatest lyric poets of all time, you could do worse than read the following passage from his 1831 collection of essays, *Thoughts on Man*. Godwin published *Thoughts on Man* at age seventy-five, near the end of his life. This excerpt seems fairly representative of his politics: "Some degree of courteous compliance and deference of the ignorant to the better informed, is inseparable from the existence of political society as we behold it. . . . Every thing however that is more than this, is evil. . . . We may admit of a moral influence; but there must be nothing, that should in the smallest degree border on compulsion."[1] Some discussion would follow. A shrewd student might ask: "So all force is evil in all cases? We should not force a dictator to step down or a murderer to be locked up?" You could tell the shrewd student that Godwin anticipates this question and answers it in the same essay. A few pages later, he proclaims that "Truth is omnipotent." Take the most hardened, the most inveterately depraved criminal; according to Godwin, the communication of "Truth" is the surest means of removing such a person from the path of error: "However corrupt he may be, however steeped in the habits of vice . . . if it [truth] be mildly, distinctly, emphatically enunciated, the colour will forsake his cheek, his speech will alter and be broken, and he will feel himself unable to turn it off lightly, as a thing of no impression and validity. In this way the erroneous man . . . stands a fair chance of being corrected."[2]

MILD COERCION

This is the notably optimistic Godwin we know and teach; it also happens to be the version of Godwin described in several studies on English penal reform. U.R.Q. Henriques writes that there were three main factions involved in prison reform in late eighteenth- and early nineteenth-century Britain: the "evangelical pietists" (e.g., Jonas Hanway), the "rational utilitarians" (e.g., Jeremy Bentham), and the "anti-coercive" "Godwinians." The first two groups wanted not "less punishment," but "more refined and effective punishment."[3] The Godwinians, according to Henriques, wanted to eliminate the need for punishment altogether, and so had virtually no effect on prison reform. Margaret DeLacy observes that British "radicals . . . were often ambivalent about the issues raised by prison reform and 'model prisons.' The only major figure to question imprisonment as such was William Godwin."[4] So for both Henriques and DeLacy, Godwin represents the anti-punishment position: namely, no institution, however reformed, can better a person by coercion, as opposed to rational persuasion. The evidence reveals that this is a mostly accurate portrait of what it means to be "Godwinian" on the subject of imprisonment, but it is a portrait that has been pushed to an extreme. Godwin was not always as unequivocal an anti-coercionist as the critical literature, or even he himself, indicates. His statements on the evils of all coercion are certainly emphatic when he expresses them, and he expresses them often, but such statements need to be balanced with certain concessions he makes, over time and on several occasions, to the necessity of healthy restraint and mild coercion in an imperfect society.

Godwin the atheist,[5] in fact, can sound very much like his "evangelical pietist" contemporaries when he writes about moral correction. Consider the words of the pious merchant and philanthropist Jonas Hanway, in *Solitude in Imprisonment*. Hanway insists that salaried Anglican chaplains should teach prayers and meditations to prisoners in solitude every day. These exercises should be easy to learn and "judiciously calculated to inspire" prisoners "by the gentle arts of persuasion."[6] The word *persuasion* is key here. Hanway mentions it again later when he claims that prisoners can be made regenerate by "the *lenient* spirit of *persuasion, blended with* rigid discipline."[7] Or take the words of the religious and political reformer John Jebb. Like the young Godwin, Jebb was attracted to Socinianism, which denied the legitimacy of the Trinity, and he was also, like Godwin, obliged at one point to resign his position as a clergyman. Jebb directed two houses of correction within a period of three years, one in Suffolk and another in Norfolk. In his essay *Thoughts on the Construction and Polity of Prisons*, he promotes the ideals of a reformed house of correction, among which are the salutary "influence of Retirement," "mild but steady Discipline, plain but frequent and affectionate Instruction," "suitable Employment" and, most important in the context of Godwin studies, "learning to feel what it is to be a rational, a moral, a social Being."[8] A less radical Anglican priest than Jebb, John Brewster, emphasizes in his own pamphlet on prison reform (1792) the need to "correct the understanding" and "convince the judgment" of prisoners.[9] All these comments by Hanway, Jebb, and Brewster are written in the general spirit of the father of prison reform, John Howard, who, in a much-quoted passage, claimed to want to replace "the gothic mode of correction, *viz.* by *rigorous severity*, which often *hardens* the heart," with "the more *rational* plan of *softening* the mind in order to its amendment."[10] This was to be the leading principle behind the first English penitentiary houses.

It is easy to overlook the extent to which Godwin himself condones "mild" coercion for the sake of reforming people morally; it is easy because Godwin makes it easy, particularly with some of his more extreme and memorable statements. In *Political Justice*, for instance, he writes that "coercion cannot convince, cannot conciliate, but on the contrary alienates the mind of him against whom it is employed. Coercion has nothing in common with reason, and therefore can have no proper tendency to the generation of virtue." It simply makes bad people worse: "all coercion sours the mind. . . . The lesson which coercion reads to . . . [a person coerced] is, 'Submit to force, and abjure reason. Be not directed by the convictions of your understanding, but by . . . the dread of present pain.'"[11] Godwin wrote these comments in 1793. In 1795, he was apparently prepared to modify his earlier opinion: he writes then that, for some men and women, "reason and expostulation . . . are not sufficient: there must be an arm to repress; a coercion, strict, but forbearing and mild." In such cases, he adds, the "real statesmen will love, will compassionate, will sympathise with those individuals, whose conduct he concludes . . . to be hostile to the general welfare. He regrets their errors, he desires their reformation and improvement."[12] I would call these last excerpts a qualification, if not a retraction, of the earlier anti-coercion position. In 1797, as it happens, Godwin is still maintaining the qualified view: "Place me in the condition of a slave, and I shall perhaps be able to endure it. Human nature is capable of accommodating itself to a state of subjection, especially when the authority of the master is exercised with mildness, and seems to be directed in a considerable degree to promote the welfare of the dependent."[13] If, therefore, in 1793, Godwin insists that all coercion is unjust because it makes no appeal to reason, in later essays he concedes that a lenient sort of coercion may, in fact, lead to "reformation and improvement." Near the turn of the century—when the first major working-class-inspired movement for constitutional reform in Britain was crushed—Godwin echoes the evangelicals who speak on prison reform. Recall that Hanway pushed for the "gentle arts" and the "*lenient* spirit of persuasion," and that Jebb promoted a "mild but steady Discipline." Godwin, in a similar vein, acknowledges that a "strict, but forbearing and mild" "coercion" can be effective for certain intractable individuals.

A mild coercion may even be, for Godwin, essential to what makes a happy home. In one of his most conservatively slanted texts, an essay in *Thoughts on Man* called "Of Love and Friendship," Godwin argues that inequality between partners is the foundation of domestic relations and the rule and measure of love. The essay could easily have been written by the forty-year-old Edmund Burke, and Mary Wollstonecraft would perhaps have turned over in her grave to read it. At one point in "Of Love and Friendship," Godwin claims that there is a "wholsome [*sic*] principle of superiority and dependence which is almost indispensable between persons of different ages dwelling under the same roof."[14] That "wholsome principle" is the late medieval concept of courtly love. It was thanks to courtly love, Godwin writes, that men and women

> were taught mutual deference. The woman regarded her protector as something illustrious and admirable; and the man considered the smiles and approbation of beauty as the adequate reward of his toils and his dangers. These modes of thinking introduced a nameless grace into all the commerce of society. It was the poetry of life. . . . It was clothed in resplendent hues, and wore all the tints of the rainbow. Equality fled and was no more; and love, almighty, perdurable love, came to supply its place.[15]

Even for an author known to contradict himself at different periods in his writing life, this is a wildly uncharacteristic passage. Here Godwin celebrates the day on which "Equality fled" from cohabitators and lovers, since there can be no true, no lasting love between equals. Real love requires a master and a subordinate: a parent and a child, a creator and a creature, a great man like Achilles and a lesser man like Patroclus. Godwin justifies the need for "unequal" partnerships by insisting that deference is a two-way street. Even though the subordinate is the one who, by definition, submits to the superior, as long as the superior occasionally defers to the subordinate—in a way Godwin leaves undefined—the love between them will flourish. It is, of course, difficult to imagine a master, a parent, or a god deferring to a servant, a child, or a creature in any way similar to or as often as the reverse. The woman in the passage looks up to the man as her "illustrious and admirable" "protector." The man, in turn, receives his "adequate reward" in the beautiful woman, who smiles at and approves of his "toils and dangers." It is easy to determine which party is more likely to defer to which, and how often.[16]

It seems, therefore, that Godwin draws a finer line than we would expect between coercion and persuasion, power and reason, inequality and equality. He claims that domestic harmony is only truly possible among unequals, without the tension and give-and-take between whom, it seems, there can be no mutual growth. My point is not to accuse Godwin of backsliding when he moves from a hatred of all coercion to a toleration of a mild form of it, in and outside the home. I only want to indicate that his political philosophy is more flexible than the critical literature in Godwin studies often assumes.

In many of his later essays, Godwin reminds readers that everyone has social obligations for which he or she will ultimately be held accountable. As social beings and as citizens, that is, we all have "duties" to perform, and "we easily reconcile ourselves to this inevitable condition of our existence, and believe that, if we neglect our duties, we must expect in some way or other to be made accountable for it."[17] Made accountable how? By rational conversation with our neighbors? Criticism from our neighbors? Mild coercion? Salutary restraint? It is almost as though, in this statement, Godwin approves of the fear of punishment as an inducement to social virtue.[18] This is by no means typical of his writing. And since we must be punished for our actions, the essay goes on to say, we ought to accept it: "we are contented to be amenable to the laws of society for our delinquencies . . . for having neglected to make the best use of our faculties."[19] This seems like periphrastic language that is essentially pro-coercion. In later editions of *Political Justice*, moreover (the following quotation does not appear in the 1793 edition of *Political Justice*), Godwin makes the same point more bluntly: he says that there are certain "principles a deviation from which the interest of the community may be supposed to render it proper to repress by sanctions and punishment."[20]

SOLITUDE

Since the 1980s, critics and scholars of Romanticism have been less and less convinced that the Romantic poets on average worked alone, or that they valued creative solitude as much as they claimed to. The alienated Romantic genius creating masterpieces on the fringes of society and culture was a myth that the Romantics invented and that the Anglo-American critical establishment has long since exploded. The story, perhaps now itself a myth, goes something like this. In late eighteenth- and early nineteenth-century Britain, some Romantic writers, mostly poets, and especially William Wordsworth and Samuel Taylor Coleridge, promoted the concept of the solitary poet-genius who thought and wrote as if somehow beyond the influence of social and commercial forces. Up until the end of the twentieth century, literary critics were more likely than not to accept this concept. But then in 1983 Jerome McGann published *The Romantic Ideology*, which warned students of Romanticism that "the scholarship and criticism of Romanticism and its works are dominated by a Romantic ideology, by an uncritical absorption in Romanticism's own self-representations."[21] By this statement McGann meant that a handful of texts written in the period we call Romantic represent that period according to a privileged set of constructs, constructs that critics once accepted as true and applied to generations of Romantic writers and to the very idea of British Romanticism. *The Romantic Ideology* was a sensible caution in 1983, and it is a sensible caution now. Numerous important studies have appeared in its wake that have "challenged the myth of the solitary Romantic speaker, emphasizing instead Romantic poetry's investment in community and collectivity."[22] Even alienated poetic geniuses, these studies insist, had to work with publishers and printers and to write for a public whose tastes they knew. Most Romantic-era poets also enjoyed collaborating with fellow poets.

Yet there is a downside to rethinking this admittedly limited critical perspective. In tearing down the idol of the solitary Romantic poet, we have put ourselves in a position to ignore the discursive importance of solitude beyond what poets felt or said about it. Late eighteenth- and early nineteenth-century Britain witnessed an explosion in writings about solitude across the professions. Not only poets, but novelists, hacks of all kinds, priests, barristers, parliamentarians, magistrates, physicians, and gentlemen were fascinated with solitude and writing about it. It was as though the culture, at this time, wanted to hash out exactly what solitude meant (it did not always mean being by oneself), how much of it was salutary, and what important effects it had or could have on the welfare of individuals, local communities, and the state.

Texts handling the theme of solitude in late eighteenth- and early nineteenth-century Britain are practically endless. I want, therefore, to narrow the focus to two main points. The first is that the period we call Romantic is unique in that texts written during this time on the subject of solitude were more likely than at any other period before it to be implicated in texts, theoretical and practical, on solitary imprisonment. Solitude as a concept was swiftly gaining new associations. It went from an idea much associated with didactic georgic poems, didactic graveyard poems, rural retirement, and pious reflection to all these things and more embodied in the slowly realized penitentiary. The second point relates specifically to Godwin. Godwin wrote more prose about the ethical implications of solitude than any major English writer of his time, save, perhaps, Hanway. Although much of this prose is hostile to solitude in general and to the possibility that solitude in prison can do anyone any good, this is not always the case. Some of Godwin's essays, letters, and novels show a surprising openness to the possibility of good things coming out of isolation, even isolation in confinement.

It has been said that "thinkers at the turn of the eighteenth and nineteenth centuries . . . made the discovery that autonomy and sociability could never be completely reconciled."[23] Godwin, for his part, never made this discovery; or if he did, he never conceded to it. He spent his whole career trying to reconcile solitude and sociability as the two sine qua non human needs; for example, "man is especially characterised by two propensities—the love of society, and the love of solitude."[24] All of his major texts expound at some point on the merits of one or the other state. His earlier writings err on the side of social development as the greater human need. *Political Justice* calls solitude a "nursery for madmen and idiots" (*PJ*, 404). *Caleb Williams* claims that a human being is no "individual" but "holds necessarily, indispensably, to his species." Alienate a person from society and he or she is all but killed: people are like "twin-births, that have two heads indeed, and four hands; but, if you attempt to detach them from each other, they are inevitably subjected to miserable and lingering destruction."[25] This is an extreme and apparently inflexible attitude. Yet if we pass ahead several years to *Thoughts on Man*, we are met, in an essay "On Leisure," with statements such as this: to be "ever and anon in solitude" is to indulge in "free and untrammelled" thought, to learn "liberty," "independence" and "self-reverence."[26] Critics have noticed this discrepancy. One admits that Godwin appears "in favour of solitude and society at the same time."[27] Another says that his devotion to "sociability as well as solitary contemplation" is one of his most "paradoxical qualities" as a writer.[28]

Godwin asks the same questions repeatedly and never decisively answers them. How much solitude is the right amount? How long should intervals of solitude last? When in the course of an individual life, and under what circumstances, is more solitude better than less solitude? How must one behave in a state of solitude? What intentions should a person have for seeking solitude? Is everyone equally capable of gleaning moral profit from solitude? And so on. What is interesting is how enmeshed this subject was in a long and inclusive debate about how to reclaim the souls of felons through solitary imprisonment. It was not a subject peculiar to philosophers or armchair thinkers. Since the 1770s, in fact, politicians, legislators, lawyers, philanthropists, and writers—including Godwin—were discussing in earnest the possible effects of prolonged isolation in prison cells: cells that would replace the old prison wards and thereby prevent "hardened" offenders from sharing a space with, and thereby corrupting, lesser offenders. These writers explored solitude in the abstract as well as in a practical and legal sense. Where Godwin stands on the subject of penal solitude and moral reform is a matter of debate. Michael Ignatieff seems to represent the critical consensus when he argues that, according to Godwin, "no one could ever be reformed in solitude. Reformation was a social process, a matter of persuasion and example rather than force. It was hopeless to expect that people would be changed by leaving them alone with their conscience."[29] This perspective requires some qualification.

The use of regulated or periodic solitude in late eighteenth- and early nineteenth-century British prisons has been well rehearsed by legal, social, and religious historians; essentially, the narrative is as follows. Jonas Hanway began his long campaign for solitary confinement in prisons in 1772. Over the next few years, most British writers had positive things to say about it. It made its way into the statute book in the 1779 Penitentiary Act ("*solitary imprisonment, accompanied by well-regulated labor, and religious instruction*") and was implemented in local gaols and houses of correction as early as 1781.[30] The consensus among reformers in the early 1780s was that solitary confinement would have generally positive results, so long as it was properly moderated. Howard accepted enforced solitude if used sparingly. But over the next few decades, the consensus began to shift in the other direction. Although, for instance, Jeremy Bentham advocated the absolute separation of prisoners in 1787, he was already changing his mind by 1791, and by 1811 he had changed it completely. Keeping scores of prisoners individually isolated all night and during part of the day was expensive, Bentham and others argued, especially to a nation at war with France. It also proved unevenly effective in practice. Some prisoners subjected to regimes of solitary confinement reformed or confessed unknown crimes; others went mad.

After 1800, the practice of solitary confinement was less rigorously enforced in British gaols and houses of correction, although it never disappeared. A sort of compromise was reached. Experiments with long periods of solitary confinement in the 1780s and 1790s gradually gave way to a new system: "since separation was impracticable, contamination [of lesser criminals by seasoned ones] could be prevented . . . by classification. Many provincial prisons in the early nineteenth century classified their inmates according to sex, type of offense, whether on trial or convicted, etc."[31] By the 1820s, classification had effectively overshadowed reformative solitary confinement as a penal discipline. The latter was more or less put on hold until it was reintroduced, more uniformly and systematically, in 1839.

Between approximately 1770 and 1790, writers on prison reform often supported enforced solitude on the grounds that it had the same benefits as elective solitude. As the chaplain John Brewster put it, in a 1790 sermon meant to be read to prisoners in solitary confinement, "the retirement which others seek by Choice, you are forced into from necessity. The good Effects, however, may be as conspicuous in you, as in other members of Society."[32] William Dodd claims that the time he spent in solitude in Newgate Prison "nor contains" "aught of punishment," since "in life's best days, / Of all most chosen, valued and belov'd, / Was soft retirement's season."[33] Hanway often conflated the penal solitude prescribed in the Penitentiary Act with "the elective, occasional solitude sought by men of culture."[34] Consider Letter IX from his epistolary text *Distributive Justice and Mercy* (1781), a letter entitled "The High Advantages of the Plan Proposed."[35] By "Plan Proposed," Hanway means a prison regime that includes solitary confinement. Yet Letter IX, as well as the theme it develops that reappears in subsequent letters, implies that any such regime will be incomplete, or less than ideal, unless the whole nation participates in it. Hanway writes:

> Let us *all* learn, that *occasional solitude*, in common life, will instruct us how to judge the mode of governing ourselves, and other men.
>
> I fear it is too true, that the fashion of the times, whether in high and elegant, or in low and vulgar life, allows but little time for *thinking*; and

> consequently that generous, pious freedom of thought is the greater stranger to our breasts.
>
> It is high time we should begin to *reform* ourselves.
>
> That it is necessary sometimes to be put under certain restraints, that we may not become the instruments of our own destruction, the experience of every hour abundantly justifies. Our *national* misfortune is, that, in common life, all kinds of restraints are become *unfashionable.*[36]

According to Hanway, certain salutary, undefined restraints need to be more fashionable in Britain. The British move licentiously this way and that; they are too much of this world; they rarely stop to think and reflect. Such freedom to do as one likes ultimately becomes another word for license; it makes for everyone a spiritual prison. True freedom, or what Hanway calls the "generous, pious freedom of thought," exists only with some measure of elective isolation and restraint. As Laurie Throness puts it: "the penitentiary's object extended beyond public order to salvation, the ultimate goal of a Christian nation."[37]

Hanway, in fact, was one of several late eighteenth-century writers to extend his moral remedies for prisoners, in some sense, to the whole nation. The antiquarian and vicar Samuel Denne wrote a reform tract in 1771 in the form of a letter to the London alderman Sir Robert Ladbroke. One minute Denne is discussing how to reform convicted lawbreakers by solitude, and the next he is prescribing reformative isolation to all England. He calls his age one of "gaiety and pleasure." England has far too many resort towns like Tonbridge and Bristol and Scarborough and Cheltenham and Bath. The metropolis, for its part, has an overabundance of playhouses and opera houses, and now, laments Denne, this new pleasure den called the Pantheon (a place of public entertainment that opened in Oxford Street in 1772). If only "all persons would . . . submit to a voluntary retirement," he adds, instead of running "from one scene of imaginary pleasure to another" to "forget themselves." But for Denne, the pursuit of pleasure is just the problem. Britons want all too much to forget themselves and drown in sensory gratifications; they refuse to be alone and think. So Denne advises "modern architects" to create buildings in London that appear as pleasure-houses on the outside, in the hope that unsuspecting hedonists will be lured into them. Inside these buildings, however, there will be no opportunities for idle pleasures, only an array of "closets" for "self-communion."[38] Even the newly built Pantheon, says Denne, should have "separate cell[s]" installed in it so that those who sin in the Pantheon by day can reflect and repent there at night.[39]

Godwin agreed with Denne on the virtues of careful, deliberate, solitary reflection. In 1812 he advised his future son-in-law, Percy Shelley, in a letter, "to keep up the intellectual, and in some sense the solitary, fermentation, and to procrastinate the contact and consequent action."[40] At the time, Shelley had tried and failed to stir up political rebellion among the working classes in Dublin. He was thus getting ahead of himself in 1812. He wanted immediate political change in all of Britain and he was trying to do his part before he was ready. Godwin accordingly advised Shelley to sit and think in solitude for a while before he went about politically educating the Irish masses. The most sensible definition of "fermentation," as Godwin uses it in his letter, is a "state of agitation tending to bring about a purer, more wholesome, or more stable condition of things."[41] Thus Shelley is supposed to isolate himself in a state of intellectual "agitation" until his ideas are "wholesome" and "stable" enough to be communicated to others. He has to "[work] out his opinions with patient scrutiny" before he can deliver them accurately, even if it means staying "shut up for weeks, or for a longer period, in his sanctuary."[42]

Speaking of sanctuaries where the intellect is purified and matured, Godwin, surprisingly, had a lot of favorable things to say about monastic solitude. He often praised medieval monks for preserving and enhancing Western intellectual tradition, even if he found their life, on the whole, too ascetic. In 1795, Godwin told a friend of his that he is

> an utter enemy to every thing of a monastic principle. I am persuaded that the true & only rational end of human life is pleasure. A wise man would . . . form to himself a scale of pleasures, and it is not probable that he would relish many pleasures that require much property to be sublimed into a small compass, which, diffused, would produce in the world a quantity of pleasure a thousand times greater. I believe we ought to be ready to sacrifice our own pleasure to a great advantage to be obtained for our neighbours, but I conceive that, to a man who has formed a just scale of pleasure, the occasion for this sacrifice will rarely occur.[43]

Here is an instance of what William Marshall calls Godwin's "hedonistic utilitarianism."[44] The letter states that the basic point of life is the pursuit of personal pleasure (hedonism). The catch is that on a few rare occasions all people will have to sacrifice small amounts of their own pleasure for the greater good (utilitarianism). How do we know when and how to do this? A "just scale of pleasure" will tell us; that is, a rational sense of which pleasures are due to us and which of our pleasures we must sacrifice for others. If everyone were to sacrifice one or two judiciously selected personal pleasures, Godwin says—pleasures "sublimed into a small compass"—then these would add up over time and enhance the general stock of pleasure. So the sacrifice of certain personal pleasures is a good thing, provided it is done economically and in view of its social usefulness.

Yet for all his interest in small, carefully chosen personal sacrifices, Godwin was fascinated with medieval monks, who sacrificed hugely disproportionate amounts of their own time and pleasure for the greater good. Monks had no "scale of pleasure" to use. They forwent all of their own pleasures, and civilization was the better for it. Godwin calls "our ancient monasteries" the "great preservers of all that is admirable in the literature of ancient Greece and Rome." Scholastic monks, he says, were a "wonderful class of men," unrivaled in "their patient labours, their voluntary self-mortification, their generous love of truth . . . their disdain of the incitements and splendours of the world" and "their exquisite subtlety of thought and accuracy of deduction in questions almost beyond the bounds of human enquiry."[45] Nor did they sacrifice individual pleasures for the sake of individual fame. Monks were "satisfied" merely "with the consciousness of their own perseverance and ingenuity."[46]

In one striking passage, Godwin speaks of scholastic monks as a self-perpetuating race of men evolved beyond the irrational desire to procreate. He writes that "perhaps the greatest debt which after ages have contracted to this remote period [the Middle Ages], arose out of the system of monasteries and ecclesiastical celibacy. Owing to these a numerous race of men succeeded to each other perpetually, who were separated from the world, cut off from the endearments of conjugal and parental affection, and who had a plenitude of leisure for solitary application."[47] Celibate monks had a "plenitude of leisure for solitary application." Is Godwin envious? He spent much of his own life in debt and taking care of five children, three of whom were not his own and none of whom was raised by the same two parents.[48] His statement that a "numerous race of men succeeded to each other perpetually" imaginatively suggests that monastic orders could reproduce themselves without women. Nor is this the first time Godwin thought along these lines. The above passage was published in *Thoughts on Man* in 1831. Yet Godwin was imagining a future race of self-perpetuating men all the way back in *Political Justice*. At the end of *Political Justice* he speculates on the possibility of a distant utopia on earth, where people "will cease to propagate. . . . The whole will be a people of men, and not of children. Generation will not succeed generation, nor truth have in a certain degree to recommence her career every thirty years" (*PJ*, 465). What kind of future society is Godwin imagining here? There seem to be two basic options. One is a prolonged but "final human society" that "would neither desire nor have a reproductive future." The other is an immortal society that has learned "to eradicate death."[49] Whichever way we read this passage, the future world that Godwin envisions is a world without children. And his vision of a childless world is perfectly in sync with his affectionate descriptions of the monastic life. The fewer children there are, the fewer slaves to adults there are, since, according to Godwin, parenting itself is of the nature of tyranny. As Cathy Collett notes about the "Generation will not succeed generation" passage: "the absence of children is central to [Godwin's] vision because it allows for a society comprised entirely of peers, a population of self-actualized adults, all equally capable of self-management."[50]

Fascination with monastic solitude textures the narrative of *Mandeville* (1817), Godwin's fourth novel. In *Mandeville*, Audley Mandeville, uncle of the narrator and eponymous protagonist, Charles Mandeville, lives in his ancestral home, which the narrator/Charles compares to "the monastery of La Trappe."[51] Here Audley leads a "sort of prison-life," where he is "so much the more completely master of the arrangement of his time; all the little machinery of his studies was about him."[52] At his fingertips is a blissful existence of "unvaried uniformity" and study. But Audley is ultimately a dead weight in this novel. He makes no use of the monastic-carceral environment that his nephew Charles apparently sees as an advantage: a lone, gloomy house built on a rock on the southern coast of England, "favourable to meditation and endless reverie."[53] Instead, Audley takes the opposite route. He falls in love with his poor cousin, Amelia, both families prevent the marriage, and Audley, in the end, is left miserable and indolent. Love and generation have derailed the monkish, carceral, intellectual life he might have had.

I noted earlier that faith in reformative penal solitude remained unshaken even after early experiments in solitary confinement (ca. 1780–1799) met with mixed results. It remained unshaken for many reasons.[54] One of the least noted of these is the diffusive influence of polite literature that apparently had nothing to do with prisons. For instance, the physician to George III, internationally renowned author and Rousseau apologist Johann Georg Zimmermann, published an enormous, four-hundred-odd-page treatise called *On Solitude* in Zurich in 1755. English translations of it began circulating in the 1790s. The timing was perfect. Scores of English gaols and houses of correction had recently been built or rebuilt in accordance with Howardian principles, including reformed prisons in Horsham, Petworth, Bodmin, Wymondham, and Gloucester. *On Solitude* is more of a long conversational essay à la Michel de Montaigne, Francis Bacon, or Joseph Addison than any explicit endorsement of the 1779 Penitentiary Act. It is not an apology for new British legislation, such as *Distributive Justice and Mercy* is. Yet it does perform similar ideological work. It promotes reformative confinement in prisons all the more effectively because its apparent aim is to do something else entirely. This is especially true when Zimmermann extends his paeans to *elective* solitude to the idea of forced, carceral solitude. He makes occasional claims such as the one quoted above: "it is certainly true that a person possessed of a fine imagination may be much happier in prison, than he could possibly be without imagination amidst the most magnificent scenery." Joseph Addison, too, made the same point in his famous *Spectator* series (nos. 411–421) on the pleasures of the imagination.

Other late eighteenth- and early nineteenth-century literary texts do related ideological work under the veil of the aesthetic. Take the 1800 poem in Spenserian stanzas by Peter Courtier, called *Pleasures of Solitude*. *Pleasures of Solitude* was popular enough to go through a second edition in 1802 and a third in 1804. Essentially, the poem upholds vigilant solitude as the precondition of sociability, morality, and piety. Courtier is no philanthropist or a moral crusader. He abandoned his clerical ambitions to work as a law clerk and publisher of textbooks. Yet like

Hanway, Denne, and others, Courtier sees elective isolation as the true path to human goodness and godliness. *Pleasures of Solitude* argues that being alone offers a person "pleasures" more "lasting and sublime" than any to be found in company. It is in isolation that the "seeds of virtue" are cultivated and the soul rises like "grateful incense," until "streams of heavenly radiance shower" on "thought[s]" otherwise "misguided."[55] The speaker claims:

> We stand indebted to the lonely hour
> Even for the sweets that public charms inspire.
> Not in the present have those charms their power,
> Not in enjoyment most their splendours fire;
> But when, in musing moment, we retire
> To make the scene of happiness our own:
> 'Tis then we hang indeed on rapture's lyre,
> Or breathe to pity's plaint congenial moan;
> Then, that the worth of each, at last is really known.[56]

The central idea in this passage is that the benefits of social interaction are not realized in the moment. The "charms" of social life are unavailable to us until after the fact: until, "in musing moment, we retire / To make the scene of happiness our own." Here Courtier echoes the famous preface to the *Lyrical Ballads* (also published in 1800). In the preface, Wordsworth says that an emotion felt in the presence of beautiful natural forms needs to be subdued by tranquility to be appreciated or properly harnessed for the sake of composing a poem. It has to be remembered when we are alone and in a quiet place, so that a new emotion, related to the old one but different, can overtake us and drive our creative energies.[57] Courtier is saying something similar in *Pleasures of Solitude*. When we are meaningfully engaged with others, he notes, we may feel hints of emotions like "rapture" or "pity" in the moment. But for Courtier these are only intimations, flashes, approximations. We have to be alone and in a reflective state if we want these emotions to "fire." Only in solitude can a person know "the worth of each" emotion he or she has had in society.

CONFINEMENT

The counterpart to solitude in the reformed prison was separate cells. At night, a prisoner would ideally sleep alone in his or her own cell. During a set part of the day, for more or fewer hours depending on the institution, he or she would work alone in that cell. Many of the new-built prison cells were accordingly designed with high windows so that inmates could not see out of them. The logic was that the less an inmate saw of the outside world, the more he or she would turn to himself or herself, look within, come to terms with his or her neglected conscience.

His or her moral and religious sensibilities would be revitalized. As Hanway puts it: prisoners "totally sequestered from the world, for a season . . . may return to it truly and literally *renewed* in *spirit*."[58] This is by now a familiar narrative. What is less familiar is how and to what extent the penal cell was part of a larger cultural interest in all things small scale in the period we call Romantic. Georgian housing, for instance, increasingly emphasized privacy and the segregation of rooms.[59] English gardens were also "devoting more and more space to seclusion" at the same time.[60] Why? The answer, according to Rachel Crawford, is that "contained spaces geared toward productivity, usually . . . of smaller dimension, took hold of the English imagination" in the late eighteenth and early nineteenth centuries.[61]

It is in the context of widespread interest in "contained spaces geared toward productivity, usually . . . of smaller dimension," that the novel *Fleetwood* (1805) becomes particularly interesting. *Fleetwood* is the third novel Godwin wrote following his masterpiece, *Caleb Williams*, and his less successful second novel, *St. Leon*. Its basic plot parallels the plot of *Othello*. Casimir Fleetwood is born and raised in Wales by his father (his mother dies early on) and rambles about the wild Welsh landscapes as a child. In time he goes to Oxford, where he lives a relatively dissipated life. Then, visiting Switzerland on the grand tour, he learns from an old family friend, Ruffigny, that his father has died. Time passes. Eventually Fleetwood travels to Cumberland and encounters the Macneil family. He falls in love with the young and talented botanist Mary Macneil, and the two marry after Mary's parents die at sea. Through a complicated subplot involving financial corruption, Mary loses her impressive fortune of 60,000 pounds and becomes penniless. To Fleetwood, however, this is a minor setback. He takes Mary back to his paternal estate in Merionethshire, Wales, where the two can start a new and happy life together.

The family seat in Wales is where the real trouble in the novel begins. In one crucial moment of the plot, Mary Macneil Fleetwood decides to take over a small room in the house that her husband has long since adored as his own personal "closet" (i.e., a small private apartment). She intends to make the closet a place where she can draw and keep her flowers. To Fleetwood this is devastating news. He is torn apart inside, though he holds in his frustration. In time, this one incident—the taking over of the closet—initiates a "career of obsession" with him.[62] He starts to see his young, attractive, and intelligent wife as a person apart, with interests of her own and a tendency to attract younger men. When he eventually learns that Mary is pregnant, Fleetwood suspects that the father is one of his own distant relatives, an army ensign named Kenrick. This maddens Fleetwood to the extent that he sets up wax dolls of Kenrick and Mary and has them act out their adultery in a tiny play for a one-man audience. At this point a villain named Gifford enters the narrative, who encourages Fleetwood in his suspicion that Kenrick is sleeping with Mary and who goes out of his way to manufacture evidence of their affair. In the end, Gifford is found out. There never was an affair. Ensign Kenrick was definitely in love with someone, but it was not Mary Macneil Fleetwood; he was instead in love with her friend, Louisa, whom Mary had met in Bath. Fleetwood, meanwhile, was too blinded by his own jealousy and the insinuations of Gifford to realize it.

Thus a single plot point—what Roland Barthes would call a "hinge" event—drives the main action of *Fleetwood*.[63] The whole plot turns on the incident with the closet. Fleetwood describes it as a "handsome, retired closet, opening into the principle drawing-room and at a short distance from . . . [his] bed-chamber."[64] It is "the scene of a thousand remembered pleasures, the object of my love."[65] He goes on:

> Here I had been permitted to con my lessons while I was yet of school-boy age; and here it had ever since been my custom to retire with some favourite author, when I wished to feel my mind in its most happy state. In this closed I meditated, I composed, I wrote. . . . I preferred this sequestered nook to all the rest of the mansion taken together. I entered it now, after a twelvemonth's absence, with a full recollection of all the castles which I had sat there and builded in the air, the odes, the tragedies, and heroic poems which, in the days of visionary childhood, upon that spot I had sketched and imagined.[66]

Fleetwood says that his child mind was "in its most happy state" when his child body was in a closet. In a different novel this would be a relatively unremarkable fact. Yet in *Fleetwood* this particular detail invites attention because it is the exact opposite of what the reader is led to expect. The novel opens on the sublime and romantic landscapes of North Wales, where Fleetwood was born and raised. We see him as a boy wandering alone along expansive, lush, endless hills and valleys in Merionethshire, tasting the "beauties of nature" at every step.[67] Yet he is never quite alone, even when alone. The life of nature surrounds and invigorates him: "Life is every where around the solitary wanderer; all is health and bloom; the sap circulates, and the leaves expand. . . . The cattle breathe, and the vegetable kingdom consumes the vital air; the herds resort to the flowing stream, and the grass drinks the moisture of the earth and the dew of heaven. Even the clouds, the winds, and the streams present us with the image of life, and talk to us of that venerable power which is operating every where, and never sleeps."[68] Here, the adult Fleetwood describes his childhood self as sensitive to everything that tells of life: from the sap circulating in a tree to the vital winds. Breath and movement and growth all speak of a pantheistic lifeforce (a "venerable power") animating all things.[69]

Yet for all his ecstatic wandering in Wales, Fleetwood says that he was happiest as a child in a closet. Why? Why is the "object of . . . [his] love" and the place where his child mind was "in its most happy state" a closet? Critics have never seriously considered this question. They pay less attention to the fact per se that Fleetwood is obsessed with his closet and more attention to the fact that this obsession advances the plot. One reader supposes that "extreme delicacy" is what makes Fleetwood "an ardent lover of the very chamber his young wife appropriates."[70] Another observes that Fleetwood is "absolutely rigid, and finds unbearable any change in his accustomed pattern, such as moving from one study to another in his own house."[71] Since he had his own way all through his childhood, he never "learn[ed] to bear the proximity to others."[72] These are sensible arguments. They help explain why an incident so apparently trivial as the taking over of a closet could move a man to become pathologically jealous of his wife. Yet the closet is important beyond its role in merely advancing the plot of *Fleetwood*. It is important in itself as a physical space and as an index of an awkward but real desire. Fleetwood is attracted to small and enclosed spaces as a means of creative stimulation. He may have had all of beautiful northern Wales to run around in, charged with the grandeur of God, but it takes a "sequestered nook" in his ancestral home to fire his imagination. As a child, he needs to be properly walled in to bring his visions to life. Victor Brombert traces a similar preoccupation in Godwin's contemporary and fellow novelist, Stendhal: "for Stendhal, as for his heroes, lucidity is conceivable only from within a shelter."[73] Their "most fundamental freedom is clearly associated with the act of writing. And this act belongs properly to the privileged world of claustration."[74]

The word *closet* bore some association with prison cells in 1805. Denne says that if British citizens were to think of their "closets" less as "dungeons" and more places of "serious reflection," they would "indulge a few minutes recollection" now and then.[75] About the county bridewell in Preston, John Howard notes that there were eleven "closets, called *boxes* . . . to sleep in."[76] Hanway had an answer prepared for anyone who doubted the virtues of solitary confinement in prisons: "Ask mankind in general, if they learn to reflect in their closet, or in the bustle of resort, amidst the business, the pleasures, the vices, and crimes of men."[77] An especially dramatic connection between personal closets and penal cells appears in *Sermons for Prisons*. One particular sermon, meant to be addressed to a prisoner, reads: "Here seated in Solitude, under the canopy of Heaven, in our closet, or *in our prison*, we turn our Eyes inward on our own hearts."[78] This passage apposes the word *closet* and the word *prison* as if to insist on their synonymity and its importance. It also uses the determiner *our* in such a way as to universalize the condition of the prisoner. Both rhetorical strategies align the virtues of coercive self-reflection with the virtues of elective self-reflection in a way that has far-reaching implications in a culture undergoing a penal revolution.

In his own writing, Godwin transformed the closet from a religious space of prayer to a humanist space of discovery and invention, never losing the qualities of austerity and isolation attached to the word. In one essay he tells readers to "*commune with your own heart in your closet, and be still.* Seek to discover your true character."[79] The first sentence in this passage, in italics, is adapted from a combination of Psalm 4 and the Gospel of Matthew, which are respectively as follows:

> Stand in awe, and sin not: *commune with your own heart* upon your bed, and *be still.* . . . Offer the sacrifices of righteousness, and put your trust in the LORD.[80]

> But thou, when thou prayest, enter into *thy closet,* and when thou hast shut thy door, pray to thy Father which is in secret; and thy Father which seeth in secret shall reward thee openly.[81]

In the essay in question, Godwin replaces the words "upon your bed," from Psalm 4:4, with the words "in your closet," from Matthew 6:6. It makes sense that he would have spliced these passages, which are clearly thematically related. What is interesting is the second sentence Godwin writes—"Seek to discover your true character"—which clarifies the first. Here Godwin makes being alone in closet an exercise in self-discovery, as opposed to an exercise in humility. Nor is this his last word on the subject of closets and reflection. In an essay in the *Enquirer*, he writes that laws were originally conceived by sages "in the tranquillity of the closet."[82] In *Mandeville*, the eponymous narrator speaks of a man "unfold[ing] the treasury of intellect in the solitude of his closet."[83]

Thus it was a special privilege to Godwin to live, in a sense and to an extent, in austere confinement. Recall that Howard refers to the sleeping cells in the Preston bridewell as "closets." A sight Godwin admired during a trip to Ireland was the ruins of a monastic settlement founded in the sixth century, by St. Kevin of Glendalough, in the county of Wicklow. Among the ruins of the settlement, Godwin singled out a bed made of rock, designed to mortify the body, in which St. Kevin was thought to have slept. Godwin respected "St Cavan's Bed," as he called it: "an excavation in the rock, with a couch, or seat, running the whole length of the cave, where the saint was accustomed to sleep, and which has the virtue, if re[sorted] to by a pregnant woman on the anniversary of the saint, of securing her a safe and easy delivery."[84] C. H. Lawrence notes that St. Kevin, renowned for his "heroic acts of mortification," is said to have remained with his arms outstretched like a cross "for seven years, unsleeping and motionless, so that the birds nested in his upturned hands."[85] It is no wonder that Godwin appreciated this peculiar spot. Here was a remote cave, an obscure cave, a site of celibacy and austerity believed to help usher in new life. In fact, we can read such a cave as an important symbol, and perhaps even a key, to certain subplots in his novels. A kind of rebirth in and through prolonged confinement is a theme Godwin explores frequently in his narrative fiction, to which we may now turn.

PRELIMINARY TO THE NOVELS

William Godwin was fascinated with imprisonment long before he became a public figure. One of his earliest childhood memories involved spending time with a Miss Godwin, his first cousin once removed, who became Mrs. Sothren when Godwin was sixteen. Mrs. Sothren lived with the Godwins in rural East Anglia and helped raise young William. She had secular pastimes, such as reading the *Spectator*, but Godwin remembers that "her whole time was engaged in solitary devotion, in . . . reading religious books, and in gardening." In this routine she made little Godwin "her companion by night and by day."[86] Consider her three activities, "solitary devotion," "gardening," and "reading religious books," in light of the reformed prison as defined by the 1779 Penitentiary Act: "*solitary imprisonment, accompanied by well-regulated labor, and religious instruction*." The two regimes seem oddly similar as indices of middle-class Protestant culture. The boy Godwin gardened with Mrs. Sothren in the morning and slept alongside her at night; "for the rest of the day, he adds," they were in the house, where he "became the *willing prisoner* of her apartment, secluded from air, secluded from sports, and having no companion but herself."[87] It was in this same apartment, too, that Godwin learned to read, around age five.

The apartment of Mrs. Sothren was, to young Godwin, a figurative prison. He could have "escaped" it if he wanted to—at least for a while—but so thoroughly did metaphors of imprisonment structure his perception that he would have felt, in some sense, walled in wherever he went. Godwin writes that, as a child, he "reflected with displeasure upon this cumbersome material machine, that we are fated to carry about us, and that places a boy at the mercy of his elders . . . or a subject at that of the government of his country."[88] He is talking, of course, about the body; even as a boy, that is, he saw the body as a carceral machine well designed to subordinate children to adults and adult subjects to the state. He held this view until the end of his life. In *Thoughts on Man*, for example, he calls the body by various carceral names: a "wall of flesh," a "cabin of flesh," a "cage."[89] According to Godwin, moreover, at some point most children will have to drag their cumbersome material machines to school, where they will be penned in like animals. In the schoolroom, in other words, children are imprisoned twice: in walls of flesh within walls of brick. The "line which is ordinarily drawn" between children and their tutors "is so forcible, that . . . [children] seem to themselves more like birds kept in a cage, or sheep in a pen, than like beings of the same nature" as adults.[90] And if an adolescent ends up making it through the prison of school, the prison of marriage awaits. In a letter to Mary Wollstonecraft, only recently his wife, Godwin compares marriage in general to a life sentence of "hard labor in the Spielberg," a Moravian fortress-prison, where the "only hope for the unfortunate captive" is that some new "despot grace his accession with a general jail delivery."[91] There may be a hint of sincerity in this last, mostly ironic comment. In every stage of life, for a writer such as Godwin, a new confinement, fortified by custom, awaits.

Godwin fills his novels with metaphors of imprisonment, the tenors of which are numerous and varied. Earth: the virtuous Ruffigny in *Fleetwood* calls Earth "the great Bridewell of the universe" and compares being outside Switzerland to "a state of solitary imprisonment." Education: Casimir Fleetwood refers to his childhood education as "a sort of shackles."[92] Power: Roderic in *Imogen* laments that "the hands of . . . [Power] are chained and fettered in links of iron."[93] Social niceties: for Reginald St. Leon, social "form" and "ceremony" are "the fetters of ages."[94] Fate: to Richard Herbert in *Cloudesley*, "fate often shuts" people "in with adamantine bars, which it is impractical for them to burst."[95] Herbert the character, here, echoes Godwin the philosopher. In one of his essays, Godwin describes the universe as a "complicated machine" and himself as an "infinitely small portion" of it, "gratefully disposed to make the most of my advantages, and not vain enough to think that I can break the adamantine chain, by which every creature is held in his appointed place."[96]

The "adamantine chain" holding everyone in place is a metaphor that Godwin uses often to describe the philosophical doctrine of Necessity. Godwin believed in this doctrine throughout his adult life (with some qualifications). Necessity holds that all mental action proceeds according to fixed laws, no less absolute than the laws of physics that govern material bodies. Our present mental actions are both the inevitable product of our past mental actions and the inevitable antecedents of our future mental actions. Motives are what cause people to act. They initiate behaviors as automatically and as invariably as physical forces propel objects. The rub is that a person cannot actually choose, willy-nilly, to have this or that motive: one either has a motive or one does not. All of this may, indeed, sound bleak when it comes to how much control we can have over our own actions; but the good news, for Godwin, is that in a necessitarian universe you are guaranteed to be able to change human minds, if you should be virtuous enough to want to. Through a limited free will—limited by Necessity itself—you can figure out how to add links to the necessitarian chains that bind the moral universe; i.e., you can replace old mental antecedents with new mental antecedents and so direct the chains of Necessity constructively. Thus an educated necessitarian has the advantage of knowing positively that his or her moral influence over others can be absolutely effective. The well-meaning necessitarian "employs real antecedents, and has a right to expect real effects" (*PJ*, 170). He or she understands that as soon as a truth takes hold on a given mind—and a truth will always take hold if it is communicated rightly—it remains fixed and unalterable in that mind: as fixed and unalterable as falsehood.

Hence in a necessitarian universe, a limitless network of invisible "chains" holds everyone and everything in place. No one can ever get out of this network, but some people can learn how to manipulate its structure for worthy or unworthy ends. A link in one of the chains of Necessity may be detached and relinked elsewhere, ideally for some benevolent and productive reason. I see a kind of tactile and extensive version of this principle at work in the Godwinian novel. Godwin places many of his fictional characters in actual prisons and fastens them there in actual chains. Yet these characters are never absolutely helpless; they learn to redirect their chains to advantage; they exploit their confinement for their own good and sometimes for the good of others. Characters are tested with isolation, walls, and chains, which they ultimately transcend. The mature novels reflect this process most clearly, particularly *Caleb Williams*, *St. Leon*, and *Deloraine.* The first of the three is the most famous Godwinian novel and the earliest.

Caleb Williams

Political Justice and *Caleb Williams* have been read as representing all aspects of any kind of coercion as irremediably bad for everyone involved. The leading lights in Godwin studies have agreed that *Caleb Williams* portrays prisons as hopeless and unequivocal evils. Peter Marshall, for instance, says that Godwin "saved his greatest indignation" in the novel "for the prisons." Marilyn Butler calls the narrativized prison in *Caleb Williams* "a place of cruelty and degradation, useless for the purpose of reform." For B. J. Tysdahl, the prison space in *Caleb Williams* "dull[s] energy and humanity."[97] These are not shocking readings. Godwin himself paved the way for such readings in *Political Justice*, a year before *Caleb Williams* appeared. In book VII of *Political Justice*, "Of Crimes and Punishments," for instance, he argues that every proposed aim of "coercion" is necessarily irrational and unjust. Coercion for the sake of restraining a person presupposes that that person will commit additional injuries if set loose; this is unfair. Coercion for the sake of reforming a person fails because it makes no appeal to the understanding of the person coerced: it simply hardens his heart against the authorities that oppress him. Nor does coercing the guilty set a meaningful example for the innocent: coercion of the few breeds only resentment among the masses; few learn anything from it; few receive moral enlightenment or are deterred from crime because the state decides to make an example of one or two unlucky persons. In a word, coercion of the guilty to deter the innocent from crime is just plain barbaric, and "barbarity possesses none of the attributes of persuasion" (*PJ*, 380).

It may seem, at first, that *Caleb Williams* advances the same basic argument—i.e., all coercion is irrational and ineffective—in narrative form. As he is on the verge of his own period of imprisonment, Caleb has an imaginary, heated conversation with John Bull:

> Thank God, exclaims the Englishman, we have no Bastile! Thank God, with us no man can be punished without a crime! Unthinking wretch! Is that a country of liberty where thousands languish in dungeons and

> fetters? Go, go, ignorant fool! and visit the scenes of our prisons! witness their unwholesomeness, their filth, the tyranny of their governors, the misery of their inmates! After that show me the man shameless enough to triumph, and say, England has no Bastile! (*CW*, 161)

Here is an authorial aside dramatizing the anti-coercion position in *Political Justice*, book VII. It lasts a full paragraph, and in the context of the novel it feels like a political set piece. Yet its depiction of imprisonment as the homogenously evil, filthy instrument of tyrants is not exactly the keynote for the rest of *Caleb Williams*. In fact, as imprisonment moves from the object of abstract speculation, as it is here, to a narrated experience, its representation, its meanings, its potentialities, gain nuance. The time Caleb spends in Newgate may rightly be said to "dull [his] energy and humanity," but it may just as easily be said to sharpen them.

What follows is a study of three Godwinian novels, *Caleb Williams*, *St. Leon*, and *Deloraine*. Each is written by a first-person narrator who recounts between one and four personal experiences of imprisonment. In every case, the imprisonment of the narrator has beneficent effects. As is to be expected, however, a few of these narrators express anger and resentment along the way. Caleb and St. Leon declaim against the horrors of their respective prisons, as well as the (mostly) tyrannical authorities that put them there. We expect such declamations to have been written by the leading anti-coercionist of the 1790s. What we do not expect is that the novels also show their heroes as redeemed and enlightened in prison to a considerable extent, and not in spite of imprisonment but because of it. The novels portray confinement simultaneously as excruciating and edifying. This may be a relatively common practice in a French Romantic novel, but for an English author with the political views of Godwin, it is remarkable.

Godwin is comparable to the French novelist Stendhal in that his novels "exploit the metaphor of the happy prison" even while revealing "unmasked indignation when confronted with degrading images of fetters and punitive walls."[98] Marilyn Butler makes a related point about *Caleb Williams* in particular. She places the novel in the Puritan literary tradition in which real seventeenth-century prisoners of conscience wrote polemics and narratives from gaols. For Butler, the Newgate sequence in *Caleb Williams* exists to assure readers that the mind of an innocent man may remain free though his body is in chains.[99] It is undeniable, of course, that parts of the novel reinforce this point. Emily Melville tells the bully Barnabas Tyrell: "you may imprison my body, but you cannot conquer my mind" (there is some irony here in the fact that Tyrell *does* end up conquering her mind: she practically goes insane) (*CW*, 62).[100] While in Newgate, Caleb adapts one of Satan's speeches from *Paradise Lost*, observing that "the mind is [its own place;] and is endowed with powers that might enable it to laugh at the tyrant's vigilance" (*CW*, 167).[101] Thus it is true that the main prison sequence in *Caleb Williams* reinforces the idea that the mind can be free while the body is confined. But this is not all the prison sequence does for Caleb. It also exercises and expands his "endowed" mental "powers" permanently. Part of Caleb flourishes within prison walls. His mind cooperates with its carceral environment to reach new levels of ingenuity and resolve. To adapt a sentence from Terry Eagleton: "the bad news is that . . . [prison] is an inhospitable place; the good news is that this mobilizes a set of admirable human resources."[102]

After the villain of the novel, the wealthy landowner Ferdinando Falkland, falsely accuses Caleb of grand larceny, he sends Caleb to what is essentially a fictionalized Newgate Prison. There Caleb spends his days (nine or ten hours) in a room with eleven other suspected felons, and his nights (fourteen or fifteen hours) alone in a 7.5 by 6.5 foot cell, in "complete darkness" (some of the other prisoners, unlike Caleb, have to sleep two or three in a cell) (*CW*, 161). Caleb tells us that, during his confinement, his mind "passed through two very different stages": in the first, his "faculties were overwhelmed"; in the second, they were "raised to a pitch of enthusiasm" (*CW*, 168). More specifically, in the first stage he felt the "iron of slavery grating upon . . . [his] soul," and he resented his "puerile eagerness to be brought to the test and have . . . [his] innocence examined" (*CW*, 162). This stage covers most of chapter 11 in volume 2, and lasts about six pages. The second, longer phase of his confinement—in which his faculties were "raised to a pitch of enthusiasm"—lasts for three chapters (chapters 12 to 14 in volume 2) and takes around eighteen pages. Clearly Godwin thought the second stage was more important.

The second stage is curious in that it reads less like the diatribe of an angry and abused inmate and more like a tutorial on how to make the most of a prison experience. Caleb reaps many of the benefits of solitude in Newgate that Zimmermann recommends in his massive treatise on that subject. Zimmermann says that "the imagination becomes more vivid, and the memory more faithful, while the senses remain undisturbed, and no external object agitates the soul." The "unencumbered mind" in solitude "recalls all that it has read; all that has pleased the eye, or delighted the ear; and reflecting on every idea which either observation, experience, or discourse, has produced, gains new information by every reflection."[103] Caleb, for his part, thrives on this kind of mental program in Newgate. He "task[s] the stores of . . . [his] memory and . . . [his] powers of invention." He "recollect[s] the history of . . . [his] life," "call[ing] to mind a number of minute circumstances which but for this exercise would have been for ever forgotten"—"whole conversations . . . their subjects, their arrangement, their incidents and frequently their very words"—until his "mind glow[s] with enthusiasm" (*CW*, 165). Next Caleb moves on from personal reflections to "imaginary adventures." He imagines "every situation in which . . . [he] could be placed," so as to master the "conduct" and the "oratory suited to these different states" (*CW*, 165–166). As a result of these and other mental exercises, he "improve[s] more in eloquence in the solitude of . . . [his] dungeon, than perhaps . . . [he] should have done in the busiest and most crowded scenes." Ultimately, Caleb turns Newgate into a sort of personalized seminary where he can methodically review his education:

> I proceeded to as regular a disposition of my time, as the man in his study who passes from mathematics to poetry, and from poetry to the law of nations in the different parts of each single day; and I seldom infringed upon my plan. . . . I went over, by the assistance of memory only, a considerable part of Euclid during my confinement, and revived day after day the series of facts and incidents in some of the most celebrated historians. (*CW*, 166)

Caleb is a protagonist especially adept at making a virtue of necessity. Zimmermann in his treatise suggests that solitude is more of a state of mind than the actual condition of being alone. Caleb proves the truth of this theory. At first he finds it hard to concentrate during the day, thanks to the noise of his eleven fellow inmates. But soon he "brought to perfection the art of withdrawing my thoughts, and saw and heard the people about me for just as short a time and as seldom as I pleased" (*CW*, 166). Caleb also learns that solitude in prison has some additional therapeutic benefits. As he puts it: "if the intercourse of our fellow men has its pleasures, solitude on the other hand is not without its advantages. In solitude we can pursue our own thoughts undisturbed; and I was able to call up at will the most pleasing avocations" (*CW*, 179). One of these avocations is practicing an Irish brogue that will come in handy later, once Caleb has to begin wearing disguises and hiding from the law.

In Newgate Caleb receives lasting moral enlightenment, à la Boethius, learning the importance of making do with very little in the way of wealth and fame. One of his epiphanies is explicitly Lear-like.[104] In *King Lear*, during the fury of the storm, Kent leads Lear to a "hovel" where the king can expect to find "friendship . . .'gainst the tempest."[105] Inside the hovel, Lear takes a good look at the wretched Edgar, who is apparently mad and dressed in rags, and then is struck with his own vanity and that of high society: "Is man no more than this? Consider him well. Thou ow'st the worm no silk, the beast no hide, the sheep no wool, the cat no perfume. Ha? here's three on 's are sophisticated. Thou art the thing itself: unaccommodated man is no more but such a poor, bare, fork'd animal as thou art."[106] Immediately, Lear tears off his clothes in an attempt to achieve solidarity with the half-naked Edgar. It so happens that Caleb dwells on a similar subject in Newgate: "Such is man in himself considered; so simple his nature; so few his wants. How different from the man of artificial society! Palaces are built for his reception, a thousand vehicles provided for his exercise, provinces are ransacked for the gratification of his appetite, and the whole world traversed to supply him with apparel and furniture. Thus vast is his expenditure, and the purchase slavery" (*CW*, 166). As the once-kingly Lear ponders in his hovel what it means to be an "unaccommodated man," "the thing itself," the once-ambitious Caleb meditates in gaol on "man in himself considered." He learns that to desire, expect, and use more goods than one needs is a violation of political justice. He sloughs off his former worldly ambitions, resolving "fully to possess the days . . . [he] had to live" (*CW*, 166). He writes: "Henceforth I will be contented with tranquil obscurity, with the cultivation of sentiment and wisdom, and the exercise of benevolence within a narrow circle" (*CW*, 171). This resolution of his has an enduring impact, reorienting Caleb morally for the rest of the novel. Eight chapters later, in volume 3, he is still thinking back "to that obscurity to which my imagination had looked forward with delight, while I was yet in . . . jail." By "obscurity" Caleb means that life of retirement in "rural solitude" that he keeps reading about in his pocket Horace (*CW*, 227). Whether he eventually lives out that life is less important, for our purposes, than where and under what conditions he first learned to desire it.

Caleb does not endorse legal imprisonment as a solid means to reform character. In one sense, in fact, his Newgate experience actually parodies the aims of the reformed prison. Instead of treading a wheel or beating hemp or chopping rags (work recommended for convicted felons in the 1779 Penitentiary Act), Caleb works steadily on his prison-break plan. Instead of receiving religious instruction from chaplains, he methodically reenacts his own liberal education. Yet Caleb does realize some of the aims of Howardian prison, in and through his experience in "Newgate," whether he wills it or not. One late eighteenth-century prison reformer has the following advice for inmates in solitary confinement: "examine your past life"; "observe what is written in your own heart"; "fix in your memory . . . good things . . . and frequently renew your resolutions to act accordingly."[107] In Newgate Caleb does just this. He learns the value of living humbly and benevolently and in obscurity, justifying the claim of Hanway that "*resolution* with regard to the future part of life, will be more sincere in the *prison*, than it usually is in the *church*."[108]

Caleb has an odd way of returning to confined spaces in the novel, almost as if he seeks them for their own sake. His first move following his escape from Newgate is to hide himself in a "black and impenetrable" cave in a valley on the outskirts of town (*CW*, 185). He calls the cave "my prison." Soon afterward he moves to a different cave, one of even "greater security" than the first, and remains there "with little variation" until nightfall. The moon appearing too bright for safe travel, Caleb finds that "my only relief during this interval was to allow myself to sink to the bottom of my cavern" (*CW*, 186). At five in the morning, the moon is finally gone and Caleb leaves his cave, traveling six miles out in the open until he is captured by a band of thieves. For a while, he is more or less confined in the thieves' hideout, where he "sigh[s] for that solitude and obscurity, that retreat from the vexations of the world . . . which I had proposed to myself when I broke my prison" (*CW*, 205). After a brief skirmish with a Gothic hag, he manages to flee the thieves' hideout and make his way into a thick forest. In the forest, his "only rule" is to "take a direction as opposite as possible to that which led to the scene of my late imprisonment" (*CW*, 209). So he wanders to a seaport town in the west of England, then to Wales, and finally to London, where Falkland's henchman, Jones, captures him and returns him to the same prison he broke out of. Things go better for Caleb in prison this time around. For one thing, his health gets better: "strange as it may seem, here, in prison . . . I recovered my health (*CW*, 325). He also learns that his recognizances have been forfeited and that he will be free to go, to his shock, in two days. For a second time, then, we find Caleb at large, and in an eerie doubling of past experience he winds up lingering near the very caves outside of town, his "prison" caves, in which he once took shelter:

> I withdrew from the town. I rambled with a slow and thoughtful pace, now bursting with exclamation, and now buried in a profound and undefinable [*sic*] reverie. Accident led me towards the very heath which had first sheltered me, when upon a former occasion I broke out of my prison. I wandered among its cavities and its vallies [*sic*]. It was forlorn and desolate solitude. I continued here for I know not how long. Night at length overtook me unperceived. (*CW*, 246)

Caleb says that it was an "accident" that led him back to the old valley, strewn with prisonlike caves. Was it also accident that made him linger there until nightfall? Partly, partly not. To some extent Caleb seems to be seeking out prisonlike spaces as the only conceivable alternatives to his problems. When he first escaped prison, he found a doubly secure cave in the vale and settled himself there. Now he returns to that same vale, as much "like a man / Flying from something that he dreads" as "one / Who sought the thing he loved."[109] It is hard to know where to draw the line here between fleeing a pain and seeking a morbid sort of safety and pleasure. Consider Robinson Crusoe finding a cave on the island in which to hide from the cannibals. Within that cave, he finds "yet another cave, deeper and far more grand than the first one," just as Caleb does on the heath. To Crusoe, the cave-within-a-cave is such a "safe and womb-like retreat" that he "admits that if he could be sure no savages would disturb him, then he would be content to spend the rest of his days there."[110] The more terrifying, worrying or monotonous the social world is—a world run by what Caleb calls "the debilitating routine of human affairs"—the more, it seems, his own "desolate solitude" can feel like a rich haven (*CW*, 195).

Of course, Caleb gravitates toward concealment and confinement in part because he has to. He is a fugitive from the law and from the magistrate Falkland, who hovers over the world menacingly like the Calvinist God. But I also think that the worst part of Newgate for Caleb is his sense of the injustice of the false accusation that brought him there, not the place itself.[111] A certain part of him learns to appreciate, in the short and in the long term, the strenuousness and mental acrobatics that prison and solitude demand from him. He may have been miserable in prison at first, but one can adapt to a lot, and habit is second nature. In fact, Caleb seems to go on and on about the ultimate value of suffering, whether in prisons or not: "persecution," he says in one instance, "at length gave firmness to my character, and taught me the better part of manhood"; he later claims that "the hardships I had endured [gave] additional mildness to my character," and that "I was probably indebted to the sufferings I had endured, and the exquisite and increased susceptibility they produced, for new energies" (*CW*, 138, 254, 328).

St. Leon

In his second novel, *St. Leon*, Godwin takes the lengthy prison scene in *Caleb Williams* and quadruples it. *St. Leon* is an expansive novel—four volumes long—and in every volume the hero is imprisoned:

> Vol. 1. In 1537, St. Leon and his family are exiled from the canton of Solothurn in northwest Switzerland. They decide to retire to a remote cottage on the north shore of Lake Constance in West Germany. Soon afterward, St. Leon goes back to Solothurn to contest the wrongful seizure of his Swiss estate. In the process he is imprisoned in Solothurn for three days. Upon his release he returns to his lakeside cottage in Germany. He and his family live there for seven years in peace.
>
> Vol. 2. In 1544, St. Leon meets the mysterious adept, Zampieri, and learns the secrets of immortal life and unlimited wealth. Six months later he is summoned before a magistrate in Constance under suspicion of having murdered Zampieri. The evidence is circumstantial: all that the authorities know is that this Zampieri died and that St. Leon acquired an enormous amount of wealth right afterward; but in Constance, one is guilty until proven innocent. So St. Leon is put in a Constance gaol. After an indeterminate period of time, he bribes the gaoler and escapes.
>
> Vol. 3. It is now March 1547, and St. Leon, suspected of being in league with Satan, is sentenced to "perpetual" imprisonment by the Spanish Inquisition. He remains in an Inquisitorial prison in Madrid for twelve years.
>
> Vol. 4. On August 27, 1559, St. Leon escapes the Inquisitorial prison and makes his way to Hungary, where he arrives in the spring of 1660. Three months later he is imprisoned in the dungeon of a castle, north of Buda, by the wild man Bethlem Gabor. (*CW*, xx)

I want to focus first on the Inquisitorial prison in Madrid, where St. Leon is confined for twelve years. By this point in the novel we suspect that St. Leon is an unreliable narrator; when he writes about what happened to him in Madrid, for instance, he seems especially evasive. He wants us to know that he is leaving certain details of his imprisonment in Spain out of his narrative, and that he has no choice in the matter. He gives three reasons for his silence. The first is that he took an "oath of secrecy" before the officers of the Inquisition to reveal nothing he had "seen" or "suffered" during his confinement (an oath his narrative eventually breaks) (*SL*, 254). The second is that there are no "surprising or agreeable adventures" to relate about his imprisonment (another statement his own narrative contradicts) (*SL*, 271). The third is that he is afraid he might "drive the most delicate or susceptible of . . . [his] readers mad with horrors" if he talks about life in his Madrilenian cell. Thus he gives these three excuses about why he has to remain silent about his imprisonment, and yet he makes a point of tantalizing us: more than once he hints that there are "secrets of . . . [his] prison-house" that he "might unfold"—secrets that "might fill the busy man of the world with thoughts and speculation almost to bursting" (*SL*, 272–273). One wonders what kind of secrets St. Leon is withholding. Would they explain why he has been confined by the Inquisition for no less than twelve years? In Switzerland his case was quickly heard and he was released; in Germany he bribed his way out of prison; but in Spain he attempts to bribe a turnkey, a keeper, and a Spanish informer (*mosca*) without success. He mentions no other visitors besides these three.

As readers we are forced to fill in a few gaps to understand why St. Leon is powerless to escape for so long. We recall that he needs certain ingredients to make the elixir of life and certain chemical apparatus to make gold. He has access to neither of these materials in his cell. It seems then that his sole option is to tempt whatever visitors he gets with the promise of extravagant sums in exchange for his release or for access to his equipment. But he is apparently never able to bribe anyone. So either only the turnkey, the keeper, and the informer were ever admitted into his cell over the course of twelve years, or St. Leon had many other visitors as well, all of whom were impossible to bribe. Any such explanation could clarify the length of his confinement. Still, it seems unusual that a (nominally) Catholic aristocrat with intelligence, unlimited wealth, and the secret to immortality could find no expedient for release or escape for twelve years, even in an Inquisitorial prison.[112]

The Madrid section of the novel is far more of a didactic set piece than it is an account of the horrors of imprisonment. St. Leon compares the tyrannical theocracy of Inquisitorial Spain to the British government during the London Treason Trials. His main point is that beliefs arrived at through private judgment are more likely to be closer to the truth than beliefs arrived at through any amount of coercion. This polemic takes up the majority of the Madrid prison narrative. This is not to say that St. Leon mentions no carceral horrors whatsoever. He recalls days of "death-like uniformity" in his Madrilenian cell (*SL*, 271)—of "dull, heavy, pestilential, soul-depressing monotony" (*SL*, 267). This is an unequivocally bleak description. But then St. Leon out-Calebs Caleb Williams in the productive use he makes of his uninterrupted solitude.[113] He says that his "faculties" were "benumbed or dead" for "days, perhaps weeks," until he became "busy, restless, impatient, and inventive" (*SL*, 272). At such times, his mind "soared to the furthest regions of the empyrean, or plunged into the deepest of the recesses in which nature conceals her operations. All systems of philosophising became familiar to me. I revolved every different fable that has been constructed respecting the invisible powers that superintend the events of the boundless universe; and I fearlessly traced out and developed the boldest conjectures and assertions of demonism or atheism" (*SL*, 272). Nor is St. Leon limited to such metaphysical speculation in prison. He also makes room for schemes of practical benevolence. He "brood[s] over" and "ruminate[s] on all the calamites of Hungary," to such an extent that his

> imagination had grown familiar with captured towns and smoking villages; with the gallant soldier stretched lifeless on the plain, and the defenseless mother and her offspring brutally insulted and massacred; with fields laid waste, and a people lifting up their hands for bread. . . . I resolved to pour the entire stream of my riches, like a mighty river, to fertilise these wasted plains, and revive their fainting inhabitants. (*SL*, 298–299)

Thus in the Inquisitorial prison St. Leon lays out his future plans for the relief of Hungary. It seems unlikely that he could do all that he says he did in a dark cell without reading or writing. How exactly was it that "all systems of philosophising became familiar" to him? *All* systems? How did he "revolv[e] every different fable that has been constructed respecting the invisible powers that superintend the events of the boundless universe"? How could he have "traced out and developed the boldest conjectures and assertions of demonism or atheism"? In what sense did he receive images of "captured towns and smoking villages" in Hungary? Either his education and his recall are both superhuman, or he was more "assisted by and in league with invisible powers" than he would have us think (*SL*, 214). Silvia Granata claims that "although trials and dungeons are . . . present" in *St. Leon*, "their efficacy is circumvented by St. Leon's magical power."[114] Perhaps, in some cases; but in his Madrilenian prison St. Leon apparently has none of the necessary apparatus with which to exercise any magical powers. The only magical power available to him is habit. The only apparatus available to him is solitary confinement. Indeed, there seems to be little that these two cannot accomplish in tandem in the Godwinian novel. St. Leon writes that "habit has a resistless empire over the human mind," and that "nothing truly great was ever achieved, that was not executed or planned in solitary seclusion" (*SL*, 244, 119).

Pure chance frees St. Leon from the grip of the Inquisition. He and several inmates are escorted one day to Valladolid to witness the execution of a heretic, when a horse throws its rider and creates a general disturbance. St. Leon escapes his guards, finds a place of safety, and drinks the elixir of life. Afterward, he travels northeast and settles in Hungary under a new name, where he makes an abortive attempt to stimulate the war-ravaged Hungarian economy. It is during this attempt that he meets Bethlem Gabor, the Turco-Hungarian soldier turned wild-man outcast. Some time ago Gabor witnessed the slaughter of his family by marauders, and has since become incurably misanthropic. For this reason he now resents the general benevolence of his new French friend St. Leon, and is determined to put an end to it. It is at this point that the fourth and final prison sequence in the novel begins.

This prison sequence is different from the others in that St. Leon practically builds his own dungeon; or at least he rebuilds the area around it so as to make the dungeon accessible and inhabitable. Gabor owns a cheerless Hungarian castle north of Buda that has been ravaged by war to the point of being uninhabitable. As a gesture of goodwill, St. Leon uses his wealth to restore the northern estate. He repairs its surrounding fields, replenishes its cattle, and "reviv[es]" its "dilapidated revenues" (*SL*, 323). The grim irony here is that all this work reestablishes access to the very dungeon that St. Leon is about to inhabit. Soon after the repairs are done, Gabor ambushes St. Leon and removes him to his freshly renovated northern castle. The two descend into its grisly dungeons, a "wild and pathless" labyrinth of underground caves (*SL*, 350). The path is so long and convoluted, in fact, that St. Leon calls the trek a "pilgrimage," a word later ironized in light of the fact that an angel visits St. Leon in his dungeon (*SL*, 332). After a "succession of dark and gloomy vaults" and two iron-barred doors, St. Leon is thrown into a cave with a bench chained to the wall, and left alone (*SL*, 331). He fasts for thirty-six hours until he is almost overcome with hunger. Right at this point Gabor revisits him, and the two engage in what Marilyn Butler and Mark Philp have called "the most powerful direct representation ever attempted by Godwin of the intellectual conflicts in which he took part." Specifically:

> St. Leon's dialogues in the dungeon with Gabor, the political optimist [St. Leon] betrayed and for a while felled by the pessimist [Gabor] . . . may be a stylized version of the severe attack recently launched on Godwin by Thomas Malthus, especially in the first chapter of *Essay of Population* (1798), in which Malthus ridicules Godwin's vision in *Political Justice* of the ever-rising curve of social progress.[115]

Another critic, quite differently, views the Hungarian dungeon sequence as a "romantic imprisonment" in which Gabor "latch[es] onto St. Leon as compensation" for the family he lost.[116]

As it turns out, the Hungarian prison is "romantic" in other ways. The first lies in the satisfaction that St. Leon takes in his own Promethean fortitude. He is never allowed to indulge in sadness or let his feelings go numb. If he is ever on the point of giving up, Gabor "sting[s] . . . [him] into life again." Or as St. Leon puts it: "refusing me the indulgence of torpor . . . [Gabor] obliged me to string myself to resistance." Whereas the officers of the Inquisition in Madrid were "indifferent whether . . . [St. Leon] died or lived," Gabor "possessed no share of their apathy; his malice was ever alive, his hatred ever ingenious and new in its devices" (*SL*, 342). St. Leon reasons that "the consequence of this was somewhat different from what Bethlem Gabor expected":

> [Gabor] taught me a better lesson. . . . He gave me a passion; he gave me an object; he gave me comparative happiness. I was roused to opposition. . . . Thus employed, I found in my employment pride. . . . I gradually ascended to the sweets of consistency, perseverance, and self-gratulation. I had for years been inured to satisfy myself with a sparing stock of pleasures; and I was less at a loss to expand and ramify those [pleasures] which I now possessed, than almost any other man would have been in my situation. If my attendant train of sensations was scanty, Bethlem Gabor took care to afford them a perpetual supply of food and employment. . . . Was it a crime in me, that this fury in my tyrant produced the operation of a sedative and a cordial? There was no malignity in the joy it gave me. I had much aversion for Bethlem Gabor, but no hatred. I took no pleasure in his agonies, because they were agonies. . . . The joy I felt . . . his fury told me . . . was the unwilling evidence of my own value. (*SL*, 342–343)

From this train of thought St. Leon segues into schemes of benevolence: "my mind would sometimes wander beyond the limits of my cavern, and remember that there were other persons beside Bethlem Gabor and myself in the world" (*SL*, 343). Specifically, he thinks of what he has already done for the Hungarian economy, and what remains to be done.

The last important event of the Hungarian prison sequence is a visionary dream that St. Leon has not long before his release. In the dream, a fully armed knight enters the cave and smiles on him like an angel (the executed forger William Dodd likewise reported to have seen an angel during his stay in Newgate in 1777; see chapter 4). The two embrace affectionately. St. Leon feels he has seen the knight before, as if the two were once "intimate friend[s]." He follows the knight out of the cave until the ground begins to tremble beneath them, as in an "earthquake." At once the knight transforms into a "female of unblemished grace and beauty," unfurling her two "radiant wings." She and St. Leon "ascen[d] together in the air" and look down as the castle of Bethlem Gabor bursts into flames (*SL*, 344). Here the dream ends. What St. Leon remembers about this dream is its testament to the powers of the imagination. He says that his rational side tried to make him dismiss the dream, but that he resisted reason:

> Reason . . . I contemplated as an abhorred intruder. It was, for a long time, part of my occupation in every day to ruminate on this vision, not with the sternness of a syllogist, but with the colouring of a painter, and the rapture of a bard. . . . It became again and again and again my vision of the night. Slumbers like these were truly refreshing. . . . Sacred and adorable power of fancy, that can thus purify and irradiate the damps of a dungeon, and extract from midnight glooms and impervious darkness perceptions more lovely and inspiriting than noontide splendor! (*SL*, 344)

There is much to observe in the entire fascinating sequence of events that constitute the Hungarian dungeon sequence.[117] One observation involves the claim made by Butler and Philp, referenced previously, that the prison scenes can be read as a "stylized" version of the dialogues between Godwin and Malthus that took place in 1797 and 1798. The textual evidence that underlies their claim is, in fact, suggestive: Gabor calls St. Leon a misguided "benefactor and parent of mankind" who assists the Hungarians only to be repaid with scorn (*SL*, 338); Malthus, likewise, refers to Godwin as an "enlightened benefactor of mankind" whose advocacy of human perfectibility ignores the salutary effects of positive and preventative checks on human population.[118] Thus Gabor and Malthus may both be called pessimists, although pessimists of a very different order. Gabor acts out of misanthropy and revenge; Malthus acts out of a conviction that mass human suffering is inevitable and ultimately for the best.

In the final chapters of his 1798 *Essay on the Principle of Population*, Malthus claims that the point of human life is "the creation and formation of mind; a process necessary to awaken inert, chaotic matter into spirit; to sublimate the dust of the earth into soul; to elicit an ethereal spark from the clod of clay." This process is made possible, he adds, by various "impressions and excitements" that try us, such as hunger, cold, pain, sorrows, disease, and various other distresses. Without them we would never learn to exert ourselves and so acquire fortitude: "extraordinary situations generally create minds adequate to grapple with the difficulties in which they are involved."[119] Nor would we ever be roused to moral exertion without examples of immorality to serve as stimulants: a "moral evil is absolutely necessary to the production of moral excellence," says Malthus, since one cannot improve "without the impressions of disapprobation which arise from the spectacle of moral evil."[120]

The fourth volume of *St. Leon* tends to reinforce this Malthusian logic. St. Leon is a man so used to "extraordinary situations" that he can live well enough in a dungeon with a "sparing stock of pleasures." The few pleasures he has there he can "expand and ramify" better than "almost any other man" in his situation. The "moral evil" he encounters in the form of Bethlem Gabor stimulates him into virtuous thought, teaching him to love the sinner and hate the sin. Though averse in principle to being held captive, he maintains no hatred for his captor, with whose "agonies" he learns to sympathize. St. Leon even says at one point that the "furious passions" of his adversary "occasionally subside[d] into a semblance of familiarity and benevolence," enough to make him "forget the complicated injuries . . . [he] had received from him" (*SL*, 345).

One point is clear: the moral insight St. Leon experiences in the cave is essentially the product of solitary confinement. In his *Essay*, Malthus reminds readers that Godwin "reprobates solitary imprisonment," despite its having "certainly been the most successful and, indeed, almost the only attempt towards the moral amelioration of offenders."[121] Malthus was most likely thinking of the anti-coercionist claims in *Political Justice* when he made this comment. But does his comment apply to *St. Leon* as well as to *Political Justice*? Does *St. Leon*, that is, reinforce the claim that Godwin "reprobates solitary imprisonment"? Yes and no. Yes, in that St. Leon says claims to undergo unjustified pain in his various prisons. No, in that he also learns a great deal along the way. In the case of the Hungarian dungeon, in fact, he learns to appreciate the intrinsic value of all human lives, both lives that endure suffering and lives that inflict it.

Zim notes that it was common for writers in prison to acknowledge "the importance of family relationships, especially the agency of a supportive feminine 'other.'"[122] We see this practice reflected in the Hungarian prison sequence. The sequence ends soon after St. Leon describes his vision of the male-knight-turned-female-angel, which he claims to have had every night since its first occurrence. The content of the vision and its position near the end of the prison narrative suggest that it anticipates his release. The female angel in the dream also alludes to certain mystical females who have solaced imprisoned male writers throughout the literature of confinement. One of these is Lady Philosophy, the allegorical comforter in *On the Consolation of Philosophy* who guides the imprisoned Boethius through the sickness of his despair into consciousness of the highest good.[123] Another is the Lady of the Lake, of Arthurian legend, as revitalized by Sir Thomas Malory in his *Le Morte Darthur* (1485).[124] Even William Dodd claims to have had such a vision in Newgate in 1777, which he called a "vision beatific." Late at night, amid the "din of desperate felons, and the roar" of "midnight orgies," he has a vision or a dream in which Lady Faith escorts him to Lady Repentance. Lady Repentance, incidentally, has the face of one of the mistresses of Louis XIV.[125]

Recall what St. Leon says about his dream: "sacred and adorable power of fancy, that can thus purify and irradiate the damps of a dungeon, and extract from midnight glooms and impervious darkness perceptions more lovely and inspiriting than noontide splendor!" This unexpected apostrophe recalls a famous point made by Joseph Addison in *Spectator* no. 411. In that issue Addison echoes the standard eighteenth-century belief that all mental images are originally received as sense impressions through the organs of sight. Once the sense impressions are stored in the mind as images, the imagination, thereafter, can "retain, alter and compound those Images, which we have once received, into all the varieties of Picture and Vision that are most agreeable to the Imagination; for by this Faculty a Man in a Dungeon is capable of entertaining himself with Scenes and Landskips more beautiful than any that can be found in the whole Compass of Nature."[126] This passage is crucial in the context of *St. Leon*. St. Leon is certainly in a "Dungeon," and in a dungeon his imagination "extract[s]" "perceptions" lovelier than any acquired in nature ("noontide splendor"). Consider his notion of "extraction." From what does the imagination of St. Leon "extract" these "perceptions"? He tells us: from "midnight glooms and impervious darkness"—i.e., from the phenomena in his dungeon. This seems to be an unexpected twist on the situation Addison describes. For Addison says that *imagined* landscapes are prettier than *seen* landscapes because of the comparative limitations of sight. The eye takes in sense impressions from a single perceptual field and the mind stores these sense impressions as images. But the imagination can do far more. It can select from thousands of stored mental images and integrate them into whatever masterful composite it wants. Addison indicates that the "Man in a Dungeon" who *imagines* a stunning landscape must have *seen* everything in that mental landscape once before. He must have seen, at one point, each of its colors, shapes, gradations, lights, shades, which his imagination has subsequently assembled into a compound picture. What is curious is that St. Leon claims that his imagination transmutes ("purif[ies]," "irradiate[s]") the grim objects in front of him and then extracts the results. In other words, he harvests beauty directly from the unsightly raw materials in his dungeon. This is not the same procedure that Addison describes: that is, assembling a set of pleasant mental images, once perceived by the physical eye, into a composite image even more pleasant.

So the vision that St. Leon has seems to be brilliant in proportion to the unpleasantness of the phenomena that his imagination "purif[ies]." A passage from Rousseau comes to mind here: "it is a very peculiar thing that my imagination never shows itself more agreeably than when my condition is the least agreeable. . . . If I want to depict the Spring I must be in the winter; if I want to describe a beautiful countryside I must be inside walls, and I have said a hundred times that if I were ever put in the Bastille, I would paint the tableau of freedom there."[127] Rousseau can best imagine a particular scene, only if his material environment is composed of or associated with conditions the opposite of that scene. This point helps explain the glorious dream that St. Leon has in his own "Bastille." Yet the imagination is not the only power that St. Leon uses to reconcile himself to his dungeon. He is also incredibly resilient, even, or maybe especially, in darkness and solitude, a trait that according to Zimmermann can work wonders: "certain it is, that patience and perseverance will, in Solitude, convert the deepest sorrow into tranquility and joy."[128] Notice the word *convert* here. For Zimmermann, a persevering person in "Solitude" can "convert" sorrow to joy. St. Leon seems to do just this. His imagination and his resilience transmute gloomy percepts into glorious percepts. His very seeing is alchemical. It works like the alchemical apparatus he lacks in the cavern that can turn base metals into gold.

With all this in mind, it seems less strange when, at one point, St. Leon almost hesitates to let his dungeon go. His release comes about by accident. One day, after St. Leon has been in the dungeon for a few months, Gabor enters it and informs his captive that the northern castle has been besieged by Austro-Hungarian forces. Gabor says that he plans to go out and die fighting his enemies, and requests that St. Leon wait twenty-four hours before attempting to escape the dungeon. St. Leon waits only six hours, and feels guilty about it. After that he "wander[s] for a considerable time among the alleys and windings of this immeasurable cavern," looking for the outlet into the castle. After a two-hour search, he thinks he sees an exit, but worries that the flames surrounding it will make egress impossible. So he relights his torch and "return[s] by the straightest road I could find to my dungeon. Arrived there, I proposed to pass the interval quietly, in the cavern where I had so long felt the weight of the Hungarian's chains." He remains in the cave for some time until he has a sudden fear. What if Gabor and his Turco-Hungarians actually repel the imperial invaders? What if Gabor is even now returning victoriously to the cavern to reclaim his captive? Fearing such a possible turn of events, St. Leon leaves his dungeon for the second time and finds somewhere else in the labyrinth to wait: "I hid myself; I deemed no cell remote enough to conceal me from the inhuman persecution of my tyrant." Twenty-four hours go by. At this point the whole subterranean network becomes "so heated and suffocating" that St. Leon has no choice but to seek the exit a second time (*SL*, 347). On this occasion he finds it passable. A faint glow leads him upward until he stumbles into a blast of sunlight. Outside, he finds the northern castle "a pile of ruins. The walls indeed for the most part remained, but choked with fragments of the falling edifice, blackened with the flames, and penetrated in every direction by the light of day" (*SL*, 348).

A good part of St. Leon has obviously craved his freedom. His tyrant has exasperated him with hunger and humiliation. And yet another part of him practically hesitates to leave his dungeon. That he even waits six of the promised twenty-four hours before attempting an escape is a little surprising. Even more surprising is that he eventually *goes back* to his dungeon to "pass the interval quietly" while the flames near the outlet die down. Is this not a counterintuitive choice? Why would he go back to the place where he felt so hungry that he seemed to be swallowing a "glowing ember" (*SL*, 334)? There are indeed practical explanations.

Maybe he waits six hours before first leaving his cave out of fear that Gabor will aggravate his punishment if he does otherwise (presuming, in such a case, that Gabor will defeat the Austro-Hungarians). Maybe he gave his word to Gabor and feels he has to honor it. Or perhaps St. Leon returns to his prison-cave after finding the exit impassable because that cave is the one place in the labyrinth from which he thinks he can find his way back to the exit. These explanations make sense, but they are not the whole picture. The lingering St. Leon does around his dungeon bespeaks a kind of affection for it, an affection, strange as it seems, for the dungeon as dungeon. It was an attachment not unheard of among actual prisoners in the late eighteenth and nineteenth centuries.

One such prisoner was the Prussian soldier and author Frederick Freiherr von der Trenck (1726–1794). Trenck served Frederick the Great in the Silesian Wars until Frederick imprisoned him in the fortress of Glatz, in southwestern Poland, under suspicion of treason. After seventeen months in Glatz, however, Trenck escaped. He wandered through Bohemia, Poland, Russia, and Austria and was eventually recaptured and re-imprisoned in the German city of Magdeburg for nine years and five months. Trenck later wrote memoirs, which became "classics in prison literature."[129] Thomas Holcroft, a close friend of Godwin, translated these memoirs into English in 1788 and asked Godwin to look over the manuscript. Holcroft published his translation as *The Life of Baron Frederic Trenck* (1788). An 1800 review of *St. Leon* in the *British Critic* compares the prison escapes in both *Caleb Williams* and *St. Leon* to the ones in "the incredible but amusing narrative of Baron Trenck"—but then leaves the topic.[130] William D. Brewer picks up on this *British Critic* review in his introduction to the Broadview edition of *St. Leon* (2005), adding the following: "both Trenck and St. Leon describe themselves as prison philosophers who mentally transcend their dungeons. However, whereas Trenck provides graphic descriptions of the sufferings he endured . . . St. Leon is vague about his prison environments and escape attempts. . . . Godwin focuses on the themes of institutional oppression and social isolation rather than horrifying his readers with the grisly details of incarceration."[131] Brewer says nothing else about Trenck and Godwin or their respective texts, though there are plenty of similarities worth noting. Both writers craved acceptance and fame. Both were puritanical in their personal habits. Trenck "devoted many hundred laborious nights to studies that might make . . . [him] useful to . . . [his] country." He "laboured in the cause of science" and "virtue" and developed a special hatred of "superstitious bigotry." He was "imbued with the heroic principles of liberty" despite living under "the despotic and iron government of Frederick."[132] Godwin made more or less the same statements about himself throughout his own life. His first two novels, moreover, draw heavily from *The Life of Baron Frederic Trenck*. Trenck writes that Frederick pursued him "through every corner of Europe" until he "suffered a martyrdom both unmerited and unexampled."[133] So also does

Falkland pursue Caleb Williams throughout England and Wales. Both Trenck and Caleb earn a living as writers: Trenck while in a prison and Caleb while in between prisons. In his German dungeon, Trenck "revolve[s] the recollection of persons, places, scenes, events" and "speeches," until he can "compose and store up in . . . [his] mind poems, satires, fables, speeches, etc."[134] We recall that Caleb performs the same mental exercises in Newgate in *Caleb Williams*. *St. Leon* also borrows several details from Trenck. St. Leon and Trenck both maintain small rural estates in Europe (respectively in Switzerland and Austria) that get devastated by hailstorms, forcing each man into manual labor. Both men assume false names at some point, are abetted in their prison escapes by a Jew, and are thought to be in league with the Devil. In his Magdeburg prison, Trenck tames a mouse to take food from his mouth and hop on his shoulder when he whistles to it. In Madrid, similarly, St. Leon muses that if a mouse were to visit him he would have cradled it and felt its heartbeat with "exultation" (*SL*, 267).

Recall that St. Leon goes back to his dungeon to wait out the battle between the imperialists and the Turks (a decision even *he* admits is strange). A related incident occurs in the memoirs of Trenck that is even more unexpected. Trenck writes that one day at dawn orders are given to remove his beloved mouse from his German prison cell. An officer wraps the mouse in a handkerchief and carries it to a guardroom a hundred yards away. In a flash, the mouse runs back to the shut prison door and conceals himself near it until the following morning. Then when the door is reopened it scurries back into the cell. The unamused guards remove the mouse again and this time give it to a lady as a pet. After its relocation, the creature is reported to have "pined, refused food, and in a few days was dead."[135] There is more to this digression in the Trenck narrative than an amusing set piece. The event foreshadows an incident in what is arguably the climax of the whole *Life of Baron Frederic Trenck*. After nine and a half years of methodical torture in his German prison and toward the end of his memoirs, Trenck is released; then, on the eve of his departure from Magdeburg, he looks out on the city and says: "who would have been so foolish as to prophesy that I should ever shed tears at leaving Magdeburg?—yet it is a fact that I did." He adds that "although I lived there for ten years I never saw the town."[136] This statement must appear striking to anyone who believes that his prison cell in Magdeburg was as bad as Trenck himself says it was. But then the idea of sadness at leaving a long-familiar cell was not unprecedented among his English contemporaries. In his account of the Gordon Riots, published almost immediately after the actual events in 1780, Holcroft recalls that Newgate, "the strongest and most durable prison in England," was "demolished" in the riots—all of it except the "bare walls," "which were too thick and strong to yield to the force of fire."[137] (In a possible echo of this fact, St. Leon notes that the only the singed walls of the Hungarian castle remained after the imperial onslaught.) Holcroft then says that even amid the burning shell of

Newgate, "several of the prisoners who had been released by the mob, had so great an affection for those scenes to which they had been long accustomed, that they could not forbear loitering about the Cells . . . and were accordingly retaken" by the military.[138] Charles Campbell reports, moreover, that "many escapees applied for readmission soon after the fire was out."[139]

Thus we have encountered three narrative representations of released prisoners lingering in or near their prisons. St. Leon goes back to his black dungeon where he almost starved to death, in order to pass the time. Trenck weeps to leave a city he lived in for ten years but never saw; he weeps for his tailor-made eight-by-ten-foot cell built into the ditch of a fortification, a cell in which the "name of Trenck was built into the wall in red brick, and under my feet was a tombstone with the name of Trenck also cut upon it and carved with a death's head."[140] The Newgate inmates risk recapture or death to hover about their charred cells, and some request readmittance. We may also add a related anecdote about Leigh Hunt. When he was released from two years of imprisonment on February 2, 1815, as we will see in the following chapter, Hunt "felt almost like running back to his cell."[141] It is difficult to say what motivated all these cell-side loiterers. Perhaps it was becoming habituated to an alien environment whose sameness one grows fond of, as a "place of endurance amidst ephemerae."[142] Maybe it was the pleasant sense of being cut off from the various responsibilities of ordinary life. For a long period of time in Magdeburg, in fact, Trenck is so busy manufacturing salable mugs, writing poems, and reading books that he almost forgets he is in a prison.[143] Hanway would have delighted in Trenck's attitude: a man once insolent enough to break out of a prison in Glatz has since learned contentment in solitary confinement with quiet and useful labor. Hanway predicted that "when *custom* shall familiarize" the prisoner to "*confinement*, and he feels his mind open to a sense of conviction . . . he will rejoice amidst his afflictions, and be *unwilling* to return into the world, till he has acquired habits, the reverse of those which brought him into the *penitentiary.*"[144] This is a utopian statement on the benefits of imprisonment if there ever was one. St. Leon and the others are probably not consciously waiting around for additional imprisonment to become more useful citizens with better manners and morals. Still, for whatever reason, they do all appear somewhat "unwilling to return into the world." Prison has inured them to a sort of macabre, yet revered, security.

Deloraine

The novel *Deloraine* was one of the last texts Godwin published in his life. Its basic plot is that a tortured Englishman named William Deloraine is writing his memoirs in a state of "deep . . . remorse."[145] He recounts how he once found his wife Margaret alone on their estate with her ex-lover, also named William. In a fit of rage, Deloraine shoots William dead. Margaret witnesses the event and bursts a blood vessel in shock, dying on the spot virtually on top of William. Her husband then flees to the Continent with their devoted daughter Catherine to avoid arrest. Meanwhile, an old friend of the deceased William, named Travers, learns of the murder and decides to hunt Deloraine down. The rest of the novel unfolds à la *Caleb Williams* in a series of stages of flight and pursuit.

While on the run Deloraine finds several places of refuge, which he describes as prison-sanctuaries. The first of these is a bookshop in Belgium. He happens to be in that shop one day when Travers suddenly shows up looking for him. Deloraine conceals himself in a small "room behind the shop, separated from it only by a window and a curtain" (*DE*, 208). He waits in stunned silence while Travers—out of sight, but still audible—interrogates the shop owner. In this situation Deloraine compares himself to a "bird" trapped in a "narrow cage," beating his wings in vain to escape (*DE*, 212). Yet once Travers leaves the shop, Deloraine realizes that someone in his circumstances is better off concealed in a "cage" than at large and exposed to capture:

> It was no longer a question of the nook that contained me, and my escape from which I anticipated with inconceivable joy. The little room behind the bookseller's shop I had regarded as my prison, and I had pined with inexpressible eagerness to be enlarged from it. Now, on the contrary, I might almost regard it as my sanctuary. The moment I should get out into the street, I should be exposed to the hazard of my enemy. . . . I must call upon darkness to cover me . . . clouds and thick darkness. (*DE*, 212–213)

Deloraine manages to flee Belgium and head east to Germany. He then makes his way down the Rhine with his faithful daughter Catherine. In time they reach a secluded German mansion built on a cliff and sheltered by woods. Its mistress invites them in, and for a while all seems well. Soon, however, the dogged Travers shows up again and informs the lady of the castle (who turns out to be Travers's cousin) about the fugitives he is after. Deloraine, overhearing their conversation, realizes that he is trapped again; he tells his daughter Catherine: "the very solitude and remoteness of this mansion render it my prison. It will be impossible for us to withdraw ourselves unseen" (*DE*, 221–222). Fortunately, Travers leaves the mansion in disappointment; his cousin has chosen not to expose Deloraine and Catherine to him. She tells them instead that their hitherto prison is now, in fact, their "sanctuary" (*DE*, 224).

What is important about these two incidents is that they herald the ultimate prison-sanctuary on the horizon in this novel. Once again, father and daughter set sail on the Rhine to stay one step ahead of Travers. In time they spot the "ruin of an old castle," set high among the "pinnacles" of "savage and romantic" "rocks." Their boatman calls the castle a "very labyrinth," and Deloraine finds it "scarcely less inaccessible than a desolate island in the South Sea." He and Catherine disembark on the "rocky and wild" shore and proceed up to the castle (*DE*, 226). Its sole inhabitant happens to be a man named Jerome, who earns a living by sheltering criminals in the castle for a fee. Deloraine is immediately "enchanted" with the "inviolable security" of the place. It is "built on a spot so remote from public view, so difficult of access, and in its aspect so like an uninhabited ruin, that . . . [he and Catherine] might probably remain here for years" (*DE*, 229). The castle also has the benefit of crannies carved out of apparently solid pillars to conceal fugitives. At first, Jerome agrees to hide his guests in the castle and keep silent, though he later changes his mind when he hears that Travers is offering a substantial reward for their apprehension.

The German castle represents the culmination of a series of prison-sanctuaries in *Deloraine*. It is both a prison and not a prison. It is a prison in that Deloraine and Catherine are forced to hide there like animals "shut up as in a pen, or like wild beasts in a cage" (*DE*, 252). Jerome, moreover, is another John Kirby. Kirby, recall, was governor of Newgate Prison from 1792 to 1804, a man Godwin met when he visited his radical friends in Newgate. Jerome, like Kirby, carries with him a "huge bunch of keys." He lives in a pair of rooms whose design and location in the fictional castle evoke the architecture of Newgate as Godwin knew it. The main castle entrance opens into a hall, for instance, at each side of which, "to the right and left, there was a door" leading to certain apartments. The apartments are located "nearest to the outer gate," where it is "most handy and convenient" for Jerome to reside. At the "further end of the hall" is a staircase heading down to "the interior and more select part of the building" (*DE*, 227–228). All of this approximates the layout of the foremost part of Newgate. In Newgate the gaoler also lives in rooms to the left and right of the main entrance hall, which terminates in a staircase descending into the prison.

Father and daughter lose no time in turning their Gothic prison into the perfect domestic retreat. The castle becomes a Shakespearean idyll, sobered, somewhat, by the chaste features of the Howardian cell. By "Shakespearean idyll" I mean a specific one—the prison-idyll in *King Lear.* Deloraine alludes to *King Lear* when he refers to Catherine as "devoted" to "a man more sinned against than sinning" (*DE*, 247). At first this allusion has the simple effect of putting *King Lear* on the mind. It later gains importance as Deloraine and Catherine begin living out a version of the carceral fantasy that Lear famously describes in act V:

> Come let's away to prison:
> We two alone will sing like birds i' th' cage;
> When thou dost ask me blessing, I'll kneel down
> And ask of thee forgiveness. So we'll live,
> And pray, and sing, and tell old tales, and laugh
> At gilded butterflies, and hear poor rogues
> Talk of court news; and we'll talk with them too—

> Who loses and who wins; who's in, who's out—
> And take upon 's the mystery of things
> As if we were God's spies; and we'll wear out,
> In a wall'd prison, packs and sects of great ones,
> That ebb and flow by th' moon.[146]

Consider the "two alone" part. Deloraine luxuriates in how remote and secluded the German castle is. He says that he and Catherine are closed in by rocks there and so "cut off from the world." In the castle there are no "places of public resort to repair to" and no "neighbours with whom to maintain an inter-change of visits" (*DE*, 235). I find it interesting that *these* are the advantages that Deloraine singles out. Never mind that he and his daughter are safe in the castle from a bloodthirsty pursuer, a murder conviction, and a death sentence. Deloraine is happy because he no longer has to go out in public, talk to his neighbors, or even see them.

We may consider these feelings of his to be symptoms of a looming guilt, of recent fatigue, or of an inveterate unsociableness. But they may also be part of a non-pathological attraction to an enclosed, prisonlike life for its own sake. The castle is certainly a kind of carceral environment. It resembles the first penitentiary in England, Millbank, in that, according to Deloraine, it is a "labyrinth" where "nothing less than the clue of Ariadne [is] necessary, to guide you through its windings" (*DE*, 228).[147] At the same time it is like the old, unreformed, eighteenth-century prisons in that it is run by a suspicious gaoler who lives by fees (i.e., who is unsalaried) and goes about his business with no bureaucratic supervision or regulation. For all Deloraine and Catherine know, the castle on the Rhine might be their long-term home. So the newfound isolation Deloraine so warmly appreciates is not a feature of some temporary hideaway or short break from harsh reality. It is the fact that the castle is about to become the new reality that it is so enticing to him. The castle will be a happy blend of unlike things: security and adventure, confinement and freedom, idleness and industry; and to Deloraine there is something pleasant about being free from all the obligations and niceties that social life requires. It is a freedom paradoxically available only through forced confinement. Deloraine and Catherine are two people "contented to inhabit a dilapidated ruin on a barren rock, having from day to day and from week to week no other society" (*DE*, 237).

Luckily, father and daughter have plenty to do by way of reading what Lear calls "old tales." The two stumble upon a "small collection of books, French, Spanish, German and Italian," as well as books in Latin and Greek, in a "neglected corner of the castle." These become an "incalculable treasure" to them, providing ever "new sources of enjoyment" (*DE*, 236). Deloraine even makes some time to teach Catherine the classical languages.[148] Not that their new curriculum is without its lighter lessons. Deloraine says that "sometimes too with our graver studies and more serious disquisitions we would intermix 'grateful digressions, and solve high dispute' with sportive interruption, and affectionate caresses, such as might best beseem the father and his daughter" (*DE*, 237). The quotation within the quotation here is from the eighth book of *Paradise Lost*:

> Her Husband the Relater she preferr'd
> Before the Angel, and of him to ask
> Chose rather: hee, she knew, would intermix
> *Grateful digressions, and solve high dispute*
> With conjugal Caresses, from his Lip
> Not Words alone pleas'd her. O when meet now
> Such pairs, in Love and mutual Honor join'd?[149]

It may seem odd for a father to compare his time locked up in a castle with his daughter to Adam and Eve talking, kissing, and caressing in their connubial garden. Deloraine alludes to the "conjugal Caresses" Adam gives Eve when he mentions (without quotation marks) his own "affectionate caresses." The marital context of *Paradise Lost* is thus thinly veiled.[150] However strange the allusion, the fact is that a Gothic prison has merged intertextually with a Miltonic paradise. Father and daughter have come to a place where, like another Adam and Eve, happily unable and unwilling to leave, they can spend their lives with "no intervals of vacuity or spleen" (*DE*, 237). This is a surreal life: reading, writing, and routine, day after day, enclosed within the same walls, and all without resentment or boredom.

In some ways the castle embodies the ideals of the reformed prison as well as those of paradise. Deloraine spends several hours alone each day writing the memoirs we are now reading. This is his special, "solitary" time during which he can find "relief" in "retrospect" (*DE*, 286), when he can experience that "creative anguish" that evangelicals thought could "alone . . . transform the spirit and reform the mind" of a prison inmate.[151] But whether he is alone or with Catherine, Deloraine is always at some kind of work. He sacrifices no time to idleness. His claustral life on the Rhine is a life "full [of] occupation," a "variety and succession of industry," "earnest employment" (*DE*, 237). Howard himself might have appreciated the general routine here; he had always insisted that a good reformative prison should involve "solitude . . . broken up by long periods of associated labor."[152] In a sense, this is precisely the sort of regimen Deloraine that has adopted for himself and his daughter.

But what is explicitly Howardian about life in the castle is Catherine. She seems modeled largely on Howard himself. And it is no wonder. Godwin called Howard one of "the most illustrious patriots and exemplary characters that are to be found in the pages of history."[153] Before Deloraine decided to wander over Europe in flight from the law, he had tried to prevent Catherine from following him; but she had insisted at the time that "if all the world hiss at and scout you, this will be an additional reason for me to be your comforter. I will be at hand to smooth your pillow, when you most need a friend. I will pour the balm of consolation into your wounds, when the world most combines to destroy you. If you go to prison, I will go with you" (*DE*, 160). "If you go to prison, I will go with you": as Howard visited every gaol and house of correction in Britain two or three times and took five similar trips to the Continent, showering consolation on the afflicted, so Catherine is a shadow of peace to her runaway father. In his words, "she voluntarily shut herself out from that world which she was so eminently qualified to adorn. She stripped herself of the glories of her character, and submitted to be my obscure and fireside companion." Nor did Catherine ever get tired. She stayed vigilant in "search[ing] out every thing that could amuse and enliven" her father in his various flights and confinements (*DE*, 214).

Catherine and Howard are also connected through a special metaphor peculiar to Howard: both are the human equivalent of a sort of moral disinfectant. Deloraine thinks of himself a "vile and loathsome weed, incumbering the earth, and infecting the air with contagion" (*DE*, 214). He tells Catherine in the end that only by turning himself in can he "remove a black and pestilential atmosphere, that suffocates your energies, that poisons your enjoyments" (*DE*, 273). Thus he describes her love for him in terms of purification, disinfection, miasmatic cleansing. Contemporary poets imagined Howard similarly. He was the superhero whose power was ventilation: the "human ventilator of divine aspect, dissipating thermometric extremes and infusing jails with healthful, temperate air."[154] And he did more than purify gaols. The many poetic paeans to Howard extended his purification practices to the entire world. Throughout his "world-spanning journey of empirically grounded atmospheric benevolence," Howard was said to "diffus[e] temperateness everywhere for the benefit of all people," in or outside of prisons.[155] In light of Godwin's allusions to Howard, it seems fitting that Deloraine refers to himself as an infectious atmosphere and to Catherine as the source of his decontamination. She will not see her father "dragged to prison" (*DE*, 275). She feels "hallowed and consecrated by every service" she can render him, even if it effects the "least mitigation" of his suffering. At one point Deloraine muses that an "unknown and a celestial energy seemed to sustain" Catherine as they went about (*DE*, 215). In a similar vein, Hanway called Howard "a star guiding us through remote regions, to discover the temporal redemption of the most miserable part of mankind."[156] Deloraine also compares Catherine to the angel of the Lord in the Book of Acts, who rescues Peter when he is chained to two soldiers in prison (*DE*, 162).

While Deloraine refers to himself figuratively as a contaminating agent, at one point in the castle-prison he actually contracts a fever. He is "seized with an inflammatory distemper, which for two days confined me to my bed." Straightaway he is treated with the "proper medicines" and recovers quickly. The actual sickness that he contracts is described in a sentence or two; the feeling of recovery is indulged in at length. His "fever" dies out, but not before it leaves a "pleasing langour" in its wake that all but deifies him. His feeling after his sickness is the pure sweetness of negative pleasure, the exquisite absence of pain: "I experienced that freshness of sensation, to which robust health is a stranger, and which comes over one like the inspiration of heaven, after a fit of sickness" (*DE*, 248). As he rises and moves about, the sensation increases:

> a life-giving breeze played upon my cheek and forehead. . . . All grief, all sorrow . . . seemed to pass away from me. I was like a new-born child, conscious only of internal sensation, swallowed up in the calm abstraction of existence. . . . [I was] a solitary green island, firm and immovable . . . in the midst of the never-reposing waves of a tumultuous sea. I gave myself up to it; and it seemed an earnest [i.e., a pledge] of everlasting existence" (*DE*, 249)

This is a wild and unexpected verbal set piece. Why is it here, in a castle-dungeon in *Deloraine*, of all places? It may not actually be gaol fever that Deloraine contracts, but one certainly thinks of it, if only because a while back in the novel he did suffer from what he then called "a species of typhus" (*DE*, 41). But his gaol sickness here in the castle no sooner arrives than it is gone. The feeling Deloraine is left with is the pleasurable absence of pain leavened with a sense of rebirth. It also suggests a regression: a return to an infant state when one is "conscious only of internal sensation" and "swallowed up in the calm abstraction of existence." The world around him feels gone as his health returns. This is pleasure and redemption in a paradise of solitude taken to an extreme. What Deloraine is feeling is far beyond the relief of getting over a sickness or of not having to talk to neighbors. He rejoices to have become his own solipsistic universe, a "solitary green island, firm and immovable" around which the peopled world rages like a "tumultuous sea." In his convalescence, Deloraine specifically receives what Wordsworth in 1815 called "Intimations of Immortality": he interprets the effects of his returning health as a living pledge, an "earnest" of "everlasting existence."[157]

The prison episodes in *Caleb Williams*, *St. Leon*, and *Deloraine* all hold out a special kind of satisfaction for the inmate, a chance at a rich, long, unthought-of enlightenment; though that enlightenment *is* either on, or on the other side of, a threshold of pain. The novels treat imprisonment with an ambiguity at odds with the unflinching anti-coercionism of *Political Justice*, book 7. This ambiguity appears to stem from the two conflicting ideologies discussed earlier in this chapter: On the one hand, Godwin preached an almost instinctual, impossibly idealistic aversion to any species of coercion since he was a child. Teachers were despots by definition. Parents were despots by definition. Both were despots no less than kings or even tyrants. On the other hand, Godwin seems to have reconciled himself over time to certain ideas and practices associated with the ideology of reformative imprisonment. The prison scenes in his novels seem to want to fuse these two lines of thought. They work to adapt a radical utopian vision of a world where no one is coerced, where everyone exercises private judgment, and where everyone is rationally benevolent, to the probability that earthly punishment in some form will always exist, will always be necessary, and will always have the potential to be, in itself or in its effects, salutary.

3

THE DESCENT OF LIBERTY

Leigh Hunt in Surrey Gaol

THE PAST SEVERAL DECADES have witnessed a renewal of critical interest in the Romantic journalist, essayist, poet, and political reformer (Henry) Leigh Hunt (1784–1859).[1] Hunt is unique among his Romantic contemporaries in that he spent two of the most fruitful years of his long life in a prison in South London, from February 3, 1813, to February 2, 1815. He was twenty-eight when he entered prison; when he was released he was never quite the same man, and he would often pine for his prison in his later life. Nowadays Hunt is primarily remembered as the literary mentor of the early John Keats and as a close friend and collaborator of Percy Shelley and Lord Byron. But he was also friends with Jeremy Bentham, Maria Edgeworth, James Mill, William Wordsworth, William Hazlitt, Charles Lamb, and other influential nineteenth-century writers. He was the first literary critic to recognize and articulate the poetic genius of Wordsworth. Several Victorian literati, including Thomas Carlyle, Elizabeth Barrett Browning, Charlotte Brontë, Elizabeth Gaskell, Alfred Lord Tennyson, Robert Browning, William Makepeace Thackeray, and Charles Dickens, had admiring things to say about Hunt. Virginia Woolf placed him among the "free, vigorous spirits [that] advance the world."[2]

If Hunt really did "advance the world," or at least his world, it was mostly through the *Examiner*. The *Examiner* was a sixteen-page, two-column quarto newspaper published on Sundays in London and founded by the brothers John and Leigh Hunt in 1808. John started as printer and publisher and Leigh as chief contributor and editor. The paper cost 7½ pence: that is, it was deliberately cheap. It allowed no advertisements on the grounds that it would be least liable to corruption or bias that way. The *Examiner* featured items as diverse as foreign and domestic news, reports on parliamentary proceedings, theatrical criticism, legal news, poems, literary sketches, death notices, and bankruptcies. Hunt himself wrote comprehensive weekly accounts of the Napoleonic Wars. In a word, the *Examiner* was one of the most eminent cultural and political newspapers of its day. The poetic talents of Keats and Shelley were introduced to the world in its pages. Hunt remained editor of the *Examiner* until he and his family left for Italy to join Shelley there in 1821.

The *Examiner* is crucial to any study of the life, thought, and writings of Leigh Hunt during his imprisonment. The events leading up to his confinement are well known. Hunt unapologetically insulted the prince regent and future George IV, by no means for the first time, in an article in the *Examiner* on March 22, 1812, in which he called the prince regent a "violator of his word, a libertine over head and ears in debt and disgrace, a despiser of domestic ties, the companion of gamblers and demireps, a man who has just closed half a century without one single claim on the gratitude of his country or the respect of posterity!"[3] The Tory British government, needless to say, was not impressed. It had already lost three different legal battles with the Hunts before this incident,[4] and was now determined to make an example of them. Leigh and John were convicted of libel and thrown in two separate prisons for two years apiece. John went to Coldbath Fields in central London; Leigh went to Surrey Gaol (also called Horsemonger Lane Gaol) in South London. Throughout their respective sentences, publication of the *Examiner* continued in earnest, and sales even improved. The imprisonment of both editors of the *Examiner* was definitely good for business.[5]

In both his private letters and the *Examiner*, Hunt consistently speaks favorably of his prison experience. How is it possible that he could feel this way? The easy answer is that Hunt had enough money and social clout to purchase better rooms at Surrey Gaol than most other inmates could afford; he was considered more or less a gentleman; his crime was political; his family was allowed to stay with him in his rooms and his friends were allowed to visit. All of this is true, and all of it would explain a confinement said to be *tolerated*. But Hunt declares that he learned in prison to be a better friend, humanitarian, thinker, and artist. Routine and restraint served him so well, in fact, that years after his release, at leisure in sunny Italy and surrounded by friends and family, he was occasionally uncertain whether he wanted to stay where he was or go back to his English prison. His uncertainty in this case seems objectively remarkable, if it is legitimate, and there is no compelling reason to think it is not.

The personal reflections, literary criticism, poems, and letters that Hunt wrote from prison, as well as his after-recollections on confinement in *Lord Byron and Some of His Contemporaries* (1828) and in his *Autobiography* (1850), reveal that Hunt was more often than not, at the very least, as happy in gaol as he was out of it. Several circumstances of his confinement attest to this fact. One such circumstance involves his having undergone a personal reformation in working habits throughout his two-year imprisonment. Although Hunt never "reformed" in gaol in the sense that he became contrite about breaking the law, or in the sense that he developed a keen (or any) awareness of his having done anything wrong, nonetheless he cultivated strong habits of intellectual industry and efficiency and developed a new and lasting sense of the value of these habits.

The development of industrious habits in prisons was, of course, a central initiative among many contemporary penal reformers and a key clause in the 1779 Penitentiary Act. The clergyman and philosopher William Paley, in his *Principles of Moral and Political Philosophy* (1785), noted that he would "measure" the solitary confinement of a prisoner "not by duration of time, but by quantity of work, in order to excite industry, and render it more voluntary."[6] The Rev. J. T. Becher, pursuant to the same logic, designed the Southwell House of Correction, erected in 1807, so as to "effect a change of life" in its inmates, not, as was the case at the Gloucester Penitentiary, "a change of heart." The Southwell House of Correction, that is, focused on prisoner "compliance" rather than on prisoner "conversion."[7] Its "leading idea" was "the encouragement of industrious habits, by the provision of comfortable conditions of life and remunerative work, in pleasant association." Inmates were supplied with "improving books," which they were "'encouraged to read to each other' round the fire."[8] If Hunt, throughout his sentence, resisted the change-of-heart model of reform, which involved penance and personal conversion, he certainly embraced a version of the change-of-life model. His remunerative prison labor was extensive, and it had strong social, professional, and intellectual ramifications.

In light of his prison experience, the most famous poem he ever wrote, *The Story of Rimini* (1816), may be read as a kind of allegorical window into his early experience of imprisonment, approximately March to June 1813.[9] *Rimini* is a verse tale, told in four cantos, describing the love affair of Francesca da Polenta and her brother-in-law Paolo Malatesta ("Paulo," in Hunt), the thirteenth-century couple whom Dante depicts briefly in his *Inferno* as burning in an eternal embrace for their adultery.[10] Hunt wrote the first canto of *Rimini* prior to his imprisonment. He drafted the second canto, a portion of the third, and possibly more in prison.[11] Most critics of *Rimini* find the circumstances of its composition, at most, incidental to its internal dynamics, which seems to me a shortsighted view. Hunt is famous for having turned his rooms at Surrey Gaol into a kind of fairyland salon, a niche of paradise in the heart of a prison. Cantos 2 and 3 of *Rimini* are very much a product of this event. Their lush, descriptive details suggest a world endlessly unfolding, endlessly alluring, with light, shade, and flora all coming to meet the senses in an almost hypnotic way. The rosy sanctuary that Hunt created in prison is inseparable from these poetic effects. Hunt chose to resume *Rimini* where and when he did—picking it up with canto 2—less as a way to escape his imprisonment (the usual critical reading), and more as a way to immortalize it, by imaginatively reproducing it. In particular, Hunt was forced in prison to refine his powers of perception so as to be able to apprehend more sensory phenomena in less space, to focus on the inexhaustible beauties of minute particulars, to see a single scene from multiple aestheticizing perspectives. *Rimini* dramatizes this process of perceptual refinement and the feelings it aroused in Hunt over time.

The writings of Hunt on early nineteenth-century penal reform offer a window into his own personal experience of confinement. Hunt denounced capital punishment in the *Examiner* as outmoded and ineffective. He also argued that non-capital punishment should refocus its energies more on the reform of the individual punished, and less on the potential reparation made by an individual to a victim or to the state. Offenders who are made miserable through punishment, he claims, are ultimately less useful to their victims and to society than offenders made "valuable, virtuous, and happy."[12] Five years after he made this claim, moreover, he validated it with the evidence of his own personal experience, showing in a variety of publications, produced during and after his imprisonment, that he himself became more valuable, virtuous, and happy in his prison, and that both he and his reading audiences were the better for his sentence.

Surrey Gaol was a reformed and relatively new prison when Hunt was admitted to it. It was comprised of two separate establishments, the Surrey county gaol and the Surrey county house of correction, each sharing a single boundary wall on Horsemonger Lane in South London. The gaol component had a chapel, a salaried chaplain, and prayers twice a week, with a sermon on Sunday. Its first inmates were received in 1798. James Neild called the gaol a "noble building [that] does honour to the County" of Surrey. It was built on "open and airy" ground, and its interiors were kept "remarkably clean" by a salaried housekeeper. Male felons were paid particular attention to. They had "a spacious court-yard, neatly paved with Yorkshire stone . . . to take air and exercise in fine weather; or, if it be otherwise, they walk under arcades paved with flag-stone." Male felons also had a "day-room . . . to dress their victuals in" and individual sleeping cells with shuttered windows, ventilators, rugs and flock-beds on elm-plank bedsteads. The cells were cleaned each morning by a housekeeper. Neild adds, approvingly, that in this "excellent Prison" there were "no less [*sic*] than four cold baths" and "one warm bath." "Excellent Rules and Orders" for the prison were posted conspicuously, and the place was regularly visited by a set of apparently conscientious magistrates who formed the prison board.[13]

THE DESCENT OF LIBERTY

The following is a list of personal and professional benefits that Hunt claims to have received during his two-year imprisonment.[14]

1. Hunt tells us that imprisonment ultimately played some part in improving his own health, as well as the health, physical and emotional, of his brother John.[15]
2. His stock of knowledge was increased in prison.[16]

3. Hunt claims that his imprisonment fostered, rather than hindered, British social and political reform.[17]
4. His imprisonment brought Hunt immediate celebrity.
5. By means of his imprisonment, Hunt met Percy Shelley, initiated his correspondence with Lord Byron, grew closer to his brother John, improved his marriage, and, not least, increased his stock of general benevolence.[18]
6. Hunt planned for and gave himself a vast and eclectic education in prison. Topics included "a full and proper knowledge . . . of history and of legislation"; "a course of epic poetry from Homer to Virgil, and so through the Italian school to the English" (all in the original languages);[19] the history of prison reform, including Bentham's *Theory of Legislation*, published in French in 1802, which Hunt meant "to enter upon regularly," as well as Howard's *State of the Prisons*;[20] the fifty-six-volume *Parnaso Italiano*, an anthology of Italian poetry edited by Andrea Rubbi, which Hunt purchased during his imprisonment and which "began his long and affectionate study of Italian literature, that not only influenced his poetic style and attitudes considerably but also produced some of his happiest translations";[21] Edmund Spenser's *Faerie Queene* (which Hunt not only read in prison but annotated intensively); the verse of Geoffrey Chaucer, John Milton, and John Dryden; and a number of other romances, travelogues, books of essays, and biographies too numerous to mention here.
7. Hunt established a methodical and lasting work ethic between 1813 and 1815. In one of many notes to the second edition of his poem *The Feast of the Poets* (1814), a note he wrote in prison, Hunt says that he hopes to master one of his old "irregular habits"—sleeping in till the afternoon.[22] It turns out that he not only mastered this old habit in prison, but developed a set of new ones to prevent any relapse. One of his great achievements during his confinement was learning intellectual discipline. As he told Marianne in April 1813: "I am . . . more regular in my reading & writing than I was, & after reading my law & history every morning for an hour & then taking my walk, go to my poetry as regularly as clock-work."[23] He continues in this strain the following month: "I am again in excellent time this week . . . I know it will please you to see me thus conquering one of my oldest & most inveterate habits:—it is a good sign for the rest of my victories."[24] His excitement over his new industriousness occasionally crops up in unexpected places. In a poem written in Surrey Gaol, *The Descent of Liberty* (1815), Hunt includes a rural scene in which a band of allegorical rustics named Stout Heart, Toil, and Exercise gather to celebrate the naturalness and felicity of hard agrarian labor, a scene, considering the circumstances of its composition, symbolic of his own revitalized work ethic in prison:

> Exercise.
> Yes, yes, we'll be up when the singing-bird starts;

TOIL.
We'll level her [Ceres's] harvests, and fill up her carts;
STOUT HEART.
And shake off fatigue with our bounding hearts[25]

Nor was this work ethic only temporary in its effects. Ann Blainey remarks that years after his imprisonment, Hunt "would attribute his habit of solitary, concentrated study to these prison schedules and he would bless them for inculcating so valuable a habit."[26]

8. The *Examiner* improved in the quality and diversity of its content between 1813 and 1815. On May 9, 1813, Hunt introduced to the *Examiner* the series of charming familiar essays collectively called "Table Talk." On August 15, his old school friend Thomas Barnes started writing weekly essays on parliamentary proceedings and on the political views of certain members of Parliament. Hunt seems to have been pleased with these additions. He writes at the end of 1813 that "our Paper has been conducted . . . in some respects better" than "could be expected under the circumstances."[27] By 1814, the *Examiner* could now lay claim to a number of "occasional articles on Literary and Philosophical Subjects," contributed by William Hazlitt.[28] Then, early in 1815, a second series of familiar essays began to appear, this time written by Hunt, Hazlitt, Lamb, and others, and eventually collected and published in 1818 as *The Round Table*. The *Round Table* essays were important as a model for colloquial columns in future magazines such as *Blackwood's* and *Fraser's*.[29] All these innovations in the *Examiner* were due in part to the fact that Hunt "suppl[ied] a place of observation seldom occupied by Journalists," that is, his "comparative abstraction from the bustle" of the outside world.[30] All improvements to the *Examiner* between 1813 and 1815 may be summarized as follows: "[Hunt's] spirits rose, his facility increased, and he delegated to others only that [*Examiner*] work which his confinement utterly prevented."[31] His prison work ethic even got to the point that "the compositors of the *Examiner* were 'petrified' by the 'volume and punctuality' of his output" from prison.[32]
9. Beginning in prison, Hunt did more than any of his contemporaries to establish the lasting reputation of Wordsworth as a literary genius.[33]
10. The last item in this list is certainly not the least. It was first in prison that Hunt helped to revolutionize the handling of the heroic couplet in English through his most famous poem, *The Story of Rimini*, which had a huge influence on Keats and especially on his irregular heroic couplets in *Endymion* (1818). *Rimini* features a host of enjambed couplets, end stops, and other caesurae in the middle of lines, rhythmic irregularities, alexandrines, and triplets. Several critics read its formal innovativeness as part of an "opposition poetics" inseparable from the social, moral, and political radicalism that Hunt advanced in the *Examiner* and elsewhere.[34]

Will Bowers has observed that the *Parnaso Italiana*, that "comprehensive survey of Italian poetry" which Hunt bought in prison, both "illuminated Hunt's incarceration and provided the source material for *Rimini*."[35] This is a perfectly reasonable claim. Hunt was certainly reading the *Parnaso* in prison, as well as theoretical texts on the literary romance and a number of actual medieval and modern romances, and he set *Rimini* in late medieval Italy. But it is equally plausible that his incarceration per se—his experience of confinement and what he wrote about it—inspired as much of the structure, tone, and poetic style of *Rimini* as the *Parnaso* did. A close reading of the middle cantos of *Rimini* strongly supports this claim, and it is to these cantos that I now want to turn.

RIMINI AS ALLEGORY

Recall that Hunt wrote canto 1 of *Rimini* before prison, whereas he wrote all of canto 2 and a part of canto 3 in Surrey Gaol. Canto 1 describes the wedding of Francesca da Polenta and Giovanni Malatesta in Ravenna. Canto 2 dramatizes the foreboding feelings of Francesca as she travels with her wedding train from her hometown of Ravenna to Rimini castle, a site of domestic and patriarchal confinement.

All of canto 1 takes place in Ravenna. In it, Francesca marries a man she thinks is Giovanni Malatesta, the elder brother, but who is actually Paulo Malatesta, the younger brother. The elder Malatesta, Giovanni, we learn, had sent his handsomer and more chivalric younger brother to Ravenna to marry Francesca as his proxy. Her own father, as it happens, was complicit in the deception, since he wanted to do all he could to force a political alliance between Ravenna and Rimini. Not long after the proxy wedding, Francesca is put in a royal chariot and swept out of Ravenna, with Paulo Malatesta riding on ahead. We are told that she can "scarce, at times, a starting cry forbear / At leaving her own home and native air" (*R*, 1.109–110). The wedding party makes its way toward Rimini in a slow descent, through a thick and winding forest, and Francesca sleeps through much of the journey. At one point in the night the travelers break from the wood, and

> turning last a sudden corner, see
> The square-lit towers of slumbering Rimini.
> The marble bridge comes heaving forth below
> With a long gleam; and nearer as they go,
> They see the still Marecchia, cold and bright,
> Sleeping along with face against the light.
> A hollow trample now,—a fall of chains,—
> The bride has entered,—not a voice remains;—

> Night, and a maiden silence, wrap the plains.
> (*R*, 2.235–243)

These lines end the second canto and evoke a sense of premonition, to be developed in cantos 3 and 4. A number of formal implications are at work in this passage. A "heaving" bridge suggests the heaving chest and heart of the bride who crosses it; the words "cold" and "hollow" anticipate the marriage to come between Francesca and her new husband—the actual husband as opposed to the proxy; the "maiden silence" that "wrap[s] the plains" implies the maiden*hood* and maiden*head* that Francesca is shortly to leave behind. Finally, there is the sound of the "fall of chains" easing the drawbridge down. By this we may imagine Francesca arriving, as one critic says, at a "prison rather than a wedding chamber."[36] And so, in a very strong sense, she has.

In his *Autobiography*, Hunt describes a similarly foreboding arrival at a literal prison. He recalls himself riding to Surrey Gaol at night in a hackney coach (not quite the royal chariot of the Ravenna party) through the illuminated streets of London. The time was early February 1813. When he saw "the prison gate and the high wall" (a "dreary business") Hunt closed his eyes and imagined he was racing on horseback across the downs of Brighton. Soon the coach pulled up to Surrey Gaol and deposited Hunt outside in a yard. He waited for what seemed like a long time to be admitted into the presence of a gaoler, by the name of James Ives. Ives was a gruff, fifty-year-old, well-meaning, red-faced man in a nightcap, who spoke with Hunt about accommodations as soon as they met.[37] (Ives initially offered to let Hunt live with him, in his own apartments, but the price was too expensive for Hunt.) The first six weeks in Surrey Gaol were trying for Hunt. He lived in a featureless garret (though it did have glazed, shuttered windows and a fireplace) located at the end of a long range of empty cells. The garret was formerly occupied by the Anglo-Irish rebel Colonel Despard, convicted of treason and executed on the roof of Surrey Gaol in 1803. At this point, Hunt could receive visits from his family only intermittently. As he tried to sleep in the garret on the first night, he heard the sound of ten or eleven locks fastening, one by one, each lock more remote sounding than the last, "till," as he says, "the weaker part of my heart died within me." Then and there he felt "suddenly alone" and "away from . . . [his] family." In a yard outside the garret were felons, whom Hunt could hear but not see, the "perpetual sound" of whose chains, "clanking from daylight" on, he recalls, "wore upon my spirits."[38]

Yet these melancholy feelings were not to last. On March 16, 1813, after six weeks in the garret, Hunt moved into new rooms in the prison infirmary, where his family was now allowed to stay with him continuously. The infirmary was a single-story building divided into four wards. Hunt took two of these wards, once old washrooms, for his own use. One room had a high window and served as his bedroom. The other was turned into a kind of salon, or drawing room, which Hunt proudly called his "noble room" and which he decorated lavishly:

> I papered the walls with a trellis of roses; I had the ceiling coloured with clouds and sky; the barred windows I screened with Venetian blinds; and when my bookcases were set up with their busts, and flowers and a pianoforte made their appearance, perhaps there was not a handsomer room on that side of the water. I took a pleasure, when a stranger knocked at the door, to see him come in and stare about him. The surprise on issuing from the Borough, and passing through the avenues of a gaol, was dramatic. Charles Lamb declared there was no other such room, except in a fairy tale.[39]

The noble room had a sofa, two windows, and a fireplace. The piano was positioned in it in such a way that Hunt could look out of the windows onto his garden as he played. (A London instrument seller, Maurice Whittaker, also lent him a lute.) Hunt had his bookcases lined with a "bright red fringe," a detail Byron remembered, and it was also installed above the piano and between the windows.[40] The upper shelf featured a selection of his favorite poets and a bust of Homer; the lower shelf held various quartos. Over the mantlepiece in the room Hunt arranged for a picture of his brother John to be mounted. A portrait of Milton was fixed elsewhere in the room. The noble room itself, moreover, was only part of the idyllic setting enjoyed the Hunt circle. Outside the room was a "little yard . . . railed off from another belonging to the neighbouring ward. This yard I shut in with green palings, adorned it with a trellis, bordered it with a thick bed of earth from a nursery, and even contrived to have a grass-plot. The earth I filled with flowers and young trees."[41] Among the flowers were wild pansies, pinks, roses, Persian lilac, daisies, White Broom, rhododendrons, polyanthuses, primroses, and lilies. Among the trees Hunt planted was an apple tree, which eventually provided the Hunts with pastries and puddings. In the autumn months Hunt could admire several scarlet runners that grew along his garden trellis, and when the weather was pleasant he would read and write in an armchair fronting the garden or take long afternoon walks. Beyond the wicket gate of his own yard was another yard, belonging strictly to the prison, in which mostly vegetables were planted and which contained a cherry tree that Hunt grew to love.[42]

Thus Hunt enjoyed a considerable degree of personal liberty once he and his family were settled in the infirmary. His good fortune is especially evident when we compare his situation to that of the Anglo-American stenographer Thomas Lloyd, another middle-aged, middle-class family man convicted of libel and thrown into a London prison. Next to Newgate Prison, where Lloyd spent three long years between 1793 and 1796, the infirmary rooms at Surrey Gaol were a pastoral idyll.

Nor was the state side of Newgate, where Lloyd lived for nine months, cheap. Lloyd tells us that prisoners admitted into the state side usually

> have each a room, for which they pay the Jailer one guinea admittance fee, and seven shillings each per week. A person, possessed of money, desirous of purchasing superior accommodations, is admitted on that side, without regard to his crime. The more frequently the lodgers are changed, the oftener the Jailer receives his admittance fee; *but if prisoners, imprisoned for misdemeanors, were to remain there of right, they could not be expected, even by avarice itself, to pay for it.*[43]

Hunt, as we saw, was not admitted to the infirmary at Surrey Gaol immediately on his arrival, but obliged to stay in the garret for over a month. He did so until it was evident to a visiting physician, one Dixon, as well as to the prison board of justices, that his health suffered considerably in the garret, and so the board decided to relocate Hunt and his family to the infirmary. Hunt most likely had to pay rent to remain there, though at what rate, weekly or monthly, and at what cost, remain unclear.

Hunt described his new environment in a series of letters to his wife, Marianne, between April 26 and June 11, 1813. During this time Marianne was away at Brighton with their sons Thornton (then two and a half) and John (less than a year old). Each of the following fascinating passages is taken from a different letter in this series. Note the lush attention to detail in some of the descriptions.

> I had some gardening yesterday. . . . No visitors this afternoon. . . . Pray tell . . . [Thornton] that I use his watering-pot, and that Marriott [John Hunt's son] (who came to see us on Sunday) mended his spade for him. . . . I will try & get my garden in good splendour. . . . At present the rains have beaten it a little, though it still {is} in nice order,—the grass has been mown,—& the look-out of the sunshine yesterday brought the apple-tree into most wanton display.
>
> Your sky at Brighton cannot be finer than our's [*sic*] was here yesterday & this morning:—this afternoon, while at dinner, we had a jovial shower, which has made all the flowers sparkle again;—the yellow globes are out & full, the Persian lilac hung with delicate bunches of blue, the daises stand up quite swelling & proud, the broom has shot out a profusion of snowy blossoms along it's [*sic*] rods, & the left-hand rhododendron is throwing up the promise of a most splendid flower;—the polyanthuses, primroses, & apple blossoms are quite gone; but the garden, you may easily imagine, looks better than ever; & by the time you return, you will be saluted with the roses & lilies.
>
> Just as I am writing this, the sun has broken out & flung a handful of his gold into the room, after a sad rainy morning. It almost looks like an omen.

> There is a pale, slim sort of gentleman, with black eyes . . . & a picturesque head of black hair (for it wants cutting) waiting for her [i.e., Marianne] with not a little impatience in a certain enchanted castle, in which s[he] can come to him though he cannot get out to her.
>
> You may imagine how well . . . [the noble room] looks with the blinds down. . . . Everything looks so neat & compact, that what with the books, the bust, & the blinds, I am sure you would quite delight in the change. Do you not long to be sitting on the sofa with me, alone, with a green light, or rather twilight, about you?
>
> There has been a fine flush of colour in it [the garden], I assure you; the rhododendrons . . . have both been magnificently diademed;—the roses however will be looking forth to meet you; so will the pinks; & there are some other colours which you may imagine, that will glow with tenfold warmth when you approach.
>
> The prison garden is as well out in leaves as it can be; there are even pinks & roses in it; & with my arm around your waist, I can fancy it absolutely pleasant by moonlight.
>
> I hope the weather will continue as fine for you as it is at present;—there is a real summer feeling about it at last, with the bees humming here & there, & every thing [*sic*] looking warm & genial;—I do not sit out in the garden however, *as I wish to keep that pleasure till you return*; then we will have out a chair or two, I shall take you on my knee, & with little Thornton running on the grass plat before us,—how much delight shall not be ours.[44]

In a related passage written years after his imprisonment, Hunt recalls the birth of his daughter, Mary Florimel, at Surrey Gaol in the summer of 1814, a birth at which he himself assisted. It is a vignette almost too painfully sweet for him to remember: "[Marianne] found many unexpected comforts: and during the whole time of her confinement, which happened to be in very fine weather, the garden door was set open, and she looked upon trees and flowers. A thousand recollections rise within me at every fresh period of my imprisonment, such as I cannot trust myself with dwelling upon."[45]

The language of these excerpts will become especially important in the forthcoming discussion of *Rimini.* I read *Rimini* as a text that imaginatively reenacts, through the character of Francesca, the real-life transition of Hunt from uncertainty to certainty, anxiety to tranquility, estrangement to intimacy, which he experienced en route to and during the early part of his stay at Surrey Gaol, and which he describes in detail in the *Autobiography.* At the same time, the poem revitalizes that sense of endless restfulness, security, and beauty peculiar to a narrow space, filled with flora and sunshine, which Hunt describes so affectionately in his letters to Marianne.

We saw that Hunt was not always sanguine in Surrey Gaol, as he had to endure the loneliness of the garret for six weeks before he lived in and grew to love the infirmary; a similar emotional arc structures the middle cantos of *Rimini*. En route to Rimini Castle, Francesca is "full of anxious thoughts" (*R*, 2.160). The forest all around her "a heavy spot . . . looks at first, / To one grim shade condemned" (*R*, 2.166–167). The same forest is also alive with the "noisome din" of "swarming insects" (*R*, 1.170–171), which we may compare to the "noise" of "dinning fetters" heard by Hunt in his garret.[46] But then the tone of the poem changes as the wedding party gets closer to Rimini: "but entering more and more, they quit the sand / At once, and strike upon a grassy land" (*R*, 2.172–173). Thus the forest, formerly condemned to one drab shade and carpeted with sand, grows greener and more inviting as Francesca and her train proceed. Hunt even dapples his imaginary Italian forest with the beautiful forms he was seeing in and around his very real infirmary rooms. The White Broom in his prison garden, for instance, which "shot out [in] a profusion of snowy blossoms," becomes, in the forest, "briony" spread "in trails of white" (*R*, 2.190). The "handful of . . . gold" "flung" by the sun into his noble room, to take another example, becomes "flings of sunshine left upon the bark" of the forest trees (*R*, 2.193).

Certain parallels between the prison infirmary and the imaginary landscape Hunt created in *Rimini* are especially evident in canto 3. In his *Autobiography*, Hunt singles out the following passage from the *Parnaso Italiano* as emblematic of the way he came to perceive his prison garden:

> *Mio picciol orto,*
> *A me sei vigna, e campo, e selva, e prato.*
> —Baldi.
> *My little garden,*
> *To me thou'rt vineyard, field, and meadow, and wood.*[47]

The lines in Italian are quoted from the poem "Celeo e L'orto [Celeo and the Garden]" (1590), one of the poems in the *Parnaso* by the Renaissance writer Bernardino Baldi. Hunt took these lines to heart during his confinement. After he quotes them, he adds that "a wicket out of the garden"—that is, out of his private garden immediately beyond the infirmary walls—"led into the large one belonging to the prison. The latter was only for vegetables; but it contained a cherry tree, which I saw twice in blossom. I parcelled out the ground in my imagination into favourite districts."[48] Thus Hunt imaginatively expanded and divided the grounds of his prison, as he tells us, after the manner of an Italian eclogue from the Renaissance. He brought a remote Italian fiction to bear on his present English reality. *Rimini* is an interesting literary experiment, as it happens, in that it performs the same operation in reverse. It brings the immediate reality of an

English prison to bear on an imaginary Italian landscape, and in such a way as to obscure any clear boundaries between fact and fiction.

In the third canto of *Rimini*, for instance, Hunt describes a "noble range" of Rimini Forest (an epithet suggesting his "noble room") where Francesca takes long walks to distract herself from her illicit love of Paulo. The noble range is divided into three districts, a garden, a dell, and a wood, with the whole of the area "walled round with trees." The garden portion of the forest is packed with walking paths and flowers, many of them varieties Hunt had in his own garden—roses, pansies, lilies, daisies (*R*, 3.382–383, 380). Meanwhile, between the garden at one end of the forest and the wood at the other,

> halfway,
> And formed of both, the loveliest portion lay,
> A spot, that struck you like enchanted ground:—
> It was a shallow dell, set in a mound
> Of sloping shrubs
> . . . .
> The ground within was lawn, with plots of flowers
> Heaped towards the centre, and with citron bowers;
> And in the midst of all, clustered about
> With bay and myrtle, and just gleaming out,
> Lurked a pavilion—a delicious sight,
> Small, marble, well-proportioned, mellowy white
> With yellow-vine-leaves sprinkled,—but no more,—
> And a young orange either side the door.
> The door was to the wood, forward, and square,
> The rest was domed at top, and circular;
> And through the dome the only light came in,
> Tinged, as it entered, with the vine-leaves thin.
> (*R*, 3.434–448, 444–455)

Naturally Francesca adores this dell, this piece of "enchanted ground." It is walled in with forest trees, shutting the gloomy Rimini Castle out of sight, not unlike the way the fantastic enclave Hunt created in the infirmary shut the rest of Surrey Gaol out of sight. Inside the dell are "plots of flowers," trees, and a "lawn"—more or less a version of the prison garden that Hunt bordered with flowers and trees and in which he "contrived to have a grass-plot." We also learn that Francesca likes to take a "lute and a few books" with her to the dell (both pastimes for Hunt in prison), and, when not playing the lute or reading, to "[look] round her with a new-born eye, / As if some tree of knowledge had been nigh" (*R*, 3.490, 525–526). It is here that she and Paulo share their first romantic tryst.

Thus Hunt has taken his prison environment, as he imaginatively reconstructed and apportioned it, and assimilated it into a coherent poetic narrative set in thirteenth-century Italy. In the process, he brings to his poetic narrative that delicacy and refinement of perception that he learned to cultivate in his narrow prison demesne over many months. *Rimini* has become, for Hunt, not so much an escape from imprisonment, as a love letter to the way he came to imagine it.

Critics tend to disagree with this claim, reading the poem as a reality completely apart from what Hunt was actually experiencing at Surrey Gaol. One such critic labels *Rimini* a "piece of belletristic escapism." Another calls it Hunt's "ambiguous and impotent effort" to deal with confinement. Another reads it as a "displacement from the painful and boring realities of imprisonment." Still another calls Hunt the "Romantic escape-artist par excellence."[49] The logic motivating these assessments is clear: an early nineteenth-century London prison is not exactly a carbon copy of a late medieval enchanted forest with a nymph-erected summerhouse in it; thus, for these readers, Hunt may be said to be trying to escape from reality to romance, pain to pleasure, boredom to engagement. But the truth is that he had no lack of meaningful occupation in prison with the result that he needed to write *Rimini* to feel useful or entertained. The critical readings here cited tend to bely the actual experience of Hunt in prison as he himself consistently described it. I especially think that the word *displacement* is off the mark here, if it is taken in anything like the sense of *re*placement. *Rimini* is as much a window *into* the experiential realities of imprisonment for Hunt as it is a means to escape them.

Additional passages from canto 3 reinforce this point. The "noble range" of the forest, we are told, is full of

> Places of nesting green, for poets made,
> Where when the sunshine struck a yellow shade,
> The slender trunks, to inward peeping sight,
> Thronged in dark pillars up the gold green light.
> (*R*, 3.430–433)

The importance of these lines lies in the way they showcase the creative element in the act of perception. The reader, that is, is not invited to see one particular sight, so much as to experience, richly, the way a poet sees that sight. We are told that the noble range is full of lush green nooks, perhaps copses, which appear to form or function as a sort of nest, especially inviting to poets. The sun often "struck a yellow shade" in these areas, with *struck* being used in the sense of made, produced, caused to appear. The yellow shade struck by the sun, moreover, blends with the green of the surrounding verdure to form a "gold green light." A lone passerby, the speaker says, may be fortunate enough to watch as the "slender trunks" of the forest trees "[throng] in dark pillars up the gold green light." This last is a curiously dense image. The monochromatic yellow shade has become a polychromatic yellow-green light; the trunks of the trees are said to resemble "dark pillars" that can "throng," or force their way, up the yellow-green light, as if that light were climbable; the very idea of tree trunks forcing their way "up" a light, furthermore, makes the trees almost seem animate, struggling, ascending, and yet they are only "pillars" after all. What we have in these four lines is a highly intensified, poetically compact version of the sort of dynamic perception that Hunt routinely displays in his letters to Marianne from Surrey Gaol. Here again is one of his descriptions of the noble room: "you may imagine how well . . . [the noble room] looks with the blinds down. . . . everything looks so neat & compact, that what with the books, the bust, & the blinds, I am sure you would quite delight in the change. Do you not long to be sitting on the sofa with me, alone, with a green light, or rather twilight, about you?" This is the perceptual stuff on which the more refined imagery in the third canto of *Rimini* is founded. For Hunt at Surrey Gaol, writing this letter, it is late May. The venetian blinds in the noble room are drawn. The slanted rays of the setting sun strike the blossomed apple tree outside. This tints the incoming light green, which then passes through the drawn blinds and settles in the room. Hunt notices the "green light" particularly around his couch—but instantly he sees it as a green "twilight" instead. He is writing to the moment, attuned to every rapid perceptual change, careful to select just the right phenomena to produce the desired image. So it is with the speaker-narrator of *Rimini* as he walks us, carefully and joyfully, through the forest.

Nearly all of the prison letters to Marianne report on the dramatic effects of natural light. The apple tree in the garden outside the noble room is "brought" into "most wanton display" by "the look-out of the sunshine." The pinks and roses in the garden are "absolutely pleasant by moonlight." The sun at one point "has broken out & flung a handful of his gold into the room, after a sad rainy morning. It almost looks like an omen." *Rimini* is full of such moments of dazzled perception. Occasionally these moments hint at latent metaphysical realities. At one point Francesca hears a stream rush through the forest, "as if it said / Something eternal" (*R*, 3. 442–443). At another she gazes on

> the sunshine and the leaves,
> The summer rain-drops counting from the eaves,
> And all that promising, calm smile we see
> In nature's face, when we look patiently.
> Then would she think of heaven. (*R*, 3.492–496)

Here a lonesome figure finds herself in the Edenic retreat of Rimini forest, a retreat nestled within an otherwise foreign and uncomfortable demesne at which she has unwillingly arrived; she sees lush green leaves glistening in the sun after a summer rain; she looks harder ("patiently"); sun and leaves and raindrops morph into a "promising, calm smile" suggesting heaven. Is this not an imaginative translation of the May 20 letter to Marianne, with its sun-flung "gold" after a "rainy morning" that looks like an "omen"?

At one point in canto 4 Francesca and Paulo revisit the forest pavilion together in sadness, where they once met lovingly in secret, "partly to see / The spot where they had last gone smilingly, / But most, from failure of all self-support" (*R*, 4.33–35). After this visit Francesca never goes to the spot again. Paulo, however, "could not refrain" from returning to the pavilion a third time, alone, and he "went again one day; and how it looked! / The calm, old shade!" (*R*, 4.50–52). Soon guilt and anguish overwhelm him and he leaves the enchanted ground. He then proceeds to isolate himself in rural niches elsewhere in the forest, similar but not identical to the forest dell, "pierc[ing] the shade / Of some enwooded field or closer glade" (*R*, 4.96–97). It is not long before Giovanni learns of the affair; Francesca alludes to it in her sleep in their marital bed. Immediately Giovanni challenges Paulo to trial by combat; and then a curious thing happens as the two brothers issue out onto the plain to fight. In the distance—we are following the perspective of Paulo—

> An opening in the trees took Paulo's eye,
> As, with his brother, mutely he went by:
> It was a glimpse of the tall wooded mound,
> That screened Francesca's favourite spot of ground:
> Massy and dark in the clear twilight stood,
> As in a lingering sleep, the solemn wood;
> And through the bowering arch, which led inside,
> He almost fancied once, that he descried
> A marble gleam, where the pavilion lay;—
> Starting he turned, and looked another way. (*R*, 4.199–208)

This fine passage works on a literal and an allegorical level. In a literal sense Paulo takes a sad last look toward the fatal spot, a place, as one critic puts it, of "freedom and enslavement."[50] In an allegorical sense the lines suggest the mixed feelings Hunt had after he left his prison. He was released on February 2, 1815, and separation was painful. He was leaving what Edmund Blunden calls his "hermitage, a home for the abstractions, a pause from the clamours of the outer world."[51] When Hunt finally rejoined the outer world he was acutely aware of "the anxiety of freedom and the deeper sense in which life holds us prisoner."[52] The first place he went after his release was across the street, to visit a friend. Roe tells us that

> From now on Hunt would try to recover the shelter and security that prison had given him. For the rest of his life, friends and acquaintance would be amazed at his spartan way of life, how he would sit wrapped in a dressing gown in a tiny study lined with books. It looked eccentric, unworldly, but what Hunt was forever trying to recreate was the infirmary in Surrey Gaol—a scene where he had been at the height of his public fame, and most fully at liberty in the imagined worlds of poetry.[53]

In the first stage of what one writer calls his "continuing, self-imposed brand of incarceration," post-prison, Hunt went to live near his brother John in Paddington, Central London, at 4 Maida Vale.[54] It was there that he reproduced the environment of his noble room at Surrey Gaol.[55] Even in the beautiful Mediterranean, in years to come, Hunt would think back on his imprisonment with quiet affection. In the *Autobiography* he admits "that in the midst of the beautiful climate which I afterwards visited," Genoa, Pisa and Florence, "I was sometimes in doubt whether I would not rather have been in gaol than in Italy."[56]

In a word, Hunt remembered his imprisonment as a special retreat from the world and its cares. Days after his release, he was writing about leaving Surrey Gaol in the *Examiner* in a leading article entitled "Departure of the Proprietors of This Paper from Prison." He notes that

> The two years' imprisonment . . . expired on Thursday last; and on that day accordingly we quitted our respective Jails. . . . There is a feeling of space and of airy clearness about every thing [*sic*], which is alternately delightful and painful. The world, in short, is new to us, and not altogether comfortably so . . . in truth, habit will dispute a point with any thing [*sic*]; there is no soil, however foreign to one's native feelings, but in the course of time will find fibres about us to grapple with it; and the sudden departure to another [soil] . . . is in some measure like being torn up by the roots.[57]

When Hunt says that "The world, in short, is new to us," he is quietly recalling the fourth-to-last line of *Paradise Lost*, "The World was all before them."[58] Hunt was leaving his own sort of Eden; the openness and clarity of real-worldly space gave him pleasure and pain in equal measure.

Early on in his confinement, Hunt told his *Examiner* audience that the "bare walls and grated windows" of his garret "seem to have borrowed a look of home."[59] This feeling only intensified when he moved into the infirmary; the "look of home" there was no longer "borrowed." Hunt wrote to Marianne four months after his move into the noble room that

> You are at length coming *home*, & in that word, all my joys & delights, you well know, are wrapped up. It is in a prison, to be sure, but our arms would make us a prison if we had not one already; & in truth, the idea of a prison has become so familiar to me, or rather is so little in my thoughts . . . that had I but decent health to enable my mind to enjoy what it really possesses, I am almost afraid I should put the prophecies of some of my friends into execution & fairly become attached to my new domesticity:—however, I think of Hampstead, & *that* idea speedily vanishes.[60]

Hunt says that he is "almost afraid" to admit to his wife what he feels is at least partially true; that is, that he has grown attached to his prison as if it were his home, that what his mind "really possesses" in prison is a world of untrammeled thought and imagination. But he puts a dash in his sentence and immediately qualifies his initial thought. Hampstead will always be his true home. He insists on it. Yet it is an extraordinary fact that, for Hunt, prison was, at the very least, a close runner-up.

HUNT ON (AND IN) REFORMATIVE CONFINEMENT

The *Examiner* consistently supported penal reform in Britain and praised the men and women who furthered it. Among its first issues was a lead article by Hunt stressing the importance of prisoner welfare as an end in penal discipline.[61] A correspondent in 1810 appealed to Hunt personally to convince Parliament to erect (what we would now call) a halfway house in London for penitent ex-convicts.[62] Several *Examiner* articles in 1814 address the need for material improvement in London prisons,[63] one of which honors the efforts of certain "wise, pious, upright, humane, and learned writers" who "have been on the side of an amelioration of the Penal Laws" and who see penal reform as essential to "improvement and progressive civilization."[64] In June of 1821, an anonymous correspondent commended the efforts of the Society for the Improvement of Prison Discipline and for the Reformation of Juvenile Offenders.[65] Another article in September maintains that "rendering all the present criminals in England happy, would be equivalent to the destruction of crime," adding, importantly, that "no power on earth can make them happy without reforming them."[66] The lead article in the segment called the Political Examiner, written in October of 1821, argues that penal reform is "demanded by the changes in society and the increased knowledge of the age."[67] About imprisonment the author adds:

> Prisoners . . . have as much a *right* to good air, wholesome and sufficient food and clothing, and *employment*, as the Judges have to their ampule emoluments. Nor are these rights the only things which should be carefully secured to them. They possess *feelings* too, which a wise government would do well to consult and improve, and which no government can long continue to outrage with impunity. Prisoners are fellow-men.

Hunt would wholeheartedly have agreed with these statements. The article goes on to applaud the ongoing success of the Eastern State Penitentiary in Philadelphia as well as the prison reform efforts of John Howard and the Quakers Thomas Fowell Buxton and Elizabeth Fry. These and other penal "Visionaries," the writer concludes, have initiated "a dawn of better times" and a "pleasant period of daylight" in England and across Europe.[68]

Hunt declared his own position on state-sanctioned punishment in the *Examiner* in 1808:

> In all public punishment there are two things generally considered; first, it's [*sic*] utility as to example; and secondly, it's [*sic*] utility as to public reparation. But there ought always to be a third consideration, it's [*sic*] utility with regard to the sufferer himself. . . . The first end of punishment is certainly it's [*sic*] social utility; but society is not indemnified by example only; there is a loss to be supplied, a detriment to be repaired; and it will be found, that the *second* and the *third* considerations necessarily depend on each other.

The point is that a healthy, happy, productive offender (third consideration) is a better reparation to society (second consideration) than an unhealthy, miserable, idle offender. The article is essentially a cry against the death penalty. Killing a few unfortunates as examples to deter the innocent masses has failed to reduce crime in Britain, a fact, Hunt reminds us, which "Sir Samuel Romilly has proved to the House of Commons, and any man of common reading may prove for himself." He adds by way of example that hanging a thief supplies no real loss to the injured person. A more effective, humane, noncapital punishment is needed. Hunt never comes out and says precisely what that punishment would look like or how it would be implemented. But whatever it may be, it should aim at "utility with regard to the sufferer himself"; that is, at the "*future repentance or happiness of the malefactor*," with the potential result that a "*thousand members of society . . . might be rendered valuable, virtuous, and happy*."[69]

Are any of these comments suitable to the case of Hunt himself? Was *he* rendered more valuable, virtuous, and happy in prison? Consider the following scenario. Hunt is in his noble room, perhaps alone, and it is a wet, cold, autumnal night in either 1813 or 1814. The rain is pouring down hard outside. Hunt settles at his table to write the third canto of *Rimini*. At this point in his poem, he has narrated up to the arrival of Francesca and her wedding train at Rimini Castle. Francesca is still under the impression that she has married Paulo Malatesta, and has yet to meet her real husband, Giovanni.

> Now why must I disturb a dream of bliss,
> Or bring cold sorrow 'twixt the wedded kiss?
> Sad is the strain, with which I cheer my long
> And caged hours, and try my native tongue;
> Now too, while rains autumnal, as I sing,
> Wash the dull bars, chilling my sicklied wing,
> And all the climate presses on my sense;
> But thoughts it furnishes of things far hence,
> And leafy dreams affords me, and a feeling
> Which I should else disdain, tear-dipped and healing;
> And shews me,—more than what it first designed,—

How little upon earth our home we find,
Or close the intended course of erring human-kind.

Enough of this. (*R*, 3.1–14)

The first two lines ask the same rhetorical question twice: Must I awaken Francesca from her happy dream? Must I relate the unhappiness that awaits her and Paulo? We know the answer: yes. So Hunt explains that it is hard for him to carry on with a "strain" so "sad." Now, he could have meant *strain* in the sense of the tale itself—its sad content—or *strain* in the sense of the exertion required to tell it. Either way, the sense of sadness is drawn out slightly at the medial caesura in line 3. But only slightly. The little dramatic pause at the comma leads almost immediately to a happy turn: "sad is the strain, with which I *cheer* my long / And caged hours." The word *cheer* crops up as a light paradox, anticipating the positive effects to come in the final six lines. But before we can get to these six lines Hunt envelops us sensually in three lines of autumnal English gloom. Lines 5 through 7 form a twofold adverbial clause on the cold and wet weather around the poet in the act of composition. We are put in his immediate position and meant to feel as he feels. It is autumn, it is raining, the rain is cold and the atmosphere seems to press down on his senses.[70] The same lines serve also to emphasize the sheer remoteness of the Italian climate sung about. Hunt sets his "native tongue," "cold sorrow," and "chilling" rains against Italian "things far hence" and "leafy dreams."[71] This is essentially the Addison-Zimmermann-Rousseau hypothesis at work, *in a real gaol.* Hunt can imaginatively create the most beautiful scenes because he is placed in material conditions the opposite of the ones he imagines.

So the climactic force builds and presses on Hunt until line 8, which initiates a rhetorical turn. Here Hunt lists three reasons why he must sustain his strain in spite of its sadness (or why the poem *makes* him sustain it). One is that *Rimini* helps him escape his own time and space with faraway thoughts and verdurous dreams. Another is that writing *Rimini* is cathartic. It arouses a feeling of pity that induces tears and "heal[s]" the poet. A third is that *Rimini* "shews . . . [Hunt],—more than what it first designed,—/ How little upon earth our home we find, / Or close the intended course of erring human kind." Critics rarely mention these last lines, let alone discuss them. I suspect this is because to take these lines seriously would be to acknowledge *Rimini* as more than simply a piece of escapist diversion.[72] Yet I would call the final lines the most interesting in the set, and the most important. The grave alexandrine at the end concludes the triplet, closes the verse paragraph, and serves as its moral-rhetorical climax. In thirteen lines we have gone from sadness, to happy thoughts and dreams, to cathartic tears, and finally to a bit of solemn reflection. Hunt ends his personal intrusion into his poetic narrative not with self-concern but with a metaphysical reflection on the ultimate fate of the human race. Writing *Rimini* "shews" the poet that our home is not on this planet and that our "intended course" is not to be fulfilled anywhere under the sun. "Erring human-kind" must leave off its wandering only when it gets to its real home, in some sort of afterlife, perhaps heaven. Immediately afterward, Hunt seems to realize he is out of character in saying as much, that it is not his place or his style to lecture his audience or to explain to his audience how he has lectured himself in prison. So he starts line 14 with "Enough of this," and moves back to sunny Italy.

Hunt once wrote the following on the "experience of evil": "it gave me an amount of reflection, such as in all probability I never should have had without it. . . . It taught me patience; it taught me charity . . . it taught me the worth of little pleasures . . . it taught me that evil itself contained good."[73] He adds that the existence of evil may be "necessary to the very bliss that supersedes it" when it is over. He goes on:

> Evil itself has its bright, or at any rate its redeeming, side. . . . [It] is the admonisher, the producer, the increaser, nay, the very adorner and splendid investitor of good; it is the pain that prevents a worse, the storm that diffuses health, the plague that enlarges cities, the fatigue that sweetens sleep, the discord that enriches harmonies, the calamity that tests affections, the victory and the crown of patience, the enrapturer of the embraces of joy.[74]

Clearly this philosophy helped Hunt thrive in prison. He also spread it to the public. His readers would have absorbed his philosophy of cheer through his personal updates in the *Examiner* written just before, throughout, and shortly after his confinement. And what did Hunt ultimately tell his readers? He told them that his imprisonment was worth the service it paid to Liberty, that a little nature could do much to support a person in straits, that he learned more philosophical habits in prison, that he underwent an aesthetic transformation in prison thanks in part to his new and rigorous work ethic. Even the government arguably got something out of his sentence in that, after 1815, Hunt kept his oppositional politics much to himself. In 1813 he started introducing more literary interests into the *Examiner* as a counterpart to its political interests.[75] He launched a new periodical in 1819, *The Indicator*, which was his most successful journal and which was "explicitly intended as a retreat from politics."[76] As Anthony Holden puts it, "prison had altered Hunt's critical priorities."[77] He became less "the hot-headed young polemicist" and more "the all-round man of letters he had always been by inclination and education, and would now always remain."[78]

4
KEATS, BYRON, AND THE IDEA OF TRANSFORMATIVE CONFINEMENT

LEIGH HUNT WAS PERHAPS the first man to live out the literary tradition of the happy prison comprehensively. In the process, he made his life imitate his art and his art imitate his life. As Samuel Taylor Coleridge, in "This Lime-Tree Bower My Prison," troped a lime-tree bower as a redemptive prison, Hunt, in *Rimini*, the *Examiner*, the *Autobiography*, and elsewhere, turned his real prison into what Keats may have indirectly referred to as a "rosy sanctuary."[1] The present chapter demonstrates how Keats and Byron both grew interested in the psychological effects of confinement through their relationship with Hunt. Byron may never have written his poem *The Prisoner of Chillon* (1816)—or written it quite as he did—had he not visited Hunt in prison between 1813 and 1815 and gotten to know him there. Keats would obviously never have written his sonnet entitled "Written on the Day that Mr. Leigh Hunt Left Prison" (1815), and neither, perhaps, would he have interlaced many of his more well-known poems, from *Endymion* (1814) to the great odes of 1819, with images and themes of happy or regenerative confinement.

KEATS, HUNT, AND THE POETICS OF CONFINEMENT

John Keats once wrote to a friend that meeting Leigh Hunt, poet, ex-convict, and radical editor of the *Examiner*, would mark "an Era in . . . [his] existence."[2] He was certainly right. The first poem by Keats to appear in print was published in the *Examiner* on May 5, 1816.[3] In October of the same year, Keats and Hunt met and became fast friends. Then in December Hunt officially introduced Keats to the world, along with Percy Bysshe Shelley and John Hamilton Reynolds, in his article in the *Examiner* entitled "Young Poets." Keats's poems, Hunt says in "Young Poets," are remarkable for the "truth of their ambition" and their "ardent grappling with nature."[4] By early 1817, the *Examiner* had published a large selection of Keats's verse.

Keats was quick to show gratitude to his mentor. His first volume of verse, published in March 1817 and unassumingly called *Poems*, begins with a sonnet dedicated to Hunt; following the sonnet is an untitled poem—"[I stood tip-toe upon a little hill]"—which features an epigraph from *The Story of Rimini* ("Places of nestling green for Poets made"); and a number of subsequent poems in the volume either name Hunt directly or reveal his influence. Hunt is thus a clear and persistent presence in the 1817 *Poems*. Consider the following sonnet, called "Written on the Day That Mr. Leigh Hunt Left Prison," one of seventeen sonnets printed in the volume. I quote the sonnet here with single-line scansion markings.

L x x Lx / x Lx L
What though, for showing truth to flatter'd state,

/ L x L x Lx L x L
Kind Hunt was shut in prison, yet has he,

x x̲ x L x Lx x̲ x L
In his immortal spirit, been as free

x x LL x L x x̲ xL
As the sky-searching lark, and as elate.

Lx x L x L x x̲ x L
Minion of grandeur! think you he did wait?

L x x L x L x L x L
Think you he nought but prison walls did see,

x Lx Lx L xL x L
Till, so unwilling, thou unturn'dst the key?

/ L/ L x L x x̲ x L
Ah, no! far happier, nobler was his fate!

x L x L x L x Lx L
In Spenser's halls he strayed, and bowers fair,

Lx x L x L x x̲ x L
Culling enchanted flowers; and he flew

x L x L x x̲ x L x L
With daring Milton through the fields of air:

xL x x̲ x L x L x L
To regions of his own his genius true

/ L x L [x] L x x L x L
Took happy flights. Who shall his fame impair

x L x L x L x L x L
When thou art dead, and all thy wretched crew?

The poem is structured around two rhetorical emphases, one minor, one major.[5] The minor emphasis involves a criticism of the Regency government. The speaker addresses a "minion of grandeur"—that is, a slave to the conscious greatness and imposing dignity of the British state—who "unwilling[ly] . . . unturn[s] the key" that releases Hunt from prison. Apparently, this minion and his "wretched crew" take a perverse delight in seeing literary talent incarcerated. The rest of the sonnet glorifies Hunt as a poetic martyr who does the opposite of simply "wait" in prison. He is all movement and action. He searches the sky, strays in Spenserian halls and bowers, culls flowers, and flies "through the fields of air" to "regions of his own" imaginative creation. His "immortal spirit" can go wherever it wants, even, or especially, when his body is placed in confinement.

The sonnet honors this experience of flight-in-confinement by imitating it. It transcends the restrictions of poetic form as Hunt has transcended his imprisonment. First, consider the volta. The volta occurs in line 8 instead of its more traditional position, in an Italian sonnet, in line 9. There is also the fact that all the lines in the sonnet except 7 and 14 feature one or more rhythmic variations. Lines 1, 5, 6, and 10, for instance, all have initial inversions (/̲ x x /̲); lines 3–5, 8, and 10–12 feature promoted syllables (x̲); and lines 2, 8, and 13 demote their first syllables (/). The variations most disruptive to iambic meter in this poem occur in lines 4 and 13: line 4 begins with a rising inversion (x x /̲ /̲), while line 13 contains a falling inversion (/̲ /̲ x x) midline. But perhaps the most virtuosic line in the sonnet is line 10. If we look at the four stress groups in line 10, labeled below, we see that the first is falling, the second is mixed, the third is falling, and the fourth is rising.

/̲ x x /̲ x /̲ x x̲ x /
Culling | enchanted | flowers; | and he flew FMFR

The stress groups are rhythmically organized in a way that has semantic implications. The third group, "FLOWers," culminates in a strong medial caesura, marked with a semicolon, which forces the reader to pause. Note how the pause is appropriate in terms of what is being described. In line 9 and up to this point in line 10, the poem has pictured Hunt as earthbound, in a bower culling flowers. Here at the caesura he seems to pause, or hesitate, as though gathering strength for an imminent flight. Immediately after the caesura, accordingly, the promoted syllable "and" (being an unstressed syllable flanked by two other unstressed syllables) speeds up the line and initiates the fourth stress group, the only rising one in the line. Thus the rhythm forces us to skim past the syllables "and" and "he" until suddenly, with "flew," we are in an expanse of white space after an enjambed line. Rhythmically, the line has taken off, mirroring the action of flight that it ascribes to Hunt.

The sonnet to Hunt, like so many other poems by Keats, doubles as a poem about either writing poetry or being a poet. The English author, Shakespearean scholar, and friend of both Hunt and Keats, Charles Cowden Clarke, recalls that

> it was upon an occasion, when walking thither [to London] to see Leigh Hunt, who had just fulfilled his penalty of confinement in Horsemonger Lane Prison for the unwise libel upon the Prince Regent, that Keats met me; and, turning, accompanied me back part of the way. At the last field-gate, when taking leave, he gave me the sonnet entitled, "Written on the day that Mr. Leigh Hunt left Prison." This I feel to be the first proof I had received of his having committed himself in verse.[6]

It is significant that Cowden Clarke considered this particular sonnet "the first proof I had received of his having committed himself in verse." For Cowden Clarke, the sonnet to Hunt was a sure sign that Keats had wholly dedicated himself to his poetic vocation over and above his abortive career in medicine. Nor did the sonnet merely mark the onset of a new career, but it was also crucial in determining the shape that that career would take. Nicholas Roe argues that Keats "sketched out his myth of poetic identity as a response to Hunt's creative survival in prison," convincing himself, as part of the myth, that "gaining poetic fame" would involve his own "self-martyrdom, a trial in a vale of soul-making, a dying into poetic life."[7] Thus the sonnet to Hunt was a way for Keats to imagine and set up his poetic career as a series of glorious trials, self-transformations, endurance tests. He would be in a constant state of divine agony as a poet. His work would repeatedly defy expectations, and more obstacles to face would mean more opportunities to transcend them.

The trial of Hunt in prison not only offered Keats an archetype of poetic identity; it also suggested an arch-metaphor in terms of which Keats would come to understand and articulate romantic desire. In June 1813, from prison, Hunt wrote the following passage in a letter to his wife Marianne. She had been away for at least three months at Brighton; Hunt, meanwhile, remained in Surrey Gaol.

> You are at length coming *home*, & in that word, all my joys & delights, you well know, are wrapped up. It is in a prison, to be sure, but our arms would make us a prison if we had not one already; & in truth, the idea of a prison has become so familiar to me, or rather is so little in my thoughts . . . that had I but decent health to enable my mind to enjoy what it really possesses, I am almost afraid I should put the prophecies of some of my friends into execution & fairly become attached to my new domesticity.[8]

The prophecies of these friends were indeed accurate. According to Roe, "prison had become home" for Hunt. It made him feel "secure, enclosed, 'wrapped up'—

exactly as he felt in Marianne's arms."[9] Nor was it any different when Marianne was away. Marianne had a younger sister, Elizabeth "Bess" Kent, a writer on botanical and horticultural topics who never married, who had always been close to Hunt, and who stayed with him in prison when Marianne was absent. Eventually, the idiosyncratic intimacy between Bess and Hunt led to scandal. Daisy Hay writes that

> When Hunt published his poem of incestuous love, *The Story of Rimini*, his critics were quick to point out that he lived in close proximity to his own sister-in-law, and the relationship became the focus of insinuation and innuendo. When the poem was published *Blackwood's* alleged in a letter to Hunt that "a sister of Mrs Hunt's resides with you, who is the mother of at least one child, of which you are the father." . . . On 15 February 1817 Bess attempted to drown herself but left no explanation for her suicide attempt and her voice is absent from all the surviving records for this period.[10]

We need not credit the story that Hunt slept with his sister-in-law to know that their relationship would have seemed unorthodox at the time. Roe says that

> by the mid-1820s Hunt and Bess had known each other for twenty-five years. Bess's childish curiosity about . . . [Hunt] had grown into the great passion of her life, and Hunt's letters reveal that he responded with equal warmth. Their adult intimacy dated from their months together in the heart of the prison, a time when Hunt also became "more of a lover" for Marianne—his most passionate letters to his wife were written while he was living with her sister. If imprisonment brought home to him the depth of his love for Marianne, it also opened the possibility of drawing others into their embrace too. Bess was the first, and there would be many more women and men whom Hunt saw as proxy partners in an extended family of love. . . . Hunt needed to be surrounded and "wrapped up" with love.[11]

Treating the infirmary at Surrey Gaol as a haven of inclusive love was one of several ways that Hunt depoliticized his punishment. Keats seems to have appropriated this act of depoliticization and taken it a step further. In his verse and in his personal letters, as with Hunt, he routinely figures ideal and intense intimacy in the language of confinement. He does this throughout his career. Often where there is an image of love, or desire, or devotion, in a poem or a letter, an image of imprisonment is not far away. He may have inherited this practice to some extent from any number of ancient, late medieval, and Renaissance writers—Apuleius, Petrarch, Ariosto, Spenser, Sidney, Shakespeare, or Burton, to name a few. Yet I suggest that what Roe calls "the aura of idealism and romance surrounding Hunt in prison" actually invigorated this practice.[12] It intensified it. Petrarch and his Elizabethan imitators frequently describe intense, unattainable love as a happy prison, compared to which any other love or way of life is unhappy freedom. Hunt, who inspired Keats to love Petrarch in the first place,[13] made these conventional Petrarchan fantasies real. He lived in an actual prison for two years that he exploited as his sanctuary of inclusive love and that he was reluctant to leave. Here is Petrarch writing about a figurative love-prison by way of juxtaposition. A nameless, lovelorn speaker says that

> Escaping from the prison where Love kept me
> while doing what he liked with me for years,
> would take too long to tell about, my ladies,
> how much my new-found liberty displeased me.
> . . . .
> sighing many times for what was past
> I said: "O my, the yoke, the chains, the shackles
> were sweeter than my living free like this!"[14]

In one sense, Love, in this poem, is a personified agent who has confined the speaker in a figurative prison; in another, love is a complex emotional state in which one happily desires an unrealistic or unattainable object. To the Petrarchan speaker in this poem, it is better to pine after an imaginary and possibly misleading version of a beloved in a condition of powerlessness, than to be free to pursue an actual person in real life or in realistic terms. In Petrarch, Sidney, and Spenser, all poets Keats admired, this idea is a commonplace.[15] Here is another Petrarchan example from canzone 296: "I respect and cherish myself more / thanks to the worthy prison, the sweet-bitter / blow that I've born now many years enclosed."[16] Recall that Hunt pined for his real prison days, months, years after he was released. This was in part because his love for his wife and sister-in-law reached new and passionate heights there. Thus we can say that Love "d[id] what he liked" to Hunt for two years in Surrey Gaol and that Hunt, like the Petrarchan speaker in the above excerpt, "sigh[ed] many times for what was past" when it was all over. Hunt effectively literalized, reified, embodied the Petrarchan conceit of love as happy imprisonment. Penal captivity became, in his letters, autobiographical texts, poetry, and literary criticism written from prison, amorous captivity. Political punishment became chivalric trial. Powerlessness was given overtones of the sweet powerlessness of Petrarchan love. This was a move that surely fascinated Keats.

The love-as-happy-prison theme is everywhere in Western literature and virtually untraceable. One or two examples of this trope specifically relevant to the Keats poems I discuss will suffice. For now I want to look briefly at the tale of Cupid and Psyche as told by Apuleius in his *Metamorphoses* (second century CE). Apuleius describes Psyche in the palace of Love (Cupid), where Love visits her nightly, as *beati carceris custodia saepta*—enclosed (*saepta*) by the confinement (*custodia*) of her luxurious prison (*beati carceris*).[17] There is considerable lexical ambiguity in this phrase. The verb *saepio* (whence the perfect passive participle *saepta*) can mean both to fence or hedge in and to protect. The noun *custodia* can mean either a confinement or a protective space. The adjective *beatus* can mean sumptuous, extravagant, luxurious, or, on the other hand, blissful or blessed. So the entire phrase can be accurately rendered as "fenced in by the confinement of her extravagant prison," or "enclosed by the protective space of her blissful prison." I mention this particular moment in Apuleius because Keats famously drew his "Ode to Psyche" from the tale of Cupid and Psyche in the *Metamorphoses*. In "Ode to Psyche," the speaker says that he plans to build a temple in his mind for Psyche, a human woman who was deified too late in antiquity to be properly worshipped. In lieu of pine trees around the temple there will be "branched thoughts, new grown with pleasant pain." The temple itself will be a "rosy sanctuary," decorated with "the wreath'd trellis of a working brain" and with endless flowers. A window in the temple will always remain open at night "to let the warm Love in," corresponding to the nightly visits from Love that Psyche received while in his palace in the *Metamorphoses*.[18]

Nicholas Roe has argued that these specific lines from "Ode to Psyche" "resemble Hunt's recollections of his prison cell, 'papered . . . with a trellis of roses,'" and his "garden[,] 'adorned with a trellis' and 'filled with flowers.'" Roe adds that "Keats's myth of soul-making in 'Ode to Psyche' apparently stands behind Hunt's accounts of his prison ordeal. And it's possible, too, that the 'rosy sanctuary' of Keats's poem had actually been suggested by Hunt's 'heart-prooving' in prison, and by what he had heard of Hunt's transformation of an oppressive scene into one of imaginative, erotic possibility."[19] Imaginative, erotic possibility born out of an oppressive and confining scene is a paradigm in Keats. From 1815 to 1820 his poems often tell us that real imaginative power, as well as real, ecstatic love, may have to be forged in and through periods of transformative isolation. In isolation, in solitude, in a pain that is also pleasure, the imagination can be vigorously chastened, the mind enlarged, the heart prepared for trial and growth.

Scenes of transformative seclusion or isolation align the path to ideal love, for instance, in *Endymion*. *Endymion*, written in 1817, numbering over 4,000 lines and divided into four books, is the first major poem Keats wrote. In book 1, we learn that Endymion of Caria (modern-day Turkey), the "brain-sick shepherd prince," has lately had several erotic dreams of the moon-goddess Cynthia.[20] His dreams overwhelm him with desire and confusion to the point that he excludes himself from the happy rites of Pan worship on Mount Latmos. Peona, his sister, takes pity on him, sets him in a boat, and sails away with him to a secluded "cove." Within the secluded cove is a "bowery island." Within the bowery island is an "arbour"[21]—that is, "a bower or shady retreat, of which the sides and roof are formed by trees and shrubs closely planted or intertwined, or of lattice-work covered with climbing shrubs and plants."[22] Within the arbor is a "couch, new made of flower leaves."[23] Thus this bowery location is a kind of nest within a nest within a nest, a series of concentric circles or enclosures, each one of which is more intimate, and more confining, than the other. Once in the arbor, Peona is setting Endymion down to rest, holding his hand as he sleeps, when, all of a sudden, the narrator exclaims:

> O magic sleep!
> . . . .
>   O unconfin'd
> Restraint! imprisoned liberty! great key
> To golden palaces, strange minstrelsy,
> Fountains grotesque, new trees, bespangled leaves,
> Echoing grottos, full of tumbling waves
> And moonlight; aye, to all the mazy world
> Of silvery enchantment!—who, upfurl'd
> Beneath thy drowsy wing a triple hour,
> But renovates and lives?—Thus in the bower,
> Endymion was calm'd to life again.[24]

This is a description of more than a bracing nap. Endymion is virtually brought back to life from a deathlike trance. He "renovates and lives"; he is "calm'd to life again." Sleep in the bower is "unconfin'd / Restraint! imprisoned liberty!" What I would ask is: why these words? Why the oxymorons—accentuated heavily by enjambment—and the prison images? Was Keats thinking of Hunt here? Of the Huntean prison narrative that he absorbed and that informed his sense of himself as a poet? The expression "imprisoned liberty" certainly recalls the central paradox—freedom in confinement—of "Written on the Day That Mr. Leigh Hunt Left Prison." Then there are the phenomena of the bower scene itself. Recall that at Surrey Gaol Hunt planted his own trees and flowers and made a trellised garden in the area outside the infirmary rooms. So he too had his own special "arbour" within otherwise unpleasant circumstances. He too had his beloved sister-in-law Elizabeth Kent to comfort him in prison when his wife was away. He too was rejuvenated physically, imaginatively, and professionally in his rosy sanctuary. In a word, Hunt lived in a state of what Keats calls "imprisoned liberty" for two years in South London.

The climactic episode of *Endymion* arguably occurs in lines 513–562 of book 4, the Cave of Quietude incident. Up to the point of this event, Endymion has only met Cynthia in dream visions. She has come at night, she has ravished his heart, and he has learned that she is more than a dream, and yet every time he wakes she is gone:

>   Straight he seiz'd her wrist;
> It melted from his grasp: her hand he kiss'd,
> And, horror! kiss'd his own—he was alone.
> Her steed a little higher soar'd, and then
> Dropt hawkwise to the earth.[25]

The Cave of Quietude episode is narrated immediately after these lines. Following the episode, Endymion leaves the cave and an aerial vision passes by him; accompanying the vision is a choric song sung in honor of his approaching marriage to Cynthia. Once the song ends, it is only a matter of time (around 400 more lines) before he and Cynthia are finally married. The Cave of Quietude is thus the last trial Endymion has to face before he and Cynthia can marry and the poem can close. But what exactly happens in this cave? Consider the following lines:

> There lies a den,
> Beyond the seeming confines of the space
> Made for the soul to wander in and trace
> Its own existence, of remotest glooms.
> Dark regions are around it, where the tombs
> Of buried griefs the spirit sees, but scarce
> One hour doth linger weeping, for the pierce
> Of new-born woe it feels more inly smart:
> And in these regions many a venom'd dart
> At random flies; they are the proper home
> Of every ill: the man is yet to come
> Who hath not journeyed in this native hell.
> But few have ever felt how calm and well
> Sleep may be had in that deep den of all.
> There anguish does not sting; nor pleasure pall:
> Woe-hurricanes beat ever at the gate,
> Yet all is still within and desolate.
> Beset with plainful gusts, within ye hear
> No sound so loud as when on curtain'd bier
> The death-watch tick is stifled. Enter none
> Who strive therefore: on the sudden it is won.
> Just when the sufferer begins to burn,
> Then it is free to him; and from an urn,
> Still fed by melting ice, he takes a draught—
> Young Semele such richness never quaft
> In her maternal longing. Happy gloom!
> Dark Paradise! where pale becomes the bloom
> Of health by due; where silence dreariest
> Is most articulate; where hopes infest;
> Where those eyes are the brightest far that keep
> Their lids shut longest in a dreamless sleep.
> O happy spirit-home! O wondrous soul!
> Pregnant with such a den to save the whole
> In thine own depth.[26]

Interpretations of these enigmatic lines vary. John Middleton Murray and Helen Vendler both read them as representative of a psychological state. Middleton Murray sees the cave as a state of "profound content" or "calm ecstasy" following despair. The "whole being of the sufferer is bathed and renewed" in such a state. Vendler says that the cave represents a mindset that processes "desolateness" as "a component within joy itself and indistinguishable" from joy. Susan Wolfson claims that Endymion loses all sensation in the cave in a way that is therapeutic. To Dorothy Van Ghent, the cave "'spiritualize[s]' Endymion for marriage" to Cynthia. Finally, Jennifer Wunder notes that the whole surreal experience actually resembles a Masonic initiation ritual in which an initiate is "isolated . . . in a darkened room" until, in desperation, he "turn[s] to his inner spiritual resources." Wunder also views the Cave of Quietude as a period of "stasis," whose "blessing is available" to Endymion without any "conscious striving" on his part.[27]

What, exactly, is the nature of this episode? Why is the Cave of Quietude in this poem, as it is and where it is? One fact to remember in answering this question is that *Endymion* is, by definition, a literary romance, and that literary romances, as Northrup Frye reminds us, usually involve a descent into a lower world in the form of a cruel prison or an oracular cave. Heroes of romance, accordingly, may experience "terror" in the one case or "uncritical awe" in the other.[28] Yet the form the lower world takes in a romance world is not static. The "dungeon or whatever" to which the hero often descends, "however dark and thick-walled" it may seem at first, is "bound to turn into a womb of rebirth sooner or later."[29] This essentially describes Endymion in the Cave of Quietude. In the cave, to repeat an earlier point, "the whole being of the sufferer is bathed and renewed," its "glooms," "tombs," "griefs," "weeping," and "woe" notwithstanding.

So we can think of the cave allegorically as a psychological state informed by the romance topos of the rejuvenating lower world. The state is one of overwhelming dejection that nonetheless offers the rare possibility of spiritual renewal. Once inside it there are basically two ways to exist. The first is to feel acute despair: to perceive the "glooms," the "dark regions," the "buried griefs" and the "new-born woe" all around as part of a living "hell," and to try to resist that feeling. It is to resent despair as an enemy to comfort and to struggle for mastery against it, which, paradoxically, only perpetuates despair. The other way to exist in the cave is to yield to despair completely, to let it take hold, tighten its grip, asphyxiate. The hero who can endure this process passes to a consequent state of emotionless, anesthetized peace, a deathlike calm that Keats compares to sleep (sleep, recall, was earlier described as "imprisoned liberty"). To the extent that the sufferer reaches this sleeplike state, he or she develops the power to see the good in evil things, the evil in good things, the joy in sorrow, the sorrow in joy. He or she no longer perceives the cave uniformly as "hell," but as a

> Happy gloom!
> Dark Paradise! where pale becomes the bloom
> Of health by due; where silence dreariest

> Is most articulate; where hopes infest;
> Where those eyes are the brightest far that keep
> Their lids shut longest in a dreamless sleep.

How exactly this process unfolds in the mind is a mystery. We are not told why or how a soul that suffers to the point of pleasant insensibility in the cave is able to perceive joy in sadness and sadness in joy, leading to extreme contentment. All we know is that Endymion has undergone a type of spiritual test in a dark, enclosed space suggestive of the prison-cave of romance. He has suffered to the point of being worthy to marry a goddess. In a way, Endymion is like Keats the poet martyring himself to his vocation, or Hunt the poet transforming his cruel prison into an oracular cave of "imaginative, erotic possibility"—a rosy sanctuary.

That the enclosed natural spaces in the poetry of Keats, such as bowers, arbors, and caves, frequently take on an intensely erotic element is generally acknowledged. Yet one such erotic, and human-made, space rarely discussed is the labyrinth. Labyrinths in Keats are often associated with unsated, uncharted, mysterious, and passionate love. Endymion, for instance, contemplates his dreams of Cynthia in a process described as "wooing . . . thoughts to steal / About the labyrinth in his soul of love" (i.e., the labyrinth of love in his soul). Near the end of the poem, Endymion is given the chance to marry an actual woman in the form of an Indian maid. Yet he confesses that "into a labyrinth now my soul would fly," and so refuses her.[30] At one point he meets Cupid, Love himself. Love recounts to Endymion how his mother Venus once "pin'd" for Adonis and strove "to bind / Him all in all unto her," at first to no avail. Adonis was initially more interested in hunting than in Venus. This preference confuses Love, since, he asks Endymion, "who would not be so prison'd" in love?[31] Endymion assuredly would be. If he had to choose between courting the immortal Cynthia, though only in the "imprison'd liberty" of sleep, or in the amorous labyrinth of mediation, and living with a mortal woman, the Indian maid, all though his waking life, he would choose Cynthia. In fact, he continues to resist his attachment to the Indian maid because, as he tells her, echoing Love, his past dreams of Cynthia still happily "prison" him.[32]

Perhaps the most extravagant love-as-labyrinth image in all of Keats comes from his poem *Lamia*. In part II of *Lamia*, the young Corinthian Lycius tells the semidivine serpent-woman Lamia, with whom, by her design, he is enamored, that he is "striving how to fill my heart / With deeper crimson, and a double smart," "How to entangle, trammel up and snare / Your soul in mine, and labyrinth you there / Like the hid scent in an unbudded rose."[33] Here Lycius first implies that his intense desire for Lamia ("deeper crimson") will almost inevitably be accompanied by intense pain ("double smart"). He then imagines his own soul as a labyrinth and the soul of Lamia as its desired inmate, with the result that he would "entangle," "trammel," "snare," and "labyrinth" her soul in his, "like the hid scent in an unbudded rose." Altogether, this is a provocative and complex simile. Essentially it portrays love as a kind of insatiable desire to captivate and imprison. It also represents what David Perkins has called "seeded potentiality," which he defines as "imagery" in Keats "which seems to contain the past and future of whatever object it describes" in an idealized way.[34] In this case, the fact that the rose is "unbudded" indicates that it is not yet in bloom, while at the same time implying that it will be in bloom at some future point. As for the "hid" "scent," a scent that is hidden in an unbudded rose is a scent that has yet to exist; or, if we say that it exists, we mean that it exists only as an eventuality, that it exists potentially. These few lines, therefore, do a considerable amount of figurative work. They portray one soul as an immaterial prison and another soul as its immaterial inmate; they image two beings as parts of one object, each inseparable from the another as a flower (Lycius) from its scent (Lamia); and they express a loving union that seems to transcend time.

There are numerous additional examples in the verse of Keats in which acts, expressions, or feelings of love are associated with imprisonment. The speaker of "Ode on Melancholy" advises an addressee to "emprison" the hands of his mistress whenever she gets irritated. A speaker in another poem longs to "[place]" his "aching arms," which he calls "tender gaolers," around the "waist" of his beloved.[35] In his letters to Fanny Brawne, moreover, Keats made such statements as: "Ask yourself my love whether you are not very cruel to have so entrammelled me, so destroyed my freedom"; "They say I must remain confined to this room for some time. The consciousness that you love me will make a pleasant prison of the house next to yours"; and "You uttered a half complaint once that I only lov'd your Beauty. Have I nothing else then to love in you but that? Do I not see a heart naturally furnish'd with wings imprison itself with me?"[36] In this last excerpt, Keats indicates that he loves Fanny for more reasons than her beauty. For what then? Her personality? Her sense of humor? Not exactly. What Keats appreciates about Fanny is his sense that her winged heart, which, being winged, can fly anywhere, has imprisoned itself voluntarily in him alone. In his eyes Fanny has willingly played the ensnared Lamia to his Lycius.

What impact does the information in this chapter have on the way we actually sit down and read Keats? For one thing it gives us a new way to understand certain crucial scenes in his poetry that involve ambiguous enclosures. Take the image of the bower. Anyone who has ever read any criticism on Keats has read something about his "bowery" poetry. Vendler has mentioned the "paradisal illusion of the bower, a conceit dear to Keats from *Endymion* on."[37] Here she means a bowery scene that creates the illusion of paradise but involves the reality of death. Stuart Curran claims that the "pastoral bower" in *Endymion* represents the "animating principle of poetry" only imperfectly.[38] Tracy Prior Seffers devotes a whole dissertation to the Keatsian bower and concludes that its meaning changes over time; in the early poetry, Seffers argues, the bower represents a "physical sanctuary from the vagaries and discomforts of the world, providing a blessed place where love and poesy may be pursued unendingly," while in the later verse it comes to represent "stasis," "an eternal hell of isolation," a "beautiful prison."[39] Ayumi Mizukoshi writes in 2001 that the "blissful bower is in constant danger of turning into a prison,"[40] and both he and Greg Kucich remind us that Keats acquired his fascination with bowers mainly from Spenser, à la Hunt.[41] All these criticisms tell us accurately what the bowers in Keats tend to represent. They suggest paradise as well as death, inspiration as well as sterility, sanctuaries as well as prisons. How and to what extent Keats internalized the image of his friend Hunt in prison as a figure for the aspiring poet helps to explain this persistent image and its range of implications.

Hunt read Spenser in prison and made a list there of all of the "beautiful sequestered scenes" he could find in *The Faerie Queene* and other poems by Spenser.[42] Then, of course, he turned the prison infirmary into his own personal Spenserian bower. Plenty of critics, as we saw in the previous chapter, have read this as an act of escapism. Yet the bowery scenes in poems like *The Faerie Queene* are not only pretty nooks where people go to escape and indulge themselves and deny their realities. They are primarily where the moral virtues of heroes are tested through trial. Hunt knew this; in prison he underscored the line, "Much dearer be the things which come through hard distresse" (iv.x.28), in his copy of *The Faerie Queene*, dating it February 4, 1813.[43] In the next month he moved into the prison infirmary, and the rest is history. I argued in the last chapter that Hunt used his imprisonment as an opportunity for personal and professional reform; that he saw his renovated rooms less as a world of make-believe and escape and more as a wandering wood, or Cave of Mammon, or Bower of Bliss, or Cave of Despair—that is, as any Spenserian locus where hardship tests integrity and enables self-transformation. It is just this sense of renovation in and through confinement and privation that structures so many of the enclosures, bowers or otherwise, that we see in Keats.

"I / REGAIN'D MY FREEDOM WITH A SIGH": *THE PRISONER OF CHILLON*

Keats was not the only second-generation Romantic poet to be fascinated with the incarcerated Hunt. Lord Byron visited Hunt twice at Surrey Gaol, once on May 20, 1813, in the company of the poet Thomas Moore, and again, three days later, alone. After these visits the two corresponded regularly—Byron occasionally sending Hunt books and game in prison, including a hare, a pheasant, and partridges—though they would not meet a third time until after Hunt was released in 1815. The first place Hunt lived after prison was on Edgeware Road, in London, near his brother. There he had "a little study overlooking the fields to Westbourne—a sequestered spot at that time embowered in trees. The study was draperied with white and green, having furniture to match; and as the noble poet [Byron] had seen me during my imprisonment in a bower of roses, he might here be said, with no great stretch of imagination, to have found me in a box of lilies."[44] Hunt and Byron grew close fairly quickly. Each began giving the other substantial advice on poetry early as 1814. Hunt attached an eight-page note to the second edition of his *Feast of the Poets* (1814), advising Byron in it not to be so misanthropic in his poetry. Byron, in turn, read drafts of Hunt's *Rimini* in 1815 (canto 3 was his favorite) and wrote detailed comments in the margins, eventually recommending *Rimini* for publication to his own publisher, John Murray. When *Rimini* finally appeared in print in January 1816, Hunt naturally, and infamously, dedicated the poem to Lord Byron.

Meeting Hunt when and how he did was fortuitous for Byron. As an artist, Byron was especially interested in the moral and psychological effects of long-term imprisonment. He wrote in his journal, dated December 1813, that

> Hunt is an extraordinary character, and not exactly of the present age. He reminds me more of the Pym and Hampden times—much talent, great independence of spirit, and an austere, yet not repulsive, aspect. If he goes on *qualis ab incepto*, I know few men who will deserve more praise or obtain it. I must go and see him again;—the rapid succession of adventure, since last summer, added to some serious uneasiness and business, have interrupted our acquaintance; but he is a man worth knowing; and though, for his own sake, I wish him out of prison, I like to study character in such situations. He has been unshaken, and will continue so.[45]

Roe speculates about this journal entry as follows:

> Byron mentioned . . . that a "rapid succession of adventure" had followed their first meetings in Surrey Gaol. We can't know, but Byron may have been intrigued by, and drawn to, Hunt's unconventional liaison with his sister-in-law. The summer of 1813 was when Byron went to live with his half-sister Augusta, and when their dangerous attraction to each other almost certainly evolved into a sexual relationship. Did Byron find the impetus for this from what he had seen of Hunt and Bess in prison? This has to be speculation, but it is clear that Byron was impressed by Hunt's example as a man unfettered by political bonds—and may also have seen him as a pioneer of sexual freedom.[46]

Byron was thus intrigued by Hunt in the summer and fall of 1813. He may even have viewed and envied Hunt as a sexual nonconformist. He in fact saw him as a modern example of the heroic spirit of seventeenth-century English republicanism.

Byron had good reason to envy the political zeal he saw in Hunt. He himself joined the Foxite wing of the Whig party in 1812. The Whigs saw themselves as spiritual successors of the seventeenth-century Parliamentarians who struggled ideologically and physically against the absolutism of Charles II. Yet in 1812, the Whigs were a relatively paralyzed party. They had initially opposed the war with France, but could not maintain that opposition in light of the increasing French military and ideological threat. So most of the Whig opposition was forced to take the conservative position on the war. Byron was a mainstream Whig theoretically dedicated to reform, but also a hereditary peer terrified of proletarian insurrection. His parliamentary career was short and relatively unproductive. Malcom Kelsall argues that "by the summer of 1813," when Byron first met Hunt, he was "already disenchanted with what he called the 'mummeries' of parliamentary government."[47] Kelsall concludes that

> Byron's political career . . . is record of failure ending in inarticulateness. There are couple of exciting "burns" of humanitarian rhetoric and indignant invective in the Luddite and Catholic debates, but they resemble a kind of hot-air ballooning. He was not fit for the long haul. In part this was the result of circumstance. The Whigs could offer nothing more than a rhetoric of opposition; and there were elements in the party who preferred it that way. But there is also an element of wilful nihilism in Byron's political career, as if the external impasse found a correspondent psychological response.[48]

Recall that, in December 1813, Byron called Hunt an "extraordinary character" of "the Pym and Hampden times—much talent, great independence of spirit, and . . . austere"—a man likely to "deserve" and "obtain" "more praise" than his contemporaries. Byron knew when he wrote this that he would never cut it as a politician himself. His own party, which theoretically inherited the spirit of the "Pym and Hampden times," was demoralized. He had personally lost faith in the efficacy of representative government. Meanwhile, his new friend Hunt was a radical journalist reaching a wide metropolitan audience and a visible martyr to his political convictions.

All this provides a curious personal context for *The Prisoner of Chillon* (1816). Its speaker, conventionally known as the Prisoner, is in one sense a radically inverted portrait of the gainfully incarcerated Leigh Hunt. Hunt was sentenced for a specific political libel. His radical politics were clear and widely known through the *Examiner*. In prison he improved in physical health, lived often with his family, educated himself, ran a widely successful periodical, received visits from philosophers and literati, and wrote enduring poetry and literary criticism. The case is nearly the exact opposite with the Prisoner. The poem implies that the Prisoner has been confined for his religious views, but these views are never revealed. His family dies around him. He does little in six years in prison except fall out of love with himself and the world. He also seems to exude a version of the "wilful nihilism" that Byron himself faced in 1816 as an abortive parliamentarian and a permanent exile from

England. More importantly, in his moral, spiritual, and physical unproductiveness, the Prisoner parodies the values of the contemporary penitentiary. *The Prisoner of Chillon* casts the Prisoner as an educated, imaginative, and articulate aristocrat who refuses to adapt himself to social realities beyond prison. He does no work. He makes no clear adjustment in moral orientation. He cares nothing about using solitude to reconcile himself to a higher power. In these ways his attitude flies in the face of the early nineteenth-century penitentiary and everything it was designed to effect.

Yet for all this, the Prisoner is not altogether unsympathetic or mentally static in his confinement. He is represented at times as pitiable and admirable, vacant and intellectually savvy, inert and imaginative, an inverted version of Hunt and a fraction of the actual Hunt, unreformable and reformable, a hopeless case and a man of ingenuity. The poem leaves these various aspects of his character in a state of unresolved tension. On the one hand, for the most part, the Prisoner appears mad or hopelessly distracted by his imagination. He leaves Chillon Castle unfit for social interaction and under the impression that life in prison is less corrupt than life in the real world. He seems more or less godless. Hence the poem has invited plenty of critics to pity or loathe the Prisoner for not having used his penal circumstances as wisely or as constructively as possible.[49] On the other hand, the Prisoner is occasionally portrayed as sympathetic, and for some readers even as admirable. Emily Bernhard Jackson, for one, calls *The Prisoner of Chillon* a "demonstration of cognitive independence, of the triumph of the individual mind over a world and a situation that seem simply to *be*: im-malleable givens." In her view, the Prisoner secures an intellectual victory in his prison; he effectively "restructure[s] his world to suit his needs, and the poem invites the reader to admire, not condemn, this action."[50] Bernhard Jackson is right in her assessment, only, I would argue, not in such a way as to invalidate the other, less charitable readings of the Prisoner. *The Prisoner of Chillon* purposely invites such disparate views of its speaker only to leave them, in the end, intact and unreconcilable.

The background of the composition of *The Prisoner of Chillon* is as follows. Byron and Shelly went on a sailing tour of Lake Geneva in Switzerland in the summer of 1816. On June 25 they visited the Château de Chillon, an island castle located off the coast of the lake in the Swiss canton of Vaud. Byron probably wrote *Chillon* between June 30 and July 2. His poetic narrative is written in the first person and tells the story of the six-year imprisonment of François Bonivard (b. 1493) in Chillon Castle from 1530 to 1536. The historical Bonivard was a Savoyard aristocrat and Catholic prior who became allied to the Protestant cause in Geneva. He resisted the attempts of Charles III, Catholic Duke of Savoy, to assert his lordship in Geneva and was consequently imprisoned. When Byron wrote *Chillon*, as he himself admits in a note to the poem, he knew very little of the historical Bonivard. His poetic version of Bonivard languishes in the castle with two of his brothers, all three of whom are initially chained to pillars. The Prisoner survives his brothers, is set free from his own pillar, endures in the castle dungeon alone, and is eventually freed. Jerome McGann reminds us that Byron

> was given more particulars of Bonivard's life after he had finished his tale, and he added the sonnet [the "Sonnet on Chillon"] in order to do further "justice to . . . [Bonivard's] courage and virtues." But even then his information was not historically unimpeachable. . . . No authority exists for the story of the death of Bonivard's brothers in prison with him, or for the alleged fact that his hair turned grey. That his father was martyred for his "faith" is likewise dubious.[51]

The "Sonnet on Chillon" that McGann refers to was written after the longer poem, and it presents the same historical person and situation in an entirely different light. Byron had the sonnet prefixed to *Chillon* when both appeared in his 1816 volume. Much of the criticism of *Chillon* centers around the fact that we should not let the triumphant tone of the sonnet—a poem written squarely in the *felix carcer* tradition—affect our interpretation of the far less affirmative narrative tale.

I have said that *Chillon* largely parodies the evangelical ideal of reformative solitude in prisons. This is especially apparent when it is compared to one of the most widely known evangelical prison poems of the eighteenth century, a verse narrative in blank verse of over 3,000 lines, called *Thoughts in Prison*. *Thoughts in Prison* was written by the Anglican priest William Dodd and published in 1777. Dodd was a Cambridge graduate, a doctor of divinity, a popular and elegant preacher in London, a supporter of a number of charities, and, at one point, a chaplain to King George III. He was also an ambitious literary man who tended to live hopelessly beyond his means and get himself into debt. In 1777, Dodd made the worst mistake of his life. He forged the signature of his former pupil, the Earl of Chesterfield, on a bond for £4,200. A broker accepted the bond on the strength of the signature and loaned Dodd the £4,200 in good faith. In time, the forgery was discovered and Dodd humbly confessed. He was arrested, convicted, and sentenced to death. The jury that convicted him, on February 24, 1777, recommended mercy, but to no avail. Dodd was to be executed. He was put in Newgate and started writing *Thoughts in Prison* the day after his trial, finishing the poem in two months. His case was widely publicized in London and in the provinces and became a sensational event. Much of the British public was vehemently sympathetic to Dodd and tried to prevent or alleviate the circumstances of his execution in several ways, some bordering on the absurd: a petition was signed by 23,000 people to spare Dodd from death, the gaoler of Newgate was bribed with £1,000 to smuggle Dodd out, a plan was formed to replace the real Dodd in prison with a wax model dressed as a priest, the hangman was bribed to make the rope press gently on the Dodd's throat as he died, and, finally, his friends tried to resuscitate his lifeless body, once removed from the gallows, with a hot bath and a surgeon.[52]

Thoughts in Prison was printed eleven times in the two decades after Dodd was executed, and it was subsequently reprinted seventeen times between 1801 and 1868.[53] Byron, therefore, was more than likely familiar with the poem. Robert Southey, for his part, was fascinated with it, and Samuel Taylor Coleridge, as Charles Rzepka has convincingly argued, almost certainly drew from it when he wrote "This Lime-Tree Bower My Prison."[54] It also seems relatively clear to me that Keats both knew of and read *Thoughts in Prison*. His famous lines from "Ode to a Nightingale," which describe the descent of the speaker from a beautiful trance to bleak reality—

> Forlorn! the very word is like a bell
> To toll me back from thee to my sole self!
> Adieu! the fancy cannot cheat so well
> As she is fam'd to do, deceiving elf.
> . . . .
> Was it a vision, or a waking dream?
> Fled is that music:—Do I wake or sleep?[55]

—seem clearly inspired, consciously or not, by the following lines from *Thoughts in Prison*:

> And can it be? or is it all a dream?
> . . . .
> A prisoner in—Impossible!—I sleep!
> 'Tis fancy's coinage!'tis a dream's delusion!
> Vain dream! vain fancy! Quickly I am rous'd
> To all the dire reality's distress[56]

Thoughts in Prison is a generically composite text. It is at once an autobiographical narrative of humility and repentance, a theodicy and a testament to the beneficent effects of reformative solitude in confinement. All three genres harmonize in the course of the poem. Its speaker implores God to make his penal solitude useful and retrospective. He sees Newgate as a haven from feeling humiliated at his trial. He warns magistrates and clerics not to make the same mistakes in judgment that he did. He anticipates that what he calls the "spirit of reformation" will one day permeate all English prisons.[57] He praises Jonas Hanway and his campaign for solitary confinement. He soaks in moral profit every minute in prison that he reflects and repents. He even has a vision, at one point, of Mercy, personified on a cloud, hinting to Dodd that his reflections in prison have earned him everlasting life.

Chillon takes this sort of religious rhetoric to task. Note the following passage from *Thoughts on Prison*. The "he" in the second line is God.

through this gloom
Of self-conviction, lowly he vouchsafes
To dart a ray of comfort, like the sun's,
All-cheering through a summer's evening shower!
Arch'd in his gorgeous sky, I view the bow
Of Grace fix'd emblem!'Tis that grace alone
Which gives my soul its firmness; builds my hope
Beyond the grave; and bids me spurn the earth![58]

Here the speaker uses an extended metaphor both to express his sense of security and to insist on his right to it. He compares the mental act of "self-conviction"—which means either self-incrimination or a strong belief proceeding from personal knowledge or experience—to a gloomy summer sky. God sends him solace in the darkness of his repentance as a lone sunray penetrates an overcast sky. Note the sense of happy certainty in this figure. The rainbow, which the speaker does not actually see but imagines in order to develop his metaphor, is a "fix'd emblem" of divine grace. It communicates its meaning strongly and clearly. The soul that envisions the rainbow is granted "firmness" and a hope that transcends death. Now compare the same figure and sentiment to a related scene in *Chillon*:

There are seven pillars of Gothic mould,
In Chillon's dungeons deep and old,
There are seven columns, massy and grey,
Dim with a dull imprison'd ray,
A sunbeam which hath lost its way,
And through the crevice and the cleft
Of the thick wall is fallen and left;
Creeping o'er the floor so damp,
Like a marsh's meteor lamp[59]

In the case of *Chillon*, the Prisoner sees an actual sunray instead of inventing a metaphorical one. The sunray, moreover, barely illuminates the three "Gothic" "pillars" to which three apparently decent men are chained. So it weakly shines, and what it does shine on is an image of horror. The ray also serves as a striking vehicle for the pathetic fallacy. It is said to have "lost its way" and "fallen" into a dungeon where it is now "imprison'd." It has been "left" there to "[creep] o'er the floor" like vermin. Clearly the Prisoner is projecting here. He perceives a natural phenomenon as an extension of his own psyche and situation. *He* has fallen; *he* has been left in imprisonment; *he* creeps around in his cell. The last line of the excerpt compares the dim sunray to a "marsh's meteor lamp." The word *meteor* in this case means "any of various luminous atmospheric phenomena, such as the . . . ignis fatuus, rainbow, etc."[60] The "marsh's meteor lamp" is the atmospheric phenomenon known as the ignis fatuus, a ghostly glow said to lure travelers into swamps or other bodies of water by assuming the appearance of a promising, flickering lantern.

Thus in both poems, *Thoughts in Prison* and *Chillon*, a "luminous atmospheric phenomen[on]" operates as a crucial sign to a man in confinement. The rainbow in *Thoughts in Prison* signifies salvation; the ignis fatuus in *Chillon* signifies deception. Each signification suits the emotional needs of its prisoner at the moment of its apprehension. Dodd naturally has the Christian afterlife to cling to as a repentant priest writing for a Protestant audience, and so he interprets the feeling he has after a bout of repentance as a sure sign of his salvation. Bonivard, apparently, has little other comfort than his own morbid imagination, so that the sun to him is either another prisoner, much like himself, or a sinister agent that wants to mislead him; to mislead him, that is, by tempting him to place his faith in the world beyond prison walls as a realm of freedom and possibility. In his own mind, he knows better.

The natural world is charged with the grandeur of God in *Thoughts in Prison*; in *Chillon* it appears prisonlike. The speaker of *Thoughts in Prison* reads the *liber Naturae* as a divinely authored text with spiritual implications. So on one bright April day, in Newgate Prison in London, he reacts to the phenomena of spring, which he has sensed, or imagined, as follows:

> Fresh from their graves,
> At his [the Sun's] resistless summons, start they ["the vegetable tribe"] forth,
> A verdant resurrection! In each plant,
> Each flower, each tree to blooming life restor'd,
> I trace the pledge, the earnest, and the type
> Of man's revival, of his future rise
> And victory o'er the grave[61]

Dodd has the old Puritan habit of reading the Book of Nature metaphorically. Plants and flowers are "resurrect[ed]" from "graves" and signify the eventual victory of humankind over death through the sacrifice on the Cross. Spring, as it were, is a holy text, and its message is a joyful one. In nature the speaker

> read[s] with joy
> Man's high prerogative; transported read[s]
> The certain, clear discovery of life
> And immortality[62]

It so happens that the Prisoner has an analogous experience in *Chillon*. He makes a footing in one of the dungeon walls so that he can climb to a lofty window and peer out of it. He says he is "curious" to see the natural world. Yet curiosity really has nothing to do with it; he already knows what he is going to see. He has already convinced himself that "the whole earth would henceforth be / A wider prison" to him, should he ever leave Chillon Castle. So when he looks out the window at the natural world, he describes a "small green isle" as "scarce broader than my dungeon floor." There are also mountains and waters and flowers and fish and eagles and everything apparently delightful and abundant—yet for all that the Prisoner wishes he had not "left . . . [his] recent chain" to observe them. He is "too much opprest" by what he sees and needs to sleep the sensation off.[63] For Bernhard Jackson, the Prisoner by this point has "refigure[d] liberty as incarceration. If the dungeon becomes his world, the world becomes his dungeon." He has "reshape[d] the outside world to mirror his cell."[64]

Here is an example of a moment in *Chillon* that the majority of its critics read as an invitation to pity or condemn the Prisoner as delusional, or willfully ignorant, at the expense of its suggestions of transcendence:

> What next befell me then and there
> I know not well—I never knew—
> First came the loss of light, and air,
> And then of darkness too:
> I had no thought, no feeling—none—
> Among the stones I stood a stone,
> And was, scarce conscious what I wist,
> As shrubless crags within the mist;
> For all was blank, and bleak, and grey;
> It was not night—it was not day,
> It was not even the dungeon-light,
> So hateful to my heavy sight,
> But vacancy absorbing space,
> And fixedness—without a place;
> There were no stars—no earth—no time—
> No check—no change—no good—no crime—
> But silence, and a stirless breath
> Which neither was of life nor death;
> A sea of stagnant idleness,
> Blind, boundless, mute, and motionless![65]

Critical reactions to this passage include that it represents a "mental breakdown"; that Bonivard is presented as "the living dead"; that he is "a mere brute, more dead than alive"; that he "loses control of spiritual, rational, and emotional behaviour"; that he is lead into "madness, solipsism, paralysis"; that he descends to a state of "inertia" without the "possibility" and "fertility" that characterizes "primal chaos"; and that he experiences a "sense of utter inertia and death-in-life."[66] These criticisms are plausible, but the Cave of Quietude experience in *Endymion* was described in similar terms, and that served Endymion perfectly well. Both experiences involve states of blankness, sensory deprivation, vacancy. Vincent Newey reads this particular moment in *Chillon* as "free-floating oneiric [dream-like] lifelessness . . . a potential transition, a way to the beyond or to a rebirth in the here and now," which is as viable a reading as any of the others.[67] Even an ultimately triumphant poem like *Thoughts in Prison* is not without such moments of disorientation. At one point Dodd says that his "whirling" and "confus'd" thought "scarce allows [him] to know / Or where, or who, or what a wretch" he is, or even whether he is "awake or acting."[68]

The ending of *Chillon*—the twenty-nine lines that make up its final, fourteenth section—is especially ambiguous and resists any definitive moral assessments of its speaker. At this point the Prisoner has discovered that he is about to be released. He is not happy about it, however, since he has now

> learn'd to love despair.
> And thus when they appear'd at last,
> And all my bonds aside were cast,
> These heavy walls to me had grown
> A hermitage—and all my own!
> And half I felt as they were come
> To tear me from a second home:
> With spiders I had friendship made,
> And watch'd them in their sullen trade,
> Had seen the mice by moonlight play,
> And why should I feel less than they?
> We were all inmates of one place,
> And I, the monarch of each race,
> Had power to kill—yet, strange to tell!
> In quiet we had learn'd to dwell;
> Nor slew I of my subjects one,
> What Sovereign hath so little done?
> My very chains and I grew friends,
> So much a long communion tends
> To make us what we are:—even I
> Regain'd my freedom with a sigh.[69]

It seems clear that the "sigh" in the last line is at least partially, if not mostly, a sigh of sadness. The Prisoner says he is leaving his "hermitage" and his "second home" when the men come to take him. He has made friends with spiders and mice and has grown to love his chains. Not every reader considers this an admirable way of thinking. Paul W. Elledge says that Bonivard sighs at the end because he has "fail[ed] . . . to recognize and capitalize upon the opportunities for spiritual growth offered by physical incarceration"; Jean Hall, that he is happy in his chains because he has "failed to revitalize his soul"; McGann, that the Prisoner sighs because he knows he is "spiritual[ly] circumscri[bed]" at the time of his release;

and Peter W. Graham, that the Prisoner probably has "Stockholm syndrome."[70] All of these statements imply that we should pity or condemn the protagonist because he did not use his time in prison to reform himself spiritually or otherwise. Yet is this really what the poem invites us to think—that if only the Prisoner had used his time in solitary confinement to reform himself morally or spiritually, or to learn industrious habits, he would have been happy or at least happier to return to the real world? I doubt it. The critics would have the Prisoner adopt the strategy for peace and salvation used by Dodd in Newgate, a strategy the poem is careful to reject.

We can read the unwillingness or inability of Bonivard to adopt the "Dodd" strategy historically. Byron wrote *Chillon* in 1816. In the period between 1815—the end of the Napoleonic Wars—and 1830—when the British philanthropist William Crawford visited America and converted to the separate system—the use of solitary confinement in Britain had yet to be perfected. Between 1815 and 1819, many of the penitentiaries built in the 1790s (including Gloucester) had to abandon the use of solitary confinement due to overcrowding.[71] Millbank was a failure as a reformative institution. The 1823 Gaols Act prohibited the use of solitary confinement except in cases of extreme misbehavior.[72] It was not until around 1830 that things began to change. Crawford brought his findings in America back to Britain. In 1832 Parliament ordered the construction of more separate cells in Millbank. By 1840, "separation" was differentiated from solitary confinement on the grounds that prisoners under the "separate system" were only isolated from other criminals, and only for an initial portion of their sentence. During that initial period of confinement, in fact, they had access to the morally uncontaminated company of prison governors, chaplains, and schoolmasters. They read the Bible and worked in their well-lit, well-ventilated, and well-heated cells. When they were not working, moreover, they could exercise outdoors, and when the period of separation was over they were allowed to interact with other prisoners.[73] It is for these reasons that the 1840s have been called the "great age of the separate system"—the decade of reformed prisons built or rebuilt at Pentonville, Preston, and Reading—and "the primary object of the separate system was reformation."[74]

The point is that in 1816, when Byron was writing *Chillon*, the separate system had not yet been systematically introduced into the British penal system, and the use of solitary confinement in the early penitentiaries was disappearing. At Millbank, solitary confinement was badly managed and ineffective. The experience of Bonivard in *Chillon* reflects this state of affairs. Bonivard finds a means of cognitive survival that works for him but that is decidedly not rehabilitative, in the sense that it prepares him to reintegrate into a human community as a decent Christian with a renewed conscience. Yet the fact remains that in prison he "rise[s] above his experience . . . by restructuring it mentally," until he is finally able to "comprehend horror as pleasure, misery as delight"—very much as Endymion was able to do in the Cave of Quietude.[75] The Cave of Quietude, in fact, is an instance of "Romantic confinement" par excellence. *Chillon* is largely a tale of frustration and exhaustion by a man who does not prepare himself to acclimate to society or to become normalized in any of the ways deemed acceptable by priests, doctors, and humanitarians. Only he does learn to live in prison as though it were a world, his world. We can pathologize this attitude anachronistically as, say, Stockholm syndrome, or we can admit that there is as much of a reason to admire the Prisoner as there is not to admire him; to admire a man who adapts cognitively to his surroundings, who successfully exercises what Coleridge called the Primary Imagination so as to turn multeity—"bonds," "heavy walls," "spiders," "mice," and "chains"—unto the unity of a "hermitage," or a peaceable monarchy.

5
JOHN CLARE
The Romantic Ascent

THE ENGLISH ROMANTIC POET JOHN CLARE (1793–1864) was certified insane on July 8, 1837. A week later he was admitted into a private asylum, owned by one Dr. Matthew Allen. The asylum was located in the village of High Beach, inside Epping Forest, eleven miles northeast of London. Clare stayed at High Beach almost four years to the day. Then, on July 20, 1841, he "escaped" and returned to his old cottage in Northborough, where his wife and five children were. Clare famously traveled four days straight on foot and nearly a hundred miles to get from High Beach to Northborough. Yet only days after his arrival, he wrote that he felt "homeless at home."[1] Clare remained in Northborough for five months, during which time he was possibly violent. His wife sought the aid of his patron, the Earl Fitzwilliam, who made certain necessary arrangements. Soon two individuals, a Peterborough doctor and a surgeon of Market Deeping, came to Northborough and recertified Clare on December 29, 1841. On the following day Clare was admitted to the Northampton General Lunatic Asylum, where he would spend the rest of his life until his death on May 20, 1864. Critics have long speculated as to whether Clare had a diagnosable mental illness that warranted his removal to the asylums, and, if so, what it was. The general, if tentative, conclusion is that he had bipolar disorder.

At best we can only make educated guesses as to the actual state of Clare's mental health. I am more interested in the way Clare acclimated to the asylums in a series of interrelated poems that, as I argue, may be read as a literary romance—a romance that conforms in many ways to the theory of romance advanced by Northrup Frye in his *Anatomy of Criticism* (1957) and *Secular Scripture* (1976)—and that would not have taken the shape it did had not Clare increasingly imagined himself as homeless, and occasionally as a captive, after 1836.[2]

Between 1837 and 1852, Clare wrote several letters to friends and family. In some of these letters he overstates the severity of the conditions at the asylums. High Beach and the Northampton General Lunatic Asylum were both based on a Quaker institution set up in York in 1796 called "the Retreat," "an Institution for Insane Persons of the Society of Friends." The Retreat was run by a new philosophy of care called "Moral Treatment." It had warm baths, fires in each room, windows without bars, a healthy diet, exercise, and opportunities to work in a garden or on a farm. At scattered points throughout his letters, nonetheless, Clare describes both High Beach and the Northampton General Lunatic Asylum variously as "the Land of sodom," as "purgatoriall hell," as the "French Bastile of English liberty," as "Captivity among the Babylonians," as "english bondage more severe then the slavery of Egypt and Affrica," and, in his most excessive description, as a "government Prison where harmless people are trapped and tortured till they die."[3] The men and women who visited Clare and wrote about their visits, however, usually described the asylums very differently, as comfortable places of relative freedom, encouragement, socialization, and humane treatment. Even Clare himself describes the asylums positively in many of his letters. Sometimes, in fact, the same letter will describe one or another asylum both positively and negatively. Consider the following excerpts:

> 1837 (to Patty). I am getting better . . . the place here is beautiful & I meet with great kindness the country is the finest I have seen.[4]

> 1841 (to Patty). I Have Been So Long In Good Health & Spirits As To Have Forgotten That I Ever Was Any Otherways. . . . I Would Sooner Be Packed In A Slave Ship For Affrica.[5]

> 1848 (to Charles Clare). Frederic and John [Clare's sons and Charles's brother] had better not come unless they wish to do so for its a *bad Place* & I have fears that they may get trapped as prisoners as I hear some have been & I may not see them nor even hear they have been here.[6]

William F. Knight, the steward at Northampton General Lunatic Asylum, 1845 to 1850, who was responsible for transcribing most of Clare's asylum verse, wrote on the back of the letter from which the excerpt immediately above comes:

> Your Father in this letter tells you that you may not see him if you come—I know not why he should say this, for he is allowed to see anyone he wishes—and he is at liberty to walk out for his pleasure—when he thinks proper—he has just left my room to walk in the garden—and if any of you think well to come and see him, I am sure he will be pleased to see you—I expect a friend of his from Shefford [Thomas Inskip] to come and see him in a day or two—he is quite well.[7]

> 1848 (to Patty). I am in the Land of sodom where all the peoples brains are turned the wrong way. . . . I write this in a green meadow by the side of the river agen. . . . The confusion & roar of Mill dams & locks is sounding very pleasant while I write it & its a very beautiful Evening the meadows are greener than usual after the shower and the Rivers are brimful.[8]

> 1848 (to Charles Clare). I am quite well and never was better. . . . Thank God for it.[9]
>
> 1850 (to Charles Clare). I shall just write to tell you that I am quite well & never was better.[10]
>
> 1852 (to Sophia Clare). I am very happy to inform, that I also am in very good health, and I think that I never have felt myself in better.[11]

What are we to make of these letters? The safest conclusion seems to be that we cannot take the words of any one letter as expressing an enduring truth. We cannot assume, that is, that any one passage in a given letter represents or even approximates the objective reality of the situation at either asylum. Nor can we assume that any one passage represents an attitude Clare held indefinitely or consistently toward one or the other institution. On one day, Clare sees the asylums as African slave ships and himself as a slave; on the next, he is stretching his body out on a grassy hill, writing at leisure on a beautiful day.

Critics are divided as to how to interpret the metaphors of imprisonment that Clare sometimes uses in his letters. J. W. Tibble and Anne Tibble argue that Clare associated High Beach with imprisonment mostly because a few of his admirers failed in their proposed scheme to raise £500 for his maintenance, and that, in fact, High Beach was a pastoral haven.[12] Edward Storey implies his own confusion as to why Clare even occasionally associated with imprisonment a living situation perfectly suited to the creative artist.[13] For Tim Chilcott and Anindita Chatterjee, Clare was simply ambivalent about the asylums. His written expressions on the subject altered as his moods altered.[14]

A few critics, such as Tim Fulford, isolate the negative language in the letters and take it as representative of a broader historical narrative, according to which the asylums were evil institutions run by heartless villains.[15] Ray Porter agrees with Fulford in this assessment, arguing that Clare was never mad till he got to a madhouse; accordingly, we can "forget about Clare as suffering from a disease syndrome" and "read his despair essentially as a product of . . . being permanently locked away."[16] The asylums, for Porter, were insidious. It was in their best interests to keep Clare unwell, he says, since Clare paid his fees on time and attracted curious visitors. Roger Sales makes the same basic argument as Fulford and Porter, but carries it to an almost incredible extreme. According to Sales, there was no conceivable offense that a late eighteenth- or early nineteenth-century asylum did not at one point commit and cover up. Sales claims, for instance, that most so-called mad doctors at one point or another perpetuated gender inequalities; invented "asylum-speak" to confuse patients; privileged inmates of a higher socioeconomic class; "exhibited" the unwell to prying visitors; invented a "sophisticated espionage system" with which to surveil patients, the underhanded methods of which the doctors then, in their case notes, projected onto the patients themselves; were habitually violent; fortified the asylums carefully, yet in such a way as to create the illusion that the buildings were not, in fact, fortified; infantilized their patients; and, along the lines of what Porter says, "produce[d] the very neuroses" they "claimed to be able to cure."[17] Sales even adds an anecdote about a chaplain at the Northampton General Lunatic Asylum who fed "reactionary nonsense" to helpless residents in a sermon in 1856.[18]

Sales, no doubt, has overstated the case. Was Clare upset or to some extent depressed at points between 1837 and 1844? Almost certainly. Was the asylum the sole or even the primary cause of it? Hardly. Well before 1837, the date at which Clare was first admitted, he was often sick and depressed. He wrote detailed descriptions in his letters of excruciating bodily pains. His marriage was problematic and he was ashamed of his extramarital sexual desires. He suffered from seizures. He was poor. He never lived up to his expectations as a writer and was hindered socially and professionally by his working-class status. He thought of adulthood as one long fall from the grace of an Eden-like childhood. He resented aging and the waning of his creative powers. The list goes on. It seems likely that the real "prison" for Clare always went beyond the asylums. In one of his well-known sonnets, for instance, he writes that "Earth's prison chilled my body with its dram / Of dullness, and my soaring thoughts destroyed." The reason for this claim is that earthly life simply cannot satisfy a "being created in the race / Of men disdaining bounds of place and time."[19] So if the asylums occasionally felt like prisons to Clare, they were as likely to be merely synecdoches for the great, all-encompassing prison of earth. As one critic puts it:

> Romantic poetry reveals its insistent awareness of states of imprisonment, as if from one point of view the great lesson of Romanticism was not the fall of the Bastille, but its survival in perpetuity. . . . The prisons that pervade Romantic fiction are both a mockery of life's promises and life's ultimate reality. No escape is possible because in the corridors of these worlds no escape is available.[20]

Although the asylums, objectively speaking, were not prisons, Clare could imagine them as prisons to suit his poetic needs. In his personal letters and in a variety of lyric poems, in fact, and especially in his long poem *Child Harold*, Clare created an epistolary and lyrical romance out of his life at the asylums, constructing the asylums as prisons or as havens as his art required it. This romance may be divided into three stages: in the first stage, Clare declares his need to dissociate himself from his domestic life as a husband and father; in the second, he has come as far as he can in this process of dissociation, treating the asylum at Epping Forest as a temporary Eden, solitary and clear of the troubling memories of his home; in the third and final stage, Clare imagines himself as having moved beyond his Edenic retreat at Epping Forest and into a dimension beyond space and time, where he deifies himself as a poet.

STAGE 1: TO CAST OFF A WORLDLY HOME

Stage 1 of the asylum romance begins at High Beach. On April 18, 1840, Clare wrote a letter to his wife, Martha "Patty" Clare.[21] At the time, he had been living at High Beach Asylum for around three years. His letter, though written in spring, is mostly, as it were, a wintry one. I quote a portion of it here:

> My dear Wife Patty:
> If you are my wife (and I am sure you used to be so—aye, ever since I was twenty-five years of age), write to me here, and acknowledge that you are so now. . . . You can claim me away from this place as your husband, the same as I was when I left you, with honest and good intention to return to my home and family in a day or two. Since then, months have elapsed, and I am still here, away from them, enduring all the miseries of solitude—which every married man must feel, through years of absence and confinement from his own home and family.[22]

This is one of several letters expressing frustration to come out of the asylum years. Clare starts off with a jab at Patty for never writing to or visiting him at High Beach; if you were really my wife, he says, you would have claimed me as your husband by this point. Then he adds pathos to his case by claiming to have endured "solitude" and "confinement" for three years. Not that he was actually alone or usually restricted in his movement at High Beach. Far from it. By the word *solitude* he means essentially separation from his wife and family, and by the word *confinement* he means the same thing. He never says he is confined *at* a place, or *in* a place, but *from* a place; that is, "from his own home" and the family that continues to live there without him. So where he *is* is less of a problem, in this letter, than where he is *not*.

The letter seems like a relatively natural one; it is no great shock to learn that a husband living in an asylum for three years would miss his home and family. Yet the letter is also misleading in an important sense. It shows us a version of Clare with a strong and confident sense of the idea of home, of what home meant, of where he belonged, of why he belonged there. In fact, Clare spent the years between 1837 and 1844 trying frantically, in poem after poem, to come to terms with the very idea of home and whether it could possibly apply to him in any consistent or meaningful way. Here in the letter, on the other hand, he seems instinctively to attach the phrase "and family" to the word "home," as if to him the two were conceptually inseparable. He does this twice. But we will see that this emotional-moral association of home with family was by no means a stable one at the time.

The 1840 letter in question was originally written on one leaf of a sheet of writing paper that is now lost; on the opposite leaf of the same sheet, Clare drafted a poem.[23] This poem, quoted in full at the end of this chapter, with line numbers (to which the reader is now directed), is uncoincidentally on the same subject as the letter—home and family. The following scheme represents the way I would classify the poem according to the critical categories established by Northrup Frye in his *Anatomy of Criticism* (I say more on these categories below):

title:	[I long to forget them]
date:	1840 or 1841
historical mode:	low mimetic
mythos:	romance (phase 3)
genre:	lyric

"I long to forget," moreover, is organized around a series of tensions, as follows:

family as love objects	fauna and flora as love objects
limitless freedom	freedom as security in enclosed spaces
Eden as domestic	Eden as solitude
Martha Clare	Mary Joyce
reality	ideality
mutability	changelessness
adulthood	childhood

"I long to forget" dramatizes the idea of home in a dynamic state of dissolution. The lists above correspond to two directions in which the speaker is being pulled, with each direction promising to lead him to a lasting sense of home and happiness, and with neither direction managing to do so.

In the first stanza of the poem, written in four-beat triple stress verse, the speaker announces his desire to forget "them." The word *them* is identified with the appositional phrase that immediately follows it, "the love of my life," which seems to represent earthly romantic love. What the speaker in line 3 calls "honey"—possibly a sweetness associated with romantic love—he describes as unhappily trapped or "cell'd" in "changeable strife" (a phrase used again in line 9). Thus the honey sweetness of love is prey to variation and decay, as all mortal things. The speaker also complains that the "love of . . . [his] life" forces him to share his personal sorrow when he would rather keep it to himself, that it threatens his sense of identity, and that it makes false promises. He needs, accordingly, a new source of love, and so he turns to the nonhuman natural world, or his memory of it, to provide that love. It so happens, however, that nonhuman nature, though appealing at first, is as yet of uncertain comfort. If the speaker can manage to forget the *human* love of his life, leaving "earth's shadows" behind in the process, the alternative source of love he seeks, nature, promises only more shadows, "shadows of hope." In a word, the speaker does not yet know where he belongs or who or what he should love. The source and object of his love are being worked out as we read, though it seems clear that he wants to break free from certain human entanglements.

The tensions in the poem between alternative sites of desire are essentially what give it its structure. The speaker says that he wants to return to a time when "flowers" were his "children" and "freedom" was his wife. In other words, he wants to go back to childhood. As a child, of course, he had neither children nor wife. His "love-ties" were fauna and flora. The robin sang him songs, the "coy thrush" was his "companion," and the "hazel-bush" kept him dry in wet weather. Linnets, bees, kites, hens, chickens, crows, snowdrops, larks, sheep, crocuses, foxgloves, and thorn hedges were, for all intents and purposes, his family. No "woman or falsehood" were "to be found." The "world and its troubles" were kept at bay. Things may have changed, the seasons may have moved on, animals may have taken their daily rounds—and yet everything felt to the speaker as though it stayed pleasantly the same. This is the childhood-as-Eden theme that practically defines the poetry of Clare as a whole.

Yet even the childhood-as-Eden theme, familiar as it is to students of Clare, rests uncomfortably within the rhetorical context of this particular poem. Other themes compete with it. In the third stanza, for instance, the speaker writes:

> To think of the joys of that once-happy spot
>   Where I lived with my children the whole summer long—
> The mother, the garden, the books, and the cot
>   The theme and affection of many a song.
> . . . .
>   down in the homestead

In these lines, the speaker reflects affectionately on his life as a married man with a home, wife, and children, a setting that is in many ways the opposite of that of his childhood. Earlier, recall, he was thinking of a time when flowers were his children and freedom was his wife and all of nature was his home. Now, he remembers a time when he lived with his actual children and their mother in a cottage. The two life scenarios are in a state of conflict.

Each way of reading the poem—that is, as a lament for the loss of childhood or a lament for the loss of wedded manhood—can be supported with relevant biographical facts. As to his childhood, Clare lived with his parents in a "thatched tenement on Helpston High street" between 1793 and 1820.[24] That thatched tenement had a vegetable garden, corresponding to the "garden" in line 19 of the poem, and there was a pond near the cottage, corresponding to the "pond" in line 24. Moving on to his adulthood, in 1820, at age twenty-six, Clare married Patty and the two moved into a different cottage. This nuptial cottage, importantly, happened to be immediately adjacent to the cottage of his own childhood, where his parents still lived. So beginning in 1820, his parents Parker and Ann Clare and his sister Sophy lived in the one thatched cottage, the cottage of his childhood, while Clare and Patty and their infant daughter Anna Maria lived in another cottage, right next door. It was here, in this second cottage, that the couple would eventually have five additional children: three sons (Frederick in 1824, John in 1826, and William Parker in 1828) and two daughters (Eliza Louisa in 1822 and Sophie in 1830). It stands to reason, therefore, that the set of images in "I long to forget" can represent either the situation of Clare as a child or the situation of Clare as a married man. In the poem, accordingly, the speaker is not sure which situation he longs for. Both situations blend together and compete for his affection. Importantly, the "home" and "family" of which Clare seemed so certain in his 1840 letter to Patty, written on the same sheet as "I long to forget," are revealed, in the poem, to be uncertain ideas, attached to different memories.

I noted earlier that the poem is written in what Frye calls the "low mimetic mode" of Western literature. There are two reasons for this categorization, the first of which is historical. Frye argues that the low mimetic mode "predominates in English literature from Defoe's time to the end of the nineteenth century."[25] It does so because it is associated with the rise of literary realism. In the ways we have outlined, "I long to forget" imitates (hence "mimetic") the realities of common, everyday (hence "low") reality. The second reason has to do with the amount of power the speaker has relative to his environment and to other individuals. He is not a god, as he would be if the poem were written in what Frye calls the "mythic mode"; nor is he god*like* ("romantic mode"); nor is he heroic or larger than life, as, say, Hamlet or King Lear ("high mimetic mode"); nor, finally, is he weak and inferior than most others ("ironic mode"). It is thus as a figure of what Frye labels the low mimetic mode that the speaker of "I long to forget" exists, as one of us, an everyman: powerless over most of the circumstances of his life, but with a will to affect or defy them if at all possible.

Even more important than the mode of the poem, however, is the fact that it corresponds to the *mythos*, or archetypical plot, of the literary romance; specifically, it corresponds to what Frye calls the "third phase" of romance, the quest. Frye defines the quest phase of a romance in psychological terms as "the search of the libido or desiring self for a fulfilment that will deliver it from the anxieties of reality but will still contain that reality."[26] "I long to forget" is one of many asylum poems to fall neatly into this pattern. Images of delivery from the "anxieties of reality" are everywhere in it. The speaker says that he wants to "hide" in a "dell" of hazel trees, to be "kept . . . unseen" in "silent solitude," to be "sheltered" by "thorn-hedges." Hid, kept, sheltered, "deliver[ed]"—from what? He tells us: from "woman," from "falsehood," from a love that "cheat[s]" and "damn[s]" his "happiness." These are the anxieties of reality from which the speaker would hide and be safe. Accordingly, he perceives the fauna and flora in the poem in terms of sought concealment and protection. The speaker sees a "bee" secreted in the "red-freckled bell" of a "tall foxglove," a "lark hid . . . in the black-bosom'd cloud," "sheep" shut up in their "whattled . . . pen." It is as though all the nonhuman living world is either seeking, maintaining, or providing a way of being protected or sheltered from something else. Yet for all this, the anxieties of reality are still "contain[ed]" in the poem. They are not entirely suppressed. Images of a wife, children, and marital cottage remain firmly in a rhetorical context that seems largely set on replacing them.

Around 1836, a year before his first certification, Clare wrote an untitled sonnet along the same lines as "I long to forget." This sonnet also seeks deliverance from the anxieties of reality while nonetheless containing that reality. It opens with the acidic line, "I hate the very noise of troublous man." The poem tells us that the domain of "troublous man" is the "world," and that the world is defined by men who are always "rushing into judgment." The speaker says that he "free from the world . . . would a prisoner be / & my own shadow all my company." He would go and live in the "lonliest shade" imaginable, in "the dearest place that quiet ever made," in order to flee the world.[27]

A single, striking image in the sonnet defines this dear and lonely place for Clare: "kingcups," which, the speaker says, "shut up green & open into gold."[28] The image is striking because it anticipates a crucial narrative arc in the asylum verse to come, the arc of darkness into light, confinement into flight, lowliness into exaltation. Thus it is worth remembering. Frye writes that the hero in a romance often lands himself in a prison or prison equivalent, which, "however dark and thick-walled," "seems bound to turn into a womb of rebirth sooner or later."[29] The asylum romance will move in just such a direction. Clare or his poetic self will find himself "shut up green," only, at the climax of his romance, to "open into gold."

The speaker of this sonnet is one who would shuffle off all worldliness, on the one hand, and yet stay connected to at least a tiny part of the world, on the other. Near the end of the sonnet Clare writes:

/ L x L xL x L x L
Take all the world away & leave me still

x L x Lx x̲x L x L
The mirth & music of a womans voice

Here we have a telling instance of double syntax. When we pause at the end of the enjambed line 12, we are left with the sense that "me" is the direct object of "leave." Leave me here, the poet seems to say, presumably alone (with "my own shadow all my company"); take the rest of the world away. We have to complete the grammatical unit by reading on to line 13 to realize that "me" is actually the *in*direct object of "leave," and that "mirth & music" are its two direct objects. Thus in the initial reading, the poet is left alone, either indefinitely—*still* in the sense of "up to and including the present time"—or in silence—*still* in the sense of "quiet, motionless, moveless." Then in line 13 we learn that not quite everything in the world is to be taken away. There will "still" be the "mirth & music of a womans voice" to cheer the speaker. Here is another instance, as in "I long to forget," where reality is partly removed from the rhetorical context of the poem and partly retained. All human judgment and harm have to be excised from the solitary prison-haven of the poet; the world and all its sharpness, even all its loves, have to be shut out. Only, the speaker requests, keep female voices; keep one sweet vestige from a world otherwise marked by criticism and trial.

The foregoing section examined two poems by Clare, one written not very long after the commencement of his life in the asylums (1840–1841) and one written immediately before he was first committed (1836). In both poems, a speaker attempts to separate himself from the conventional adult world of marriage, family, and domesticity; to shut himself out of a world of criticism and strife and live peacefully, with no companions save the fauna and flora dear to him in childhood. Yet we also saw that the adult world that he would flee manages to creep into the ideal world from his childhood that he would recreate. In this way the two poems mark the beginning period of a romance quest, a quest which, in psychological terms, we defined (via Frye) as "the search of the libido or desiring self for a fulfilment that will deliver it from the anxieties of reality but will still contain that reality." Several other poems, written in the heart of the asylum years and examined in the following sections, reveal the more advanced stages of this romance quest. They show us a Clare who ultimately does cast off everything earthly, not only his domestic life, the life he originally wanted to escape (an accomplishment represented in stage two), but also the Edenic life of his childhood, the life he imagined, at first, would serve as a desirable alternative to the domestic life (an accomplishment that characterizes stage 3). Ultimately, Clare as a poet will move beyond both worlds in an effort to transcend space and time altogether. In the process, too, he will attempt to make his relationship with Mary Joyce, a woman who was not his wife, but whom Clare nonetheless idealized as and called his wife, permanent, timeless, the sort of relationship only available in a literary romance. The asylum poems as a whole, that is, come to suggest that love, for Clare, is only real insofar as it is ideal, and it is the romance quest that can make it so.

STAGE 2: EDENIC REPRIEVE

In May 1841, Clare was visited at High Beach Asylum by a man he had never met. That man was Cyrus Redding, wine specialist, editor, literary enthusiast, and founder, in 1841, of the short-lived periodical the *English Journal*. Redding was so fascinated with his visit to Clare that he wrote an article about it almost immediately, publishing it in the *English Journal* in two parts on May 15 and 29, 1841. Redding writes the following about High Beech Asylum:

> The situation is lofty; and the patients inhabit several houses at some distance from each other. These houses stand in the midst of gardens, where the invalids may be seen walking about, or cultivating the flowers, just as they feel inclined. The utmost politeness was exhibited upon making our object known; and we were informed that CLARE was in an adjacent field, working with four or five of the other patients.
>
> We accordingly proceeded thither, and saw the "Peasant Poet," apart from his companions, busily engaged with a hoe, and smoking. On being called, he came down at once, and very readily entered into conversation. Our friend [a man accompanying Redding who had known Clare] was surprised to see how much the poet was changed in personal appearance, having gained flesh, and being no longer, as he was formerly, attenuated and pale of complexion. . . . He was communicative, and answered every question put to him in a manner perfectly unembarrassed. He spoke of the quality of the ground which he was amusing himself by hoeing, and the probability of its giving an increased crop the present year, a continued smile playing upon his lips.[30]

Clare apparently gave Redding twenty original poems in manuscript during the visit. Redding subsequently had all twenty poems transcribed and inserted into his May article in the *English Journal*. These poems, including "Sighing for Retirement," "The Forest Maid," "A Walk in the Forest," "The Water Lilies," "A Walk on High Beach, Loughton," "London *versus* Epping Forest," and "The Botanist's Walk," all fit the idyllic description above that Redding gives of High Beach.

The twenty poems featured in the *English Journal* in 1841 show Clare at a high point in his quest to "forget" the "love of . . . [his] life." The "silent solitude" that he coveted in "I long to forget" is now his in Epping Forest. Consider the poem "Sighing for Retirement." Almost everything in this poem is associated with the idea of an idyllic and inviolable quietness. At Epping, the speaker no longer has to "bear the noise" of the "busy crowd," since "Nature's voice is never loud" where he is; all the joys there are "quiet joys."[31] The speaker likes to read in the forest, naturally, but not the sort of books that have "idle words" in them; his book is the *liber Naturae*. In a word, as the speaker puts it, "quiet Epping pleases well."[32] Tranquility is the order of the day at High Beach and its environs.

In the *English Journal* poems, Clare and his poet-speakers live in what Redding calls "the midst of gardens," surrounded by the comfortable seasonal rhythms of Epping Forest. The forest is described as a remote and secure haven; it is high up, whereas the competitive social world is down below. In "A Walk in the Forest," for instance, the speaker celebrates the "break neck hills, that headlong go, / And leave me high, and half the world below."[33] In a related poem, "A Walk on High Beach, Loughton," the Epping Forest District is defined both in terms of its geographical and its moral altitude. The lofty forest is set in contradistinction to the geographical and moral lowness of London. From the high ground at Loughton the speaker sees "Giant London" as "nothing but a guess among the trees," a place "hardly known to quiet and repose." The ruling passion of London is frenetic "ambition." All of Epping Forest above it, on the contrary, "seem[s] to live with joy."[34] This same London-Epping contrast is established more palpably in another *English Journal* poem, "London *versus* Epping Forest." In this poem it is spring, and "brakes" "come up" from the earth "like young stag's horns." Like the city, the forest is "crowd[ed]," but with "ling and holly-bush" and "woods of beach" instead of people. In its tangled mass of verdurous growth there is "room enough to walk and search for flowers" along the winding forest paths.[35]

The gist of most of the *English Journal* poems, in the words of "London *versus* Epping Forest," is that

> Nature is lofty in her better mood,
> She leaves the world and greatness all behind;
> Thus London, like a shrub among the hills,
> Lies hid and lower than the bushes here.[36]

London has dwindled into a mere "shrub," lower than the shrubs at Epping. The twenty poems printed in the *English Journal* in 1841 are relatively unified in tone, mood, and image. This is crucial in light of the fact that the numerous songs and stanzas that make up the asylum poem *Child Harold*, which follows the *English Journal* poems chronologically and which I consider in the next section, are full of clearly disparate voices and attitudes ("moods" that "change at lightening speed," according to Jonathan Bate).[37] In the *English Journal* verse, on the contrary, there is little tension. The uncertainty and anxiety of "I long to forget" (1840–1841) and "I hate the very noise of troublous man" (1836) have been temporarily lifted. The wishes expressed in these two earlier poems are presented as fulfilled. Nightingales resound almost supernaturally among the forest of beech trees. The seasons move in and out with a comforting earthly rhythm. God directs the flight of birds and cares especially for all meaner and humbler things. Pride and ambition have no place; true merit alone is rewarded. The passion of courtship does not abate when courtship moves on to love. Women are mostly ideal creatures like forest maids, who carry pitchers as they walk, ankle-deep in flowers, through the woods. In Epping Forest, a poet can stop and look for hours at water lilies on a lake—which, in an allusion to the Arthurian cycle of romances, Clare calls "Ladies of the Lake"—and imagine the sort of garden they would make, lying on the water like "Pleasure in a quiet place."[38] Animals are not startled by the presence of humans. Poets join in choruses with larks. Kindness is linked indissolubly with greatness.

It turns out, however, that this sense of repose is only temporary. The idyllic peacefulness which Clare associates with Epping Forest yields, over time, to the awful, near-apocalyptic vistas of *Child Harold*.

The apocalyptic verse of *Child Harold* is, however, subtly anticipated in the third- and second-to-last stanzas of "Sighing for Retirement," lines 21–28. In these stanzas, Clare explains the difference between an ordinary perception of the natural world and a heightened one. To explain an ordinary perception of natural phenomena, he uses what Frye calls "demonic" imagery; to explain a heightened perception of natural phenomena, he uses what Frye calls "apocalyptic" imagery. In his *Anatomy of Criticism*, Frye claims that the so-called demonic imagery we sometimes find in a literary romance—imagery rooted in myth—corresponds to a world like hell, a "world that desire totally rejects."[39] Apocalyptic imagery, on the other hand, also rooted in myth, is the opposite; it corresponds to a world like heaven, a "reality" conceived precisely "in the forms of human desire."[40] Among the images Frye associates with the demonic, or hellish, world are "deserts, rocks, and waste land"; among the images he associates with the apocalyptic, or heavenly, world are the "garden" and the "grove."[41] Here are the stanzas of "Sighing for Retirement" in question, with emphases added:

> I love to seek the brakes and fern,
> And rabbits up and down;
> And then the pleasant autumn comes,
> And turns them all to brown.
>
> To common eyes they only seem
> A *desert waste* and *drear*;
> To taste and love they *always shine*,
> A *garden through the year*.[42]

Where an ordinary perception sees the autumn landscape at Epping as decaying, with its vital greens having turned, sadly, to a "desert waste and drear," this speaker, apparently a man of "taste and love," sees the same landscape as a "garden through the year" that "always shine[s]." Nor does he perceive the landscape in this way merely as a happy optimist. In fact, he is beginning to see the ordinary world in terms of an apocalyptic world, a world "eternally unchanging . . . where there is continuous life but no *process* of life," no "alternation of success and decline, effort and repose, life and death which is the rhythm of process." The phrases "always shine" and "garden through the year" suggest such a condition of changeless apocalyptic purity. If the rest of "Sighing for Retirement" tends to adapt myth to nature as it exists in the real world, to displace the paradisal garden "at the final goal of human vision" with an earthly version of that garden in the form of Epping Forest, these two stanzas offer a hint of apocalyptic vision.[43] They anticipate a later stage in the mythopoeic narrative that structures many of the asylum poems written between 1841 and 1844, a stage in which the cyclical world of nature, of earth, space, and time, and the undisplaced apocalyptic world beyond nature will come momentarily, dazzlingly, into alignment. It is to this third and final stage of the asylum romance that we may now turn.

STAGE 3: EDEN TO APOCALYPSE

In the spring of 1841 Clare began drafting one of his best, if not his best, long poems, *Child Harold*.[44] The earliest version of *Child Harold* exists in a small notebook known as Northampton MS 8.[45] When he started the poem, Clare had been living at High Beach for nearly four years, and he worked on the draft while there for a few months. Then, on July 20, 1841, he decided to leave High Beach and return to his former home in Northborough, where his wife and children were. In Northborough, rather than continue the draft he started in MS 8, which may or may not have approximated a complete poem, Clare began to copy out a revised version of the MS 8 draft. This project took him into the late summer and through the autumn of 1841. This revised version of the *Child Harold* draft—the more authoritative edition of the poem—exists in a different notebook, known as Northampton MS 6. MS 6 takes us as far as line 965 in the 1,300-line poem as we have it, with lines 966 to 1,300 remaining essentially the unrevised draft material in MS 8. After Clare was recertified in December 1841 and sent to Northampton General Lunatic Asylum, he apparently abandoned the revision process.

Child Harold marks the beginning of a creative renaissance for Clare, dating from 1841 to about 1850. Critics have noted that during this period Clare reached the height of his "lyric genius" and possessed a "new quality of vision"; that he began to write with "visionary power"; that his "astonishing creativity" at the time suggests a poetic renascence; that several poems from this decade are marked by an "imperturbable lucidity" and a lyricism having reached its "full development"; that contemporaries and friends of Clare were impressed at this time with a new kind of "poetic power" they never knew he had; and so on.[46] All of this is not to say that everything Clare wrote between 1841 and 1850 deserves the word *visionary*. Many more poems from the asylum period stay out of print than get in it, and are not visionary in the least. But it seems accurate to say that the above descriptions apply to more lyrics written between 1841 and 1850 than before 1841. The poems to which the above critics refer also have a special role to play in the narrative structure of the asylum verse so far discussed.

The visionary poems written between 1841 and 1844 make the most sense when read as part of a sustained lyrical narrative comprising several of the poems written in the asylums between 1837 and 1844. This lyrical narrative has a relatively traceable romance plot. The plot is by no means perfectly linear; it does not begin with one lyric written in, say, 1837, and then steadily advance in subsequent lyrics up to 1844 without any backtracking or variation in theme. Yet a general narrative progression is observable nonetheless. Poems of class *x* work to anticipate poems of class *y*, where the *y* poems represent a kind of emotional or attitudinal advancement from the poems of class *x*. If, for instance, a set of poems written up to early 1841 shows us an artist looking for a place analogous to Eden but not yet having found it (class *x*), the poems published in the *English Journal* in May 1841 (class *y*) show us a poet who has apparently found that Eden and is more or less happy in it. A remaining set of poems, beginning in 1841 and including lyrics from *Child Harold* and a few others written up to 1844—say, class *z*—constitutes the third and final major advancement in the narrative.

The class *z* poems are characterized primarily by a tension between what a speaker really desires and what he apparently desires. Poems in this class may approach, and do eventually reach, what Frye calls a purely mythic world. Yet the effort to reach that world is repeatedly stymied by the seductive pull of Eden, Eden in the form of recollection, reminiscence, a loving fixation on the past that ultimately gets the poet nowhere. Eden as the past tempts Clare even up to the brink of 1844; it remains for him a *locus amoenus*; but its hold on him yields increasingly to desires with a strongly mythic element.

Some class *z* poems tend boldly to approach a mythic world; others tend to retreat from a mythic world to an Edenic one. Recall that the mythic world, as it is represented in any verbal structure, can be characterized by either apocalyptic imagery or demonic imagery. In the first case, a literary text is symbolically organized around a mythic world analogous to heaven; in the second case, a literary text is symbolically organized around a mythic world analogous to hell. On a number of occasions in *Child Harold*, the poet may advance out of a clear type of Eden and head in either of the two mythic directions; he may do this at any given moment. Images, that is, may be primarily apocalyptic in one song or stanza of *Child Harold* and primarily demonic in the next. At times, too, both kinds of image may occur in the same poem. Overall, *Child Harold* represents what Frye calls the fourth phase of romance, the phase following the quest, which he defines as "maintaining . . . the integrity of the innocent world against the assault of experience."[47] This is essentially what the songs and stanzas in *Child Harold* attempt to do. They try to maintain a hold on the Edenic world of the past, even as they are drawn increasingly toward a lasting and more perfect bliss, in the mythic apocalyptic world, or toward a lasting and more perfect despair, in the mythic demonic world.

Thus an ongoing tension between the apocalyptic and demonic aspects of the mythic world is part of the fundamental structure of any romance plot. Frye explains this point in *Anatomy of Criticism*, arguing that, in romance, "these two structures"—that is, the verbal structures organized around apocalyptic imagery and the verbal structures organized around demonic imagery—"operate dialectically, pulling the reader toward the . . . mythical undisplaced core of the work."[48] So in *Child Harold* demonic images threaten to overtake the poet and bring him to a point of despair, whereas apocalyptic images encourage in him a dim and as-yet-unrealized hope for a bliss beyond time and space. And meanwhile, the temptation to stay still in the haven of the Edenic past, to make no advance in any direction toward a mythic world, maintains its lulling pull.

It is well known that *Child Harold* is as mixed in poetic forms as it is in emotional tones. It opens with a Spenserian stanza with a final pentameter line in lieu of the alexandrine. A song in two-beat triple meter follows. Then there is another Spenserian stanza like the first and after that another song. So, single stanza, song, single stanza, song. The second song, lines 51–91, introduces a happy prison theme that runs intermittently through the whole 1,300-line poem. One stanza of this song reads:

> Though cares still will gather like clouds in my sky
> Though hopes may grow hopeless & fetters recoil
> While the sun of existance sheds light in my eye
> I'll be free in a prison & cling to the soil
> I'll cling to the spot where my first love was cherished
> Where my heart nay my soul unto Mary I gave
> & when my last hope & existance is perished
> Her memory will shine like a sun on my grave.[49]

The "prison" in these lines is, essentially, the past. Clare was seven when he first met Mary Joyce in a provisional schoolroom in the parish church at Glinton, and he became immediately smitten with her. But his crush never amounted to anything more serious than a crush—at least not physically. Clare spent much of his adult imaginative life idealizing Mary as the embodiment of everything pure and good in romantic and spiritual love. Hence the dilemma of these lines. The poet implies that he is free as long as he can maintain his memory of and faith in what Mary represents to him. Yet he is unfree for the same reason; the mental solace that Mary brings him is only as strong as his imagination.

The real interest in these lines has to do less with Clare and more to do with the pattern they make as a verbal structure. All eight lines are organized around an extended metaphor that remains carefully subtle and implicit. To read the poem quickly is to miss it. The poet imagines himself as one day metamorphosed into a flower. A series of interconnected images in the stanza communicates this. The "cares" of the poet are compared to "clouds" (clouds being the hypothetical cares of a flower). The hopes of the poet "grow" hopeless. His "existance" is owing to sunlight shed in his "eye" (a word commonly used to refer to the center of a flower). To remember Mary is to "cling to the soil" where they first met, as, naturally, a flower clings to any good soil. And when the poet has died, when the "sun of existance" has finally "perished," "her memory will shine like a sun on . . . [his] grave." In this last line, 82, the sun is associated with memory, memory conceived as a beneficent human power beyond death. The poet will die; he will be put in his grave; yet the sun will remain to shine on it, just as his memory of Mary, or her memory of him, will remain to exert some positive influence over him when he is gone. The solar imagery in the final line also has important implications for the rest of *Child Harold.* Later in the poem, the sun will become associated with apocalyptic vision and the immortality of the soul. Here, however, it is not; it is very much the sun we know.

The poet-speakers of *Child Harold* tend to be peripatetic, as heroes in a traditional romance usually are. One says he "wander[s] many a weary mile." Another "wander[s] . . . hid in a palace green," "roaming" on "paths unseen" anywhere from "leaf hid forest" to "lonely shore."[50] Occasionally a speaker ends up in a landscape resembling what Frye calls the demonic or lower world of romance. In the lower world, the hero is customarily "trapped in labyrinths or prisons." He endures "prevailing moods . . . of terror or uncritical awe."[51] He encounters mostly images of "perverted or wasted work, ruins and catacombs, instruments of torture and monuments of folly." All around are "the vast, menacing, stupid powers of nature. . . . Symbols of heaven in such a world tend to become associated with the inaccessible sky, and the central idea that crystallizes from it is the idea of inscrutable fate or external necessity. The machinery of fate is administered by a set of remote invisible gods."[52] We know such places in *Child Harold* when we see them. One grim lyric is set in a land of "Madhouses Prisons wh—re shops"—that is, "monuments of folly." Note the lack of punctuation in this list. This is nothing unusual in Clare, but here it seems to blend an asylum, a prison, and a brothel into a single deadly institution. All three cooperate in the complicated process of demoralization. All take in humans made of "refined clay" and turn them into "stagnant" bodies.[53]

Another largely demonic lyric is "Written in a Thunder storm July 15th 1841," lines 217–236 of *Child Harold.* This poem takes place during a violent summer storm in which "the heavens are wrath" and "the thunders rattling peal / Rolls like a vast volcano in the sky." Here is a clear instance of what Frye has called the "inaccessible sky" in the demonic world. The heavens hold nothing meaningful or sublime for this speaker. They produce, at least in the first three stanzas of the lyric, no sense of security or comfort in the midst of terror; quite the opposite, in fact. The "soul" of the speaker who sees the storm is himself a "ruin vast," living amid "worlds" of "ruins." His "heart & soul [are] cased in obdurate steel."[54] These self-images are especially appropriate to a lyric set mostly in the lower or demonic world of romance, in which, according to Frye, human beings may be turned into "mechanical" or "subhuman creatures."[55] All of this is to say that, by line 217 in *Child Harold*, the wandering poet has hit a critical low point. His autonomy is threatened, the heavens are inscrutable, and the world is as much in ruins—what Frye calls "perverted or wasted work"—as his soul.

Yet there is a moment of exaltation even in this very lyric, when the speaker is suddenly extracted from the threatening demonic world. Recall that, in a romance narrative, "however dark and thick-walled" a lower-world prison seems, it is "bound to turn into a womb of rebirth sooner or later." The second part of "Thunder storm" enacts such a rebirth. After three stanzas of demonic images, of images of entrapment and dehumanization (lines 217–227), we move toward the apocalyptic in lines 228–236. At line 229, for instance, we read:

> I live in love sun of undying light
> & fathom my own heart for ways of good
> In its pure atmosphere day without night
> Smiles on the plains the forest & the flood[56]

Note the first of these four lines, "I live in love sun of undying light." Here is an explicit love metaphor where "love" is the tenor and "sun of undying light" is the vehicle, a vehicle to which the tenor is grammatically apposed. Love is compared to a sun that shines eternally. This comparison is significant insofar as "romance . . . eventually takes us into the great Eros theme in which a lover is driven by his love to ascend to a higher world."[57] The speaker of "Thunder storm," in fact, ascends to such a world. By "love" the poet means more or less an idealized version of Mary Joyce, or his love for such an idealized person. She is his muse and, in a sense, the guiding principle of all of *Child Harold*. The poet identifies his love for Mary with an ascent to a "pure atmosphere" where there is "day without night." Thus in these four lines the sun as it exists in nature, seeming to rise and set, as well as love that exists in nature, subject to fluctuation and decay, are both abandoned for the apocalyptic imagery of the timeless. Not love, but timeless love; not sunlight by day followed by night, but "undying" sunlight: these images mark the ascent of the poet toward an apocalyptic world.

"Thunder storm" marks an important transition in *Child Harold* in that its speaker is momentarily within sight of an apocalyptic vision of reality. Recall that in an earlier stanza from *Child Harold*, beginning "Though cares still will gather," sunlight was associated not with the timeless but primarily with the movement of clouds, with organic growth and decay, with vitality and death. This sort of natural, rhythmic sun imagery is customary in a romance that is heading toward, but has not yet reached, mythical proportions:

> the nearer the romance is to myth, the more attributes of divinity will cling to the hero. . . . The conflict . . . takes place in, or at any rate primarily concerns, our world, which is in the middle, and which is

> characterized by the cyclical movement of nature. . . . If it is a story within this general area, cyclical imagery is likely to be present, and solar imagery is normally prominent among cyclical images.[58]

So whereas the solar imagery in the stanza beginning "Though cares still will gather" is centered, accordingly, around the cyclical rhythm of day and night, in "Thunder storm" the sun becomes a sun of "undying light." The poet has moved decidedly closer toward the imagery of the timeless, of the world of myth.

In a purely mythic world, Frye notes, everything can be metaphorically identified with everything else. In other words, in a pure or undisplaced *myth* there may exist, say, a sun god. The sun equals god. The two are identical terms. In a *romance*, on the other hand, this metaphorical equivalence becomes displaced, made suitable to a new verbal context. Instead of the sun god of myth, that is, in a romance there may a hero "who is significantly associated with the sun," but not identical to it or absolutely divine: "what can be metaphorically identified in a myth can only be linked in romance by some form of simile: analogy, significant association, incidental accompanying imagery, and the like."[59] This is how we can understand what happens at the end of "Thunder storm." Its poet-hero at that point is linked to the sun by significant association in a way that approaches myth very closely but does not quite reach it. He imagines his love, Mary, or his affection for her, as undying sunlight in which he also happens to live, as "day without night" that "smiles on the plains the forest & the flood." The speaker of "Thunder storm" is thus close to mythic apotheosis in a way that is not evident in the more earth-oriented stanza beginning "Though cares still will gather."

As the terms and classifications from Frye are many and liable to confusion, a recapitulation of their application is often helpful. The second song from *Child Harold*, including the stanza beginning "Though cares still will gather," is essentially a longing for Eden as the past. It contains sun imagery that is cyclical and rhythmic and its speaker is essentially an ordinary person. Then in "Thunder storm" we find that the speaker has temporarily abandoned his interest in an Edenic world. As the demonic imagery in "Thunder storm" gives way to the apocalyptic, the speaker associates himself with the sun as "undying light"; he approaches divinity but is not yet presented as fully divine. The full divinity of the hero of *Child Harold* comes in a different poem, written three years later, an 1844 poem entitled "A Vision." In "A Vision," the speaker is virtually apotheosized as a sun god. I will return to "A Vision" shortly. I mention it now only because "Thunder storm" approaches and anticipates its apocalyptic intensity.

There are a few more temptations to revert to the Edenic world of the past, in the rest of the 1,300 lines of *Child Harold*, which must be overcome before we reach the apocalyptic climate of "A Vision." In one song, lines 444–476, Clare writes that

> Dying gales round a prison
> To fancy may sigh
> But day here hath risen
> Over prospects of joy
> Here Mary would toy
> When the sun it got low
> Even gales whisper joy
> & never sigh so.[60]

A paraphrase of these lines may look as follows:

> Weakening winds round a prison may sound like sighs to the imagination. But here, in this prison, it is daytime and the future looks joyful. Here Mary used to move about playfully each evening as the sun set. Winds communicate a joyful rather than a melancholy sensation.

The sun imagery in this poem, as in "Though cares will still gather," is presented in terms of natural cycles. The sun rises and sets in an unspecified place where Mary once was. The fact that she was once present, or, more likely, the act of imagining or recollecting her onetime presence, renders an otherwise prisonlike space no prison. Winds communicate pleasure rather than sadness. The speaker appears tempted to isolate his consciousness in the happy prison of an imagined past.

Even near the end of *Child Harold* we find the poet clinging to an imagined past as a happy prison. In one stand-alone stanza, lines 1,265–1,273, we read:

> Her looks was like the spring her very voice
> Was springs own music more then song to me
> Choice of my boyhood nay my souls first choice
> From her sweet thralldom I am never free
> Yet here my prison is a spring to me
> Past memories bloom like flowers where e'er I rove
> My very bondage though in snares is free
> I love to stretch me in this shadey Grove
> & muse upon the memories of love[61]

What makes this stanza powerful and complex is its threefold association. The speaker associates spring with (1) Mary herself, with (2) the act of recollecting Mary, and with (3) the environment in which she is recollected.

1. The first two lines identify Mary with spring in terms of her appearance and her voice. Perhaps the speaker means to say that her beauty seemed newly alive to

him, lush, energetic, a harmony of lights and shades. Her voice was full of springlike vitality and drive.

2. In line 1,268, the poet says that "from her sweet thralldom I am never free"; that is, we have the Petrarchan convention of love as a happy prison. Here, the "sweet thralldom" is the act of remembering Mary.
3. The act of remembering Mary, in turn, enables the poet to recreate a spring around him wherever he is. This is what he means by "past memories bloom like flowers where e'er I rove." He may be hopelessly chained to the past, enthralled, bound, ensnared, but his imprisonment in the past allows him to live in a perennial spring.

There is a kind of wild circularity to all of this. Mary is like the spring, or in a sense *is* the spring; the act of recollecting Mary creates a figurative spring around the poet; in this figurative spring around the poet he is reminded of Mary, who is the spring. Thus the object of recollection, the act of recollecting, and the environment in which recollection occurs are all intertwined in the single figure of Mary Joyce. Her pull is such that even at the end of *Child Harold* the poet cannot come quite to the end of his quest. He may continue to "rove," as he says in this stanza, but he is not roving very far, or if he is roving at all he is moving in circles. He is all too ready to lie down in a "shadey Grove" alone and muse upon what he can never have.

I noted earlier that love in the asylum poems is only real in proportion as it is ideal. A love that is vital and rich and enduring must be born in a literary romance. Mary is to Clare what Cynthia is to Endymion; that is, the more remote and inaccessible she is, the more, it seems, he can love and remain in love with her. We saw that in one stanza of *Child Harold* ("Though cares will still gather") a speaker compares himself to a flower and Mary to the sun that nourishes it. In another ("Her looks was like the spring") he compares Mary to the springtime that brings flowers into being. In each case Mary is pleasurably, imaginatively unreachable, and in each case the imagery of the happy prison is involved. In the former poem, the speaker says that he will "be free in a prison & cling to the soil" where he gave his soul to Mary. In the latter, he says that his "prison is a spring" to him and that his "bondage" and "snares" are free, provided that he can continue to locate Mary in an imagined past. We have seen this pattern before. It is a version of the concept articulated by Joseph Addison, Johann Georg Zimmermann, Jean-Jacques Rousseau, Samuel Taylor Coleridge, Leigh Hunt, and others, according to which confinement of the body is inversely proportionate to the freedom, the pleasures and the powers of imagination.

Here is the full text of the poem "A Vision." It is dated August 2, 1844, three years after Clare abandoned his work on *Child Harold*.

I lost the love, of heaven above;
I spurned the lust, of earth below;
I felt the sweets of fancied love,—
And hell itself my only foe.

I lost earths joys, but felt the glow,
Of heaven's flame abound in me:
'Till loveliness, and I did grow,
The bard of immortality.

I loved, but woman fell away;
I hid me, from her faded fame:
I snatched the sun's eternal ray,—
And wrote 'till earth was but a name.

In every language upon earth,
On every shore, o'er every sea;
I give my name immortal birth
And kep't my spirit with the free.[62]

"A Vision" invites us to read it as an apocalyptic sequel to "Thunder storm." Both texts feature noncyclical solar imagery closely associated with the idea of poetic immortality. In "Thunder storm," the poet "live[s] in love sun of undying light," an eternally "pure atmosphere" without darkness. In "A Vision," "heaven's flame abound[s]" in him until he is essentially immortalized as a poetic sun god. The "sun's eternal ray" is no longer a figure for Mary or his love of Mary, but his writing instrument. He harnesses it as the medium of poetic creation. We also see that in both poems an immortality associated with the sun is set in contradistinction to earthly vanities. At the end of "Thunder storm," the speaker announces his desire to be free of "earth & its delusions." In "A Vision," in which earth is "but a name," and earthly "delusions" such as "lust" and "fancied love" are unnecessary to poetic inspiration, he has apparently achieved that freedom. The love of his life that, since 1840, the poet "long[ed] to forget" has finally been forgotten. Martha Clare and Mary Joyce and all their idealized female surrogates have become so many earthly "name[s]," names whose "loveliness" "grow[s]" within the poet and immortalizes him.

I said earlier that *Child Harold* represents the fourth phase of romance: "maintaining . . . the integrity of the innocent world against the assault of experience"; "A Vision"—not part of *Child Harold*—seems to represent the fifth phase. Frye defines the fifth phase of romance as one in which the hero has arrived at a "reflective, idyllic view of experience from above," a view characterized by "contemplative withdrawal from or sequel to action."[63] Experience is no longer a mystery or a threat in this phase, as it was in phase 4, so much as a thing comprehended. The main action of the hero is over and he is able to contemplate the results of his quest. "A Vision," in fact, emphasizes what Frye describes as "the point at which the undisplaced apocalyptic world and the cyclical world of nature come into alignment, and which we propose to call the point of epiphany. . . . The movement from one world to the other may be symbolized by the golden fire that descends from the sun."[64]

As to the poetic form of "A Vision," a rhymical variation that stands out occurs in line 5:

x ∠ /   ∠ x ∠ x ∠
I lost earths joys, but felt the glow

This is the only rhythmical variation of its kind in the poem. Here the stressed monosyllable "earths" has to be metrically demoted in order to function as an offbeat and complete the four-beat rhythm of the line. This is perfectly an appropriate action, considering the moral-rhetorical context of the poem. Everything in "A Vision" associated with the earth—love, lust, joy, mortality, woman—is mentioned only as what is no longer important. The metrical demotion of "earth" in form corresponds to its moral-rhetorical demotion in content. Then there is the issue of all these uncharacteristic and grammatically supererogatory commas in some of the lines. Normally, Clare leaves all kinds of punctuation out of his poems; in "A Vision" he includes far more punctuation than is required. So we have these unusual caesuras:

I lost the love, of heaven above

I spurn'd the lust, of earth below

I felt the glow, / Of heaven's flame

'Till loveliness, and I did grow

I hid me, from her faded fame

The first three medial caesuras are marked by commas that separate nouns—"love," "lust," and "glow"—from the prepositions that logically bind them and specify of what kind they are. The fourth medial caesura features a comma between two one-word grammatical subjects. The fifth (initial) caesura separates a reflexive pronoun from a simple prepositional phrase indicating that from which the "I" has hid himself. It is hard to say what effects these commas have, but, if anything, they encourage slow reading. The otherwise swift movement of a poem written in four by four meter (four beats per line in stanzas of four lines each) is brought to a steady, and perhaps stately, pace, a pace appropriate for someone reflecting on a former experience or quest that is no longer threatening or central.

Another point of note is the logical discrepancy in the poem surrounding the idea of heaven. In line 1 the poet says that he "lost the love, of heaven above," though five lines later he says that "heaven's flame abound[s]" in him. How does this make sense? How can you lose the love of heaven and be full of heaven's flame? The answer may have to do with the ambiguity of the word *heaven*. Line 1 could mean that the poet lost his love of heaven where *of* is an objective genitive; that is, the poet lost his love *for* heaven in the sense of the Christian heaven; or it could mean that he lost the love that *heaven* once had for *him* (subjective genitive). If the first scenario is true, then the "heaven's flame" in line 6 probably has less to do with the Christian heaven and more to do with the sun. If the second scenario is true, the same conclusion may follow: the God of heaven has ceased to love the poet, and so he himself has become his own god, a poetic creator, immortal, free from sexual love, identified with the sun, universally known.

It should not surprise us that *Child Harold* reads as a literary romance. Its title comes from one of the most popular romances of the early nineteenth century, and to list all the parallels between *Child Harold* and the romance mode would require another chapter.[65] What I have attempted to show is that Clare creates a romantic narrative out of his confinement in which he begins as a poet unfettered by worldly distraction, leaves his home and family, faces temptations in the form of stasis and peaceful inactivity, descends into a kind of demonic underworld where the physical or magical perils of romance are displaced as existential crises, escapes that underworld, and then, finally, ascends to the heavens where he lays hold of his desired identity—no longer an earthly but an unearthly or divine poet. He has "move[d] upward toward [that] self-recognition" which Frye says is "central to romance."[66] He has quite literally romanticized his confinement.

Yet I want to be clear that I have no interest in romanticizing the experience of Clare in the asylums. Clare was certainly treated better in the asylums than some of the nastier language in his letters suggests. He was allowed to walk to neighboring towns, work in the garden, write, socialize, idle about the landscape, and so on. But he could be consigned to his room on occasion, as he once was when he got drunk in town, and he was especially pained by sexual abstinence and the inability to tell whether asylum employees were his real friends. So High Beach and the Northampton General Lunatic Asylum were no twin paradises. But that ambiguity is the whole point of the happy prison tradition in Western literature. Clare wrote some of the best poems of his life in the asylums. This does not mean that any poet who would excel should be locked up, but it does mean that a number of Romantic poets, whether actually confined like Hunt or Clare, or figuratively confined like John Keats or Coleridge, were fascinated with the idea of the loss of freedom and its implications with respect to the psyche and to art. When Clare says that he wants to be a "prisoner" "free from the world," with no friend but his "own shadow," he is manifesting this fascination. He is meditating on what it would mean for the creative imagination, were his body and soul to be taken to the limits of endurable isolation and enclosure.

[I long to forget them—the love of my life—]

I long to forget them—the love of my life—
To forget them, and keep this lorn being my own;
The honey is cell'd in such changeable strife,
I long to keep sorrow and trouble my own—
To live in myself, and to be what I am,
And to leave earth's delusions and shadows behind,
Where love may not cheat, nor its happiness damn:
The shadows of hope I with nature may find.

O, bear me away from this changeable strife,
To the childhood of nature, the linnet and bee!
Let her flowers be my children, her freedom my wife,
Where God, my Creator, is constant and free.
The flower on the white bush, the nest in the ground,
Which my own happy childhood once shouted to find;
Let me live in those scenes, with the wind blowing round,
And I shall be happy to bear it in mind,

To think o the joys of that once-happy spot
Where I lived with my children the whole summer long—
The mother, the garden, the books and the cot,
The theme and affection of many a song.
The snowdrop and crocus are first in the year,
And there the tall foxglove its red-freckled bell
To the summer and bee was delicious and dear;
And down in the homestead, the pond and the dell

Would hide me an hour in its hazel so green,
While the world and its troubles kept far, far away;
And there silent solitude kept me unseen,
With love-ties around me the whole of the day.
And there was the robin, perch'd on the ash tree,
Would sing me a tune, and then drop for a worm;
And there the coy thrush my companion would be,
While the hazel-bush sheltered my seat from a storm.

And there came the linnet, with wool in its bill,
To build its new nest in the hedge or the thorn;
And there I could see the black sails of the mill,
And the spire in the gray, sleeping light of the morn.
And there came the heavy-wing'd kite o'er the lea,
And the old hens they call'd for their chickens aloud;
And there the black crow came and perch'd on the tree,
And the lark hid itself in the black-bosom'd cloud.

O, bear me away from this tumult and strife
    Where woman or falsehood is not to be found—
To the scenes which I loved in the childhood of life,
    In the fields which the thorn-hedges sheltered around;
Where trees without order in spinney clumps stand,
    And in corners the aged or the whattled sheep pen;
O bear me to those dearest spots in the land,
    And the peace of my lowly thatch'd cottage again!

6

JANE AUSTEN AND PENITENTIAL SPACE

BETWEEN 1804 AND 1808, Edward Austen Knight, the third eldest brother of Jane Austen, helped conceive, design, and oversee a reformed gaol and house of correction in the city of Canterbury, in East Kent. The new Canterbury Gaol and House of Correction, as it was called, was a progressive penal institution: it employed a salaried gaoler, a chaplain, and a surgeon; was well cleaned, heated, and ventilated; disinfected old clothes and issued "plain Dresses" bought with county rates; provided for regular exercise; contained forty-one individual sleeping cells; posted its rules and regulations within plain view, in accordance with recent legislation; allowed no fees to be exacted by goalers from prisoners; abolished the garnish (the fee customarily paid by new inmates to old inmates); and emphasized the reform of character and manners through regular work and religious education.[1] The gaol component of the new building housed up to seventeen male felons, including men awaiting trial and those convicted; the house of correction component held up to twenty-four men and women sentenced to hard labor in a bridewell; more serious criminals—men and women tried and convicted at the assizes—were sent not to Canterbury but to the gaol at Maidstone in West Kent. In the Canterbury Gaol and House of Correction, moreover, there was no accommodation for debtors, on the one hand, and limited space for male fines (i.e., men held for nonpayment of a fine) and female felons, on the other. Austen accompanied Austen Knight on a periodical inspection of the new prison at least one time that we know about: Wednesday, November 2, 1813.[2] How may she have felt feel about what she saw?

Terry Eagleton has claimed that Austen was essentially a Tory Christian pessimist who thought of human beings, lawbreakers or not, as "irreparably flawed" and not much capable of serious reform.[3] From this perspective, if we choose to accept it, it follows that Austen probably regarded reformed prisons as incapable of doing anything for human nature that human nature could do for itself. Yet, as we will see, the matter is not as simple as this. Austen, of course, certainly felt that women could be improved, socially, morally, and intellectually, beyond the limits explicitly set for them by the male-authored educational treatises of the eighteenth century. Particularly since the work of Claudia Johnson, critics now routinely agree that Austen's novels consistently advance "modest but distinctly reformist positions about female manners" and education.[4]

Nor was Austen a pessimistic Christian who had little confidence in the spiritual reformation of individuals. Her own prayers, for instance, stress "stringent moral self-examination" for the purpose of self-improvement.[5] Her novels, moreover, are "allied with the goals of Anglican Evangelicalism, the heart of . . . calls for reform" in her day,[6] and they insist on the importance of "local government and individuals working together in their parish communities" to minister to the unfortunate.[7] It also helps to recall that the men who helped influence and pass the 1779 Penitentiary Act, men such as William Blackstone and William Eden, were likewise "advocates of . . . character reformation within the Church of England."[8] What is true of Blackstone and Eden is true of Austen. Her novels repeatedly chastise "selfish and irreligious" members of the gentry and middle classes who act "lawlessly, without attention to the need for humility, charity, truthfulness, or self-examination."[9] This last fact alone implies that Austen would not be opposed or indifferent to efforts on the part of local government to reinforce "humility, charity, truthfulness," and "self-examination" in reformed penal institutions. Prisons and houses of correction even had a special role to play in her own life. Her aunt spent seven months in an unreformed prison for shoplifting (more on this below), and her brother was a magistrate responsible for helping to design, erect, and oversee a reformed prison and house of correction in Kent.

The personal exposure Austen had to the administration of criminal justice at the local level, through the news and through her acquaintances, friends, family, and especially her brother Edward Austen Knight, helped to shape a pattern of relations in her novels between critical mental activity and physical space. In particular, *Sense and Sensibility*, *Persuasion*, and *Mansfield Park* use what I call penitential space to mark and authenticate accounts of intensive growth or insight. We may, for instance, observe as a character is illuminated with self-awareness, possibly in a few moments, or possibly over the course of a few days. We may witness the critical end result of her long process of adaptation to a set of painful inevitabilities. We may watch as a character learns the value of personal integrity in the face of ongoing social opposition. In such cases, the physical space a character inhabits as she undergoes a decisive mental experience often serves to texture, complement, or validate that experience. A peculiar sort of room—usually small, and with a prevailing mood of seclusion, reflection, adaptation, or resignation—becomes associatively linked to the psychological advances made in it, with the result that the room remains significant in its own right. We can read the massive ideological thrust behind the shift from executions and corporal punishment to unreformed prisons, and from unreformed prisons to penitentiaries, in modern Britain, as a broad cultural frame within which to evaluate the close relation in the novels between accounts of space and accounts of moral, emotional, or intellectual development.

THE AUSTENS AND THE CANTERBURY GAOL AND HOUSE OF CORRECTION

The Austen family was exposed to important developments in late eighteenth-century penal reform through a provincial newspaper called the *Hampshire Chronicle*.[10] The *Chronicle*, for instance, announced the passing of the Penitentiary Act in 1779.[11] In August 1784, it summarized recent debates in the House of Commons on what the attorney general called "a matter of considerable importance," the inability of the average British prison to maintain the health or even the lives of its increasing number of inmates. Readers of the *Chronicle* would know that William Eden was present in the Commons on July 29, 1784, and that he pled to the Commons on behalf of the penitentiary, a plea that preceded a report on the proverbially bad conditions at Newgate.[12] On February 14, 1785, the *Chronicle* published a public letter by the agriculturalist Sir Thomas Beevor on a new bridewell and penitentiary built in Wymondham, Norfolk. Sir Thomas and a handful of justices had helped erect these two institutions on Howardian lines, "under such regulations and discipline as promise, with God's blessing, to work a thorough reformation" of the "manners" of both petty and serious offenders.[13] The new penitentiary at Wymondham, in particular, had "separate cells for each prisoner, airy, neat, and healthy, in which they sleep, and when necessary, work the whole day alone. This solitude is found to affect the most unfeeling and hardened among them beyond either fetters or stripes, and is that part of their punishment from which reformation is chiefly expected."[14] Following this account, Sir Thomas proudly announces a new set of new rules and orders, which he and others drew up according to the recommendations made in the 1784 Gilbert Act,[15] which specified that prisoners should be divided into classes, put to work, and given religious education. The assize judge Lord Loughborough, who himself would write a pamphlet on prison reform in 1793, was so impressed with the two new institutions at Wymondham that he told Sir Thomas that "he would send thither every convict" tried at the Norfolk Circuit and "sentenced to confinement."[16]

Yet the most famous penitentiary in all England before 1816, The Gloucester Penitentiary House (opened in 1791 on the site of Gloucester Castle), would soon take the lead in prison reform and inspire other counties to imitate its success. On January 24, 1791, for instance, the *Hampshire Chronicle* reported on a recent meeting of the county justices held at the Epiphany Quarter Sessions. The justices therein resolved to petition Parliament for an act granting them "certain powers and authorities" "for the better government of the jails" in Hampshire, adding that the privileges they were to request were based on certain powers previously granted to county justices in the 1785 Gloucester Gaol Act,[17] "*An Act for building a new Gaol, a Penitentiary House, and certain [four] new Houses of Correction, for the County of Gloucester, and for regulating the same.*"[18] Thus the Hampshire justices based their request for additional authority in the administration of local prisons on "powers and authorities" granted six years earlier to magistrates in Gloucester. The article goes on to say that, since the present petition is "of a public nature, and highly interesting to this county," it should be "inserted in the provincial papers to entreat the favour of those gentlemen, who make the public concerns of this county an object of their attention, to communicate their sentiments on this very important subject."[19] Edward Austen Knight was one such gentleman operating in the county of Kent. He was commissioned as a justice in 1791, and it is to his work in Kent that I now want to turn.

The fact is that whole families were often involved in the administration of local government in Kent in the late eighteenth and early nineteenth centuries. According to one scholar, in a small book on Kentish magistrates, the late eighteenth century witnessed "the formation of small dynasties, as brothers, uncles, sons, nephews and sons-in-law are all co-opted in what sometimes appears as a frenzied effort to ensure an imposing family presence" in the execution of local justice.[20] The Austen name was firmly rooted in its time in local affairs in Kent. Here is a list of Austens, their relation to Jane, and their government post in Kent around the late eighteenth and early nineteenth centuries:

John Austen VI (1726–1807). First cousin once removed. Magistrate, West Kent.[21]
Francis Motley Austen (1747–1815). First cousin once removed. Clerk of the peace for the county of Kent (1773–1808), governor of Sevenoaks School, trustee of multiple turnpike trusts.[22]
Captain/Major John Austen (1761–1831). First cousin once removed. Magistrate, West Kent.[23]
Edward Austen Knight (1768–1852). Third eldest brother. Magistrate, East Kent.
Francis Lucius Austen (1773–1815). Second cousin. Magistrate, West Kent. Matriculated at Oxford in 1792 at nineteen, was declared insane in 1813 and died in 1815.[24]
Col. Thomas Austen (1775–1859). Second cousin. Magistrate, West Kent.[25]
Rev. John Austen VII (1777–1851). Second cousin. Magistrate, West Kent.[26]

Thus at least seven Austens were active government officials in Kent around the time the new gaol and house of correction, above mentioned, was conceived and built (1804–1808). All seven would most likely have known about the project. Two of the seven Austens had a hand in the process of realizing it. As clerk of the peace for the county of Kent, Francis Motley Austen drafted a bond on July 15, 1806 (on order from the assize judges) between the builder Charles Hedge and nine East Kent magistrates responsible for every decision about the new prison.[27] Edward Austen Knight was one of these nine magistrates and his signature is on the bond. The signatures of four other men with connections to Jane Austen are also on the bond:

Sir Edward Knatchbull, 8th baronet (1759–1819). Magistrate, East Kent. He chaired the committee of the nine East Kent justices responsible for the prison. His son, Sir Edward Knatchbull, 9th baronet (1781–1849), married Jane Austen's niece, Fanny Knight, and the two had nine children.

Nicholas Roundell Toke (1764–1837). Magistrate, East Kent. Of Godinton House, near Ashford. Jane dined in his company in Nackington at some point between September 5 and 15, 1796.[28]

William Deedes II (1761–1834). Magistrate, East Kent, deputy lieutenant, chairman of the Quarter Sessions for East Kent, MP for Hythe (1807–1812).[29] He and Edward Austen Knight had a double wedding on December 27, 1791, with the Bridges sisters. William married Sophia Bridges and Austen Knight married Elizabeth Bridges. On September 7, 1805, Jane and Cassandra went to stay with William and Sophia Deedes at their country house in Sandling.[30] This couple had the almost unbelievable amount of *nineteen* children, and Jane knew eighteen of them. She wrote to Cassandra on October 26, 1813, that she liked William Deedes II "a great deal."[31] In a little over a week after writing this comment, she would see the new prison at Canterbury. Might William Deedes II have recommended such a visit for Jane?

James Wildman (1747–1816). Magistrate, East Kent. Of Chilham Castle, near Godmersham. Here is an interesting detail. Recall that Jane toured the reformed gaol on November 2, 1813. Two days later, on November 4, 1813, she attended a musical party with both Edward Austen Knight and James Wildman at Chilham Castle.[32] Surely the prison must have come up in discussion. Jane Austen herself, the author of *Sense and Sensibility*, the author of *Pride and Prejudice*, had just toured it! About this lively party Jane says to Cassandra in a letter: "as I must leave off being young [she would be thirty-eight next month], I find many Douceurs [i.e., pleasures] in being a sort of Chaperon[e,] for I am put on the Sofa near the Fire & can drink as much wine as I like." Perhaps she drank enough wine to whisper her thoughts on the prison to James Wildman, as he "sat close by & listened, or pretended to listen" to his daughter play the piano.[33]

A few more personages worth noting are as follows. The attorney and justice Thomas Brett (1758–1822), of Spring Grove, met with several East Kent magistrates on November 2, 1804. By law they had to advertise in Kentish newspapers that they would consider what to do about the dilapidated state of the old gaol and house of correction in Canterbury. This was the substance of their meeting.[34] Jane happened to dine with Edward Austen Knight and Thomas Brett on August 22, 1805, a week after the builder for the new gaol was decided on.[35] Yet another magistrate involved with the gaol was the Canterbury MP Edward Taylor (1774–1843).[36] Apparently, Jane not only knew Taylor but had an adolescent crush on him. She once rode by his home at Bifrons on a moonlit autumn night in her early twenties, and as the carriage passed by she felt a frisson of mixed emotions. She told Cassandra: "We went by Bifrons, & I contemplated with a melancholy pleasure, the abode of Him [Taylor], on whom I once fondly doated."[37] And finally there is Edward Austen Knight's father-in-law, Sir Brook Bridges (1733–1791). Both Austen Knight and Sir Brook were present at a meeting at Canterbury Castle on January 14, 1806, to help decide that a "grinding machine" (i.e., a machine for grinding wheat) was to be built "to employ Prisoners in the present House of Correction."[38]

I realize that I have gone into a fair amount of detail about old manuscripts relating to the gaol/bridewell at Canterbury; but these details are important.[39] If one considers only the letter Jane wrote to Cassandra on November 3, 1813, one will probably assume that she visited the gaol only once and knew little about it beforehand. But it is quite possible, if not probable, that she visited the gaol more than once. The place received its first inmate in late 1808.[40] That gives us around five years in which Austen could have had an earlier tour than the one we know of. And it is almost certainly the case that she *knew* a good deal about the gaol prior to 1813. Several times between 1804 and 1813 she met or dined with a number of men, including, of course, her brother, who were directly involved in the design, construction, and management of the new prison.

We can recreate vividly what Austen probably saw and heard when she visited the new Canterbury Gaol and House of Correction. We have the actual blueprints before us[41] and detailed descriptions of the place by contemporaries.[42] First of all, the day of the visit was overcast. It had started out pleasant enough, but by the time Austen and her brother Edward returned home, it was raining. The new prison was located a little way from the town of Canterbury. The first thing Austen saw as she approached it was its huge octagonal boundary wall of imposing stone, fixed under the louring clouds. She would have known that the prison was built on the site of the old monastery of St. Augustine of Canterbury. For centuries the monastery had been dissolved and dismantled. Now its monastic cells were replaced with monastic-like prison cells, as the design in Figure 6.1 shows.[43]

There was a single entrance into the prison the whole way round the stone octagon. A massive, twelve-inch iron lock was heard from the inside, unbolting. When you entered the place you walked immediately into a hall. To your left was a washhouse with a "boiler, warm and cold baths, and an oven to purify foul or infected clothes."[44] Up and to the right was a small, brick-paved room where the turnkey lodged. If you glanced over his door you knew immediately that you were in a reformed prison. You knew in part—aside from the scents and sounds of clothes being washed and disinfected—because a set of "fetters and Chains of cast Iron [were] fix'd" above the head jamb.[45] This was a relatively common practice at the time. In the course of the eighteenth century, architects began to design prisons with "speaking architecture," *architecture parlante*, as it was called, suppos-

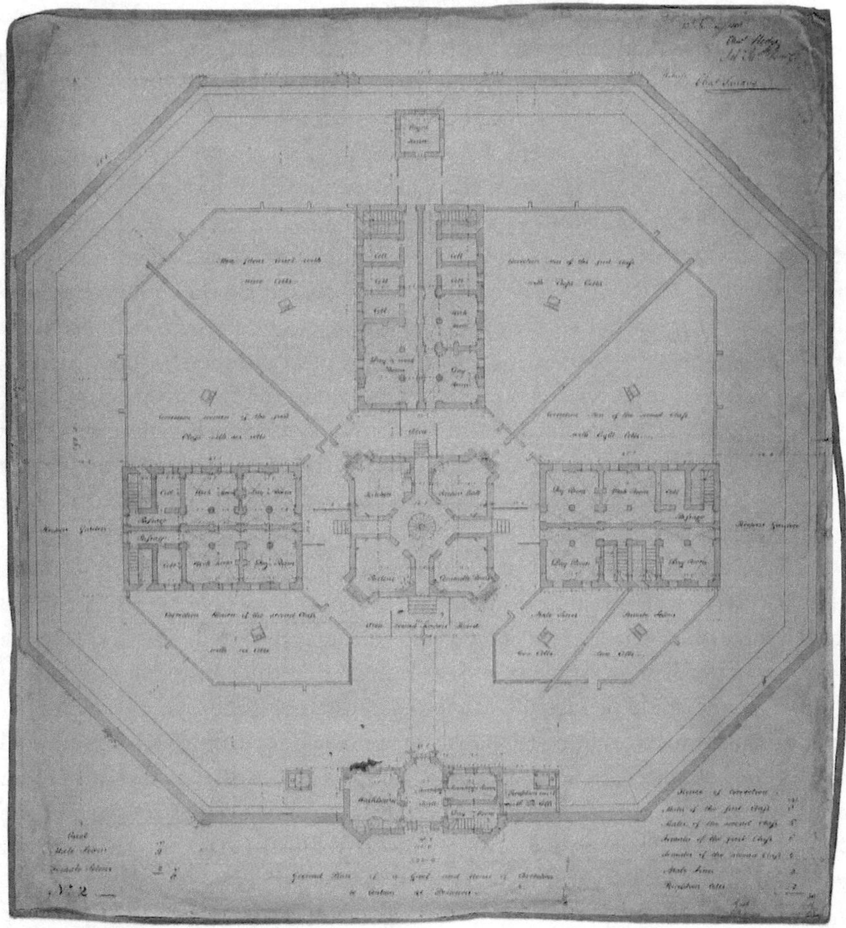

Figure 6.1 Ground plan of a gaol and house of correction. Reproduced with the permission of the Kent Archive and Local History Service.

edly to strike terror into onlookers. The hanging fetters were a sort of sensational Gothic image meant to overawe whoever saw them and, in a way that almost contradicts the overawing, to remind visitors that such fetters in reformed prisons were no longer needed on actual legs. Fetters were not used to restrain prisoners in the reformed Canterbury Gaol and House of Correction. The giant stone wall around the prison did much of the job of securing inmates. To your immediate right on entering the prison was a sitting room where the turnkey spent much of his day. Austen probably walked into the sitting room, but she likely steered clear of the room adjoining it. *That* was the reception room, where new inmates were inspected, cleaned, and examined for infectious disorders.

Thus Austen would have glided through the hall for around thirty feet and then found herself outside again. She was on a stone avenue, lined with iron rails, each rail liked with chains. The avenue was forty feet long and led to the prison interior, "a handsome stone-fronted building, with the Gaoler's house in the centre," also "of an octagon construction."[46] On either side of the avenue a flourishing vegetable garden was planted, the happy yet practical pastime of the gaoler Samuel Aris. From the avenue you could only see a small part of the garden. The rest of it spanned the length of the perimeter of the prison, between its inner and outer octagonal walls. So Edward and Jane advanced along the stone avenue and up the steps that led to the interior of the prison. Right after the entrance there was another open-air space, where visitors could meet prisoners without entering a single room or courtyard. Twelve feet ahead stood the two-story house of the gaoler Samuel Aris. Extending from the open-air space circling his house were three wings: to the north was a wing for male felons; to the east and west were wings for men and women sentenced to hard labor in a house of correction. Between all three wings were roofless courtyards.

Surely Jane visited none of the wings or the courtyards adjacent to them. Nor was there any need. The two-floor hub of the prison where the gaoler Samuel Aris lived satisfied whatever modest curiosity she may have had to see the inmates: all the courtyards were visible from his house, raised three feet above the rest of the prison, and could be carefully inspected. Austen probably saw one or two felons or misdemeanants taking the air (this prison held no debtors). On the ground floor of the house were a parlor, a kitchen, a hall for Aris, and the committee room where Edward and the other justices periodically met, together with the prison chaplain William Chasey and prison surgeon William Chandler. Such regular inspections of prisons by justices were required by law.

PENITENTIAL SPACES IN *SENSE AND SENSIBILITY, PERSUASION,* AND *MANSFIELD PARK*

Perhaps the earliest penitential space in the Austen canon is Barton Cottage, the second home of the Dashwoods in *Sense and Sensibility*. Mrs. Dashwood and her daughters, the elder Elinor and the younger Marianne, are forced to relocate to Barton Cottage from their comparatively massive estate at Norland. The move happens at the onset of the novel, and Austen stresses the change from a large habitation to a small one. When they arrive at the cottage, the Dashwoods find their new home in "good repair," even if it is "poor and small indeed."[47] Everyone makes the best of the small size, and we learn that "to add and improve was a delight" to Mrs. Dashwood (*SS*, 34). Soon, in a few chapters, everyone is in love with the place: "the ordinary pursuits which had given to Norland half its charms, were engaged in again with far greater enjoyment than Norland had been able to afford" (*SS*, 48).

Why, one wonders? Why are the Dashwoods instantly happy in this cottage after growing up in what was probably a sprawling maze of a great house? Is it because of their adaptability? their selective memory? an optimism required by necessity? Julie Park argues that the Dashwoods adjust as easily and quickly to the cottage as they do, not in spite of its smallness, but because of it. For Park, the tininess of Barton Cottage allows for a kind of mental expansion:

> Even as enclosure . . . appears to constrict the main characters, it also provides the medium through which the imagination, a central aspect of interiority, achieves the depth and movement of its expression. . . . The tolerable snugness of the cottage as the family's new home provides the architectural setting for the novel's predominating mode of enclosure as both a psychological and physical habitation that constricts the self even as it expands it.[48]

According to Park, the "tolerable snugness" of Barton Cottage is the "medium" in and through which the imaginative expression of the Dashwoods is deepened and vitalized. The mental powers of the inhabitants of the cottage are expanded specifically because these powers are activated in a narrow space. It may be no coincidence, moreover, that a very similar concept was justifying the construction of reformed prisons in the 1790s, right as the novel in its first form was being written (c. 1795–1797). Now, of course, a tolerably snug cottage in the English countryside is hardly the same setting as a clean, well-run, reformed prison with individual sleeping cells. Yet common to both locations is the implication that architecture can condition thought. The narrowness of the living space in each environment is implied to be able to condition how its inhabitants process serious or life-altering events. As Robin Evans remarks about the new late eighteenth-century prisons: "the program of reformatory discipline outlined by the philanthropists, which put great faith in the redeeming effects of separation and seclusion, could only be implemented" in a certain kind of space; thus architecture "was acknowledged to be the crucial factor setting the [reformatory] process in motion."[49]

Reliance on individual cells to isolate criminals and facilitate their rehabilitation was the hallmark of the separate system of prison discipline. The more time an inmate spent in his or her cell by night and, to varying extents, by day, the more he or she could reflect, grow, adapt, repent. An alternative model to the separate system of prison discipline was the silent system.[50] In the silent system, inmates slept alone, but assembled each day to eat and work in the prison shops, where they were not allowed to talk, whisper, touch, or even exchange looks. If they exhibited any of these behaviors, they were probably whipped. Thus, whereas seclusion and religious meditation were crucial to the reformative process of the separate system, learning the value of hard work, of property, and of cooperative social interaction was crucial to the reformative process of the silent system.

One vignette of the Dashwood women at work in Barton Cottage features uncanny silent-system undertones:

> Without shutting herself up from her family, or leaving the house in determined solitude to avoid them, or lying awake the whole night to indulge meditation, Elinor found every day afforded her leisure enough to think of Edward. . . . There were moments in abundance, when, if not by the absence of her mother and sisters, at least by the nature of their employments, conversation was forbidden among them, and every effect of solitude was produced. Her mind was inevitably at liberty; her thoughts could not be chained elsewhere; and the past and the future, on a subject so interesting, must be before her, must force her attention, and engross her memory, her reflection, and her fancy. (*SS*, 121)

Here we learn that Elinor has no need to lock herself in her room, or to leave the house "in determined solitude," or to lie up at night and "indulge meditation." These are separate-system behaviors, not silent-system behaviors. Yet Elinor receives the benefits of solitude, seclusion, and reflection anyway in the silent-system-like space of the cottage. Note the second sentence in the above passage: "by the nature of their employments, conversation was forbidden among them, and every effect of solitude was produced." This is a relatively clear and compact description of silent-system discipline. The Dashwoods work side by side without speaking. And the practice was both novel and familiar at the time. Several of the fifty-plus gaols and bridewells erected between 1778 and 1795 were experimenting with degrees of silent work in association. The county gaol at Horsham in Sussex, for instance, which opened in 1778, was the first penitentiary house in England and a forerunner of the silent system. Even at the famous Gloucester Penitentiary, where a prototypical separate system prevailed, prisoners met for washing, for attending divine service, and for exercise. They also left their day cells at times to labor in pairs.[51]

The third and final sentence in the passage contains a metaphor involving chains, which evolves into a paradox. While Elinor works at the cottage with her sister and mother, in silence, "her mind was inevitably at liberty; her thoughts could not be chained elsewhere." Inevitably at liberty to do what? Austen tells us: to think exclusively about Edward Ferrars. Now, this is exactly what Elinor wants to do at this point in the novel. The past and the future as either relates to Edward is an "interesting" subject to her and a personal one. She wants her thoughts "chained" on Edward, not "chained elsewhere." Still, consider that the word "inevitable" is somewhat at odds with a state of perfect liberty. An "inevitable" freedom to have one's thoughts "chained" on a single object seems at least a touch coercive. Then there is the last clause in the sentence: we read that thoughts about Edward "*must* be before her, *must* force her attention, and *engross* her memory, her reflection, and her fancy." Who is saying or thinking these words? Is it Elinor, thinking through free indirect discourse, indulging in hedonistic thoughts of love, panting daydreamingly at each emphatic "must"? Or is the narrator simply telling us what *must* happen to Elinor, whether she likes it or not?

The passage is paradoxical in the sense that Elinor both acts and is acted on. She both wills Edward-centered thoughts and Edward-centered thoughts are thrust upon her by her immediate environment. Whether she remembers ("memory"), thinks ("reflection"), or wonders ("fancy"), it is, it must be, in this space and under these conditions, about Edward. It is as though her mind in all of its faculties is stiflingly, yet productively, channeled by her surroundings. Recall that Park calls Barton Cottage a "psychological and physical habitation that constricts the self even as it expands it." Her comment is especially relevant in the context of this passage, but not only because Elinor is constricted in body though free in mind. It is more that, in mind, she is simultaneously restricted and free: in her breadth of thought Elinor is severely confined to Edward; yet in depth of thought she can go as far as she likes—or as far as she "must."

Thus Elinor meditates silently and works methodically alongside her sister and mother in a small room, in which she learns to regulate feelings which, for her, exceed the limits of propriety and may lead to unrealistic expectations. Edward has just left the cottage after only a weeklong visit and in a state of extreme melancholy. He apparently has no prospect of a profession and hardly knows what to do with himself. Elinor is consequently forced to come to terms with the fact that she is in love with a man who is morose, directionless, and quite possibly hiding something important. She has to correct internally what she feels is an overbalance of emotion, and she must set her interiority to order. The setting of the cottage as a compact, austere, and industrious space, as it has been characterized up to the point of the scene in question, is an element inseparable from this self-corrective process and important in its own right.

This scene takes place in the first novel Austen published (1811); in her final novel, *Persuasion* (1818), the penitential space returns dramatically and self-consciously. Every Janeite will recall the odd addition of the character of Mrs. Smith, who appears in the final pages of *Persuasion.* Late in the novel, the hero Anne Elliot has yet to find out that her suitor, Mr. Elliot, is a scoundrel. So in a sort of deus ex machina maneuver Austen introduces a Mrs. Smith, née Hamilton, in volume 2, chapter 5. At this point, the denouement of *Persuasion* is in full swing. The subplot with Mrs. Smith goes like this: Miss Hamilton and Anne Elliot were once old schoolfriends. But unlike Anne, Miss Hamilton married an improvident and reckless man, named Smith, who died and left her in financial straits. At his time of death, Smith owned property in the West Indies whose profits could have spared his widow from ruin. His friend and the executor of his will, Mr. Elliot, had a chance to reclaim the property on behalf of Mrs. Smith.

She even begged him to. But Mr. Elliot never bothered to look into it, and Mrs. Smith ended up a poor widow whose rheumatism eventually all but immobilized her as a semipermanent invalid in Bath. Anne visits her twice near the end of *Persuasion*, learns the whole backstory about Mr. Elliot, and discovers, through the testimony of her old friend, that Mr. Elliot is a villain. All of this useful information straightens her primrose path to the much worthier Captain Wentworth.

Thus Mrs. Smith is essentially a homebound invalid when we meet her in the final pages of *Persuasion*. She is confined to a house in a relatively ungenteel part of town, near two baths, the Hot Bath and the Cross Bath, whose heated waters invalids either immersed their bodies in or had pumped onto their pained extremities. What is most interesting about her confinement are its carceral and penitential undertones. One such undertone is historically rooted. The editors of the *Cambridge Edition of the Works of Jane Austen* argue that Mrs. Smith was based in part on Charlotte Turner Smith (1765–1806), novelist, poet, and Romantic revitalizer of the sonnet. They make a convincing case: both Mrs. Smiths married men who had ties to property in the West Indies and who left their wives in financial straits.[52] Yet the editors overlook another parallel that happens to be crucial in this context. Charlotte Smith spent seven months in a London prison with her husband after he was arrested for debt and embezzlement in late 1783. It was there, in King's Bench Prison, that she negotiated the sale of the first edition of her groundbreaking volume, *Elegiac Sonnets* (1784). The fictional Mrs. Smith, as it happens, finds herself in a similar predicament. She also ends up in a long, dramatic confinement thanks to the improvidence of her husband. She, of course, is a bit more coddled in Bath than Charlotte would have been in King's Bench Prison, and instead of arranging to sell sonnets to the middle classes, the fictional Mrs. Smith survives by making "thread-cases, pincushions and card-racks" for the poor.[53] Her solicitous caretaker Nurse Rooke helps her distribute them.

Anne is rightfully shocked to find out how cheerfully Mrs. Smith handles her situation. Charlotte Smith is said to have had a "natural buoyancy of . . . temperament," which made her imprisonment bearable.[54] By comparison, Mrs. Smith is almost supernaturally resilient in her confinement, and the narrator makes sure to communicate the extent of her adversity. She has lost her "bloom" since Anne last saw her at age fifteen (Mrs. Smith is now twenty-seven) (*P*, 166). She loved her husband, and had to bury him. Like the vicar of Wakefield, she lived well, even in "affluence," and then lost everything. She has no children, no relatives, and bad health. She cannot move without assistance, and when she does move it is mainly to go to a thermal bath. Yet for all this, her days are full of "hours of occupation and enjoyment." Why? Anne suspects that her friend is simply gifted with a rare disposition to make the best of a bad situation, a disposition Anne calls the "choicest gift of Heaven" (*P*, 167). This may be true, but there is something more to Mrs. Smith than a stoic temperament. She has acquired a sort of monkish, *contemptus mundi* attitude that has altered her worldview and that is clearly complemented by her virtual incarceration in Bath. Mrs. Smith tells Anne that, until recently, she has "lived very much in the world" (*P*, 167), and that she has "seen too much of the world," in fact, "to expect sudden or disinterested attachment any where" (*P*, 168). To Anne she laments: "'generally speaking . . . it is selfishness and impatience rather than generosity and fortitude, that one hears of. There is so little real friendship in the world!—and unfortunately' (speaking low and tremulously) 'there are so many who forget to think seriously till it is almost too late'" (*P*, 169). To "think seriously" about what, and before "it is almost too late" for what? In this last, "low" and "tremulously" uttered sentence, Mrs. Smith is recalling her role in what the narrator calls certain "dissipations of the past," and regretting it (*P*, 167). A reconciliation with God is in order. She now sees human existence as divided into the dichotomous realms of living in the world and living out of it, and as someone about to live out of it, permanently, a penitential confinement seems to suit her. She works, serves the poor, reviews her past life, meditates on last things.

The last novel I want to examine is a text "explicitly set in the contemporary world, and with several references to current events and controversies"—*Mansfield Park*.[55] Of all six novels, *Mansfield Park* has the closest ties to the historical reality of reformative confinement in early nineteenth-century Britain. Mark Canuel, in fact, has read *Mansfield Park* as an important "contribution . . . to the broader eighteenth- and nineteenth-century discourse on the reformed aims of punishment." Canuel claims that the "unrelenting public notice" and "omnipresent pattern of judgments" endured by Fanny Price at Mansfield Park effectively construct her subjectivity. Fanny would have no personality, no moral agency, no sense of self, that is, were she not constantly visible and repeatedly punished by the adults at Mansfield Park. Canuel also views the home of the Prices at Portsmouth as the opposite of the great house at Mansfield Park, insofar as, at Portsmouth, Fanny is utterly "exclu[ded] and invisib[le]."[56] According to Canuel, because Fanny goes relatively unnoticed at Portsmouth, she can receive no punishment, and as a consequence she undergoes no real development. I agree with Canuel that we can view Mansfield Park as a sort of panoptic manor house where the protagonist is virtually punished into selfhood. Yet we cannot fully appreciate Mansfield Park as a "reformed" penal space unless it is set in clear contradistinction to the Portsmouth house as an "unreformed" penal space. Austen draws a firm line of demarcation between the two houses and dramatically juxtaposes them. Portsmouth, as a carceral space, is defined by promiscuous association, swearing, bad lighting, poor ventilation, drunkenness, dirtiness, noise, and wastefulness. Mansfield Park, as a carceral space, is defined by order, enforced restrictions, relative solitude, evangelical religiosity, reflection, exercise, and economy.

Austen began planning *Mansfield Park* in 1811, and she composed it between 1812 and 1813; one current event that receives implicit attention in this novel is the decision of the British government to adopt penitential imprisonment as *the* mode of incarceration. The root of this decision is in a report published by a parliamentary committee on May 31, 1811. That committee was the Holford Committee. The Holford Committee was chaired by George Holford in 1810 to reexamine the issues of the 1779 Penitentiary Act. It was created at the behest of Samuel Romilly as a way to mitigate the statutory reliance on capital punishment in British jurisprudence. Holford and his committee set out to determine "whether existing prisons could be adapted for the purposes of penitentiary imprisonment, or whether a new type of administration and management was necessary."[57] The report of the committee to the House of Commons generally views the prison/penitentiary at Gloucester as the model to be emulated. It says that "many offenders may be reclaimed by a system of penitentiary imprisonment; by which, your committee mean a system of imprisonment, not confined to the safe custody of the person, but extending to the reformation and improvement of the mind, and operating by *seclusion*, *employment*, and *religious instruction*."[58] These words were the death knell of the panopticon, and probably gave its creator, Jeremy Bentham, many sleepless nights. The panopticon model of prison discipline, administration, and management never put much stress on religious education or reformation, and for men like John Howard, George Onesiphorus Paul, and Holford, the salvation of imprisoned souls was highly important. The eventual result of the Holford report was the erection of the first national penitentiary at Millbank in 1816, whose design, construction, and opening Holford supervised, and whose reformative effects, at least at first, he praised.

It is not exactly new to associate *Mansfield Park* with the *ahistorical* idea of imprisonment. Critics other than Nina Auerbach have made such associations in response to the amount of prison metaphors the novel uses.[59] Mr. Rushworth, for instance, calls his home at Sotherton Court "a prison—quite a dismal old prison" that "wants improvement." Rushworth, in fact, "never saw a place that wanted so much improvement in . . . [his] life; and it is so forlorn."[60] His fiancé, Maria Bertram, sees Sotherton Court as a prison in a different sense. The iron gate and the fence on its grounds give her a "feeling of restraint and hardship. I cannot get out, as the starling said"; that is, Maria cannot get out of her impending marriage to a blockhead and her eventual domestic confinement as a result of it (*MP*, 115–116). To Fanny Price, the very presence of the coquettish Henry Crawford is a "grievous imprisonment of body and mind" (*MP*, 398). Of these metaphors, the first is the most evocative of imprisonment in a historical sense. That Rushworth feels he has to renovate his "dismal old prison" of an estate, with its "tall iron palisades and gates" and its "forlorn" feel—not to mention its dramatically defunct chapel—more than hints at the three decades of remodeling and rebuilding "dismal old" English prisons that precede the setting of *Mansfield Park* (*MP*, 99).

Mansfield Park is less critical of the promise of reformed imprisonment than, say, *Northanger Abbey*. The former drifts more into alignment with the spirit and letter of the Holford Committee report.[61] As a structure and as a disciplinary space, Northanger Abbey suggests an awkward mixture of unreformed and reformed prison environments. On the one hand, it has a Newgate-ish feel to it. It is an architectural hybrid whose new pantries, sculleries, cellars, and laundries sit glaringly next to the "ancient kitchen of the convent, rich in the massy walls and smoke of former days."[62] General Tilney, the owner of Northanger Abbey, is as unscrupulous and exploitative as the old gaolers who drained their inmates dry with fees. There is also a strong resemblance between Northanger Abbey and Newgate Prison as repositories of thrilling horrors.[63] Yet for all its Gothic creepiness, the abbey is perfectly modern in lighting, sleeping conditions, fenestration, air quality, ventilation, and safety. The narrator takes us on a kind of proud periodical inspection of the place. We learn that the fireplace in the main hall is a Rumford.[64] Catherine finds the "air" of her bedroom "altogether far from uncheerful" (*NA*, 167). The abbey is even "so guarded" that she can move about "securely" on its premises (*NA*, 171). Thus the Newgate-ish-ness of Northanger Abbey exists alongside its modern appearance and amenities. At Mansfield Park, on the other hand, the environment is entirely unmixed as a penal space. It is bright, modern, and completely, even ruthlessly, efficient.

When Fanny Price arrives at Mansfield Park as a nine-year-old girl from Portsmouth, her uncle, Sir Thomas Bertram, sees "much to wish altered" in his niece: "gross ignorance, some meanness of opinions, and very distressing vulgarity of manner." He adds, however, that these are "not incurable faults," and so may not be "dangerous for her associates"—that is, for her twelve- and thirteen-year-old cousins Julia and Maria and for her older cousins Edmund and Tom (*MP*, 11). But then Sir Thomas ends up stashing Fanny in the diminutive "white attic" anyway, at the advice of Mrs. Norris (*MP*, 10). (It is worth noting that the idea of "vulgarity of manner[s]" "dangerous for . . . associates" invokes the much-feared threat of moral contamination inside unreformed prisons.) So Fanny sleeps in the white attic. And sleeping is about all she can do there, thanks to its "deficiency of space and accommodation" (*MP*, 177).[65] When Fanny has any leisure time at all at Mansfield Park, she spends it in the old schoolroom immediately below the attic, called the East room. There she is comfortable enough. The East room is shabbily furnished with an old stool, a few transparencies on a few windows, some inferior pictures of the Bertrams, and a sketch made by her brother William Price.

Fanny is happy with the plainness of the East room; she prefers it; she "would not have changed its furniture for the handsomest in the house" (*MP*, 178). The "bright bars of her empty [fire] grate"—"bright" because there is never a fire there—cause her no unease (*MP*, 197). All she needs is a "gleam of sunshine" to warm up the East room, even in the wintertime (*MP*, 177). It is a kind of mind-over-matter situation with Fanny. As someone who is earnest, pious, and reflective, she can handle, if not thrive under, a few material "privations and restrictions"

(*MP*, 361). In fact, it is because of the sparseness and "solitude of the East room," not in spite of it, that she has often "worked and meditated . . . undisturbed" (*MP*, 187, 197).

All these facts resonate with an important exchange between Edmund Bertram and Mary Crawford in the chapel at Sotherton Court. The exchange in question occurs when the young people are all touring Sotherton Court, where Maria Bertram will presumably end up living with her fiancé Mr. Rushworth. Mary implies, in the presence of Edmund and Fanny, that someone whose mind wanders in the midst of a congregation at divine service will be no more devout if alone in a small room. She asks Edmund: "Do you think the minds which are suffered, which are indulged in wanderings in a chapel, would be more collected in a closet?" Edmund argues that they would be; in a "closet," he says, there is "less to distract the attention" and more to confirm devotional habits (*MP*, 102). He could have looked to Fanny at this point for corroboration. She is a fine example of religious diligence in small spaces. She sleeps and prays, night and morning, in her little cell of an attic, and reads and meditates in the East room when she is not working for her aunts. Add to this that she exercises regularly, receives evangelical religious education at the hands of Sir Thomas and Edmund, and lives in a "modern-built house," "well placed" and "airy" (*MP*, 55, 517). Mansfield Park may be no paradise, but it is a spotless house and a methodizing one. Next to the Price home in Portsmouth, in contradistinction to which it is dramatically and deliberately positioned, Mansfield Park functions as a domestic analogue to the happy prison of British literary tradition.

We may also compare the comment by Edmund, that there is "less to distract the attention" and more to confirm devotional habits in a "closet," to the following comment by Holford:

> Each of the inmates of the common [i.e., shared] cell will probably, at times, be disposed to serious reflection . . . but unless the disposition to seriousness should come on all of them at the same time, (which is not to be supposed,) it is not likely to be so cultivated as to produce any lasting benefit. It is not likely that a man should . . . apply himself to his Bible, or kneel down in prayer, while his companions in the same cell are indulging in light or profligate conversation.[66]

This is essentially the same point that Edmund makes to Mary, who tends to indulge in light or profligate conversation. If "inmates" is replaced with "parishioners" and "common cell" with "chapel," the argument is essentially the same. Holford adds: it is a "common . . . practice (*not confined to prisoners*) for men to jest or sneer at those who treat any subject more gravely than they are themselves disposed to do."[67] One almost has to think of Mary Crawford in light of this last comment. She tells Edmund that the "the good people who used to kneel and gape" in the chapel at Sotherton Court would probably have much preferred to stay longer in bed than to go to chapel in the first place. After a few more irreverent statements of this sort, Mary gets scolded: Edmund tells her that her "lively mind can hardly be serious even on serious subjects" (*MP*, 102).

In the third volume of the novel, Sir Thomas sends (sentences?) his niece Fanny to Portsmouth to "spend a little time with her own family" (*MP*, 425). Sir Thomas, at the time, is bewildered and incensed over the fact that Fanny has just rejected a marriage proposal from the charming and landowning Henry Crawford. After hearing her evidence for her refusal, Sir Thomas is not satisfied. He thinks that Fanny is acting too proud in light of her social station and limited expectations. So he executes a kind of summary justice: he hears her case, convicts her of unreasonableness, and sends her off to live at Portsmouth for a short time, a time that ends up running through the season of Lent. He wants Fanny to learn what one miserable alternative can be to what he imagines would have been a respectable marriage settlement with Henry Crawford. At first he is proud of his plan. He thinks of it as

> a medicinal project upon his niece's understanding, which he must consider as at present diseased. A residence of eight or nine years in the abode of wealth and plenty had a little disordered her powers of comparing and judging. Her father's house would, in all probability, teach her the value of a good income; and he trusted that she would be the wiser and happier woman, all her life, for the experiment he had devised. (*MP*, 425–426)

Essentially, his "experiment" to put Fanny in captivity for a while works. This is not to say that she ends up changing her mind about marrying Henry Crawford; she and the reader both know that that Crawford is a scoundrel. But at Portsmouth she does come to realize "the value of a good income" and is made to reflect on where her real "home" is, or should be.

The subplot involving the Price home at Portsmouth is more or less one long assault on the senses, reading like a version of the literary tradition of a descent into hell. When Fanny and her brother William arrive at the Price house they are greeted by the "trollopy-looking" maid Rebecca. Rebecca is immediately pushed aside by the eleven-year-old Sam Price running out of the house. The first thing Fanny hears once she and William are inside is a "squabble" between Sam and Rebecca about who can carry her trunk upstairs. Enter Mr. Price, head of the household, half-drunk, swearing and kicking luggage out of his way. It is dark enough for him to request a candle, though no candle is forthcoming. He greets and hugs Fanny and leaves on her the scent of rum and water. The eight- and nine-year-old Tom and Charles Price then rush into the house all "ragged and dirty." Things go on like this over the next several days. Everyone in the Price house seems to be "tumbling about and hallooing" at once. Mr. Price shouts at Sam for interrupting his paper. The "threat" is "palpably disregarded." The boys "are kicking each other's shins, and hallooing out at sudden starts immediately under their father's eye" (*MP*, 435, 438, 440, 441, 442, 443). We also learn that the Price children were supposed to have been sent a few prayer books from Mansfield Park, but that the books never arrived.

Thus the Price house is "the abode of noise, disorder, and impropriety. Nobody was in their right place, nothing was done as it ought to be" (*MP*, 450).[68] It is a "scene of mismanagement and discomfort from beginning to end" (*MP*, 451–452), a place of "ceaseless tumult" (*MP*, 454), "closeness . . . confinement, bad air, bad smells" (*MP*, 500).[69] Even the sun looks in on the Prices with a kind of sickened gaze: "here, its power was only a glare, a stifling, sickly glare, serving but to bring forward stains and dirt that might otherwise have slept." On most days, Fanny sits in a

> blaze of oppressive heat, in a cloud of moving dust; and her eyes could only wander from the walls marked by her father's head [has Mr. Price been slamming his head into walls?], to the table cut and notched by her brothers, where stood the tea-board never thoroughly cleaned, the cups and saucers wiped in streaks, the milk a mixture of motes floating in thin blue, and the bread and butter growing every minute more greasy than even Rebecca's hands had first produced it. (*MP*, 508)[70]

At Mansfield, on the other hand, "no sounds of contention, no raised voice, no abrupt bursts, no tread of violence was ever heard; all proceeded in a regular course" (*MP*, 453).

Compare how Austen describes the Price house, quoted above, to how her aunt Mrs. Leigh-Perrot describes time spent in Somerset County Gaol at Ilchester, where she and her husband lived with the prison governor and his family for seven months. The following comes from a letter from Mrs. Leigh-Perrot to her cousins in Lincolnshire, and is dated October 1799:

> Vulgarity, Dirt, Noise from Morning till Night. . . . This Room joins to a Room where the Children all lie, and not Bedlam itself can be half so noisy, besides which, as not one particle of Smoke goes up the Chimney, except you leave the door or window open, I leave you to judge of the Comfort I can enjoy in such a Room. . . . No! my Good Cousin, I cannot subject even a Servant to the suffering <u>we</u> daily experience. . . . My dearest Perrot with <u>his</u> sweet composure adds to <u>my</u> Philosophy. . . . Cleanliness has ever been his greatest delight and yet he sees the greasy

> toast laid by the dirty Children on his Knees, and feels the small Beer trickle down his sleeves on its way across the table unmoved.[71]

The parallels in the two descriptions seem too close to go unnoticed. In both cases, a respectable female used to a comfortable life is suddenly transplanted to a foreign, decrepit, and disordered space full of unruly children: a "scene of mismanagement and discomfort from beginning to end" (Portsmouth); "Vulgarity, Dirt, Noise from Morning till Night" (Ilchester); "the abode of noise, disorder, and impropriety" (Portsmouth); "not Bedlam itself can be half so noisy" (Ilchester); "the bread and butter growing every minute more greasy" (Portsmouth); "the greasy toast laid by the dirty Children" (Ilchester). I should add that Mrs. Austen offered to send her daughters, either Jane, Cassandra, or both, to live with and support their aunt during her seven months in prison. But Mrs. Leigh-Perrot gratefully refused the offer: she could not let "those Elegant young Women be . . . Inmates in a Prison."[72] Perhaps the Portsmouth episode in *Mansfield Park* was a mediated and belated way for Austen to acknowledge a family misfortune she almost had to, but never did, share.

The pattern to which I have drawn attention in this chapter is hardly a complete account. There are surely more domestic spaces in the novels—relatively small, enclosed, and marked by a certain aura of piety or austerity—readily associated with an instance of moral exertion, clarity, resolve, or improvement. A study similar to the present one could expand the temporal and generic parameters significantly. It could examine, say, a series of domestic novels published between 1777 (the date of the publication of *State of the Prisons*) and 1816 (the establishment of the first national penitentiary in England), novels set primarily in the English provinces, and trace how and to what extent an author is careful to associate a specified type of physical environment with a specified type of moral or spiritual improvement. Is a character suddenly enlightened in a way in which spatial form plays a crucial role? Is his or her gradual resolve to be better to any extent accommodated by the physical environment(s) in which this resolve is explored? Is a novel concerned with qualities such as room size, wholesome air, exercise, degrees of socialization, eating habits, regulated labor, available reading material, religious counsel, strict timekeeping schedules, or prayer, in connection with the reintegration of one or more characters into society? Is something similar to what Edward Austen Knight accomplished in the sphere of local government accomplished, or at least attempted, in the domestic fiction of the age? How and to what extent, in short, may a novel, on the one hand, and a political, evangelical, or legal pamphlet, on the other, be said to reflect and reinforce a social order increasingly reliant on confined spaces designed "to reconstruct the . . . mind and heart"?[73]

CODA

IN THE LAST THIRD OF THE EIGHTEENTH CENTURY and the first third of the nineteenth century, cultural awareness of crime and of the prison experience was strong.[1] The lived experiences of prisoners and the rampant abuses of prison administrators were frequently reported in the news and in the writings of reformers, philosophers, and legislators.[2] Old prisons and houses of correction were being torn down and new ones erected based on Howardian principles in several counties with the help of private acts of Parliament. A spate of radical texts emerged from the careful collaboration of political prisoners in Newgate and their friends in the opposition press. The government was on the lookout for a site for its first national penitentiary. Commoners like Sir Francis Burdett were building political campaigns on penal reform. The moral and material film of imprisonment clung to the bodies of both inmates and the friends, relatives, spies, philanthropists, and government officials who went in and out of prisons like Newgate to visit them.[3] Crimping houses were viewed as a kind of prison that the state winked at. And so on. It was in this particular cultural climate that the British literary tradition we now call Romantic emerged and developed. The vision of the Howardian prison took root in the same soil as new developments in poetics, narrative fiction, intertextuality, the social meaningfulness of art, and the creative imagination.[4] I have focused on what I believe to be the most important examples of how and to what extent the language and ideology of prison discourse informed the language and ideology of contemporary literary discourse, and vice versa, suggesting that the boundaries between these two discourses were often porous, and that this porousness has important implications for how we understand either one.

I have also argued that this book connects the form and historicity of literary texts imaginatively organized around themes of imprisonment to the rise of penal reform and the birth of the modern prison in late eighteenth- and early nineteenth-century Britain. The nature of one or another such connection varies from text to text. The poems tend to romanticize or aestheticize conditions of limitation or restraint, voluntary or otherwise. "This Lime-Tree Bower My Prison," for instance, exploits an opportunity for religious meditation in a situation of solitary confinement, a confinement that is technically involuntary, but otherwise a prison only in name. The prisons described in the verse of John Keats and Lord Byron are either figurative or fictional, though they are real to the extent that the raw elements of their creation include the experience of the incarcerated Leigh Hunt. The chapters on Hunt and John Clare examined cases in which actual and forced confinement is manipulated in art to yield positive results, moral, imaginative, aesthetic, or otherwise. The prose texts, for the most part, operate differently from the poems. William Godwin is capable of romanticizing imprisonment in his novels even as he foregrounds its fundamental destructiveness and inhumanity. Jane Austen associates heightened powers of introspection, social awareness, and piety with seclusion in austere or restrictive domestic spaces.

All such texts, however different in rhetoric or genre, create cultural conditions amenable to the theory and practice of reformative imprisonment in late eighteenth- and early nineteenth-century Britain. Even texts that romanticize elective solitude or confinement cultivate sensibilities serviceable to penal reform in a culture in which the modern prison was veritably born. These texts glorify the paradoxical idea of freedom in and through restraint. They valorize the hermetic or monastic cell in a culture in which the idea of isolating inmates in reformatory cells was first authorized by one of the most important acts of penal legislation in history. I have said that the imaginative treatment of solitude and seclusion in literary texts was more likely to be implicated in penal discourse in the late eighteenth and early nineteenth centuries than in any previous period. It follows that numerous other texts, and other kinds of text, are suitable to the present or a similar project, such as the graveyard poems of the so-called pre-Romantics, gothic novels, familiar essays, plays, didactic poems, didactic essays, and so on. More work remains to be done. This book is only part of the small but increasing cadre of critical texts that explore and document an area of literary scholarship that has proven both fruitful and neglected.

ACKNOWLEDGMENTS

This book would hardly have been possible without several research-related awards granted by the California State University, Sacramento, including four Research and Creative Activity (RCA) awards, sponsored by the Offices of Research, Innovation, and Economic Development, and two Scholarly and Creative Activity (SCA) awards, sponsored by the College of Arts and Letters. I would also like to thank the Kent Archival and Local History Service for allowing me to reproduce archival materials. My greatest debt, however, is to my partner, Mary, who listened patiently to me as I articulated the inchoate arguments of each and every one of these chapters, and who waited patiently for me as I worked far too long, for far too many years, on all of them. I would also like to thank my friend Noah Heringman, without whose consummate wisdom and advice I would hardly have arrived where I am.

NOTES

INTRODUCTION

1. Thus Lorenz Eitner writes that "the trend of progressive emancipation from every sort of constraint—thematic, aesthetic, or technical—was a steady undercurrent beneath the surface turbulence of Romanticism, unaffected by its contradictions and inconsistences. This libertarian impetus was perhaps the only pervasive force in Romanticism, and the best reason for considering it, despite its lack of unity and coherence, as one movement" (Lorenz Eitner, "Cages, Prisons, and Captives in Eighteenth-Century Art," in *Images of Romanticism: Verbal and Visual Affinities*, ed. Karl Kroeber and William Walling [New Haven, CT: Yale University Press, 1978], 13).
2. Another reason literary critics tend to study the advent of the modern prison in tandem with Victorian literature is that the so-called Newgate novels—novels glamorizing the lives of famous criminals—became popular in the 1830s, as Romanticism started to wane. Still another is the establishment of the first bona fide national penitentiary at Pentonville in 1842, five years after the ascension of Victoria.
3. Judith Thompson, "An Autumnal Blast, a Killing Frost: Coleridge's Poetic Conversation with John Thelwall," *Studies in Romanticism* 36, no. 3 (1997): 451; John Bugg, *Five Long Winters: The Trials of British Romanticism* (Stanford, CA: Stanford University Press, 2013), 50; and Jon Mee, "Treason, Seditious Libel, and Literature in the Romantic Period," in *Oxford Handbook Topics in Literature*, online ed. (Oxford: Oxford Academic, 2016), http://doi.org/10.1093/oxfordhb/9780199935338.013.113. LeGette enlarges on the work of Bugg by examining not only "the ways in which radical [nineteenth-century] prisoners made the Romantic lyric their own, but also the ways in which imprisonment conditioned Romanticism itself" (Casie LeGette, "The Lyric Speaker Goes to Gaol: British Poetry and Radical Prisoners, 1820–1845," *Nineteenth-Century Literature* 67, no. 1 [2012]: 4).
4. Judith Scheffler, "Romantic Women Writing on Imprisonment and Prison Reform," *The Wordsworth Circle* 19, no. 2 (1988): 99. See also Gabriel Cervantes and Dahlia Porter, "Extreme Empiricism: John Howard, Poetry, and the Thermometrics of Reform," *The Eighteenth Century* 57, no. 1 (2016): 95–119; and Gabriel Cervantes and Dahlia Porter, "Walking with John Howard: Itineracy and Romantic Reform," *Romanticism* 27, no. 1 (2021): 4–15.
5. See, for instance, Ralph A. Manogue, "The Plight of James Ridgway, London Bookseller and Publisher, and the Newgate Radicals, 1792–1797," *The Wordsworth Circle* 27, no. 3 (1996): 158–166; Iain McCalman, "Newgate in Revolution: Radical Enthusiasm and Romantic Counterculture," *Eighteenth-Century Life* 22, no. 1 (1998): 95–110; Michael T. Davis, Iain McCalman, and Christina Parolin, eds., *Newgate in Revolution: An Anthology of Radical Prison Literature in the Age of Revolution* (London: Continuum, 2005); Gary Kelly, introduction to *Newgate Documents*, vol. 1 of *Newgate Narratives*, ed. Gary Kelly (London: Pickering and Chatto, 2008); and Christina Parolin, *Radical Spaces: Venues of Popular Politics in London, 1790-c. 1845* (Acton, Australia: ANU Press, 2010).
6. Sal Nicolazzo, *Vagrant Figures: Law, Literature, and the Origins of the Police* (New Haven, CT: Yale University Press, 2020), 3, 251.

7. Carrie D. Shanafelt, *Uncommon Sense: Jeremy Bentham, Queer Aesthetics, and the Politics of Taste* (Charlottesville: University of Virginia Press, 2022), 49.
8. Mark Canuel, *The Shadow of Death: Literature, Romanticism, and the Subject of Punishment* (Princeton, NJ: Princeton University Press, 2007), 5.
9. Quentin Bailey, *Wordsworth's Vagrants: Police, Prisons and Poetry in the 1790s* (Farnham, UK: Ashgate, 2011), 3, 87.
10. David Philips, "'A Just Measure of Crime, Authority, Hunters and Blue Locusts': The 'Revisionist' Social History of Crime and the Law in Britain, 1780–1850," in *Social Control and the State*, ed. Stanley Cohen and Andrew Scull (New York: St. Martin's Press, 1983), 50.
11. Aileen Ward, "Romantic Castles and Real Prisons: Wordsworth, Blake, and Revolution," *The Wordsworth Circle* 30, no. 1 (1999): 11.
12. Ward, "Romantic Castles and Real Prisons," 12.
13. Uwe Böker, "The Prison and the Penitentiary as Sites of Public Counter-Discourse," in *Sites of Discourse—Public and Private Spheres—Legal Culture: Papers from a Conference Held at the Technical University of Dresden, December 2001*, ed. Uwe Böker and Julie A. Hibbard (Amsterdam: Editions Rodopi B. V., 2002), 233, 237.
14. Ulrich Broich, "The Politicization of the Prison Motif in the English Literature of the 1790s," *Poetica* 39, no. 1/2 (2007): 120.
15. Broich, "The Politicization of the Prison Motif," 115.
16. Kelly, *Newgate Documents*, x.
17. Cervantes and Porter, "Extreme Empiricism," 97.
18. Mary Ellen Snodgrass, *Encyclopedia of Gothic Literature: The Essential Guide to the Lives and Works of Gothic Writers* (New York: Facts on File, 2005), s.v. "dungeons and prisons."
19. Snodgrass, *Encyclopedia of Gothic Literature*.
20. Joseph Addison, "No. 411: Saturday, June 21, 1712," in *The Spectator*, ed. Donald F. Bond, vol. 3 (Oxford: Clarendon Press, 1965), 537; Johann Georg Zimmermann, *On Solitude. Or the Effects of Occasional Retirement on the Mind, the Heart, General Society, in Exile, in Old Age, and on the Bed of Death. In Which the Question is Considered Whether It is Easier to Live Virtuously in Society, or in Solitude* (London: Vernor and Hood; J. Cuthell; J. Walker; Lackington, Allen and Co.; J. Nunn, Ogilvy and Son; Darton and Harvey; W. Otridge and Son; R. Lea, 1798), 120; Jean-Jacques Rousseau, *The Confessions, and Correspondence, Including the Letters to Malesherbes*, trans. Christopher Kelly, ed. Christopher Kelly, Roger D. Masters and Peter G. Stillman, vol. 5 of *The Collected Writings of Rousseau*, ed. Christopher Kelly, Roger D. Masters, and Peter G. Stillman (Hanover, NH: University Press of New England, 1995), 144.
21. Thomas Fowler, *The Prison: A Poem* (London: Printed for the Author; W. Moore; C. Stalker, 1790), lines 104–110.
22. Elizabeth Inchbald, *Such Things Are; A Play, in Five Acts. As Performed at the Theatre Royal, Covent Garden*, 2nd ed. (London: G. G. J. and J. Robinson, 1788), 3.2.
23. The critical literature on the history of imprisonment in Europe is vast. A useful starting point for this history is Norval Morris and David J. Rothman, eds., *The Oxford History of the Prison: The Practice of Punishment in Western Society* (Oxford: Oxford University Press, 1998). Two magisterial traditionalist histories of imprisonment are Sidney Webb and Beatrice Webb, *English Prisons under Local Government*, 1922, repr. (Hamden, CT: Archon Books, 1963); and Leon Radzinowicz, *The Movement for Reform*, vol. 1 of *A History of English Criminal Law and Its Administration from 1750*, 1948, repr. (London: Stevens and Sons, 1969). The first prominent revisionist histories were Michel Foucault, *Discipline and Punish: The Birth of the Prison*, trans. Alan Sheridan, 2nd ed. (New York: Vintage, 1995); and Michael Ignatieff, *A Just Measure of Pain: The Penitentiary in the Industrial Revolution, 1750–1850* (London: Penguin, 1978). Other landmark studies include surveys of prison architecture, such as Robin Evans, *The Fabrication of Virtue: English Prison Architecture, 1750–1840* (Cambridge: Cambridge University Press, 1982); and Helen Johnston, "Architecture and Contested Space in the Development of the Modern Prison,"

in *Architecture and Justice: Judicial Meanings in the Public Realm*, ed. Jonathan Simon, Nicholas Temple, and Renée Tobe, 23–35 (Farnham, UK: Ashgate, 2013). Studies of imprisonment in the British Isles, of specific British prisons, or of specific areas of British penal administration became popular in 1970s, continuing on to the present. These include Anthony Babington, *The English Bastille: A History of Newgate Gaol and Prison Conditions in Britain, 1188–1902* (London: Macdonald, 1971); J. R. S. Whiting, *Prison Reform in Gloucestershire, 1776–1820: A Study of the Work of Sir George Onesiphorus Paul, Bart.* (London: Phillimore, 1975); W. J. Sheehan, "Finding Solace in Eighteenth-Century Newgate," in *Crime in England, 1550–1800*, ed. J. S. Cockburn, 229–245 (London: Methuen, 1977); Eric Stockdale, *A Study of Bedford Prison, 1660–1877* (London: Phillimore, 1977); Christopher Harding, Bill Hines, Richard Ireland, and Philip Rawlings, *Imprisonment in England and Wales: A Concise History* (Dover, NH: Croom Helm, 1985); Margaret DeLacy, *Prison Reform in Lancashire, 1700–1850: A Study in Local Administration* (Stanford, CA: Stanford University Press, 1986); Frank McLynn, *Crime and Punishment in Eighteenth-Century England* (Oxford: Routledge, 1989); Charles Campbell, *The Intolerable Hulks: British Shipboard Confinement, 1776–1857* (Bowie, MD: Heritage, 1993); Simon Deveraux and Paul Griffiths, *Penal Practice and Culture, 1500–1900: Punishing the English* (Basingstoke, UK: Palgrave Macmillan, 2004); and Clive Emsley, *Crime and Society in England, 1750–1900*, 4th ed. (Harlow, UK: Pearson Education, 2010). Critical accounts of literary authors and imprisonment soon followed. Among the most important are W. B. Carnochan, *Confinement and Flight: An Essay on English Literature of the Eighteenth Century* (Berkeley: University of California Press, 1977); John Bender, *Imagining the Penitentiary: Fiction and the Architecture of Mind in Eighteenth-Century England* (Chicago: University of Chicago Press, 1987); Ioan Davies, *Writers in Prison* (Cambridge, MA: Basil Blackwell, 1990); Sean Grass, *The Self in the Cell: Narrating the Victorian Prisoner* (New York: Routledge, 2003); Jason Haslam and Julia M. Wright, eds., *Captivating Subjects: Writing Confinement, Citizenship, and Nationhood in the Nineteenth Century* (Toronto: University of Toronto Press, 2005); Jan Alber and Frank Lauterbach, eds., *Stones of Law, Bricks of Shame: Narrating Imprisonment in the Victorian Age* (Toronto: University of Toronto Press, 2009); Philip Edward Phillips, ed., *Prison Narratives from Boethius to Zana* (New York: Palgrave Macmillan, 2014); Anne Schwan, *Convict Voices: Women, Class, and Writing about Prison in Nineteenth-Century England* (Durham, NH: University of New Hampshire Press, 2014); and Rivkah Zim, *The Consolations of Writing: Literary Strategies of Resistance from Boethius to Primo Levi* (Princeton, NJ: Princeton University Press, 2014). A few scholars have written critical surveys of the modern histories of imprisonment extant around the late twentieth century. The most important of these are Michael Ignatieff, "State, Civil Society and Total Institutions: A Critique of Recent Social Histories of Punishment," in *Legality, Ideology and the State*, ed. David Sugarman, 183–211 (London: Academic Press, 1983); and George Fisher, "The Birth of the Prison Retold," *The Yale Law Journal* 104, no. 6 (1995): 1235–1324. Other key studies of imprisonment and penal reform in the British Isles include Seán McConville, *A History of English Prison Administration* (London: Routledge, 1981); J. M. Beattie, *Crime and the Courts in England, 1660–1800* (Oxford: Clarendon Press, 1986); and Laurie Throness, *A Protestant Purgatory: Theological Origins of the Penitentiary Act, 1779* (Aldershot, UK: Ashgate, 2008). As long as it is, this list is hardly exhaustive.

24. Fisher, "Birth of the Prison," 1273.
25. Webb and Webb, *English Prisons*, 16–17.
26. Randall McGowen, "The Problem of Punishment in Eighteenth-Century England," in *Penal Practice and Culture, 1500–1900: Punishing the English*, ed. Simon Deveraux and Paul Griffiths (Basingstoke, UK: Palgrave Macmillan, 2004), 211.
27. Randall McGowen, "The Well-Ordered Prison: England, 1780–1865," in *The Oxford History of the Prison: The Practice of Punishment in Western Society*, ed. Norval Morris and David J. Rothman (Oxford: Oxford University Press, 1998), 75.

28. Kelly, *Newgate Documents*, xcix; Sheehan, "Finding Solace," 242.
29. See Harold D. Kalman, "Newgate Prison," *Architectural History* 12 (1969): 50–61, 108–112.
30. Kelly, *Newgate Documents*, c.
31. Throness, *Protestant Purgatory*, 195.
32. Webb and Webb, *English Prisons*, 38.
33. David W. Chapman, "The Legendary John Howard and Prison Reform in the Eighteenth Century," *The Eighteenth Century* 54, no. 4 (2013): 549.
34. Radzinowicz, *Movement for Reform*, 275.
35. Radzinowicz, *Movement for Reform*, 282.
36. Janet Semple, *Bentham's Prison: A Study of the Panopticon Penitentiary* (Oxford: Clarendon Press, 1993), 69.
37. McGowen, "Well-Ordered Prison," 77–78.
38. Tessa West, *The Curious Mr Howard, Legendary Prison Reformer* (Hook, UK: Waterside Press, 2011), 174.
39. McGowen, "Well-Ordered Prison," 79.
40. John Jebb, *Thoughts on the Construction and Polity of Prisons, with Hints for Their Improvement*, ed. Capel Lofft (Bury St. Edmund's, UK: J. Rackham, 1785), 3.
41. Capel Lofft, "Prefatory Address," in *Thoughts on the Construction and Polity of Prisons, with Hints for their Improvement*, by John Jebb (Bury St. Edmund's, UK: J. Rackham, 1785), viii.
42. Semple, *Bentham's Prison*, 76.
43. McGowen, "Well-Ordered Prison," 78.
44. Simon Deveraux, "The Making of the Penitentiary Act, 1775–1779," *The Historical Journal* 42, no. 2 (1999): 405.
45. Semple, *Bentham's Prison*, 98.
46. William Blackstone, *Commentaries on the Laws of England, Book the Fourth* (Oxford: Clarendon Press, 1769), 18.
47. J. A. Sharpe, *Crime in Early Modern England, 1550–1750* (London: Longman, 1984), 145.
48. Fisher, "Birth of the Prison," 1238–1239.
49. As Grass points out, between 1790 and 1820 Parliament "whittled the 'Bloody Code' from more than 200 capital offenses to fewer than ten" (Grass, *Self in the Cell*, 23).
50. Ignatieff, *Just Measure of Pain*, 87.
51. Randall McGowen, "'He Beareth the Sword in Vain': Religion and the Criminal Law in Eighteenth-Century England," *Eighteenth-Century Studies* 21, no. 2 (1987–1988): 209. The assizes were "sessions held periodically in each county of England, for the purpose of administering civil and criminal justice, by judges acting under certain special commissions" (McGowen, "Well-Ordered Prison," 73). Assize judges toured the country twice a year to try serious cases. The majority of criminal business, however, was carried out not by assize judges but by county justices, presiding locally at what were called the quarter sessions.
52. McConville, *English Prison Administration*, 60–61.
53. Semple, *Bentham's Prison*, 70.
54. Semple, *Bentham's Prison*.
55. Emsley, *Crime and Society*, 261.
56. See Throness, *Protestant Purgatory*.
57. Lissa Paul, *Eliza Fenwick: Early Modern Feminist* (Newark: University of Delaware Press, 2019), 35.
58. Richard R. Follett, *Evangelicalism, Penal Theory and the Politics of Criminal Law Reform in England, 1808–30* (Basingstoke, UK: Palgrave, 2001), 3.
59. Hilary M. Carey, *Empire of Hell: Religion and the Campaign to End Convict Transportation in the British Empire, 1788–1875* (Cambridge: Cambridge University Press, 2019), 19–20.

60. U.R.Q. Henriques, "The Rise and Decline of the Separate System of Prison Discipline," *Past and Present* 54 (1972): 91.
61. Nicholas Roe, *Fiery Heart: The First Life of Leigh Hunt* (London: Pimlico, 2005), 192.
62. See Helen Vendler, *The Odes of John Keats* (Cambridge, MA: Belknap Press, 1983); Jacqueline Labbe, *Romantic Visualities: Landscape, Gender and Romanticism* (New York: Palgrave Macmillan, 1998); and Rachel Crawford, *Poetry, Enclosure and the Vernacular Landscape, 1700–1830* (Cambridge: Cambridge University Press, 2002).
63. The manuscripts I use, housed in the Kent History and Library Centre in Maidstone, include the contract to build the prison, negotiated by one Francis-Motley Austen, Jane's first cousin once removed; extracts from meetings of East Kent justices (1804–1806) concerning the construction of the prison; architectural plans for the prison (1805–1806); and reports of Kent justices, including Edward Austen Knight, who drafted and administered rules for the new prison (1806–1811). See East Kent Gaol at Canterbury (Q/AGe), Kent Archives and Local History, Kent History and Library Centre, Maidstone, England.
64. See, for instance, Susannah Fullerton, *Jane Austen and Crime*, 3rd ed. (Madison, WI: Jones Books, 2006); Laura Mooneyham White, *Jane Austen's Anglicanism* (Burlington, VT: Ashgate, 2011); Stephen Wade, *Jane Austen's Aunt behind Bars: Writers and Their Criminal Relatives and Associates, 1700–1900* (London: Thames Rivers Press, 2013); and Sheryl Craig, *Jane Austen and the State of the Nation* (Basingstoke, UK: Palgrave Macmillan, 2015).

CHAPTER 1 — SOLITARY CONFINEMENT

1. Samuel Taylor Coleridge, "The Rime of the Ancyent Marinere," in *Poetical Works: Part 1. Poems (Reading Text)*, ed. J. C. C. Mays, no. 16 of *The Collected Works of Samuel Taylor Coleridge*, ed. Kathleen Coburn and Bart Winer (Princeton, NJ: Princeton University Press, 2001), lines 125, 195, 185–186. J. C. C. Mays prints the 1798 version of "The Rime of the Ancyent Marinere" side by side with the 1834 version. All references to the poem in the notes are from the 1798 version in this edition. I refer to the 1834 version once to cite a marginal comment by Coleridge.
2. Coleridge, "Ancyent Marinere," lines 177–180.
3. Michael O'Neill, "Poetry of the Romantic Period: Coleridge and Keats," in *A Companion to Romance: From Classical to Contemporary*, ed. Corinne Saunders (Malden, MA: Blackwell Press, 2007), 308.
4. See John Howard, *The State of the Prisons in England and Wales, with Preliminary Observations, and an Account of Some Foreign Prisons and Hospitals*, 3rd ed. (London: T. Cadell, J. Johnson and C. Dilly, 1784), 28–29.
5. DeLacy, *Prison Reform*, 91.
6. See Campbell, *Intolerable Hulks*, 35.
7. Coleridge, "Ancyent Marinere," lines 189.1.3–189.1.5, 192.
8. Coleridge, "Ancyent Marinere," line 202.1.
9. Coleridge, "Ancyent Marinere," lines 220–223.
10. In the 1834 version of the poem, Coleridge writes in a marginal note that "the ancient Mariner . . . proceedeth to relate his horrible penance" (Samuel Taylor Coleridge, "The Rime of the Ancient Mariner," in *Poetical Works*, no. 16 of *The Collected Works of Samuel Taylor Coleridge*, 391).
11. Coleridge, "Ancyent Marinere," lines 232–233, 234, 245–247, 282–283, 288–291.
12. Michael Murphy, "John Thelwall, Coleridge, and *The Ancient Mariner*," *Romanticism* 8, no. 1 (2002): 71.
13. Coleridge, "Ancyent Marinere," line 235.
14. Coleridge, "Ancyent Marinere," line 284.
15. *Oxford English Dictionary*, s.v. "dell, n.1," July 2023, https://doi.org/10.1093/OED/1045085729.

16. Coleridge, "This Lime-Tree Bower My Prison," in *The Collected Works of Samuel Taylor Coleridge*, line 10.
17. Reeve Parker, *Coleridge's Meditative Art* (Ithaca, NY: Cornell University Press, 1975), 45; Lucy Newlyn, *Coleridge, Wordsworth, and the Language of Allusion* (Oxford: Clarendon Press, 1986), 18; Charles J. Rzepka, "Thoughts in Prison/Imprisoned Thoughts: William Dodd's Forgotten Poem and the Incarceration Trope of Coleridge's 'This Lime-Tree Bower My Prison,'" *Romantic Circles*, October 2010, https://romantic-circles.org/editions/prison/HTML/poetryEEd.28intro.html, par. 72.
18. Coleridge, "This Lime-Tree Bower," lines 8, 14, 17, 27.
19. Coleridge, "Ancyent Marinere," lines 282, 285, 273.
20. Coleridge, "This Lime-Tree Bower," line 71.
21. W. B. Carnochan, "The Literature of Confinement," in *The Oxford History of the Prison: The Practice of Punishment in Western Society*, ed. Norval Morris and David J. Rothman (Oxford: Oxford University Press, 1998), 382.
22. John Colmer, "Coleridge and Politics," in *Writers and Their Background: S. T. Coleridge*, ed. R. L. Brett (Athens: Ohio University Press, 1972), 256.
23. Colmer, "Coleridge and Politics," 269, 246.
24. Colmer, "Coleridge and Politics," 245.
25. Peter J. Kitson, "Coleridge's Lectures 1795: On Politics and Religion," in *The Oxford Handbook of Samuel Taylor Coleridge*, online ed. (Oxford: Oxford Academic, 2009), 145.
26. Henriques, "Separate System," 91.
27. Ignatieff, *Just Measure of Pain*, 67.
28. Crawford, *Poetry, Enclosure*, 231.
29. Jeffrey C. Robinson, *The Current of Romantic Passion* (Madison: University of Wisconsin Press, 1991), 67.
30. Bugg, *Five Long Winters*, 77.
31. In marginalia written in 1833, Coleridge divides criminal offenders into three classes. Class one includes murderers, rapists, arsonists, and violent burglars, who, he claims, deserve death. Class two includes men and women who commit "crimes against the positive institutions of the Land," and who ruin their reputation in the process. These individuals deserve transportation for life. Class three includes all other offenses: "offences leaving hope of reform.—Restraint, Labor, &c—but without inflicting *ignominy*" (Coleridge, "Robert Southey, *History of Brazil*," in *Marginalia: Sherlock to Unidentified*, ed. H. J. Jackson and George Whalley, no. 12 of *The Collected Works of Samuel Taylor Coleridge*, 103). I read "This Lime-Tree Bower My Prison" as rationalizing the punishment of at least the third class of offenders, though I suspect that, in 1797, a younger and less conservative Coleridge may have had more hope than he did in 1833 even for criminals of the first and second classes.
32. Böker, "The Prison," 233, 237.
33. Coleridge, "Greek Epitaph for Howard's Tomb," in *The Collected Works of Samuel Taylor Coleridge*, 72.
34. Coleridge, "Reflections on Having Left a Place of Retirement," in *The Collected Works of Samuel Taylor Coleridge*, lines 49–50.
35. Coleridge, "Review of Count Rumford's Essays," in *The Watchman*, ed. Lewis Patton, no. 2 of *The Collected Works of Samuel Taylor Coleridge*, 176.
36. Coleridge, "The Dungeon," in *The Collected Works of Samuel Taylor Coleridge*, line 15.
37. Coleridge, "A Moral and Political Lecture," in *Lectures 1795 on Politics and Religion*, ed. Lewis Patton and Peter Mann, no. 1 of *The Collected Works of Samuel Taylor Coleridge*, 14; Coleridge, "Children in the Cotton Factories (31 Mar)," in *Essays on His Times*, ed. David Erdman, vol. 2, no. 3 of *The Collected Works of Samuel Taylor Coleridge*, 486.
38. See Coleridge, "On the Present War," in *Lectures 1795 on Politics and Religion*, ed. Lewis Patton and Peter Mann, no. 1 of *The Collected Works of Samuel Taylor Coleridge*, 65.
39. Jebb, *Polity of Prisons*, 7.

40. Jonas Hanway, *Solitude in Imprisonment . . . and Freedom from Violence* (London: J. Bew, 1776), 115.
41. Coleridge, "The Dungeon," lines 3, 23–24.
42. Coleridge, that is, was not a member of that radical sect, influenced by the French Revolution and its aftermath, which the *Edinburgh Review* in 1813 called "fanatics in politics, religion, or sentiment, who would have no imprisonment because it violates liberty" (Anonymous, "Art. I. *Theorie des Peines et des Recompenses.* Par M. Jeremie Bentham, Jurisconsulte Anglois. Redigée en Francois d'apres les Manuscrits, par M. Et. Dumont de Génève. 2 vol. 8vo. pp. 800. à Londres, Dulau, 1811," *Edinburgh Review* 22, no. 43 [1813]: 12).
43. Coldbath Fields had a reputation for brutality, especially in the first few decades of the nineteenth century. See Ignatieff, *Just Measure of Pain*, 131–141; J. Ann Hone, *For the Cause of Truth: Radicalism in London, 1796–1821* (Oxford: Clarendon Press, 1982), 122–128; Semple, *Bentham's Prison*, 255–257; Böker, "The Prison," 232; and Parolin, *Radical Spaces*, 49–82.
44. Coleridge, "The Devil's Thoughts," in *The Collected Works of Samuel Taylor Coleridge*, lines 29–32.
45. Coleridge attributes this stanza to Southey in three different notes to the poem, in his 1828, 1829, and 1834 *Poetical Works*. See J. C. C. Mays, editor, *Poetical Works II*, no. 16 of *The Collected Works of Samuel Taylor Coleridge*, 731–732.
46. Daniel Stuart, "The Abuse of Prisons," in *Essays on His Times*, ed. David Erdman, vol. 2, no. 3 of *The Collected Works of Samuel Taylor Coleridge*, 110.
47. Sara Coleridge, appendix to *Essays on His Own Times, Forming a Second Series of The Friend, by Samuel Taylor Coleridge, Edited by His Daughter* (London: William Pickering, 1850), 1033.
48. David Erdman, introduction to *Essays on His Times*, ed. David Erdman, vol. 1, no. 3 of *The Collected Works of Samuel Taylor Coleridge*, cxlvi.
49. Qtd in Lynda Pratt, "Interaction, Reorientation, and Discontent in the Coleridge-Southey Circle, 1797: Two New Letters by Robert Southey," *Notes and Queries* 47, no. 3 (2000): 317–318.
50. Pratt, "Interaction," 316.
51. Pratt, "Interaction," 316–317.
52. Labbe, *Romantic Visualities*, 101.
53. Labbe, *Romantic Visualities*, 101, 94–95.
54. It may be relevant that, from the late sixteenth century on, the word *rook* could mean a "disreputable" person, a "cheat, swindler, or sharper," as well as a Eurasian crow (*Oxford English Dictionary*, s.v. "rook, n.1," July 2023, https://doi.org/10.1093/OED/9481705620).
55. Coleridge, "This Lime-Tree Bower," lines 69–77; italics mine.
56. *Oxford English Dictionary*, s.v. "creak, v.," July 2023, https://doi.org/10.1093/OED/3963218266.
57. Coleridge, "The Dungeon," lines 25–30; italics mine.
58. Coleridge, "The Dungeon," line 21; *Oxford English Dictionary*, s.v. "distempered, adj.1," July 2023, https://doi.org/10.1093/OED/5909885705.
59. Michael Raiger, "The Poetics of Liberation in Imaginative Power: Coleridge's 'This Lime Tree Bower My Prison,'" *European Romantic Review* 3, no. 1 (1992): 72.
60. John Brewster, *Sermons for Prisons. To Which Are Added Prayers for the Use of Prisoners in Solitary Confinement* (Stockton: R. Christopher, 1790), 35–37. Or take James Neild, twenty-two years later, in 1812: "Solitary Confinement, as affording an opportunity to the reflective powers"—"an advantage which the hurrying scenes of vice are calculated to deny"—"presents a scheme of reform that at first sight warmly recommends itself for adoption." The key for Neild is to make sure that some "controuling power" exists in a prison to "check the apprehended evils of Total Seclusion" (James Neild, *State of the Prisons in England, Scotland, and Wales . . . to Explain and Improve the Condition of Prisoners in General* [London: John Nichols and Son, 1812], liv).
61. Coleridge, "This Lime-Tree Bower," lines 65–67.

62. The moralizing lines from "This Lime-Tree Bower My Prison"—"sometimes / 'Tis well to be bereft of promised good, / That we may lift the Soul"—imply that adding a restraint or privation to solitude is occasionally preferable, if it is morally required or advantageous. This is the poetic analogue of a third class of punishments that Jeremy Bentham calls "restrictive," which "consist in preventing the offender from enjoying, or doing something agreeable or useful to him" (Anonymous, "Art I. *Theorie des Peines*," 14). Compare Neild, who claims that "privations patiently endured, are the certain forerunners of reform" (Neild, *State of the Prisons*, lvii).
63. Brewster, *Sermons for Prisons*, xii.
64. Brewster, *Sermons for Prisons*, 152.
65. Brewster, *Sermons for Prisons*, 152, 177.
66. Anonymous, *The Prisoner's Companion; Containing Religious and Moral Advice, Adapted to Persons in Solitary Confinement* (London: Dodsley, 1785), 19.
67. J. H. D. Scourfield, "Consolatio," in *The Oxford Classical Dictionary*, revised 3rd ed., ed. Simon Hornblower and Antony Spawforth (Oxford: Oxford University Press, 2003), 378.
68. See, for instance, Anne E. Fernald, "Loneliness and Consolation," *Harvard Review* 12 (1997): 46–52. The poem has also been associated with pious texts written by seventeenth-century English Protestants, who saw earth as a prison and wrote meditations on Heaven so as to achieve "full affective awareness" of the afterlife (Parker, *Coleridge's Meditative Art*, 29).
69. Ulmer argues that the poem is exclusively meant to solace Lamb, not Coleridge. Coleridge and Lamb exchanged a series of letters between 1794 and 1798 that involved their shared Unitarian faith. Unitarianism became especially important to Charles after the tragic incident with his sister Mary in September 1796. In a few letters to Lamb, Coleridge encourages his friend "to adopt an attitude of Necessitarian resignation, to believe that the apparent evils of human experience are vehicles of divine benevolence, and that sufferings are the educative means of spiritual improvement" (William A. Ulmer, "The Rhetorical Occasion of 'This Lime-Tree Bower My Prison,'" *Romanticism* 13, no. 1 [2007]: 17). British evangelicals made similar points when discussing the administrative roles proper to penitential prisons. In 1782, the lawyer Manasseh Dawes advised prison chaplains that, while an inmate "suffers on the one hand his punishment with resignation, every hope should be awakened in him, that according to his sorrow and regret will be his future advantage and happiness" (M[anasseh] Dawes, *An Essay on Crimes and Punishments . . . of Morality [as the Source of all Good]* [London: C. Dilly; J. Debrett, 1782], 131).
70. Qtd. in Parker, *Coleridge's Meditative Art*, 53.
71. Zim, *Consolations of Writing*, 6.
72. K. M. Wheeler, *The Creative Mind in Coleridge's Poetry* (Cambridge, MA: Harvard University Press, 1981), 129; Raiger, "Poetics of Liberation," 75; Rachel Crawford, "Accident and Strange Calamity in 'This Lime-Tree Bower My Prison,'" *Romanticism* 2, no. 2 (1996): 201; Felicity James, "Agreement, Dissonance, Dissent: The Many Conversations of 'This Lime-Tree Bower,'" *The Coleridge Bulletin* 26 (2005): 49.
73. Labbe, *Romantic Visualities*, 94, 100.
74. Donald Davie, *Articulate Energy: An Inquiry into the Syntax of English Poetry* (London: Routledge and Paul, 1955), 73.
75. Stuart Curran, *Poetic Form and British Romanticism* (Oxford: Oxford University Press, 1986), 110.
76. James Engell, "Imagining into Nature: 'This Lime-Tree Bower My Prison,'" in *Critical Essays on Samuel Taylor Coleridge*, ed. Leonard Orr (New York: G. K. Hall, 1994), 111.
77. Wheeler, *Creative Mind*, 139.
78. Raiger, "Poetics of Liberation," 66.

CHAPTER 2 — WILLIAM GODWIN, "MILD COERCION," AND THE HAPPY PRISON TRADITION

1. William Godwin, "Of Ballot," in *Essays*, ed. Mark Philp and Austin Gee, vol. 6 of *PPW*, 210.
2. Godwin, "Of Ballot," 214–215.
3. Henriques, "Separate System," 63.
4. DeLacy, *Prison Reform*, 138.
5. Peter Marshall writes that Godwin officially became an atheist in 1792, although in 1800, at the instigation of Coleridge, he adopted a sort of "broad pantheism" (Peter Marshall, *William Godwin: Philosopher, Novelist, Revolutionary* [Oakland, CA: PM Press, 2017], 239).
6. Hanway, *Solitude in Imprisonment*, 44.
7. Hanway, *Solitude in Imprisonment*, 87; italics in original.
8. Jebb, *Polity of Prisons*, vii.
9. John Brewster, *On the Prevention of Crimes, and on the Advantages of Solitary Imprisonment* (London: W. Clark, J. Debrett and J. Johnson, 1792), 17.
10. John Howard, *An Account of the Principle Lazarettos in Europe . . . in Great Britain and Ireland*, 2nd ed. (London: J. Johnson, C. Dilly and T. Cadell, 1791), 226; italics in original.
11. William Godwin, *An Enquiry concerning Political Justice*, ed. Mark Philp and Austin Gee, vol. 3 of *PPW*, 378–379. Text references *Political Justice* are hereafter abbreviated *PJ*.
12. William Godwin, "Considerations on Lord Grenville's and Mr Pitt's Bills, concerning Treasonable and Seditious Practices and Unlawful Assemblies, by a Lover of Order," in *Political Writings II*, ed. Mark Philp and Austen Gee, vol. 2 of *PPW*, 126, 131.
13. William Godwin, "Of Reasoning and Contention," in *Educational and Literary Writings*, ed. Pamela Clemit, vol. 5 of *PPW*, 122.
14. Godwin, "Of Love and Friendship," in *Essays*, ed. Mark Philp and Austin Gee, vol. 6 of *PPW*, 192.
15. Godwin, "Of Love and Friendship," 198–199.
16. Dorothea von Mücke disagrees that the essay is generally uncharacteristic of Godwin, insisting that "Of Love and Friendship" is not as conservative as it seems: "in contrast to Edmund Burke . . . Godwin firmly believes that all inequality among men . . . derives from culture, not nature." She explains: "to the extent that it relates inequality to the specific cultural construction of courtly love, the citation . . . fits into . . . [Godwin's] political perspective" (Dorothea von Mücke, "'To Love a Murderer'—Fantasy, Sexuality, and the Political Novel: The Case of *Caleb Williams*," in *Cultural Institutions of the Novel*, ed. Deidre Lynch and William B. Warner [Durham, NC: Duke University Press, 1996], 308). This claim seems true in the letter, if not in the spirit, of Godwin's essay. "Of Love and Friendship" clearly indicates that Godwin is in no hurry to correct an enduring cultural construct like courtly love, which wears "all the tints of the rainbow" and makes modern love the wonderful institution that it is.
17. William Godwin, "On Liberty (Fragment)," in *Religious Writings, with Index to the Political and Philosophical Writings of Godwin*, ed. Mark Philp and Austin Gee, vol. 7 of *PPW*, 204.
18. McGowen claims, on a related note, that for most conservative, eighteenth-century Anglican priests, "fear was a most valuable human motive, not just for the criminal but for all members of society" (McGowen, "'He Beareth the Sword in Vain,'" 201).
19. Godwin, "On Liberty (Fragment)," 204.
20. William Godwin, *An Enquiry concerning Political Justice, Variants*, ed. Mark Philp, vol. 4 of *PPW*, 60.
21. Jerome McGann, *The Romantic Ideology: A Critical Investigation* (Chicago: University of Chicago Press, 1983), 1.

22. LeGette, "Lyric Speaker," 3. Two influential studies on this topic are Gillian Russell and Clara Tuite, eds., *Romantic Sociability: Social Networks and Literary Culture in Britain, 1770–1840* (Cambridge: Cambridge University Press, 2002); and Jeffrey N. Cox, "Communal Romanticism," *European Romantic Review* 15, no. 2 (2004): 329–334.
23. Rowland Weston, "Politics, Passion and the 'Puritan Temper': Godwin's Critique of Enlightened Modernity," *Studies in Romanticism* 41, no. 3 (2002): 445.
24. Godwin, "On Liberty (Fragment)," 205.
25. William Godwin, *Caleb Williams*, ed. Pamela Clemit, vol. 3 of *Collected Novels and Memoirs of William Godwin*, ed. Mark Philp (London: William Pickering, 1992), 332. Text references to *Caleb Williams* are hereafter abbreviated *CW.*
26. William Godwin, "Of Leisure," in *Essays*, ed. Mark Philp and Austin Gee, vol. 6 of *PPW*, 132.
27. Mona Scheuermann, "The Study of Mind: The Later Novels of William Godwin," *Forum for Modern Language Studies* 19, no. 1 (1983): 17.
28. Pamela Clemit, introduction to *The Letters of William Godwin*, vol. 1, *1778–1797* (Oxford: Oxford University Press, 2011), xlvi.
29. Ignatieff, *Just Measure of Pain*, 118.
30. Danby Pickering, ed., *The Statutes at Large, from Magna Charta to the End of the Eleventh Parliament of Great Britain, Anno 1761, Continued*, vol. 32 (London: Charles Bathurst, 1778), 419.
31. Henriques, "Separate System," 66.
32. Brewster, *Sermons for Prisons*, 33.
33. William Dodd, *Thoughts in Prison . . . with Some Account of the Author* (London: J. Mawman; Longman, Hurst, Rees, Orme and Brown; Baldwin, Cradock and Joy; Sherwood, Neely and Jones; Gale, Curtis and Fenner; and J. Walker and Co., 1815), 73.
34. Evans, *Fabrication of Virtue*, 71.
35. The aim of *Distributive Justice and Mercy* was to promote the principles behind the 1779 Penitentiary Act with an emphasis on what Hanway, on the title page, calls the "real Solitary Imprisonment of Convicts." It was published two years after the act passed. That same year, 1781, witnessed the well-known portrait of Sir Brooke Boothby, by Joseph Wright of Derby. In the portrait, a landowning amateur poet and philosopher lies by a sylvan stream, smartly dressed, pointing to his vellum-bound volume of Rousseau with a kind of distracted expression as he lifts his mind above the cares of the world. He seems to elevate his mind not despite, but because his body is so dramatically earthbound. His dun clothing and near-horizontal attitude make his body one with the earth he lies on. What is important is that each cultural text, *Distributive Justice and Mercy* and *Sir Brooke Boothby*, works to legitimate the other by serving as an ideological extension of it. Boothby is a leisured version of the man in the cell, and the man in the cell is a penal version of Boothby. The one has his Rousseau; the other, perhaps, a sermon left by the chaplain. Each is where he is to undo the injurious effects of worldliness.
36. Jonas Hanway, *Distributive Justice and Mercy . . . Safety, Honour, and Reputation of the People* (London: J. Dodsley, 1781), 42–43, 50–51, 195. On a related note, the founder of Methodism, John Wesley, argued that the "gestures, images, and phrases" at the assizes—the "ritual of the law" that was performed there—were addressed not only to criminals or potential criminals, but "to all of society." Wesley also believed that these rituals were rooted in the "religious principles which supported justice" (McGowen, "'He Beareth the Sword,'" 193).
37. Throness, *Protestant Purgatory*, 300.
38. Samuel Denne, *Letter to Sir Robert Ladbroke, Knt., Senior Alderman . . . the Confinement of Criminals in Separate Apartments* (London: J. and W. Oliver and J. Rivington, 1771), 38–40.
39. Denne, *Letter to Sir Robert Ladbroke*, 43.
40. Qtd. in Marshall, *William Godwin*, 298–299.

41. *Oxford English Dictionary*, s.v. "fermentation, n.," July 2023, https://doi.org/10.1093/OED/8522959678.
42. William Godwin, "Of Belief," in *Essays*, ed. Mark Philp and Austin Gee, vol. 6 of *PPW*, 177.
43. Godwin to Thomas Wedgwood, September 22, 1795, in *The Letters of William Godwin*, ed. Pamela Clemit, vol. 1, *1778–1797* (Oxford: Oxford University Press, 2014), 125.
44. Marshall, *William Godwin*, 158.
45. William Godwin, *Of Population. . . . Being an Answer to Mr. Malthus's Essay on that Subject*, in *Political Writings II*, ed. Mark Philp and Austen Gee, vol. 2 of *PPW*, 281.
46. William Godwin, "Of the Durability of Human Achievements and Productions," in *Essays*, ed. Mark Philp and Austin Gee, vol. 6 of *PPW*, 82.
47. Godwin, "Of the Durability."
48. In December 1801, Godwin married his second wife, Mary Jane Clairmont, and so "made a deep plunge indeed into domestic life since his celibate days before 1796." The "burdens and turmoils of this new life," moreover, weighed on Godwin, as he "struggled to support his family by the kind of writing which required quiet study" (Gary Kelly, *The English Jacobin Novel, 1780–1805* [Oxford: Clarendon Press, 1976], 257).
49. Cathy Collett, "Every Child Left Behind: *St. Leon* and William Godwin's Immortal Future," *European Romantic Review* 25, no. 3 (2014): 331.
50. Collett, "Every Child Left Behind."
51. William Godwin, *Mandeville*, ed. Pamela Clemit, vol. 6 of *CNM*, 43.
52. Godwin, *Mandeville*, 32. The similarities between the reformative prison cell, more or less invented in the early nineteenth century, and the monastic cell have frequently been noted. See, for instance, Foucault, *Discipline and Punish*, 143; Ignatieff, *Just Measure of Pain*, 53; Victor Brombert, *The Romantic Prison*: *The French Tradition* (Princeton, NJ: Princeton University Press, 1978), 3; McConville, *English Prison Administration*, 31; and Evans, *Fabrication of Virtue*, 60–65. Hilary M. Carey, in 2019, put the matter succinctly: in the late eighteenth and early nineteenth centuries, she writes, "across Christendom, the monastery had been the model for penal discipline in Christian states" (Carey, *Empire of Hell*, 13).
53. Godwin, *Mandeville*, 58, 24–25.
54. As James Neild put it in 1812: "When a principle is intrinsically good, it ought not to be relinquished, merely on the ground of difficulty to carry it into effect: And even should every attempt hitherto made of putting prisons for Solitary Confinement on an eligible footing be found to have failed, it would not follow from thence, that Solitary Confinement ought to be abandoned, as unequal to the beneficial ends proposed from it: But, so long as its possible utility is acknowledged, new attempts should be made to adopt such checks, as may effectually prevent the abuses apprehended, or complained of" (Neild, *State of the Prisons*, lv).
55. Peter Courtier, *Pleasures of Solitude. A Poem* (London: T. Gillet, 1800), 39–40.
56. Courtier, *Pleasures of Solitude*, 24.
57. William Wordsworth, "Preface to Lyrical Ballads, 1800," in *Lyrical Ballads, and Other Poems, 1797–1800*, ed. James Butler and Karen Green (Ithaca, NJ: Cornell University Press, 1992), 756–757.
58. Jonas Hanway, *The Neglect of the Effectual Separation of Prisoners, and the Want of Good Order and Religious Decorum in Our Prisons . . . in Fifteen Letters* (London: Dodsley; Sewell; Bew, 1784), 14; italics in original.
59. See Ian Watt, *The Rise of the Novel: Studies in Defoe, Richardson and Fielding* (Berkeley: University of California Press, 1957), 187–188.
60. Evans, *Fabrication of Virtue*, 70–71.
61. Crawford, *Poetry, Enclosure*, 5.
62. P. N. Furbank, "Godwin's Novels," *Essays in Criticism* 5, no. 37 (1955): 220.
63. See Roland Barthes, "An Introduction to the Structural Analysis of Narrative," *New Literary History* 6, no. 2 (1975): 247–248.

64. William Godwin, *Fleetwood*, ed. Pamela Clemit, vol. 5 of *CNM*, 193.
65. Godwin, *Fleetwood*, 195.
66. Godwin, *Fleetwood*, 194.
67. Godwin, *Fleetwood*, 17.
68. Godwin, *Fleetwood*, 18.
69. This passage reflects the pantheism to which Godwin converted, in 1800, at the instigation of Coleridge (see Marshall, *William Godwin*, 193).
70. B. J. Tysdahl, *William Godwin as Novelist* (London: Althone Press, 1981), 104.
71. Scheuermann, "Study of Mind," 19.
72. Julie Carlson, *England's First Family of Writers: Mary Wollstonecraft, William Godwin, Mary Shelley* (Baltimore: Johns Hopkins University Press, 2007), 49.
73. Brombert, *The Romantic Prison*, 81.
74. Brombert, *The Romantic Prison*, 87.
75. Denne, *Letter to Sir Robert*, 40.
76. Howard, *State of the Prisons*, 435.
77. Hanway, *Distributive Justice*, 93.
78. Brewster, *Sermons for Prisons*, 32; italics in original.
79. William Godwin, "Sketches of History. In Six Sermons," in *Religious Writings, with Index to the Political and Philosophical Writings of Godwin*, ed. Mark Philp and Austin Gee, vol. 7 of *PPW*, 21; italics in original.
80. Ps. 4:4–5 (KJV); italics mine.
81. Mat. 6:6 (KJV); italics mine.
82. William Godwin, "Of Trades and Professions," in *Educational and Literary Writings*, ed. Pamela Clemit, vol. 5 of *PPW*, 175.
83. Godwin, *Mandeville*, 91.
84. William Godwin, "Essay on Sepulchres: Or, a Proposal for Erecting Some Memorial of the Illustrious Dead in All Ages on the Spot Where Their Remains Have Been Interred," in *Essays*, ed. Mark Philp and Austin Gee, vol. 6 of *PPW*, 15.
85. C. H. Lawrence, *Medieval Monasticism: Forms of Religious Life in Western Europe in the Middle Ages*, 2nd ed. (London: Longman, 1989), 46.
86. William Godwin, "Autobiography," in *Autobiography, Autobiographical Fragments and Reflections, Godwin/Shelley Correspondence, Memoirs*, ed. Mark Philp, vol. 1 of *CNM*, 11–12.
87. Godwin, "Autobiography," 12; italics mine.
88. Godwin, "Autobiography," 26.
89. William Godwin, "Of the Rebelliousness of Man," in *Essays*, ed. Mark Philp and Austin Gee, vol. 6 of *PPW*, 94–95. Viewing the body as the prison of the soul is at least as old as Plato (e.g., *Phaedo*), not to mention commonplace among British and continental Protestants, including especially John Calvin. See Throness, *A Protestant Purgatory*, 61–62; and Zim, *Consolations of Writing*, 14–15.
90. William Godwin, "Of Deception and Frankness," in *Educational and Literary Writings*, ed. Pamela Clemit, vol. 5 of *PPW*, 126.
91. Godwin to Mary Wollstonecraft, June 9–10, 1797, in *The Letters of William Godwin*, ed. Pamela Clemit, vol. 1, *1778–1797* (Oxford: Oxford University Press, 2014), 216–217; Marshall, *William Godwin*, 158.
92. Godwin, *Fleetwood*, 27; Marshall, *William Godwin*, 158.
93. William Godwin, "Imogen," in *Damon and Delia, Italian Letters and Imogen*, ed. Pamela Clemit, vol. 2 of *CNM*, 231.
94. William Godwin, *St. Leon*, ed. Pamela Clemit, vol. 4 of *CNM*, 17. Text references to *St. Leon* are hereafter abbreviated *SL*.
95. William Godwin, *Cloudesley*, ed. Maurice Hindle, vol. 7 of *CNM*, 85.
96. William Godwin, "Of Religion," in *Religious Writings, with Index to the Political and Philosophical Writings of Godwin*, ed. Mark Philp and Austin Gee, vol. 7 of *PPW*, 71.

97. Marshall, *William Godwin*, 151; Marilyn Butler, *Jane Austen and the War of Ideas* (Oxford: Clarendon Press, 1975), 62; Tysdahl, *William Godwin as Novelist*, 37.
98. Brombert, *The Romantic Prison*, 63.
99. See Butler, *Jane Austen and the War of Ideas*, 62–72.
100. Cp. the Lady in Milton's *Comus*: "Thou canst not touch the freedom of my mind / With all thy charms, although this corporal rind / Thou hast immanacl'd" (John Milton, *A Mask Presented at Ludlow Castle, 1634 . . . Honorable Privy Council*, in *John Milton, Complete Poems and Major Prose*, ed. Merritt Y. Hughes (Indianapolis: Hackett, 2003), lines 663–665.
101. Cp. Milton's Satan: "The mind is its own place, and in itself / Can make a Heav'n of Hell, a Hell of Heav'n" (John Milton, *Paradise Lost*, in *John Milton, Complete Poems and Major Prose*, ed. Merritt Y. Hughes (Indianapolis: Hackett, 2003), Book 1, lines 254–255.
102. Terry Eagleton, *The English Novel: An Introduction* (Malden, MA: Blackwell, 2005), 35.
103. Zimmermann, *Solitude*,18–19.
104. Zim notes that "Shakespeare's notable historic prisoners, including King Lear and Richard II, consistently reflect the idea that prisoners are heroic representatives of humanity who gain philosophical and ethical enlightenment from their misfortunes, and even redeem themselves through various kinds of resistance as prisoners, and become capable of articulating important truths for others" (Zim, *Consolations of Writing*, 15).
105. William Shakespeare, *King Lear*, in *The Riverside Shakespeare*, ed. G. Blakemore Evans et al., 2nd ed. (Boston: Houghton Mifflin, 1997), 3.2.61–62.
106. Shakespeare, *King Lear* 3.4.102–108.
107. Anonymous, *Prisoner's Companion*, 7–8.
108. Hanway, *Solitude in Imprisonment*, 98–99; italics in original.
109. William Wordsworth, "Lines Written a Few Miles above Tintern Abbey, on Revisiting the Banks of the Wye during a Tour, July 13, 1798," in *Lyrical Ballads, and Other Poems, 1797–1800*, ed. James Butler and Karen Green (Ithaca, NY: Cornell University Press, 1992), lines 71–73.
110. Carnochan, *Confinement and Flight*, 42–43. Throness notes that, in the eighteenth century, "the search for innocence, the pastoral ideal, retirement, solitude and removal from conversation were all interwoven into a fictional genre," the Robinsonade, "patterned after its most famous example, *Robinson Crusoe*" (Throness, *Protestant Purgatory*, 222). In these eighteenth-century Robinsonades, solitude is never "freely chosen." Providence subjects heroes to it for their own good: "after a period of torment and difficulty each protagonist experienced moral development. . . . Although involuntary solitude might be painful at first, reflections upon Christian themes in a secluded environment could have a profoundly beneficial effect" (Throness, *Protestant Purgatory*, 228).
111. Godwin makes a similar point regarding his own affairs. In an 1801 letter of uncertain date to an unknown addressee, he remarks that being the victim of "misconstruction & censure" is actually "worse than a prison" (Godwin to Unknown, February–March 1801, in *The Letters of William Godwin*, ed. Pamela Clemit, vol. 2, *1798–1805* [Oxford: Oxford University Press, 2014], 210). On a related note, when, at one point in the novel, Caleb Williams calls himself "a prisoner, in the most intolerable sense of that term," he means nothing that has to do with a gaol. His "most intolerable" kind of imprisonment is being "tormented with a [conscious] secret, of which I must never disburthen myself" (*CW*, 124).
112. Bribery in such a situation seems to have been at least possible historically. Norman Roth notes that suspected heretics sentenced to "perpetual" imprisonment by the Spanish Inquisition, as St. Leon was, may not have been obliged to stay in prison until death. What was intended by "perpetual" imprisonment remains uncertain: "whether this was literally 'perpetual,' i.e., until death, or whether it was possible to bribe one's way out of prison eventually, is unclear from the sources" (Norman Roth, *Conversos, Inquisition, and the Expulsion of the Jews from Spain* [Madison: University of Wisconsin Press, 2002], 222). Henry Kamen,

on a related note, observes that two sixteenth-century heretical Christians, Isabel and Alcaraz de Cazalla, although "condemned to 'perpetual' prison" by the Inquisition, "were released after a few years" in the late 1530s (Henry Kamen, *The Spanish Inquisition: A Historical Revision*, 4th ed. [New Haven, CT: Yale University Press, 2014], 97).

113. St. Leon may be compared to Caleb Williams, or to Robinson Crusoe, in that he adapts to solitary confinement to considerable advantage. According to John Bender, for both Caleb Williams and Robinson Crusoe, "prison" becomes "equated with solitary reflection" and "is first viewed as negative, random, punitive, vengeful; but it slides into another thing entirely—something salubrious, beneficent, reformative, and productive of wealth and social integration" (Bender, *Imagining the Penitentiary*, 55). Compare this statement to one by Hanway on the ultimate virtues of solitary confinement: Hanway writes that although solitude in prison is, "for a time, nauseous to the taste, or terrible to the imagination," eventually it becomes a "balmy remedy" (Hanway, *Solitude in Imprisonment*, 42).
114. Silvia Granata, "Poisonous Language: Mental Slavery and Self-Recognition in Godwin's *Mandeville*," *Confronto Letterario: Quaderni del Dipartimento di lingue e Letterature Straniere Moderne dell'Università di Pavia* 26, no. 51 (2009): 85.
115. Marilyn Butler and Mark Philp, introduction to *Autobiography, Autobiographical Fragments and Reflections, Godwin/Shelley Correspondence*, ed. Mark Philp, vol. 1 of *CNM*, 33.
116. Anne Chandler, "Romanticizing Adolescence: Godwin's 'St. Leon' and the Matter of Rousseau," *Studies in Romanticism* 41, no. 3 (2002): 405.
117. Ellen Lévy has rightly noted that, "in the course of [his] successive imprisonments," St. Leon "moves from indignation to metaphysical speculation to the discovery of the powers of the imagination" (Ellen Lévy, "The Philosophical Gothic of *St Leon*," *Caliban* 33 (1996): 52–53.
118. Thomas Malthus, *An Essay on the Principle of Population*, ed. Geoffrey Gilbert (Oxford: Oxford University Press, 1993), 10.
119. Malthus, *Principle of Population*, 149.
120. Malthus, *Principle of Population*, 151.
121. Malthus, *Principle of Population*, 105.
122. Zim, *Consolations of Writing*, 6.
123. At one point in the *Consolation*, Lady Philosophy tells Boethius that she has "swift and speedy wings / With which to mount the lofty skies, / And when the mind has put them on / The earth below it will despise" (Boethius, *On the Consolation of Philosophy*, trans. and ed. Victor Watts, revised ed. [New York: Penguin, 1999], 86). Lady Philosophy goes on to dramatize the ascent of the mind to God, who both she and Boethius have agreed is the source and center of the universe. St. Leon, for his part, seems destined never to leave the earth, though in the end he does come to despise it. *His* winged lady carries him just high enough to foresee the destruction of the Hungarian castle. Note that Godwin read a translation of the *Consolation* by Chaucer. His sale catalogue also lists a 1609 translation (by one J. T.) of Book 5 of the *Consolation*. See William Godwin, *The Diary of William Godwin*, ed. Victoria Myers, David O'Shaughnessy and Mark Philp (Oxford: Oxford Digital Library, 2010), http://godwindiary.bodleian.ox.ac.uk/bibl/te1306.html. The *Consolation* is not the only text written by a Catholic martyr from inside a prison to which *St. Leon* alludes. The Hungarian setting at the beginning of the novel's fourth volume recalls the setting used by Thomas More in his theodicy, *A Dialogue of Comfort against Tribulation*. More wrote *A Dialogue* in 1534 while imprisoned in the Tower of London and awaiting execution. But the actual events of his text—a dialogue between the young Vincent and his old uncle Antony—are set not in London but in Buda, capital of the Kingdom of Hungary, between 1527 and 1528, about a year after Suleiman the magnificent defeated the last native Hungarian king, Louis II, in 1526. As it happens, St. Leon mentions the defeat of Louis II when giving the background for his own adventures in Hungary, which begin in 1560.

124. Amy S. Kaufman observes that the Lady of the Lake, Nynyve, "is based on a character in French legends on whom Malory greatly expands" in his own version of Arthurian legend, adding that as an "imprisoned writer suffering from the distance of love and the fickleness of his leaders," Malory "may have found comfort in the fantasy of an objective and omnipotent guardian angel"—i.e., the Lady of the Lake—"who acts as an agent of justice in the material world" (Amy S. Kaufman, "'For This Was Drawyn by a Knyght Presoner': Sir Thomas Malory and *Le Morte Darthur*," in *Prison Narratives from Boethius to Zana*, ed. P. Phillips [New York: Palgrave Macmillan, 2014], 46–47).
125. Dodd, *Thoughts in Prison*, 115, 110.
126. Addison, "No. 411," 537.
127. Rousseau, *Confessions*, 144.
128. Zimmermann, *Solitude*, 238.
129. Brombert, *The Romantic Prison*, 36.
130. Anonymous, "Art. IX. *St. Leon, a Tale of the Sixteenth Century*, by William Godwin. . . . 1799," *The British Critic* 15 (1800): 48.
131. William D. Brewer, introduction to *St. Leon: A Tale of the Sixteenth Century* (Peterborough, ON, Canada: Broadview, 2005), 22–23.
132. Frederick Freiherr von der Trenck, *The Strange Adventures of Frederick Baron Trenck*, ed. Philip Murray (New York: Frederick A. Stokes, 1927), 2–3.
133. Trenck, *Strange Adventures*, 101–102.
134. Trenck, *Strange Adventures*, 173.
135. Trenck, *Strange Adventures*, 227.
136. Trenck, *Strange Adventures*, 239.
137. Thomas Holcroft [as T. Strickland], *A Plain and Succinct Narrative of the Late Riots and Disturbances in the Cities of London and Westminster, and Borough of Southwark. . . . with an Account of the Commitment of Lord George Gordon to the Tower, and Anecdotes of His Life*, 3rd ed. (London: Fielding and Walker, 1780), 28.
138. Holcroft, *Plain and Succinct Narrative*, 38.
139. Campbell, *Intolerable Hulks*, 42.
140. Trenck, *Strange Adventures*, 157.
141. Ann Blainey, *Immortal Boy: A Portrait of Leigh Hunt* (New York: St Martin's Press, 1985), 79.
142. Martha Grace Duncan, *Romantic Outlaws, Beloved Prisons: The Unconscious Meanings of Crime and Punishment* (New York: New York University Press, 1996), 11.
143. As he says: "I read, wrote, and became so busy that I almost forgot I was a prisoner" (Trenck, *Strange Adventures*, 196).
144. Hanway, *Distributive Justice*, 177; italics in original.
145. William Godwin, *Deloraine*, ed. Maurice Hindle, vol. 8 of *CNM*, 8. Text references to *Deloraine* are hereafter abbreviated *DE*.
146. Shakespeare, *King Lear*, 5.3.8–19.
147. Arthur Griffiths calls Millbank a "labyrinth" with "angles every twenty yards, winding staircases, dark passages, innumerable doors and gates." He recalls that "an old warder" who served there for years was "unable, to the last, to find his way about the premises" without a "piece of chalk" (Arthur Griffiths, *Memorials of Millbank and Chapters in Prison History* [London: Chapman and Hall, 1884], 27). Ignatieff describes Millbank as an "enormous warren of passages and cells built in the style of a turreted medieval fortress near the Houses of Parliament" (Ignatieff, *Just Measure of Pain*, 188).
148. Deloraine and Godwin happen to have similar work routines, the one in his castle-prison and the other in his London home. William St. Clair recalls how in the early 1790s Godwin "settled to a pattern which he was to maintain for most of his life. He rose early and would read from the work of a Greek or Latin author before breakfast." For the rest of the morning he would write and read. In the afternoons he would make and receive visits (William St. Clair, *The Godwins and the Shelleys: The Biography of a Family* [Baltimore: Johns Hopkins University Press, 1989], 59).

149. Milton, *Paradise Lost*, Book 1, lines 254–255; italics mine.
150. Ranita Chatterjee suggests that Catherine serves Deloraine both as his dutiful daughter and as his devoted wife (she is around the age of his deceased wife Margaret), as if "all heterosexual relations under patriarchy are figuratively incestuous" (Ranita Chaterjee, "Filial Ties: Godwin's *Deloraine* and Mary Shelley's Writings," *European Romantic Review* 18, no. 1 [2007]: 37).
151. DeLacy, *Prison Reform*, 207.
152. Ignatieff, *Just Measure of Pain*, 102.
153. William Godwin, "On the History and Effects of the Christian Religion," in *Religious Writings, with Index to the Political and Philosophical Writings of Godwin*, ed. Mark Philp, vol. 6 of *PPW*, 202.
154. Cervantes and Porter, "Extreme Empiricism," 106.
155. Cervantes and Porter, "Extreme Empiricism," 106–107.
156. Hanway, *Solitude in Imprisonment*, 61.
157. Note that Deloraine feels transcendent joy as an illness is *leaving* his body. Charles Mandeville in *Mandeville*, on the other hand, feels the same kind of ecstasy when he is *actually* bedridden and enervated with pain. The one pleasure is negative—pleasure exclusively in the absence of something bad; the other pleasure is positive—indulging in an ostensible misfortune for its own sake. At one point in *Mandeville*, Charles is thrown from his horse and severely injured. He spends several weeks at a farmhouse in Derbyshire, "confined to . . . [his] bed under the care of . . . surgeons" and nursed by the villainous Mallison. For fourteen days, Mandeville is "required to continue in one attitude, my body straitened, and my face turned toward the zenith." He says that his "situation perfectly resembled that of a prisoner," since, after all, he "had no real sickness, and suffered only a compulsory confinement." *Only* a compulsory confinement—as though that were a small price to pay for the joy of being attended by a villain for weeks on end in a supine and locked position. Yet his immobility on a prison bed and the attendance of someone like Mallison bring Mandeville undeniable joy. In his rigid confinement he has the privilege of being "shut up within the circle of his actual sensations," so that "a sort of deadness as to external things comes over him." On his sickbed, as with Deloraine in his convalescence, the "world is nothing to him; its vexations and embarrassments are absolutely annihilated and forgotten." He feels "ashamed to own," in fact, "that this was to me a period of unwonted enjoyment" (Godwin, *Mandeville*, 239, 246–247).

CHAPTER 3 — THE DESCENT OF LIBERTY

1. Prominent among twenty-first-century studies of Hunt is *The Selected Writings of Leigh Hunt*, a six-volume collection published in 2003 by Pickering and Chatto, totaling 2,784 pages. In 2005, the first scholarly, full-length biographies of Hunt appeared: Nicholas Roe's *Leigh Hunt: Life, Poetics, Politics* (Pimlico) and Anthony Holden's *The Wit in the Dungeon* (Little, Brown).
2. Virginia Woolf, *The Diary of Virginia Woolf*, ed. Anne Olivier Bell and Andrew McNellie, 1st Harvest ed., vol. 2, *1920–1924* (Orlando: Harcourt, Brace, 1980), 130. The entry is for August 13, 1921.
3. Leigh Hunt, "The Prince on St Patrick's Day," *Examiner*, no. 221, March 22, 1812, 179, *British Newspaper Archive*, http://www.britishnewspaperarchive.co.uk.
4. See Edmund Blunden, *Leigh Hunt and His Circle* (New York: Harper and Brothers, 1930), 68–69.
5. Stewart writes that "by the end of the *Examiner*'s first year, Leigh Hunt estimated sales of 2,200, but this increased, particularly during his time in prison from 1813–1815, to above 7,000 weekly" (David Stewart, *Romantic Magazines and Metropolitan Literary Culture* [New York: Palgrave Macmillan, 2011], 123).
6. Radzinowicz, *Movement for Reform*, 253.

7. McConville, *English Prison Administration*, 117.
8. Webb and Webb, *English Prisons*, 62.
9. All quotations from *Rimini* come from the 1816 version of the poem, as printed in the first volume of *SWLH*. Text references to *Rimini* are hereafter abbreviated *R* and formatted as follows: *R*, 3.12 for *Rimini*, canto 3, line 12.
10. Hunt expands on the tale, as found in Dante, considerably: "Whilst it takes only thirteen lines to relate the consummation of illicit passion in Francesca's bower in Cary's Dante (*Inferno* V. 123–135), Hunt's *Rimini* takes more than 100 lines merely to describe the garden" (Ayumi Mizukoshi, *Keats, Hunt and the Aesthetics of Pleasure* [Basingstoke, UK: Palgrave Macmillan, 2001], 67).
11. It is difficult to say exactly how much of the third canto—or even the poem as a whole—Hunt actually wrote in prison. On the one hand, in the first edition of *Rimini*, published in 1816, Hunt included a single note at the start of Canto 3: "The preceding canto, and a small part of the present, were written in prison" (*R*, 182). On the other hand, in his *Autobiography* he says that "the greater part" of *Rimini* "was written in prison" (Leigh Hunt, *The Autobiography of Leigh Hunt*, ed. J. E. Morpurgo [London: The Cresset Press, 1948], 257).
12. Leigh Hunt, "Upon the Necessity of a Reform in the Criminal Law of England," *Examiner*, no. 22, May 29, 1808, 338, *British Newspaper Archive*, http://www.britishnewspaperarchive.co.uk.
13. Neild, *State of the Prisons*, 547, 551, 548, 549, 550.
14. Critics are divided on how to interpret the statements, both private and public, that Hunt made about his time in prison. Blainey argues that "Hunt's imprisonment was, publicly and personally, a triumph. Deriving maximum pleasure from his study and work, enjoying an ever enlarging group of friends and rejoicing in the support of his family, he escaped what had seemed an inevitable breakdown" (Blainey, *Immortal Boy*, 73). This comment was made in 1985; Eberle-Sinatra reinforces it twenty years later: "Most critics now consider Hunt's imprisonment for seditious libel to have been one of the most positive events in his life" (Michael Eberle-Sinatra, *Leigh Hunt and the London Literary Scene: A Reception History of His Major Works, 1805–1828* [New York: Routledge, 2005], 31). "Most critics" felt this way when Eberle-Sinatra was writing, but not all. Clarice Short, for one, claims that Hunt wrote *Rimini* "to palliate the dreariness of his term in prison"; Kucich, that Hunt was "beset in prison by . . . the psychological anxiety of entrapment"; Hessell, that "Hunt's brave attempts to make jail bearable should not necessarily be construed as delight in the prison experience"; and Webb, that prison for Hunt was comprised of "painful and boring realities" (Clarice Short, "The Composition of Hunt's 'The Story of Rimini,'" *Keats-Shelley Journal* 21/22 [1972/1973]: 207; Greg Kucich, "Leigh Hunt and Romantic Spenserianism," *Keats-Shelley Journal* 37 [1988]: 116; Nikki Hessell, "Jailhouse Journalism: Leigh Hunt and the 'Examiner,' 1813–1815," *Keats-Shelley Journal* 54 [2005]: 82; and Timothy Webb, "Stories of Rimini: Leigh Hunt, Byron and the Fate of Francesca," in *Dante in the Nineteenth Century: Reception, Canonicity, Popularization*, ed. Nick Havely [Bern, Switzerland: Peter Lang, 2011], 43). These latter four statements read more as inferences than evidence-based conclusions.
15. In 1813, Hunt wrote to his wife Marianne that "there was no getting at his [i.e., John's] tendernesses before, through that iron philosophy of his; but by the help of this additional metal coating [i.e., Coldbath Fields, where John was sentenced], the other [i.e., John's "iron philosophy"] is melting away a little,—as far as it ought" (Hunt to Marianne Hunt, May 31, 1813, in *Leigh Hunt: A Life in Letters, Together with Some Correspondence of William Hazlitt*, ed. Eleanor M. Gates [Essex, CT: Falls River Publications, 1999], 45). Around halfway through their sentences, Hunt told his *Examiner* audience: "My brother has not enjoyed better health for years:—indeed, a little after his going to prison, I had a letter from him in which he told me that for years he had not enjoyed health so good; and I rejoice to say, that with the exception of that overwhelming week of fog, it has remained

uninterrupted" (Leigh Hunt, "Expiration of the First Year's Imprisonment of the Proprietors," *Examiner*, no. 310, February 6, 1814, 82, *British Newspaper Archive*, http://www.britishnewspaperarchive.co.uk). As to his own health, at the end of his sentence Hunt wrote in the *Examiner* that "The Editor . . . is now about to emerge from prison, better in health than when he entered it" (Leigh Hunt, "New Prospectus of *The Examiner*," *Examiner*, no. 365, December 25, 1814, 819, *British Newspaper Archive*, http://www.britishnewspaperarchive.co.uk).

16. Near the end of his sentence, Hunt reports to the *Examiner*: "We must mention also a two-year's [*sic*] imprisonment, as a circumstance that has increased our stock of ideas" (Leigh Hunt, "The Round Table, No. 1," *Examiner*, no. 366, January 1, 1815, 12, *British Newspaper Archive*, http://www.britishnewspaperarchive.co.uk).
17. "Even the freer side of the party papers have rather raised than lowered their tone since our condemnation: and by the direct and loud increase in that of some of our brother Reformists, some persons have supposed, as they did of us, that they would rather court than avoid our fate" (Leigh Hunt, "Expiration of the First Year's Imprisonment of the Proprietors," 82).
18. Hunt himself notes that he first met Shelley in prison (Hunt, *Autobiography*, 247). His correspondence with Lord Byron, moreover, began soon after Byron started visiting him at Surrey Gaol (Timothy Webb, "After Horsemonger Lane: Leigh Hunt's London Letters to Byron [1815–1816]," *Romanticism* 16, no. 3 [2010]: 233). In their respective prisons, "John and he, though separated in flesh, had never been closer in spirit" (Blainey, *Immortal Boy*, 61). Roe observes that the "adult intimacy" between Hunt and Marianne "dated from their months together in the heart of the prison, a time when Hunt also became 'more of a lover' for Marianne" (Roe, *Fiery Heart*, 195). In the *Examiner*, at the onset of his sentence, Hunt wrote: "separation has only brought the hearts of our friends into closer contact with us; and we have had even from strangers those cordial graspings of the hand, which speak volumes of manly good-will.—I trust, that when the hand that is now writing shall have grown too feeble to hold a pen, the feel of that strenuous honesty shall still be living in it's [*sic*] palm" (Leigh Hunt, "Sentence Against the Examiner, with an Observation or Two on Some Proposals of a Subscription," *Examiner*, no. 269, February 21, 1813, 113, *British Newspaper Archive*, http://www.britishnewspaperarchive.co.uk). Along these same lines, Roe says that the prison years "provided the basis for the inclusive 'family of love' . . . [that Hunt] would endeavor to establish with Marianne, her sister Bess, the Shelleys, and a wider circle of men and women" (Nicholas Roe, preface to *Fiery Heart: The First Life of Leigh Hunt* [London: Pimlico, 2005], xvi.
19. Leigh Hunt, *The Correspondence of Leigh Hunt. Edited by His Eldest Son. With a Portrait. In Two Volumes*, ed. Thornton Hunt, vol. 1 (London: Smith, Elder and Co., 1862), 79.
20. Hunt, *Correspondence*, 80.
21. James Thompson, *Leigh Hunt* (Boston: G. K. Hall & Co., 1977), 28.
22. Leigh Hunt, *The Feast of the Poets*, in *Poetical Works, 1801–21*, edited by John Strachan, vol. 5 of *SWLH*, 78n26.
23. Hunt to Marianne Hunt, April 29, 1813, in *Leigh Hunt: A Life in Letters*, 31.
24. Hunt to Marianne Hunt, May 29, 1813, in *Leigh Hunt: A Life in Letters*, 40.
25. Leigh Hunt, *The Descent of Liberty*, in *Poetical Works, 1801–21*, edited by John Strachan, vol. 5 of *SWLH*, lines 568–570.
26. Blainey, *Immortal Boy*, 64. Adherence to strict time schedules is a running theme in the prison letters: "I have not been idle with my pen, I assure you,—as you will find when you return"; "Betsy tells me my time [for writing this letter] is almost out"; "Betsy tells me, all of a sudden, that I have but ten minutes" (Hunt to Marianne Hunt, May 4, 1813, in *Leigh Hunt: A Life in Letters*, 36; Hunt to Marianne Hunt, May 10, 1813, in *Leigh Hunt: A Life in Letters*, 38; Hunt to Marianne Hunt, May 31, 1813, in *Leigh Hunt: A Life in Letters*, 47). The dinners he hosted for his friends in prison became as regularly scheduled as his studies. He wrote to Marianne: "Moore & Lord Byron dine with me today at *4*; so I have just been taking my luncheon at 2, & then sat down to write to you" (Hunt

to Marianne Hunt, May 20, 1813, in *Leigh Hunt: A Life in Letters*, 40). He also sent two letters to Charles Cowden Clark, respectively on July 13, 1813, and January 5, 1814, to the same effect: "Remember, we dine at three!"; "You know our dinner-hour" (qtd. in John Barnard, "Leigh Hunt and Charles Cowden Clark, 1812–18," in *Leigh Hunt: Life, Poetics, Politics*, ed. Nicholas Roe [London: Routledge, 2003], 35, 38).

27. Leigh Hunt, "Postscript," in *Periodical Essays, 1805–14*, ed. Greg Kucich and Jeffrey N. Cox, vol. 1 of *SWLH*, 307.
28. Leigh Hunt, "New Prospectus of *The Examiner*," 820.
29. See Stewart, *Romantic Magazines*, 129.
30. Leigh Hunt, "The Prince and Princess of Wales," *Examiner*, no. 271, March 7, 1813, 145, *British Newspaper Archive*, http://www.britishnewspaperarchive.co.uk. A week after he wrote these words, Hunt reminded his audience that he was still "abstracted from the rest of the bustle" (Leigh Hunt, "Prince and Princess of Wales," *Examiner*, no. 272, March 14, 1813, 161, *British Newspaper Archive*, http://www.britishnewspaperarchive.co.uk).
31. Blainey, *Immortal Boy*, 63.
32. Anthony Holden, *The Wit in the Dungeon: The Remarkable Life of Leigh Hunt—Poet, Revolutionary, and the Last of the Romantics* (New York: Little, Brown, 2005), 85.
33. Hunt added over a hundred or so pages of endnotes, drafted in prison, for the 1814 edition of *The Feast of the Poets*, originally published in *The Reflector* in 1811. The longest of these notes is a twenty-three-page disquisition, mostly positive, on Wordsworth's poetic genius. For Wordsworth, the note could not have come at a better time. His 1807 *Poems, in Two Volumes* had been badly reviewed, and his massive poem *The Excursion* (1814) had received a scathing critique in November 1814 by Francis Jeffrey. Thus in his note on Wordsworth in *The Feast of the Poets*, Hunt not only developed "increasing confidence as a literary critic," but also "took the lead in identifying the beauties and explaining the defects of Wordsworth's poetry, thereby initiating the critical reassessment which would establish Wordsworth's reputation for the nineteenth and twentieth centuries" (Eberle-Sinatra, *Leigh Hunt and the London Literary Scene*, 33; Roe, *Fiery Heart*, 5).
34. Greg Kucich, "Cockney Chivalry: Hunt, Keats and the Aesthetics of Excess," in *Leigh Hunt: Life, Poetics, Politics*, ed. Nicholas Roe (London: Routledge, 2003), 125. Blainey calls *Rimini* a "milestone in English literature" (Blainey, *Immortal Boy*, 77). Kucich adds that this one poem made Hunt a "leading poet," "establish[ed] an important model of progressive gender relations among the period's second generation of writers" and advanced an "aesthetic excess that mocks authority and blurs social and political hierarchies" (Kucich, "Leigh Hunt and Romantic Spenserianism," 121; Greg Kucich, "'The wit in the dungeon': Leigh Hunt and the Insolent Politics of Cockney Coteries," *European Romantic Review* 10, nos. 1–4 [1999]: 243; and Kucich, "Cockney Chivalry," 121).
35. Will Bowers, *The Italian Idea: Anglo-Italian Radical Literary Culture, 1815–1823* (Cambridge: Cambridge University Press, 2010), 33.
36. Rodney Stenning Edgecombe, *Leigh Hunt and the Poetry of Fancy* (Madison, NJ: Fairleigh Dickinson University Press, 1994), 71.
37. Hunt, *Autobiography*, 236.
38. Hunt, *Autobiography*, 241–242.
39. Hunt, *Autobiography*, 243.
40. Roe, *Fiery Heart*, 2.
41. Hunt, *Autobiography*, 244.
42. Hunt, *Autobiography*,
43. Thomas Lloyd, "Impositions and Abuses in the Management of the Jail of Newgate; Pointed Out and Exposed, in a Letter Addressed to the Late Grand Juries of the City of London and County of Middlesex," in *Newgate in Revolution: An Anthology of Radical Prison Literature in the Age of Revolution*, ed. Michael T. Davis, Iain McCalman and Christina Parolin (London: Continuum, 2005), 72.

44. Hunt to Marianne Hunt, May 4, 1813; Hunt to Marianne Hunt, May 10, 1813; Hunt to Marianne Hunt, May 20, 1813; Hunt to Marianne Hunt, May 25, 1813; Hunt to Marianne Hunt, May 29, 1813; Hunt to Marianne Hunt, May 31, 1813; Hunt to Marianne Hunt, June 10, 1813; Hunt to Marianne Hunt, June 11, 1813; all in *Leigh Hunt: A Life in Letters*, 33–35, 37, 40, 42, 44–45, 46, 52, 53.
45. Hunt, *Autobiography*, 245.
46. Leigh Hunt, "Sentence Against the Examiner, and Summary of Objections to the Whole of the Proceedings Connected with It (*Concluded.*)," *Examiner*, no. 270, February 28, 1813, 129, *British Newspaper Archive*, http://www.britishnewspaperarchive.co.uk.
47. Hunt, *Autobiography*, 244.
48. Hunt, *Autobiography*.
49. Karl Kroeber, *Romantic Narrative Art* (Madison: University of Wisconsin Press, 1960), 122; Thomas Goggans, "Deferred Desire and the Management of Tone in Leigh Hunt's 'The Story of Rimini,'" *Keats-Shelley Journal* 50 (2001): 98; Webb, "Stories," 43; and Howard Felperin, *Shakespearean Romance* (Princeton, NJ: Princeton University Press, 1972), 40.
50. Jane Stabler, "Leigh Hunt's Aesthetics of Intimacy," in *Leigh Hunt: Life, Poetics, Politics*, ed. Nicholas Roe (London: Routledge, 2003), 109.
51. Blunden, *Leigh Hunt and His Circle*, 89.
52. Thompson, *Leigh Hunt*, 22.
53. Roe, *Fiery Heart*, 225.
54. Holden, *Wit in the Dungeon*, 91.
55. Holden notes that Hunt's "ornate little study" at Maida Vale, "looking out from Edgware Road across the fields towards rural Westbourne," was "for all the world a re-creation of his prison 'salon'" (Holden, *Wit in the Dungeon*, 93).
56. Hunt, *Autobiography*, 251.
57. Leigh Hunt, "Departure of the Proprietors of This Paper from Prison," *Examiner*, no. 361, February 5, 1815, 81, *British Newspaper Archive*, http://www.britishnewspaperarchive.co.uk.
58. Milton, *Paradise Lost*, Book IX, line 646.
59. Leigh Hunt, "Sentence Against the Examiner (*Continued from last week's*)," *Examiner*, no. 268, February 14, 1813, 97, *British Newspaper Archive*, http://www.britishnews paperarchive.co.uk.
60. Hunt to Marianne Hunt, June 10, 1813, in *Leigh Hunt: A Life in Letters*, 51.
61. Leigh Hunt, "Upon the Necessity of a Reform in the Criminal Law of England," 337–338.
62. The anonymous correspondent writes: "As you, Mr. Examiner, have *heretofore* been the mighty means of exciting Ministers to *many* despicable deeds of anger, I trust that you may *now* be the gentler means of inciting them to *one grand and noble one*" (Thismiames, "Penitentiary House," *Examiner*, no. 131, July 1, 1810, 408, *British Newspaper Archive*, http://www.britishnewspaperarchive.co.uk).
63. See, for instance: Anonymous, "Newgate Prison," *Examiner*, no. 316, January 16, 1814, 44–45, *British Newspaper Archive*, http://www.britishnewspaperarchive.co.uk; Anonymous, "Newgate Prison," *Examiner*, no. 318, January 30, 1814, 78–79, *British Newspaper Archive*, http://www.britishnewspaperarchive.co.uk; and Anonymous, "London and Southwark Prisons," *Examiner*, no. 338, June 19, 1814, 390–391, *British Newspaper Archive*, http://www.britishnewspaperarchive.co.uk.
64. Anonymous, "General View of the Arguments in Favour of an Amelioration of the Penal Laws," *Examiner*, no. 352, September 25, 1814, 621, *British Newspaper Archive*, http://www.britishnewspaperarchive.co.uk. This article is continued in no. 365, December 25, 1814, 828–830.
65. Anonymous, "Prison Discipline," *Examiner*, no. 701, June 10, 1821, 360, *British Newspaper Archive*, http://www.britishnewspaperarchive.co.uk.
66. J. F., "Prison Discipline," *Examiner*, no. 717, September 30, 1821, 621, *British Newspaper Archive*, http://www.britishnewspaperarchive.co.uk.

67. Anonymous, "Mr. Justice Park—Prison Discipline," *Examiner*, no. 721, October 28, 1821, 673, *British Newspaper Archive*, http://www.britishnewspaperarchive.co.uk.
68. Anonymous, "Mr. Justice Park—Prison Discipline," 674.
69. Leigh Hunt, "Upon the Necessity of a Reform in the Criminal Law of England," 338; emphasis mine.
70. An example of Huntean spontaneity: using the "illusion" of spontaneity "to create a sense" that a poem "fulfil[s] laws and articulate[s] insights that exist only in the process of composition" (Michael O'Neill, "'Even now while I write': Leigh Hunt and Romantic Spontaneity," in *Leigh Hunt: Life, Poetics, Politics*, ed. Nicholas Roe [London: Routledge, 2003], 135).
71. Edgecombe likewise notes that "a cold north" here is "set in opposition to the 'warm south' of the poem, and so measures the strength of the imaginative flights that have gone into its creation" (Edgecombe, *Leigh Hunt and the Poetry of Fancy*, 72).
72. One critic claims—wrongly, I would say—that "Hunt's poetic escapism retains an ironic consciousness of its own artificiality. Though this therapeutic exercise provides him with a 'tear-dipped and healing' catharsis, nevertheless Hunt actively parodies this sort of indulgence through Francesca's dangerous tendency to indulge in the reading of romances" (Goggans, "Deferred Desire," 97).
73. Hunt, *Autobiography*, 164.
74. Hunt, *Autobiography*, 165–166.
75. Stewart notes that Hunt created a new *Examiner* that combined "a 'literary air' with political comment" (Stewart, *Romantic Magazines*, 40).
76. Gregory Dart, *Metropolitan Art and Literature, 1810–1840: Cockney Adventures* (Cambridge: Cambridge University Press, 2012), 30.
77. Holden, *Wit in the Dungeon*, 91.
78. Holden, *Wit in the Dungeon*, 92. Yet we should note that the general editors of *The Selected Works of Leigh Hunt*, Robert Morrison and Michael Eberle-Sinatra, warn us not to assume that Hunt simply gave up political activism after 1815. They say rather that Hunt grew "increasingly inclined toward political positions of reconciliation and moderation" while nonetheless staying "deeply committed to radical objectives" (Robert Morrison and Michael Eberle-Sinatra, introduction to *Periodical Essays, 1805–14*, ed. Greg Kucich and Jeffrey N. Cox, vol. 1 of *SWLH*, xvi).

CHAPTER 4 — KEATS, BYRON, AND THE IDEA OF TRANSFORMATIVE CONFINEMENT

1. Nicholas Roe is the first and, to my knowledge, the only critic to have noticed a connection between the "rosy sanctuary" set up in the poet's brain, in Keats's "Ode to Psyche," and the literal rosy sanctuary that was Hunt's noble room in Surrey Gaol (see Roe, *Fiery Heart*, 192).
2. Keats to C. C. Clarke, October 9, 1816, in *The Letters of John Keats*, ed. Hyder Edward Rollins (Cambridge, MA: Harvard University Press, 1958), 1:113.
3. The poem, "To Solitude," is signed "J. K."
4. Leigh Hunt, "Young Poets," *Examiner*, no. 466, December 1, 1816, 761.
5. John Keats, "Written on the Day That Mr. Leigh Hunt Left Prison," in *John Keats: Complete Poems*, ed. Jack Stillinger (Cambridge, MA: Harvard University Press, 1982). In this and in the following chapter, when poems are scanned in the text, I follow the practice of beat scansion invented by Derek Attridge and explored in his *Rhythms of English Poetry* (1982), *Poetic Rhythm: An Introduction* (1995), *Metre and Meaning in Poetry* (2003) (co-authored with Thomas Carper) and *Moving Words* (2013). Beat scansion differentiates between stresses and beats. In the lines from the sonnet, an underscore above a syllable represents a syllable that takes a metrical beat. The absence of an underscore above one or more syllables represents a syllable or pair of syllables taking a metrical offbeat. Syllables

that take beats are often, but not always, stressed; the syllable "of" in line 12, for instance, is an unstressed beat, also called a "promoted" syllable. Likewise, syllables that take offbeats are often, but not always, unstressed; the syllable "Kind" in line 2 is a stressed offbeat, also called a "demoted" syllable. Furthermore, I occasionally divide one or another line in a poem into stress groups, which, importantly, have nothing to do with the traditional concept of a poetic "foot." Attridge defines a stress group as "a word or group of words consisting of one full stress and one or more weaker syllables attached to it" (Derek Attridge, *Poetic Rhythm: An Introduction* [Cambridge: Cambridge University Press, 1995], 223). I use "R" to designate a rising stress group, "F" to designate a falling stress group, and "M" to designate either a monosyllabic stress group or a mixed stress group—a stress group that is neither rising nor falling.

6. Charles Cowden Clarke and Mary Cowden Clarke, *Recollections of Writers*, 2nd ed. (London: Sampson Low, Marston, Searle and Rivington, 1878), 127.
7. Roe, *Fiery Heart*, 227.
8. Hunt to Marianne Hunt, June 10, 1813, in *Leigh Hunt: A Life in Letters*, 51.
9. Roe, *Fiery Heart*, 192.
10. Daisy Hay, "Adventures of an Unromantic Biographer," *Life Writing* 14, no. 2 (2017): 250.
11. Roe, *Fiery Heart*, 195.
12. Roe, *Fiery Heart*, 192.
13. According to Mary Anne Myers, "Keats encountered Petrarch as mediated by Spenser, Shakespeare, and Milton as well as in the original Italian and in Romantic translations and images." She adds that Hunt "enhanced the younger poet's appreciation for Petrarch," and identifies "Written on the Day That Mr. Leigh Hunt Left Prison" as a "Petrarchan-patterned sonnet" (Mary Anne Myers, "Keats and the Hands of Petrarch and Laura," *Keats-Shelley Journal* 62 [2013]: 101, 104).
14. Petrarch, *canzone* 89, in Petrarch, *The Canzoniere, or Rerum bulgarium fragmenta*, trans. and ed. Mark Musa (Bloomington: Indiana University Press, 1996), lines 1–4, 9–11.
15. Here is a random example of countless such examples in Sidney. In *The Old Arcadia* (completed in 1550), the Macedonian prince Pyrocles, in love with the princess Philoclea, says that he is "bound, and bound by so noble bands as loath to be unbound, / Gaoler I am to myself, prison and prisoner to mine own self. / Yet be my hopes thus placed" (Philip Sidney, *The Old Arcadia*, ed. Catherine Duncan-Jones [Oxford: Oxford University Press, 2008], 78). Pyrocles "hopes" that the princess will "transform" and "reform" him in and through his imprisonment in love.
16. Petrarch, canzone 296, in Petrarch, *The Canzoniere*, lines 2–4.
17. Apuleius, *Metamorphoses*, ed. and trans. J. Arthur Hanson, 2 vols. (Cambridge, MA: Harvard University Press, 1989), 260.
18. John Keats, "Ode to Psyche," in *John Keats: Complete Poems*, ed. Jack Stillinger (Cambridge, MA: Harvard University Press, 1982), lines 52, 59–60, 67.
19. Nicholas Roe, "Leigh Hunt: Some Early Matters," in *Leigh Hunt: Life, Poetics, Politics* (London: Routledge, 2003), 29–30.
20. John Keats, *Endymion*, in *John Keats: Complete Poems,* ed. Jack Stillinger (Cambridge, MA: Harvard University Press, 1982), 2.43.
21. Keats, *Endymion*, 1.430, 428, 431.
22. *Oxford English Dictionary*, s.v. "arbour | arbor, n.," July 2023, https://doi.org/10.1093/OED/9337928661.
23. Keats, *Endymion*, 1.438.
24. Keats, *Endymion* , 1.453–464.
25. Keats, *Endymion*, 4.508–512.
26. Keats, *Endymion*, 4.513–545.
27. John Middleton Murray, *Studies in Keats* (New York: Haskell, 1972), 42; Vendler, *Odes of John Keats*, 182; Susan J. Wolfson, *Reading John Keats* (Cambridge: Cambridge University Press, 2015), 45; Dorothy Van Ghent, "Keats's Myth of the Hero," *Keats-Shelley Journal* 3

(1954): 8; and Jennifer N. Wunder, *Keats, Hermeticism, and the Secret Societies* (London: Routledge, 2008), 171.

28. Northrop Frye, *The Secular Scripture: A Study of the Structure of Romance* (Cambridge, MA: Harvard University Press, 1976), 129.
29. Frye, *Secular Scripture*, 134.
30. Keats, *Endymion*, 3.141, 4.630.
31. Keats, *Endymion*, 2.458–459, 461.
32. Keats, *Endymion*, 4.691.
33. John Keats, *Lamia*, in *John Keats: Complete Poems*, ed. Jack Stillinger (Cambridge, MA: Harvard University Press, 1982), 2.50–54.
34. David Perkins, *The Quest for Permanence: The Symbolism of Wordsworth, Shelley, and Keats* (Cambridge, MA: Harvard University Press, 1959), 199.
35. John Keats, "Ode on Melancholy," in *John Keats: Complete Poems*, ed. Jack Stillinger (Cambridge, MA: Harvard University Press, 1982), line 19; John Keats, "What Can I Do to Drive Away," in *John Keats: Complete Poems*, ed. Jack Stillinger (Cambridge, MA: Harvard University Press, 1982), lines 50–51.
36. Keats to Fanny Brawne, July 1, 1819; Keats to Fanny Brawne, February 4 (?), 1820; Keats to Fanny Brawne, March (?) 1820; all in *The Letters of John Keats*, 2:123, 250, 275.
37. Vendler, *Odes of John Keats*, 92.
38. Curran, *Poetic Form*, 149.
39. Tracy Prior Seffers, "'A Bowery Nook Will Be Elysium': The Image of the Bower in the Poetry of John Keats," PhD diss., College of William and Mary, 1993, iii, 10.
40. Mizukoshi, *Aesthetics of Pleasure*, 65.
41. See Mizukoshi, *Aesthetics of Pleasure*; and Kucich, "Romantic Spenserianism."
42. Leigh Hunt, qtd. in Kucich, "Romantic Spenserianism," 119.
43. See Kucich, "Romantic Spenserianism," 123.
44. Hunt, *Autobiography*, 252–253.
45. George Gordon, Lord Byron, *Byron's Letters and Journals*, ed. Leslie A. Marchand, vol. 3, *1813–1814* (Cambridge, MA: Harvard University Press, 1974), 228.
46. Roe, *Fiery Heart*, 197.
47. Malcom Kelsall, "Byron's Politics," in *The Cambridge Companion to Byron*, ed. Drummond Bone (Cambridge: Cambridge University Press, 2006), 48.
48. Kelsall, "Byron's Politics," 50.
49. Almost every reader of *Chillon* has read the Prisoner as perverse, selfish, or delusional. Andrew Rutherford argues that we are "not invited to accept or admire . . . [the Prisoner's] delusions" as he tries to survive in prison (Andrew Rutherford, *Byron: A Critical Study* [Stanford, CA: Stanford University Press, 1961], 69), a sentiment echoed by William H. Marshall (William H. Marshall, *The Structure of Byron's Major Poems* [Philadelphia: University of Pennsylvania Press, 1962], 82–83). Newey sees the happy-prison topos as implied everywhere in *Chillon*, only to be denied in the end (see Vincent Newey, "Byron's 'Prisoner of Chillon': The Poetry of Being and the Poetry of Belief," *Keats-Shelley Memorial Bulletin, Rome* 35 [1984]: 54–70). Hall says that the Prisoner is "wretched" and that his "personality is annihilated" in the course of the narrative (Jean Hall, "The Evolution of the Surface Self: Byron's Poetic Career," *Keats-Shelley Journal* 36 [1987]: 142). Stafford warns us not to mistake the Prisoner's expressions of "guilt, resentment, self contempt [*sic*] and sheer misery" as signs of his "patience and heroism" (Fiona J. Stafford, *The Last of the Race: The Growth of a Myth from Milton to Darwin* [Oxford: Clarendon Press, 1994], 181).
50. Emily A. Bernhard Jackson, "Underground Knowledge: *The Prisoner of Chillon* and the Genesis of Byronic Knowing," *Romanticism* 17, vol. 2 (2011): 222.
51. Jerome McGann, ed., *Lord Byron: The Complete Poetical Works*, vol. 4 (Oxford: Clarendon Press, 1986), 449.
52. See Radzinowicz, *Movement for Reform*, 466–467.
53. Rzepka, "Imprisoned Thoughts," par. 8.

54. See Southey to Grosvenor Charles Bedford, March 22, [1806], in Robert Southey, *The Collected Letters of Robert Southey*, ed. Lynda Pratt et al., *Romantic Circles*, March 2009, https://romantic-circles.org/editions/southey_letters, n.p. As to Coleridge, according to Rzepka, "That *Thoughts in Prison* played a part in shaping Coleridge's solitary reflections in Thomas Poole's lime-tree bower on that July day in 1797 when he first composed 'This Lime-Tree Bower My Prison' is, I believe, undeniable" (Rzepka, "Imprisoned Thoughts," par. 22).
55. John Keats, "Ode to a Nightingale," in *John Keats: Complete Poems*, ed. Jack Stillinger (Cambridge, MA: Harvard University Press, 1982), lines 71–74, 79–80.
56. Dodd, *Thoughts in Prison*, 49.
57. Dodd, *Thoughts in Prison*, 32. This phrase is in a note at the bottom of the page.
58. Dodd, *Thoughts in Prison*, 17.
59. George Gordon, Lord Byron, *The Prisoner of Chillon*, in *Lord Byron: The Complete Poetical Works*, ed. Jerome J. McGann, vol. 4 (Oxford: Clarendon Press, 1986), lines 27–35.
60. *Oxford English Dictionary*, s.v. "meteor, n.[1] & adj.,[1]" July 2023, https://doi.org/10.1093/OED/9689090112.
61. Dodd, *Thoughts in Prison*, 130–131.
62. Dodd, *Thoughts in Prison*, 131.
63. Byron, *Prisoner of Chillon*, lines 328, 322–323, 344–345, 358, 364.
64. Bernhard Jackson, "Underground Knowledge," 230, 232.
65. Byron, *Prisoner of Chillon*, lines 231–250.
66. Rutherford, *Byron: A Critical Study*, 71; Robert Gleckner, *Byron and the Ruins of Paradise* (Baltimore: Johns Hopkins University Press, 1967), 196; Paul W. Elledge, *Byron and the Dynamics of Metaphor* (Nashville: Vanderbilt University Press, 1968), 51; Gordon E. Slethaug, "Patterns of Imagery in 'The Prisoner of Chillon,'" *Queen's Quarterly* 78 (1971): 452; Sandra M. Gilbert and Susan Gubar, *The Madwoman in the Attic: The Woman Writer and the Nineteenth-Century Literary Imagination*, 1979, Veritas Paperback ed. (New Haven, CT: Yale University Press, 2020), 279; Frederick Garber, *Self, Text, and Romantic Irony* (Princeton, NJ: Princeton University Press, 1988), 123; and Stafford, *Last of the Race*, 181.
67. Newey, "Byron's 'Prisoner of Chillon,'" 56.
68. Dodd, *Thoughts in Prison*, 5, 49.
69. Byron, *Prisoner of Chillon*, lines 374–394.
70. Elledge, *Byron and the Dynamics of Metaphor*, 46; Hall, "The Evolution," 144; Jerome McGann, *Fiery Dust: Byron's Poetic Development* (Chicago: University of Chicago Press, 1968), 167; and Peter W. Graham, "Byron and Prisoners: Politics, Poetry, and Myth," *Essays on Byron in Honour of Dr Peter Cochran: Breaking the Mould*, ed. Malcom Kelsall, Peter Graham, and Mirka Horová (Newcastle upon Tyne: Cambridge Scholars Publishing, 2018), 90.
71. See Ignatieff, *Just Measure of Pain*, 155–156.
72. Harding et al., *Imprisonment in England and Wales*, 144.
73. Henriques, "Separate System," 75–77.
74. Henriques, "Separate System," 78, 83.
75. Bernhard Jackson, "Underground Knowledge," 227.

CHAPTER 5 — JOHN CLARE

1. Clare to Mary Joyce, July 27, 1841, in *The Letters of John Clare*, ed. Mark Storey (Oxford: Clarendon Press, 1985), 649.
2. I use the theory of romance as advanced by Frye because it continues to be the most methodical and comprehensive account of the romance as a total literary-cultural system, incorporating nearly a millennium of Western verse and prose.

3. Clare to Patty Clare, July 19, 1848 ("Sodom, "purgatoriall hell," "French Bastile"); Clare to Charles Clare, April 28, 1849 ("Captivity"); Clare to Patty Clare, [1849–1850] ("English bondage," "government Prison"); all in *The Letters of John Clare*, 657, 661, 669.
4. Clare to Patty Clare, November 23, 1837, in *The Letters of John Clare*, 642.
5. Clare to Patty Clare, March 17, 1841, in *The Letters of John Clare*, 643.
6. Clare to Charles Clare, June 15, 1847, in *The Letters of John Clare*, 654.
7. Mark Storey, ed., *The Letters of John Clare* (Oxford: Clarendon Press, 1985), 655n6.
8. Clare to Patty Clare, July 19, 1848, in *The Letters of John Clare*, 657.
9. Clare to Charles Clare, October 17, 1848, in *The Letters of John Clare*, 658.
10. Clare to Charles Clare, April 24, 1850, in *The Letters of John Clare*, 672.
11. Clare to Sophia Clare, October 8, 1852, in *The Letters of John Clare*, 682.
12. J. W. Tibble and Anne Tibble, *John Clare: A Life*, 1932, rev. ed. (London: Michael Joseph, 1972), 344.
13. Storey writes that throughout his time at the Northampton General Lunatic Asylum, "Clare was looked after most sympathetically. . . . Visitors were often surprised . . . to find such a robust character. . . . All his physical wants were cared for and he no longer had the responsibility of providing for his family. His time was his own now to read and write. But he needed more than such comforts or benefits. However considerate his superiors might have been, and however accommodating the asylum was, Clare could only see himself as a helpless captive" (Edward Storey, *A Right to Song: The Life of John Clare* [London: Methuen, 1982], 291).
14. See Tim Chilcott, *"A Real World & Doubting Mind": A Critical Study of the Poetry of John Clare* (Hull: Hull University Press, 1985), 168; and Anindita Chatterjee, "'I Think I have Been Here Long Enough': John Clare and the Poetry of His Asylum Years," *Rupkatha Journal on Interdisciplinary Studies in Humanities* 3, no. 4 (2011): 434.
15. See Tim Fulford, "Personating Poets on the Page: John Clare in His Asylum Notebooks," *John Clare Society Journal* 32 (2013): 27–48.
16. Roy Porter, "'All madness for writing': John Clare and the Asylum," in *John Clare in Context*, ed. Hugh Haughton, Adam Phillips, and Geoffrey Summerfield (Cambridge: Cambridge University Press, 1994), 273.
17. Roger Sales, *John Clare: A Literary Life* (New York: Palgrave, 2002), 111, 119–120, 128.
18. Sales, *John Clare*, 105.
19. John Clare, "Sonnet: '*I am*,'" in *The Later Poems of John Clare, 1837–1864*, ed. Eric Robinson, David Powell, and Margaret Grainger, vol. 1 (Oxford: Clarendon Press, 1984), lines 3–4, 7–8.
20. Nina Auerbach, *Romantic Imprisonment: Women and Other Glorified Outcasts* (New York: Columbia University Press, 1985), 6, 11.
21. Bate says the letter in question was probably written in 1840, whereas Mark Storey proposes that it could have been written either in 1840 or 1841 (Jonathan Bate, *John Clare: A Biography* [London: Picador, 2004], 433; and Storey, ed., *Letters of John Clare*, 644).
22. Clare to Patty Clare, [April 18, 1841], in *Letters of John Clare*, 644–665.
23. John Clare, "[I long to forget them—the love of my life—]," in *The Later Poems of John Clare, 1837–1864*, ed. Eric Robinson, David Powell, and Margaret Grainger, vol. 1 (Oxford: Clarendon Press, 1984).
24. Bate, *John Clare*, 13.
25. Northrup Frye, *Anatomy of Criticism: Four Essays*, 1957, Princeton Classics ed. (Princeton, NJ: Princeton University Press, 2020), 34.
26. Frye, *Anatomy of Criticism*, 193.
27. John Clare, "[I hate the very noise of troublous man]," in *Poems of the Middle Period, 1822–1837*, ed. Eric Robinson, David Powell, and P. M. S. Dawson, vol. 5 (Oxford: Clarendon Press, 2003), lines 1, 6, 3–4, 7–8.
28. Clare, "[I hate the very noise of troublous man]," lines 9–10.

29. Frye, *Secular Scripture*, 134.
30. Qtd. in Mark Storey, *John Clare: The Critical Heritage* (New York: Routledge, 1996), 248.
31. John Clare, "Sighing for Retirement," in *The Later Poems of John Clare, 1837–1864*, ed. Eric Robinson, David Powell, and Margaret Grainger, vol. 1 (Oxford: Clarendon Press, 1984), lines 2, 1, 3–4.
32. Clare, "Sighing for Retirement, lines 6, 17.
33. John Clare, "A Walk in the Forest," in *The Later Poems of John Clare, 1837–1864*, ed. Eric Robinson, David Powell, and Margaret Grainger, vol. 1 (Oxford: Clarendon Press, 1984), lines 3–4.
34. John Clare, "A Walk on High Beach, Loughton," in *The Later Poems of John Clare, 1837–1864*, ed. Eric Robinson, David Powell, and Margaret Grainger, vol. 1 (Oxford: Clarendon Press, 1984), lines 4–5, 8, 7, 14.
35. John Clare, "London *versus* Epping Forest," in *The Later Poems of John Clare, 1837–1864*, ed. Eric Robinson, David Powell, and Margaret Grainger, vol. 1 (Oxford: Clarendon Press, 1984), lines 1, 3–5.
36. Clare, "London *versus* Epping Forest," lines 7–10.
37. Bate, *John Clare*, 442.
38. John Clare, "The Water Lilies," in *The Later Poems of John Clare, 1837–1864*, ed. Eric Robinson, David Powell, and Margaret Grainger, vol. 1 (Oxford: Clarendon Press, 1984), lines 12, 9.
39. Frye, *Anatomy of Criticism*, 147.
40. Frye, *Anatomy of Criticism*, 141.
41. Frye, *Anatomy of Criticism*, 150, 141.
42. Clare, "Sighing for Retirement," lines 21–28.
43. Frye, *Anatomy of Criticism*, 158.
44. In the fourteenth and fifteenth centuries, the word *child*, or *childe*, probably meant a young man of noble birth. The title *Child Harold* comes from *Childe Harold's Pilgrimage* (1812–1818), by Lord Byron, the "quintessential romance of the [Romantic] period" (Stuart, *Poetic Form*, 151).
45. MS 8 aside, poetic material related to *Child Harold* also appears in Northampton MSS 7, 49, and 57, as well as Bodleian MSS Don. a. 8 and Don. c. 64 (see Lynn Pearce, "John Clare's 'Child Harold': A Polyphonic Reading," *Criticism* 31, no. 2 [1989]: 155n4).
46. Mark Storey, *The Poetry of John Clare: A Critical Introduction* (London: Macmillan, 1974), 175; Mark Minor, "Clare, Byron, and the Bible: Additional Evidence from the Asylum Manuscripts," *Bulletin of Research in the Humanities* 85, no. 1 (1982): 105; Storey, *Right to Song*, 270; Chilcott, *"A Real World,"* 145, 210; Bate, *John Clare*, 488.
47. Frye, *Anatomy of Criticism*, 201.
48. Frye, *Anatomy of Criticism*, 151.
49. John Clare, *Child Harold*, in *The Later Poems of John Clare, 1837–1864*, ed. Eric Robinson, David Powell, and Margaret Grainger, vol. 1 (Oxford: Clarendon Press, 1984), lines 75–82.
50. Clare, *Child Harold*, lines 92, 175, 201.
51. Frye, *Secular Scripture*, 129.
52. Frye, *Anatomy of Criticism*, 147.
53. Clare, *Child Harold*, lines 147, 161.
54. Clare, *Child Harold*, lines 217–218, 221, 226–227.
55. Frye, *Secular Scripture*, 129.
56. Clare, *Child Harold*, lines 229–232.
57. Frye, *Secular Scripture*, 151.
58. Frye, *Anatomy of Criticism*, 187–188.
59. Frye, *Anatomy of Criticism*, 137.
60. Clare, *Child Harold*, lines 460–467.
61. Clare, *Child Harold*, lines 1,265–1,273.

62. Clare, "A Vision," in *The Later Poems of John Clare, 1837–1864*, ed. Eric Robinson, David Powell, and Margaret Grainger, vol. 1 (Oxford: Clarendon Press, 1984).
63. Frye, *Anatomy of Criticism*, 202.
64. Frye, *Anatomy of Criticism*, 203.
65. One last parallel is worth mentioning. In his letters and poems written during the asylum years, Clare repeatedly mentions that he has two wives, his actual wife Patty/Martha Clare and his make-believe wife Mary Joyce. Most critics of the later poems make some mention of this fact. Usually it is seen as a delusion or wish fulfillment. But it actually has a literary precedent in a romance mythos organized around demonic imagery. Frye writes that in the process of "demonic modulation," which he defines as the process whereby a poet takes an archetype with apocalyptic associations and reverses these associations, "true love may be symbolized by the triumph of an adulterous liaison over marriage" (Frye, *Anatomy of Criticism*, 157).
66. Frye, *Secular Scripture*, 152.

CHAPTER 6 — JANE AUSTEN AND PENITENTIAL SPACE

1. See East Kent Gaol at Canterbury (Q/AGe), Kent Archives and Local History, Kent History and Library Centre, Maidstone, England. I will cite each quotation from an archived item by date, the archival series in which the item is located and the archival number of the item. For instance, the phrase "plain Dresses" in this paragraph comes from January 9, 1809, Q/AGe/4, no. 22.
2. See Austen to Cassandra Austen, November 3, 1813, in Jane Austen, *Jane Austen's Letters*, ed. Deirdre Le Faye, 4th ed. (Oxford: Oxford University Press, 2008), 258.
3. Eagleton, *The English Novel*, 114.
4. Claudia Johnson, *Jane Austen: Women, Politics, and the Novel* (Chicago: University of Chicago Press, 1988), 22.
5. Mooneyham White, *Jane Austen's Anglicanism*, 26. Compare the following passages, from prayers attributed to Jane Austen, to similar passages in a pamphlet on sermons for reformed prisons (1790): "make us feel . . . [our sins] deeply, that our Repentance be sincere" (Jane Austen, "Prayers," in *Later Manuscripts*, ed. Janet Todd and Linda Bree [Cambridge: Cambridge University Press, 2008], 573); "grant . . . that I may not deceive myself by a counterfeit repentance" (Brewster, *Sermons for Prisons*, 157); "give us a stronger desire of resisting every evil inclination" (Austen, "Prayers," 574); "dispose and correct my Inclinations" (Brewster, *Sermons for Prisons*, 155); "bring to our knowledge every . . . evil Habit" (Austen, "Prayers," 573); "break off all evil habits" (Brewster, *Sermons for Prisons*, 157).
6. Mooneyham White, *Jane Austen's Anglicanism*, 25.
7. Craig, *Jane Austen and the State*, 18. This point links Austen with the evangelical Anglican Hannah More, whose literary campaign for moral reform "was directed at the decadence of the aristocracy; at the moral laxness of the clergy; at the lack of education, sobriety, cleanliness, and thrift among the working classes; and at the poor education and irresponsible behavior of women of all classes" (Anne Kostelanetz Mellor, "Were Women Writers 'Romantics'?", *Modern Language Quarterly* 62, no. 4 [2001]: 401).
8. See Throness, *Protestant Purgatory*, 132.
9. Mooneyham White, *Jane Austen's Anglicanism*, 81, 82.
10. As David Wilson has observed, the "flurry of prison building at the local level . . . helped to keep the issue of incarceration in public and parliamentary discourse" (David Wilson, "Millbank, The Panopticon and Their Victorian Audiences," *The Howard Journal* 41, no. 4 [2002]: 384).
11. Two anonymous advertisements in the *Hampshire Chronicle*—one on October 4, 1779, and another on October 18, 1779—describe the act as: "Act for erecting Penitentiary Houses for the confinement of offenders convicted of transportable crimes."

12. Anonymous, "London, Thursday, July 29. House of Commons," *Hampshire Chronicle*, August 2, 1784, *British Newspaper Archive*, https://www.britishnewspaperarchive.co.uk.
13. Sir Thomas Beevor, "A Letter from Sir Thomas Beevor, bart., of Hethel in Norfolk, on the New Construction of Prisons," *Hampshire Chronicle*, February 14, 1785, *British Newspaper Archive*, https://www.britishnewspaperarchive.co.uk.
14. Sir Thomas Beevor, "A Letter."
15. 24 Geo. III, c. 55.
16. Sir Thomas Beevor, "A Letter."
17. 25 Geo. III, c. 10.
18. Anonymous, "Hants Epiphany Session, 1791," *Hampshire Chronicle*, January 24, 1791, *British Newspaper Archive*, https://www.britishnewspaperarchive.co.uk.
19. Anonymous, "Hants Epiphany Session, 1791."
20. Shirley Burgoyne Black, *The Kentish Justice, 1791–1834* (Oxford: Darenth Valley Publications, 1987), 5.
21. Burgoyne Black lists an "Austen, John (of Horsmonden)" as included in the commissions of the peace of 1791 and 1799 (Burgoyne Black, *Kentish Justice*, 10). John Austen VI inherited the Broadford estate at Horsmonden from his father, John Austen V.
22. See Deirdre Le Faye, *A Chronology of Jane Austen and Her Family, 1600–2000*, 2nd ed. (Cambridge: Cambridge University Press, 2013), 56.
23. Burgoyne Black lists an "Austen, John (of Swift's Place)" as included in the commissions of the peace of 1799, 1814, and 1820 (Burgoyne Black, *The Kentish Justice*, 11). Captain/Major John Austen purchased Swift's Place, a country estate and manor house a half mile east of the parish of Cranbrook, from one Thomas Adams in 1789 (see Peter Allen, "The History of Great Swifts," *Cranbrook Journal* 16 [2005]: 3–6).
24. Burgoyne Black lists an "Austen, Francis Lucius" as included in the commissions of the peace of 1799 (Burgoyne Black, *The Kentish Justice*, 10). For the information on Francis Lucius, see Le Faye, *A Chronology*, 151, 453, 499.
25. Burgoyne Black lists an "Austen, Thomas" as included in the commissions of the peace of 1814, 1820, and 1830 (Burgoyne Black, *The Kentish Justice*, 11).
26. Burgoyne Black lists an "Austen, Rev. John" as included in the commissions of the peace of 1814, 1820, and 1830 (Burgoyne Black, *The Kentish Justice*, 10).
27. East Kent Gaol at Canterbury (Q/AGe), July 15, 1806, Q/AGe/2, nos. 2–3.
28. See Austen to Cassandra Austen, September 15, 1796, in *Jane Austen's Letters*, 9.
29. This William Deedes II should not be confused with his father, William Deedes I, of St. Stephens, Canterbury, and Hythe (see John Burke and John Bernard Burke, *A Genealogical and Heraldic Dictionary of the Landed Gentry of Great Britain and Ireland*, vol. 1, *A to L* [London: Henry Colburn, 1847], 320). William Deedes I, like his son and heir, was also chairman of the Quarter Sessions for East Kent, from 1776 to 1792 (Burgoyne Black, *The Kentish Justice*, 17).
30. See Le Faye, *A Chronology*, 317.
31. Austen to Cassandra Austen, October 26, 1796, in *Jane Austen's Letters*, 254.
32. See Le Faye, *A Chronology*, 466.
33. Austen to Cassandra Austen, November 6, 1796, in *Jane Austen's Letters*, 261–262.
34. See East Kent Gaol at Canterbury (Q/AGe), November 2, 1804, Q/AGe/1, no. 15.
35. See Le Faye, *A Chronology*, 466. For the acceptance of Charles Hedge as builder of the Canterbury Gaol and House of Correction, see East Kent Gaol at Canterbury (Q/AGe), August 16, 1805, Q/Age/1, nos. 34–36.
36. See East Kent Gaol at Canterbury (Q/AGe), January 16, 1805, Q/AGe/1, no. 16.
37. Austen to Cassandra Austen, September 15–16, 1796, in *Jane Austen's Letters*, 10.
38. See East Kent Gaol at Canterbury (Q/AGe), January 14, 1806, Q/AGe/1, no. 41.
39. Finn says that "the half century from 1780 to 1830" was "the period in which the highly personalized justice of the county magistracy was arguably at its zenith" (Margot C.

Finn, *The Character of Credit: Personal Debt in English Culture, 1740–1914* [Cambridge: Cambridge University Press, 2003], 155).

40. See Neild, *State of the Prisons*, 101.
41. See figure 6.1 for the design of the ground floor.
42. The most reliable contemporary text on the prison itself is Neild, *State of the Prisons*.
43. It is interesting in this context to remember that Catherine Morland in *Northanger Abbey* imagines the late Mrs. Tilney to have languished and died in a stone monastic cell, where she was held captive by her estranged husband. Canterbury Gaol and House of Correction contained a total of forty-one prison cells.
44. Neild, *State of the Prisons*, 102.
45. See East Kent Gaol at Canterbury (Q/AGe), July 15, 1806, Q/AGe/2, no. 5.
46. Neild, *State of the Prisons*, 102.
47. Jane Austen, *Sense and Sensibility*, ed. Edward Copeland (Cambridge: Cambridge University Press, 2006), 33. Text references to *Sense and Sensibility* are hereafter abbreviated *SS*.
48. Julie Park, "The Poetics of Enclosure in Sense and Sensibility," *Studies in Eighteenth-Century Culture* 42 (2013): 244.
49. Evans, *Fabrication of Virtue*, 169.
50. Both systems eventually became matters of national debate in Britain in the 1830s. As DeLacy writes: "ever since the introduction of cellular prisons in the late eighteenth century, a trend toward the separation of prisoners had been growing; the separate and silent systems were merely its logical conclusion" (DeLacy, *Prison Reform*, 222).
51. Gloucester Penitentiary had a regimen of "separate sleeping and separate employment in isolated cells, varied with daily chapel, twenty-minutes' tread-wheel and twenty minutes' walk—all in silent association—and professedly tempered, every day or every few days, by regular visits from and conversation with the master and the chaplain, the surgeon and the Visiting Justice. Other reformed prisons adopted similar combinations of cellular isolation during the night, and non-intercourse during the day" (Webb and Webb, *English Prisons*, 90–91).
52. Janet Todd and Antje Blank, introduction to *Persuasion*, by Jane Austen (Cambridge: Cambridge University Press, 2006), liii–liv.
53. Jane Austen, *Persuasion*, ed. Janet Todd and Antje Blank (Cambridge: Cambridge University Press, 2006), 109. Text references to *Persuasion* are hereafter abbreviated *P*. Note that manufacturing small gifts for the poor was an activity associated with late eighteenth-century prisoners. Howard mentions that debtors at the York City and County Gaol "sell nets, purses, laces, &c" at a window, over which is "an inscription on a stone tablet, '*He that giveth to the poor, lendeth to the Lord*'" (Howard, *State of the Prisons*, 409).
54. Loraine Fletcher, *Charlotte Smith: A Critical Biography* (Basingstoke, UK: Macmillan, 1998), 67.
55. John Wiltshire, introduction to *Mansfield Park*, by Jane Austen (Cambridge: Cambridge University Press, 2005), xxv–xxvi.
56. Canuel, *Shadow of Death*, 84, 83.
57. McConville, *English Prison Administration*, 111.
58. George Holford et al., "Reports from the Committee on the Laws Relating to Penitentiary Houses," *The Literary Panorama, Being a Compendium of National Papers and Parliamentary Reports . . . Forming an Annual Register*, vol. XI (London: C. Taylor, 1812), 199.
59. One critic observes that Fanny and her cousins Maria and Julia all "suffer from enclosure, limitation, and inspection" in the "enclosed world of the home" (Margaret Doody, *Jane Austen's Names: Riddles, Persons, Places* [Chicago: University of Chicago Press, 2015], 338–339). This is an understandably negative take on the prison metaphors in the novel, which Doody reads as gendered domestic confinements. Lionel Trilling views the same

metaphors in the opposite sense. He argues that "no other great novel has so anxiously asserted the need to find security, to establish, in fixity and enclosure, a refuge from the dangers of openness and chance" (Lionel Trilling, "*Mansfield Park*," in *The Moral Obligation to Be Intelligent: Selected Essays*, ed. Leon Wieseltier [Evanston, IL: Northwestern University Press, 2000], 295). The only critic to my knowledge who has read *Mansfield Park* in light of historical imprisonment in Regency Britain, aside from Mark Canuel, is Susannah Fullerton; see Fullerton, *Jane Austen and Crime*, 171–196.

60. Jane Austen, *Mansfield Park*, ed. John Wiltshire (Cambridge: Cambridge University Press, 2005), 62. Text references to *Mansfield Park* are hereafter abbreviated *MP*.
61. Mooneyham White notes that "most of the social and religious reforms Anglican Evangelicals promoted can be found as issues in . . . *Mansfield Park*: non-residency [of clergymen in their designated parishes], the abolition of the slave trade, the irreligiosity of urban elites, the importance of family prayers, the distrust of amateur acting, and the call to intense private self-examination" (Mooneyham White, *Jane Austen's Anglicanism*, 27). To this list we can add the evangelical concern with penal reform.
62. Jane Austen, *Northanger Abbey*, ed. Barbara M. Benedict and Deirdre Le Faye (Cambridge: Cambridge University Press, 2006), 188–89. Text references to *Northanger Abbey* are hereafter abbreviated *NA*.
63. Gary Kelly reminds us that eighteenth- and nineteenth-century accounts "tended to regard Newgate as a 'Gothic' relic from an earlier, less enlightened and moral age, an incorrigible repeat offender, a tourist attraction, a warning, an occasion for titillation or the arousal of such sensations of 'horror,' like a Gothic romance" (Kelly, introduction to *Newgate Documents*, xvii). Thus what Newgate was to provincial English tourists, Northanger Abbey is to the provincial Catherine. She arrives expecting to witness "past scenes of horror being acted within the solemn edifice" (*NA*, 165). Note the phrase "scenes of horror." A 1792 pamphlet on John Howard used the same words to describe the interiors of unreformed English prisons (Anonymous, "John Howard, F. R. S.," in *An Interesting Collection of Modern Lives . . . Illustrated with the Heads of Several of the Above, Finely Engraved* [London: G. Riebau, 1792], 13).
64. Edgerton says that "by the 1790s . . . house-warming principles had found an unchallenged expert in Count Rumford, an American expatriate in England, who was so widely read . . . that almost all new chimneys and fireplaces were subsequently designed to his specifications" (Samuel Y. Edgerton, "Heat and Style: Eighteenth-Century House Warming by Stoves," *Journal of the Society of Architectural Historians* 20, no. 1 [1961]: 21). Edward Austen Knight and the proprietors of the Canterbury Gaol and House of Correction chose to purchase a Pantheon stove instead of a Rumford, the Pantheon being one of several new "architecturally-shaped iron stoves to heat large rooms" manufactured in London (Edgerton, "Heat and Style," 23).
65. The white attic functions more or less as a solitary sleeping cell in a reformed prison. Here is Holford: "of all the points to be attended to in a place of confinement, in which any hope of reformation is entertained, that of giving to each person a separate night-cell is the most important" (George Holford, "Prefatory Remarks," in *The Convict's Complaint in 1815, and the Thanks of the Convict in 1825; Or, Sketches in Verse of a Hulk in the Former Year, and of the Millbank Penitentiary in the Latter* [London: Rivingtons; Hachard, 1825], xi).
66. Holford, "Prefatory Remarks," xii.
67. Holford, "Prefatory Remarks," xii; italics mine.
68. All this is much alleviated when Fanny launches a new "method of reform" at the Price house (*MP*, 458). She teaches her fourteen-year-old sister Susan the value of "active indispensable employment" (*MP*, 513) and acts as the ideal visiting magistrate: securing a "powerful influence over the objects of . . . [her] care," "discouraging the rapid progress of evil," and "fanning the feeble flame of expiring virtue" (Joseph Gurney, *Notes on a Visit Made to Some of the Prisons in Scotland and the North of England, in Company with Elizabeth Fry;*

with Some General Observations on the Subject of Prison Discipline [London: Archibald Constable; Longman, Hurst, Rees, Orme and Brown; Hurst, Robinson, 1819], 147).

69. Mrs. Price extends the sense of confinement at the Portsmouth house to the whole town: she notes that her daughters are "very much confined—Portsmouth was a sad place—they did not often get out" (*MP*, 466).
70. Portsmouth as a whole was also associated with unreformed imprisonment owing to the military and criminal prison hulks harbored there. Francis William Austen was responsible for discharging French prisoners into prison ships at Portsmouth Harbor in 1808 (see Le Faye, *A Chronology*, 357). In one of her letters, moreover, Austen mentions that lieutenant Earle Harwood, part of a squirarchical family living at the Dean House near the church where the Rev. George Austen was rector, received an "appointment to a Prison ship at Portsmouth [the *Prothee*], which he has been for some time desirous of having; & he & his wife are to live on board for the future" (Austen to Cassandra Austen, December 19, 1798, in *Jane Austen's Letters*, 27–28). It was common for the wives of British military officers to live on board the hulks during the Revolutionary and Napoleonic Wars. In 1813, when Austen was writing *Mansfield Park*, there were at least fifteen hulks at Portsmouth being used as military prisons, and one being used as a criminal prison. The *Prothee* was a French ship captured by the British in 1780 (see Richard Rose, ed., "Appendix A: Prisoner of War Hulks at Portsmouth," in *The Floating Prison: The Remarkable Account of Nine Years' Captivity on the British Prison Hulks during the Napoleonic Wars, 1806 to 1814*, by Louis Garneray [London: Conway Maritime Press, 2003], 232–233).
71. Qtd. in Deidre Le Faye, *Jane Austen: A Family Record*, 2nd ed. (Cambridge: Cambridge University Press, 2004), 121.
72. Mr. Mountague Cholmeley to Mrs. Leigh-Perrot, January 11, 1800, qtd. in Le Faye, *Jane Austen: A Family Record*, 122.
73. Beattie, *Crime and the Courts*, 636.

CODA

1. See Bailey, *Wordsworth's Vagrants*, 15–16.
2. Hanway claimed in 1776 that British "*news-papers daily* exhibit" more "commitments to prisons . . . than extraordinary *births* or *marriages*" (Hanway, *Solitude in Imprisonment*, 62). McCalman observes that newspapers in the 1790s regularly reported on the "visitors, routines, and private li[ves]" of state prisoners in Newgate (McCalman, "Newgate in Revolution," 96).
3. Discharged prisoners were often feared as spreaders of disease in the late eighteenth century (see McConville, *English Prison Administration*, 85). In Fanny Burney's 1796 novel *Camilla*, for instance, the frenetic governess Miss Margland warns her young female charges to steer clear of a family whose father has recently been in a Northwick gaol: "Miss Margland . . . suddenly called out: 'Miss Lynmere! Miss Eugenia! come away directly! It's ten to one but these people have all got the gaol distemper!'" (Fanny Burney, *Camilla*, ed. Edward A. Bloom and Lillian D. Bloom [Oxford: Oxford University Press, 2009], 111).
4. Cervantes and Porter have called attention to a "virtually unexplored archive of poetry and periodical writing" in the 1780s and 1790s about John Howard, adding that the poems on Howard are problematically "written off as a litany of dreadful couplets dripping with inflated, banal sentimentalism" (Cervantes and Porter, "Extreme Empiricism," 97, 98).

BIBLIOGRAPHY

Addison, Joseph. "No. 411: Saturday, June 21, 1712." In *The Spectator*, edited by Donald F. Bond, vol. 3, 535–539. Oxford: Clarendon Press, 1965.

Alber, Jan, and Frank Lauterbach, eds. *Stones of Law, Bricks of Shame: Narrating Imprisonment in the Victorian Age*. Toronto: University of Toronto Press, 2009.

Allen, Peter. "The History of Great Swifts." *Cranbrook Journal* 16 (2005): 3–6.

Anonymous. "Art. I. *Theorie des Peines et des Recompenses*. Par M. Jeremie Bentham . . . à Londres, Dulau, 1811." *Edinburgh Review* 22, no. 43 (1813): 1–31.

———. "Art. IX. *St. Leon, a Tale of the Sixteenth Century. By William Godwin. . . . 1799*." *The British Critic* 15 (1800): 47–52.

———. "General View of the Arguments in Favour of an Amelioration of the Penal Laws." *Examiner*, no. 352, September 25, 1814, 621–622. *British Newspaper Archive*, http://www.britishnewspaperarchive.co.uk.

———. "Hants Epiphany Session, 1791." *Hampshire Chronicle*, January 24, 1791. *British Newspaper Archive*, https://www.britishnewspaperarchive.co.uk.

———. "John Howard, F. R. S." In *An Interesting Collection of Modern Lives . . . Illustrated with the Heads of Several of the Above, Finely Engraved*, 9–36. London: G. Riebau, 1792.

———. "London, Thursday, July 29. House of Commons." *Hampshire Chronicle*, August 2, 1784. *British Newspaper Archive*, https://www.britishnewspaperarchive.co.uk.

———. "London and Southwark Prisons." *Examiner*, no. 338, June 19, 1814, 390–391. *British Newspaper Archive*, http://www.britishnewspaperarchive.co.uk.

———. "Mr. Justice Park—Prison Discipline." *Examiner*, no. 721, October 28, 1821, 673–674. *British Newspaper Archive*, http://www.britishnewspaperarchive.co.uk.

———. "Newgate Prison." *Examiner*, no. 316, January 16, 1814, 44–45. *British Newspaper Archive*, http://www.britishnewspaperarchive.co.uk.

———. "Newgate Prison." *Examiner*, no. 318, January 30, 1814, 78–79. *British Newspaper Archive*, http://www.britishnewspaperarchive.co.uk.

———. "Prison Discipline." *Examiner*, no. 701, June 10, 1821, 360. *British Newspaper Archive*, http://www.britishnewspaperarchive.co.uk.

———. *The Prisoner's Companion; Containing Religious and Moral Advice, Adapted to Persons in Solitary Confinement*. London: Dodsley, 1785.

Apuleius. *Metamorphoses*. Edited and translated by J. Arthur Hanson. 2 vols. Cambridge, MA: Harvard University Press, 1989.

Attridge, Derek. *Poetic Rhythm: An Introduction*. Cambridge: Cambridge University Press, 1995.

Auerbach, Nina. *Romantic Imprisonment: Women and Other Glorified Outcasts*. New York: Columbia University Press, 1985.

Austen, Jane. *Jane Austen's Letters*. Edited by Deirdre Le Faye. 4th ed. Oxford: Oxford University Press, 2008.

———. *Mansfield Park*. Edited by John Wiltshire. Cambridge: Cambridge University Press, 2005.

———. *Northanger Abbey*. Edited by Barbara M. Benedict and Deirdre Le Faye. Cambridge: Cambridge University Press, 2006.

———. *Persuasion*. Edited by Janet Todd and Antje Blank. Cambridge: Cambridge University Press, 2006.

———. "Prayers." In *Later Manuscripts*, edited by Janet Todd and Linda Bree, 573–576. Cambridge: Cambridge University Press, 2008.

———. *Sense and Sensibility*. Edited by Edward Copeland. Cambridge: Cambridge University Press, 2006.

Babington, Anthony. *The English Bastille: A History of Newgate Gaol and Prison Conditions in Britain, 1188–1902*. London: Macdonald, 1971.

Bailey, Quentin. *Wordsworth's Vagrants: Police, Prisons and Poetry in the 1790s*. Farnham, UK: Ashgate, 2011.

Barnard, John. "Leigh Hunt and Charles Cowden Clark, 1812–18." In *Leigh Hunt: Life, Poetics, Politics*, edited by Nicholas Roe, 32–57. London: Routledge, 2003.

Barthes, Roland. "An Introduction to the Structural Analysis of Narrative." *New Literary History* 6, no. 2 (1975): 237–272.

Bate, Jonathan. *John Clare: A Biography*. London: Picador, 2004.

Beattie, J. M. *Crime and the Courts in England, 1660–1800*. Oxford: Clarendon Press, 1986.

Beevor, Sir Thomas. "A Letter from Sir Thomas Beevor, bart., of Hethel in Norfolk, on the New Construction of Prisons." *Hampshire Chronicle*, February 14, 1785. *British Newspaper Archive*, https://www.britishnewspaperarchive.co.uk.

Bender, John. *Imagining the Penitentiary: Fiction and the Architecture of Mind in Eighteenth-Century England*. Chicago: University of Chicago Press, 1987.

Bernhard Jackson, Emily A. "Underground Knowledge: *The Prisoner of Chillon* and the Genesis of Byronic Knowing." *Romanticism* 17, vol. 2 (2011): 222–239.

Blackstone, William. *Commentaries on the Laws of England. Book the Fourth*. Oxford: Clarendon Press, 1769.

Blainey, Ann. *Immortal Boy: A Portrait of Leigh Hunt*. New York: St. Martin's Press, 1985.

Blunden, Edmund. *Leigh Hunt and His Circle*. New York: Harper and Brothers, 1930.

Boethius. *On the Consolation of Philosophy*. Translated and edited by Victor Watts. Revised ed. New York: Penguin, 1999.

Böker, Uwe. "The Prison and the Penitentiary as Sites of Public Counter-Discourse." In *Sites of Discourse—Public and Private Spheres—Legal Culture: Papers from a Conference Held at the Technical University of Dresden, December 2001*, edited by Uwe Böker and Julie A. Hibbard, 211–247. Amsterdam: Editions Rodopi B. V., 2002.

Bowers, Will. *The Italian Idea: Anglo-Italian Radical Literary Culture, 1815–1823*. Cambridge: Cambridge University Press, 2010.

Brewer, William D. Introduction to *St. Leon: A Tale of the Sixteenth Century*, 11–39. Peterborough, ON, Canada: Broadview, 2005.

Brewster, John. *On the Prevention of Crimes, and on the Advantages of Solitary Imprisonment*. London: W. Clark, J. Debrett and J. Johnson, 1792.

———. *Sermons for Prisons. To Which Are Added Prayers for the Use of Prisoners in Solitary Confinement*. Stockton: R. Christopher, 1790.

Broich, Ulrich. "The Politicization of the Prison Motif in the English Literature of the 1790s." *Poetica* 39, no. 1/2 (2007): 111–133.

Brombert, Victor. *The Romantic Prison: The French Tradition*. Princeton, NJ: Princeton University Press, 1978.

Bugg, John. *Five Long Winters: The Trials of British Romanticism*. Stanford, CA: Stanford University Press, 2013.

Burgoyne Black, Shirley. *The Kentish Justice, 1791–1834*. Oxford: Darenth Valley Publications, 1987.

Burke, John, and John Bernard Burke. *A Genealogical and Heraldic Dictionary of the Landed Gentry of Great Britain and Ireland*. Vol. 1, *A to L*. London: Henry Colburn, 1847.

Burney, Fanny. *Camilla*. Edited by Edward A. Bloom and Lillian D. Bloom. Oxford: Oxford University Press, 2009.

Butler, Marilyn. *Jane Austen and the War of Ideas*. Oxford: Clarendon Press, 1975.
Butler, Marilyn, and Mark Philp. Introduction to *Autobiography, Autobiographical Fragments and Reflections, Godwin/Shelley Correspondence*, edited by Mark Philp, 7–46. Vol. 1 of *Collected Novels and Memoirs of William Godwin*, edited by Mark Philp. London: William Pickering, 1992.
Byron, Lord George Gordon. *Byron's Letters and Journals*. Edited by Leslie A. Marchand. Vol. 3, *1813–1814*. Cambridge, MA: Harvard University Press, 1974.
———. *The Prisoner of Chillon*. In *Lord Byron: The Complete Poetical Works*, edited by Jerome J. McGann, vol. 4, 4–15. Oxford: Clarendon Press, 1986.
Campbell, Charles. *The Intolerable Hulks: British Shipboard Confinement, 1776–1857*. Bowie, MD: Heritage, 1993.
Canuel, Mark. *The Shadow of Death: Literature, Romanticism, and the Subject of Punishment*. Princeton, NJ: Princeton University Press, 2007.
Carey, Hilary M. *Empire of Hell: Religion and the Campaign to End Convict Transportation in the British Empire, 1788–1875*. Cambridge: Cambridge University Press, 2019.
Carlson, Julie. *England's First Family of Writers: Mary Wollstonecraft, William Godwin, Mary Shelley*. Baltimore: Johns Hopkins University Press, 2007.
Carnochan, W. B. *Confinement and Flight: An Essay on English Literature of the Eighteenth Century*. Berkeley: University of California Press, 1977.
———. "The Literature of Confinement." In *The Oxford History of the Prison: The Practice of Punishment in Western Society*, edited by Norval Morris and David J. Rothman, 381–406. Oxford: Oxford University Press, 1998.
Cervantes, Gabriel, and Dahlia Porter. "Extreme Empiricism: John Howard, Poetry, and the Thermometrics of Reform." *The Eighteenth Century* 57, no. 1 (2016): 95–119.
———. "Walking with John Howard: Itineracy and Romantic Reform." *Romanticism* 27, no. 1 (2021): 4–15.
Chandler, Anne. "Romanticizing Adolescence: Godwin's 'St. Leon' and the Matter of Rousseau." *Studies in Romanticism* 41, no. 3 (2002): 399–414.
Chapman, David W. "The Legendary John Howard and Prison Reform in the Eighteenth Century." *The Eighteenth Century* 54, no. 4 (2013): 545–550.
Chatterjee, Anindita. "'I Think I have Been Here Long Enough': John Clare and the Poetry of His Asylum Years." *Rupkatha Journal on Interdisciplinary Studies in Humanities* 3, no. 4 (2011): 425–436.
Chatterjee, Ranita. "Filial Ties: Godwin's *Deloraine* and Mary Shelley's Writings." *European Romantic Review* 18, no. 1 (2007): 29–41.
Chilcott, Tim, *"A Real World & Doubting Mind": A Critical Study of the Poetry of John Clare*. Hull: Hull University Press, 1985.
Clare, John. "Child Harold." In *The Later Poems of John Clare, 1837–1864*, edited by Eric Robinson, David Powell, and Margaret Grainger, vol. 1, 40–88. Oxford: Clarendon Press, 1984.
———. "[I hate the very noise of troublous man]." In *Poems of the Middle Period, 1822–1837*, edited by Eric Robinson, David Powell, and P. M. S. Dawson, vol. 5, 248. Oxford: Clarendon Press, 2003.
———. "[I long to forget them—the love of my life—]." In *The Later Poems of John Clare, 1837–1864*, edited by Eric Robinson, David Powell, and Margaret Grainger, vol. 1, 14–15. Oxford: Clarendon Press, 1984.
———. *The Letters of John Clare*. Edited by Mark Storey. Oxford: Clarendon Press, 1985.
———. "London *versus* Epping Forest." In *The Later Poems of John Clare, 1837–1864*, edited by Eric Robinson, David Powell, and Margaret Grainger, vol. 1, 28. Oxford: Clarendon Press, 1984.
———. "Sighing for Retirement." In *The Later Poems of John Clare, 1837–1864*, edited by Eric Robinson, David Powell, and Margaret Grainger, vol. 1, 19–20. Oxford: Clarendon Press, 1984.

———. "Sonnet: '*I am.*'" In *The Later Poems of John Clare, 1837–1864*, edited by Eric Robinson, David Powell, and Margaret Grainger, vol. 1, 397–398. Oxford: Clarendon Press, 1984.

———. "A Vision." In *The Later Poems of John Clare, 1837–1864*, edited by Eric Robinson, David Powell, and Margaret Grainger, vol. 1, 297. Oxford: Clarendon Press, 1984.

———. "A Walk in the Forest." In *The Later Poems of John Clare, 1837–1864*, edited by Eric Robinson, David Powell, and Margaret Grainger, vol. 1, 24. Oxford: Clarendon Press, 1984.

———. "A Walk on High Beech, Loughton." In *The Later Poems of John Clare, 1837–1864*, edited by Eric Robinson, David Powell, and Margaret Grainger, vol. 1, 27. Oxford: Clarendon Press, 1984.

———. "The Water Lilies." In *The Later Poems of John Clare, 1837–1864*, edited by Eric Robinson, David Powell, and Margaret Grainger, vol. 1, 25–26. Oxford: Clarendon Press, 1984.

Clemit, Pamela. Introduction to *The Letters of William Godwin*, vol. 1, *1778–1797*, xxiii–xlvi. Oxford: Oxford University Press, 2011.

Coleridge, Samuel Taylor. "Children in the Cotton Factories (31 Mar)." In *Essays on His Times*, edited by David Erdman, vol. 2, 484–489. No. 3 of *The Collected Works of Samuel Taylor Coleridge*. Edited by Kathleen Coburn and Bart Winer. Princeton, NJ: Princeton University Press, 2001.

———. "The Devil's Thoughts." In *Poetical Works: Part 1. Poems (Reading Text)*, edited by J. C. C. Mays, 560–567. No. 16 of *The Collected Works of Samuel Taylor Coleridge*, edited by Kathleen Coburn and Bart Winer. Princeton, NJ: Princeton University Press, 2001.

———. "The Dungeon." In *Poetical Works: Part 1. Poems (Reading Text)*, edited by J. C. C. Mays, 333–334. No. 16 of *The Collected Works of Samuel Taylor Coleridge*, edited by Kathleen Coburn and Bart Winer. Princeton, NJ: Princeton University Press, 2001.

———. "Greek Epitaph for Howard's Tomb." In *Poetical Works: Part 1. Poems (Reading Text)*, edited by J. C. C. Mays, 71–72. No. 16 of *The Collected Works of Samuel Taylor Coleridge*. Edited by Kathleen Coburn and Bart Winer. Princeton, NJ: Princeton University Press, 2001.

———. "A Moral and Political Lecture." In *Lectures 1795 on Politics and Religion*, edited by Lewis Patton and Peter Mann, 3–19. No. 1 of *The Collected Works of Samuel Taylor Coleridge*. Edited by Kathleen Coburn and Bart Winer. Princeton, NJ: Princeton University Press, 2001.

———. "On the Present War." In *Lectures 1795 on Politics and Religion*, edited by Lewis Patton and Peter Mann, 51–74. No. 1 of *The Collected Works of Samuel Taylor Coleridge*. Edited by Kathleen Coburn and Bart Winer. Princeton, NJ: Princeton University Press, 2001.

———. "Reflections on Having Left a Place of Retirement." In *Poetical Works: Part 1. Poems (Reading Text)*, edited by J. C. C. Mays, 260–263. No. 16 of *The Collected Works of Samuel Taylor Coleridge*. Edited by Kathleen Coburn and Bart Winer. Princeton, NJ: Princeton University Press, 2001.

———. "Review of Count Rumford's Essays." In *The Watchman*, edited by Lewis Patton, 175–180. No. 2 of *The Collected Works of Samuel Taylor Coleridge*. Edited by Kathleen Coburn and Bart Winer. Princeton, NJ: Princeton University Press, 2001.

———. "The Rime of the Ancient Mariner." 1834. In *Poetical Works: Part 1. Poems (Reading Text)*, edited by J. C. C. Mays, 365–419. No. 16 of *The Collected Works of Samuel Taylor Coleridge*. Edited by Kathleen Coburn and Bart Winer. Princeton, NJ: Princeton University Press, 2001.

———. "The Rime of the Ancyent Marinere." 1798. In *Poetical Works: Part 1. Poems (Reading Text)*, edited by J. C. C. Mays, 365–419. No. 16 of *The Collected Works of Samuel Taylor Coleridge*. Edited by Kathleen Coburn and Bart Winer. Princeton, NJ: Princeton University Press, 2001.

———. "Robert Southey, *History of Brazil*." In *Marginalia: Sherlock to Unidentified*, edited by H. J. Jackson and George Whalley, 101–107. No. 12 of *The Collected Works of Samuel Taylor Coleridge*. Edited by Kathleen Coburn and Bart Winer. Princeton, NJ: Princeton University Press, 2001.

———. "This Lime-Tree Bower My Prison." In *Poetical Works: Part 1. Poems (Reading Text)*, edited by J. C. C. Mays, 349–354. No. 16 of *The Collected Works of Samuel Taylor Coleridge*.

Edited by Kathleen Coburn and Bart Winer. Princeton, NJ: Princeton University Press, 2001.

Coleridge, Sara. Appendix to *Essays on His Own Times, Forming a Second Series of The Friend, by Samuel Taylor Coleridge, Edited by His Daughter*, 1031–1034. London: William Pickering, 1850.

Collett, Cathy. "Every Child Left Behind: *St. Leon* and William Godwin's Immortal Future." *European Romantic Review* 25, no. 3 (2014): 327–336.

Colmer, John. "Coleridge and Politics." In *Writers and Their Background: S. T. Coleridge*, edited by R. L. Brett, 244–270. Athens: Ohio University Press, 1972.

Courtier, Peter. *Pleasures of Solitude. A Poem*. London: T. Gillet, 1800.

Cowden Clarke, Charles, and Mary Cowden Clarke. *Recollections of Writers*. 2nd ed. London: Sampson Low, Marston, Searle and Rivington, 1878.

Cox, Jeffrey N. "Communal Romanticism." *European Romantic Review* 15, no. 2 (2004): 329–334.

Craig, Sheryl. *Jane Austen and the State of the Nation*. Basingstoke, UK: Palgrave Macmillan, 2015.

Crawford, Rachel. "Accident and Strange Calamity in 'This Lime-Tree Bower My Prison.'" *Romanticism* 2, no. 2 (1996): 188–203.

———. *Poetry, Enclosure and the Vernacular Landscape, 1700–1830*. Cambridge: Cambridge University Press, 2002.

Curran, Stuart. *Poetic Form and British Romanticism*. Oxford: Oxford University Press, 1986.

Dart, Gregory. *Metropolitan Art and Literature, 1810–1840: Cockney Adventures*. Cambridge: Cambridge University Press, 2012.

Davie, Donald. *Articulate Energy: An Inquiry into the Syntax of English Poetry*. London: Routledge and Paul, 1955.

Davies, Ioan. *Writers in Prison*. Cambridge, MA: Basil Blackwell, 1990.

Davis, Michael T., Iain McCalman, and Christina Parolin, eds. *Newgate in Revolution: An Anthology of Radical Prison Literature in the Age of Revolution*. London: Continuum, 2005.

Dawes, M[anasseh]. *An Essay on Crimes and Punishments, with a View of, and Commentary upon Beccaria, Rousseau, Voltaire, Montesquieu, Fielding, and Blackstone. In Which Are Contained Treatises . . . of Morality (as the Source of all Good)*. London: C. Dilly; J. Debrett, 1782.

DeLacy, Margaret. *Prison Reform in Lancashire, 1700–1850: A Study in Local Administration*. Stanford, CA: Stanford University Press, 1986.

Denne, Samuel. *Letter to Sir Robert Ladbroke, Knt., Senior Alderman, and One of the Representatives of the City of London: with An Attempt to Shew the Good Effects Which May Reasonably Be Expected from the Confinement of Criminals in Separate Apartments*. London: J. and W. Oliver and J. Rivington, 1771.

Deveraux, Simon. "The Making of the Penitentiary Act, 1775–1779." *The Historical Journal* 42, no. 2 (1999): 405–433.

Deveraux, Simon, and Paul Griffiths. *Penal Practice and Culture, 1500–1900: Punishing the English*. Basingstoke, UK: Palgrave Macmillan, 2004.

Dodd, William. *Thoughts in Prison . . . with Some Account of the Author*. London: J. Mawman; Longman, Hurst, Rees, Orme and Brown; Baldwin, Cradock and Joy; Sherwood, Neely and Jones; Gale, Curtis and Fenner; J. Walker and Co., 1815.

Doody, Margaret. *Jane Austen's Names: Riddles, Persons, Places*. Chicago: University of Chicago Press, 2015.

Duncan, Martha Grace. *Romantic Outlaws, Beloved Prisons: The Unconscious Meanings of Crime and Punishment*. New York: New York University Press, 1996.

Eagleton, Terry. *The English Novel: An Introduction*. Malden, MA: Blackwell, 2005.

East Kent Gaol at Canterbury (Q/AGe). Kent Archives and Local History, Kent History and Library Centre, Maidstone, England.

Eberle-Sinatra, Michael. *Leigh Hunt and the London Literary Scene: A Reception History of His Major Works, 1805–1828*. New York: Routledge, 2005.

Edgecombe, Rodney Stenning. *Leigh Hunt and the Poetry of Fancy*. Madison, NJ: Fairleigh Dickinson University Press, 1994.

Edgerton, Samuel Y. "Heat and Style: Eighteenth-Century House Warming by Stoves." *Journal of the Society of Architectural Historians* 20, no. 1 (1961): 20–26.

Eitner, Lorenz. "Cages, Prisons, and Captives in Eighteenth-Century Art." In *Images of Romanticism: Verbal and Visual Affinities*, edited by Karl Kroeber and William Walling, 13–38. New Haven, CT: Yale University Press, 1978.

Elledge, Paul W. *Byron and the Dynamics of Metaphor*. Nashville: Vanderbilt University Press, 1968.

Engell, James. "Imagining into Nature: 'This Lime-Tree Bower My Prison.'" In *Critical Essays on Samuel Taylor Coleridge*, edited by Leonard Orr, 108–123. New York: G. K. Hall, 1994.

Emsley, Clive. *Crime and Society in England, 1750–1900*. 4th ed. Harlow, UK: Pearson Education, 2010.

Erdman, David. Introduction to *Essays on His Times*, edited by David Erdman, vol. 1, lix–clxxix. No. 3 of *The Collected Works of Samuel Taylor Coleridge*. Edited by Kathleen Coburn and Bart Winer. Princeton, NJ: Princeton University Press, 2001.

Evans, Robin. *The Fabrication of Virtue: English Prison Architecture, 1750–1840*. Cambridge: Cambridge University Press, 1982.

Felperin, Howard. *Shakespearean Romance*. Princeton, NJ: Princeton University Press, 1972.

Fernald, Anne E. "Loneliness and Consolation." *Harvard Review* 12 (1997): 46–52.

Finn, Margot C. *The Character of Credit: Personal Debt in English Culture, 1740–1914*. Cambridge: Cambridge University Press, 2003.

Fisher, George. "The Birth of the Prison Retold." *The Yale Law Journal* 104, no. 6 (1995): 1235–1324.

Fletcher, Loraine. *Charlotte Smith: A Critical Biography*. Basingstoke, UK: Macmillan, 1998.

Follett, Richard R. *Evangelicalism, Penal Theory and the Politics of Criminal Law Reform in England, 1808–30*. Basingstoke, UK: Palgrave, 2001.

Foucault, Michel. *Discipline and Punish: The Birth of the Prison*. Translated by Alan Sheridan. 2nd ed. New York: Vintage, 1995.

Fowler, Thomas. *The Prison: A Poem*. London: Printed for the Author; W. Moore; C. Stalker, 1790.

Frye, Northrup. *Anatomy of Criticism: Four Essays*. 1957. Princeton Classics edition. Princeton, NJ: Princeton University Press, 2020.

———. *The Secular Scripture: A Study of the Structure of Romance*. Cambridge, MA: Harvard University Press, 1976.

Fulford, Tim. "Personating Poets on the Page: John Clare in His Asylum Notebooks." *John Clare Society Journal* 32 (2013): 27–48.

Fullerton, Susannah. *Jane Austen and Crime*. 3rd ed. Madison, WI: Jones Books, 2006.

Furbank, P. N. "Godwin's Novels." *Essays in Criticism* 5, no. 37 (1955): 214–228.

Garber, Frederick. *Self, Text, and Romantic Irony*. Princeton, NJ: Princeton University Press, 1988.

Gilbert, Sandra M., and Susan Gubar. *The Madwoman in the Attic: The Woman Writer and the Nineteenth-Century Literary Imagination*. 1979. Veritas Paperback ed. New Haven, CT: Yale University Press, 2020.

Gleckner, Robert F. *Byron and the Ruins of Paradise*. Baltimore: Johns Hopkins University Press, 1967.

Godwin, William. "Autobiography." In *Autobiography, Autobiographical Fragments and Reflections, Godwin/Shelley Correspondence, Memoirs*, edited by Mark Philp, 3–38. Vol. 1 of *Collected Novels and Memoirs of William Godwin*, edited by Mark Philp. London: William Pickering, 1992.

———. *Caleb Williams*. Edited by Pamela Clemit. Vol. 3 of *Collected Novels and Memoirs of William Godwin*, edited by Mark Philp. London: William Pickering, 1992.

———. *Cloudesley*. Edited by Maurice Hindle. Vol. 7 of *Collected Novels and Memoirs of William Godwin*, edited by Mark Philp. London: William Pickering, 1992.

———. "Considerations on Lord Grenville's and Mr Pitt's Bills, concerning Treasonable and Seditious Practices and Unlawful Assemblies, by a Lover of Order." In *Political Writings II*, edited by Mark Philp and Austen Gee, 123–162. Vol. 2 of *Political and Philosophical Writings of William Godwin*, edited by Mark Philp. London: William Pickering, 1993.

———. *Deloraine*. Edited by Maurice Hindle. Vol. 8 of *Collected Novels and Memoirs of William Godwin*, edited by Mark Philp. London: William Pickering, 1992.

———. *The Diary of William Godwin*. Edited by Victoria Myers, David O'Shaughnessy, and Mark Philp. Oxford: Oxford Digital Library, 2010. http://godwindiary.bodleian.ox.ac.uk.

———. *An Enquiry concerning Political Justice*. Edited by Mark Philp and Austin Gee. Vol. 3 of *Political and Philosophical Writings of William Godwin*, edited by Mark Philp. London: William Pickering, 1993.

———. *An Enquiry concerning Political Justice, Variants*. Edited by Mark Philp. Vol. 4 of *Political and Philosophical Writings of William Godwin*, edited by Mark Philp. London: William Pickering, 1993.

———. "Essay on Sepulchres: Or, a Proposal for Erecting Some Memorial of the Illustrious Dead in All Ages on the Spot Where Their Remains Have Been Interred." In *Essays*, edited by Mark Philp and Austin Gee, 1–30. Vol. 6 of *Political and Philosophical Writings of William Godwin*, edited by Mark Philp. London: William Pickering, 1993.

———. *Fleetwood*. Edited by Pamela Clemit. Vol. 5 of *Collected Novels and Memoirs of William Godwin*, edited by Mark Philp. London: William Pickering, 1992.

———. "Imogen." In *Damon and Delia, Italian Letters and Imogen*, edited by Pamela Clemit, 163–267. Vol. 2 of *Collected Novels and Memoirs of William Godwin*, edited by Mark Philp. London: William Pickering, 1992.

———. *The Letters of William Godwin*. Edited by Pamela Clemit. 2 vols. Oxford: Oxford University Press, 2014.

———. *Mandeville*. Edited by Pamela Clemit. Vol. 6 of *Collected Novels and Memoirs of William Godwin*, edited by Mark Philp. London: William Pickering, 1992.

———. "Of Ballot." In *Essays*, edited by Mark Philp and Austin Gee, 209–217. Vol. 6 of *Political and Philosophical Writings of William Godwin*, edited by Mark Philp. London: William Pickering, 1993.

———. "Of Belief." In *Essays*, edited by Mark Philp and Austin Gee, 172–180. Vol. 6 of *Political and Philosophical Writings of William Godwin*, edited by Mark Philp. London: William Pickering, 1993.

———. "Of Deception and Frankness." In *Educational and Literary Writings*, edited by Pamela Clemit, 124–127. Vol. 5 of *Political and Philosophical Writings of William Godwin*, edited by Mark Philp. London: William Pickering, 1993.

———. "Of Leisure." In *Essays*, edited by Mark Philp and Austin Gee, 129–137. Vol. 6 of *Political and Philosophical Writings of William Godwin*, edited by Mark Philp. London: William Pickering, 1993.

———. "Of Love and Friendship." In *Essays*, edited by Mark Philp and Austin Gee, 187–200. Vol. 6 of *Political and Philosophical Writings of William Godwin*, edited by Mark Philp. London: William Pickering, 1993.

———. *Of Population. An Enquiry concerning the Power of Increase in the Numbers of Mankind, Being an Answer to Mr. Malthus's Essay on that Subject*. In *Political Writings II*, edited by Mark Philp and Austen Gee, 267–296. Vol. 2 of *Political and Philosophical Writings of William Godwin*, edited by Mark Philp. London: William Pickering, 1993.

———. "Of Reasoning and Contention." In *Educational and Literary Writings*, edited by Pamela Clemit, 121–124. Vol. 5 of *Political and Philosophical Writings of William Godwin*, edited by Mark Philp. London: William Pickering, 1993.

———. "Of Religion." In *Religious Writings, with Index to the Political and Philosophical Writings of Godwin*, edited by Mark Philp and Austin Gee, 59–73. Vol. 7 of *Political and*

Philosophical Writings of William Godwin, edited by Mark Philp. London: William Pickering, 1993.
———. "Of the Durability of Human Achievements and Productions." In *Essays*, edited by Mark Philp and Austin Gee, 79–90. Vol. 6 of *Political and Philosophical Writings of William Godwin*, edited by Mark Philp. London: William Pickering, 1993.
———. "Of the Rebelliousness of Man." In *Essays*, edited by Mark Philp and Austin Gee, 91–101. Vol. 6 of *Political and Philosophical Writings of William Godwin*, edited by Mark Philp. London: William Pickering, 1993.
———. "Of Trades and Professions." In *Educational and Literary Writings*, edited by Pamela Clemit, 171–183. Vol. 5 of *Political and Philosophical Writings of William Godwin*, edited by Mark Philp. London: William Pickering, 1993.
———. "On Liberty (Fragment)." In *Religious Writings, with Index to the Political and Philosophical Writings of Godwin*, edited by Mark Philp and Austin Gee, 204–206. Vol. 7 of *Political and Philosophical Writings of William Godwin*, edited by Mark Philp. London: William Pickering, 1993.
———. "On the History and Effects of the Christian Religion." In *Religious Writings, with Index to the Political and Philosophical Writings of Godwin*, edited by Mark Philp, 181–203. Vol. 6 of *Political and Philosophical Writings of William Godwin*, edited by Mark Philp. London: William Pickering, 1993.
———. "Sketches of History. In Six Sermons." In *Religious Writings, with Index to the Political and Philosophical Writings of Godwin*, edited by Mark Philp and Austin Gee, 1–57. Vol. 7 of *Political and Philosophical Writings of William Godwin*, edited by Mark Philp. London: William Pickering, 1993.
———. *St. Leon*. Edited by Pamela Clemit. Vol. 4 of *Collected Novels and Memoirs of William Godwin*, edited by Mark Philp. London: William Pickering, 1992.
Goggans, Thomas. "Deferred Desire and the Management of Tone in Leigh Hunt's 'The Story of Rimini.'" *Keats-Shelley Journal* 50 (2001): 84–99.
Graham, Peter W. "Byron and Prisoners: Politics, Poetry, and Myth." In *Essays on Byron in Honour of Dr Peter Cochran: Breaking the Mould*, edited by Malcom Kelsall, Peter Graham, and Mirka Horová, 78–90. Newcastle upon Tyne: Cambridge Scholars Publishing, 2018.
Granata, Silvia. "Poisonous Language: Mental Slavery and Self-Recognition in Godwin's *Mandeville*." *Confronto Letterario: Quaderni del Dipartimento di lingue e Letterature Straniere Moderne dell'Università di Pavia* 26, no. 51 (2009): 81–102.
Grass, Sean. *The Self in the Cell: Narrating the Victorian Prisoner*. New York: Routledge, 2003.
Griffiths, Arthur. *Memorials of Millbank and Chapters in Prison History*. London: Chapman and Hall, 1884.
Gurney, Joseph John. *Notes on a Visit Made to Some of the Prisons in Scotland and the North of England, in Company with Elizabeth Fry; with Some General Observations on the Subject of Prison Discipline*. London: Archibald Constable; Longman, Hurst, Rees, Orme and Brown; Hurst, Robinson, 1819.
Hall, Jean. "The Evolution of the Surface Self: Byron's Poetic Career." *Keats-Shelley Journal* 36 (1987): 134–157.
Hanway, Jonas. *Distributive Justice and Mercy: Shewing, That a Temporary Real Solitary Imprisonment of Convicts, Supported by Religious Instruction, and Well-Regulated Labour, Is Essential to Their Well-Being, and the Safety, Honour, and Reputation of the People*. London: J. Dodsley, 1781.
———. *The Neglect of the Effectual Separation of Prisoners, and the Want of Good Order and Religious Decorum in Our Prisons . . . in Fifteen Letters*. London: Dodsley; Sewell; Bew, 1784.
———. *Solitude in Imprisonment . . . and Freedom from Violence*. London: J. Bew, 1776.
Harding, Christopher, Bill Hines, Richard Ireland, and Philip Rawlings. *Imprisonment in England and Wales: A Concise History*. Dover, NH: Croom Helm, 1985.
Haslam, Jason, and Julia M. Wright, eds. *Captivating Subjects: Writing Confinement, Citizenship, and Nationhood in the Nineteenth Century*. Toronto: University of Toronto Press, 2005.

Hay, Daisy. "Adventures of an Unromantic Biographer." *Life Writing* 14, no. 2 (2017): 247–256.

Henriques, U.R.Q. "The Rise and Decline of the Separate System of Prison Discipline." *Past and Present* 54 (1972): 61–93.

Hessell, Nikki. "Jailhouse Journalism: Leigh Hunt and the 'Examiner,' 1813–1815." *Keats-Shelley Journal* 54 (2005): 72–92.

Holcroft, Thomas [as T. Strickland]. *A Plain and Succinct Narrative of the Late Riots and Disturbances in the Cities of London and Westminster, and Borough of Southwark. . . . with an Account of the Commitment of Lord George Gordon to the Tower, and Anecdotes of His Life.* 3rd ed. London: Fielding and Walker, 1780.

Holden, Anthony. *The Wit in the Dungeon: The Remarkable Life of Leigh Hunt—Poet, Revolutionary, and the Last of the Romantics.* New York: Little, Brown, 2005.

Holford, George. "Prefatory Remarks." In *The Convict's Complaint in 1815, and the Thanks of the Convict in 1825; Or, Sketches in Verse of a Hulk in the Former Year, and of the Millbank Penitentiary in the Latter*, v–xiv. London: Rivingtons; Hachard, 1825.

Holford, George, et al. "Reports from the Committee on the Laws Relating to Penitentiary Houses." *The Literary Panorama, Being a Compendium of National Papers and Parliamentary Reports . . . Forming an Annual Register*, vol. XI, 193–206. London: C. Taylor, 1812.

Hone, J. Ann. *For the Cause of Truth: Radicalism in London, 1796–1821.* Oxford: Clarendon Press, 1982.

Howard, John. *An Account of the Principle Lazarettos in Europe . . . and Additional Remarks on the Present State of Those in Great Britain and Ireland.* 2nd ed. London: J. Johnson, C. Dilly and T. Cadell, 1791.

———. *The State of the Prisons in England and Wales, with Preliminary Observations, and an Account of Some Foreign Prisons and Hospitals.* 3rd ed. London: T. Cadell, J. Johnson and C. Dilly, 1784.

Hunt, Leigh. *The Autobiography of Leigh Hunt.* Edited by J. E. Morpurgo. London: The Cresset Press, 1948.

———. *The Correspondence of Leigh Hunt. Edited by His Eldest Son. With a Portrait. In Two Volumes.* Edited by Thornton Hunt. Vol. 1. London: Smith, Elder and Co., 1862.

———. "Departure of the Proprietors of This Paper from Prison." *Examiner*, no. 361, February 5, 1815, 81. *British Newspaper Archive*, http://www.britishnewspaperarchive.co.uk.

———. *The Descent of Liberty.* In *Poetical Works, 1801–21*, edited by John Strachan, 83–122. Vol. 5 of *The Selected Writings of Leigh Hunt*, edited by Robert Morrison and Michael Eberle-Sinatra. London: Pickering and Chatto, 2003.

———. "Expiration of the First Year's Imprisonment of the Proprietors." *Examiner*, no. 310, February 6, 1814, 81–82. *British Newspaper Archive*, http://www.britishnewspaperarchive.co.uk.

———. *The Feast of the Poets.* In *Poetical Works, 1801–21*, edited by John Strachan, 27–81. Vol. 5 of *The Selected Writings of Leigh Hunt*, edited by Robert Morrison and Michael Eberle-Sinatra. London: Pickering and Chatto, 2003.

———. *Leigh Hunt: A Life in Letters, Together with Some Correspondence of William Hazlitt.* Edited by Eleanor M. Gates. Essex, CT: Falls River Publications, 1999.

———. "New Prospectus of *The Examiner.*" *Examiner*, no. 365, December 25, 1814, 819–820. *British Newspaper Archive*, http://www.britishnewspaperarchive.co.uk.

———. "Postscript." In *Periodical Essays, 1805–14*, edited by Greg Kucich and Jeffrey N. Cox, 307. Vol. 1 of *The Selected Writings of Leigh Hunt*, edited by Robert Morrison and Michael Eberle-Sinatra. London: Pickering and Chatto, 2003.

———. "Prince and Princess of Wales." *Examiner*, no. 272, March 14, 1813, 161–163. *British Newspaper Archive*, http://www.britishnewspaperarchive.co.uk.

———. "The Prince and Princess of Wales." *Examiner*, no. 271, March 7, 1813, 145–147. *British Newspaper Archive*, http://www.britishnewspaperarchive.co.uk.

———. "The Prince on St. Patrick's Day." *Examiner*, no. 221, March 22, 1812, 177–180. *British Newspaper Archive*, http://www.britishnewspaperarchive.co.uk.

———. "The Round Table, No. 1." *Examiner*, no. 366, January 1, 1815, 11–13. *British Newspaper Archive*, http://www.britishnewspaperarchive.co.uk.

———. "Sentence Against the Examiner, and Summary of Objections to the Whole of the Proceedings Connected with It (*Concluded*.)." *Examiner*, no. 270, February 28, 1813, 129–130. *British Newspaper Archive*, http://www.britishnewspaperarchive.co.uk.

———. "Sentence Against the Examiner (*Continued from last week's*)." *Examiner*, no. 268, February 14, 1813, 97–99. *British Newspaper Archive*, http://www.britishnewspaperarchive.co.uk.

———. "Sentence Against the Examiner, with an Observation or Two on Some Proposals of a Subscription." *Examiner*, no. 269, February 21, 1813, 113–114. *British Newspaper Archive*, http://www.britishnewspaperarchive.co.uk.

———. *The Story of Rimini*. In *Poetical Works, 1801–21*, edited by John Strachan, 161–206. Vol. 5 of *The Selected Writings of Leigh Hunt*, edited by Robert Morrison and Michael Eberle-Sinatra. London: Pickering and Chatto, 2003.

———. "Upon the Necessity of a Reform in the Criminal Law of England." *Examiner*, no. 22, May 29, 1808, 337–338. *British Newspaper Archive*, http://www.britishnewspaperarchive.co.uk.

Ignatieff, Michael. *A Just Measure of Pain: The Penitentiary in the Industrial Revolution, 1750–1850*. London: Penguin, 1978.

———. "State, Civil Society and Total Institutions: A Critique of Recent Social Histories of Punishment." In *Legality, Ideology and the State*, edited by David Sugarman, 183–211. London: Academic Press, 1983.

Inchbald, Elizabeth. *Such Things Are; A Play, in Five Acts. As Performed at the Theatre Royal, Covent Garden*. 2nd ed. London: G. G. J. and J. Robinson, 1788.

James, Felicity. "Agreement, Dissonance, Dissent: The Many Conversations of 'This Lime-Tree Bower.'" *The Coleridge Bulletin* 26 (2005): 37–57.

Jebb, John. *Thoughts on the Construction and Polity of Prisons, with Hints for Their Improvement*. Edited by Capel Lofft. Bury St Edmund's, UK: J. Rackham, 1785.

J. F. "Prison Discipline." *Examiner*, no. 717, September 30, 1821, 620–621. *British Newspaper Archive*, http://www.britishnewspaperarchive.co.uk.

Johnson, Claudia. *Jane Austen: Women, Politics and the Novel*. Chicago: University of Chicago Press, 1988.

Johnston, Helen. "Architecture and Contested Space in the Development of the Modern Prison." In *Architecture and Justice: Judicial Meanings in the Public Realm*, edited by Jonathan Simon, Nicholas Temple, and Renée Tobe, 23–35. Farnham, UK: Ashgate, 2013.

Kalman, Harold D. "Newgate Prison." *Architectural History* 12 (1969): 50–61, 108–112.

Kamen, Henry. *The Spanish Inquisition: A Historical Revision*. 4th ed. New Haven, CT: Yale University Press, 2014.

Kaufman, Amy S. "'For This Was Drawyn by a Knyght Presoner': Sir Thomas Malory and *Le Morte Darthur*." In *Prison Narratives from Boethius to Zana*, edited by P. Phillips, 35–55. New York: Palgrave Macmillan, 2014.

Keats, John. *Endymion*. In *John Keats: Complete Poems*, edited by Jack Stillinger, 64–162. Cambridge, MA: Harvard University Press, 1982.

———. *Lamia*. In *John Keats: Complete Poems*, edited by Jack Stillinger, 342–359. Cambridge, MA: Harvard University Press, 1982.

———. *The Letters of John Keats*. Edited by Hyder Edward Rollins. 2 vols. Cambridge, MA: Harvard University Press, 1958.

———. "Ode on Melancholy." In *John Keats: Complete Poems*, edited by Jack Stillinger, 283–284. Cambridge, MA: Harvard University Press, 1982.

———. "Ode to a Nightingale." In *John Keats: Complete Poems*, edited by Jack Stillinger, 279–281. Cambridge, MA: Harvard University Press, 1982.

———. "Ode to Psyche." In *John Keats: Complete Poems*, edited by Jack Stillinger, 275–277. Cambridge, MA: Harvard University Press, 1982.

———. "What Can I Do to Drive Away." In *John Keats: Complete Poems*, edited by Jack Stillinger, 374–376. Cambridge, MA: Harvard University Press, 1982.

———. "Written on the Day That Mr. Leigh Hunt Left Prison." In *John Keats: Complete Poems*, edited by Jack Stillinger, 6. Cambridge, MA: Harvard University Press, 1982.

Kelly, Gary. Introduction to *Newgate Documents*, ix–ciii. Vol. 1 of *Newgate Narratives*, edited by Gary Kelly. London: Pickering and Chatto, 2008.

———. *The English Jacobin Novel, 1780–1805*. Oxford: Clarendon Press, 1976.

Kelsall, Malcom. "Byron's Politics." In *The Cambridge Companion to Byron*, edited by Drummond Bone, 44–55. Cambridge: Cambridge University Press, 2006.

Kitson, Peter J. "Coleridge's Lectures 1795: On Politics and Religion." In *The Oxford Handbook of Samuel Taylor Coleridge*. Online ed. Oxford: Oxford Academic, 2009.

Kroeber, Karl. *Romantic Narrative Art*. Madison: University of Wisconsin Press, 1960.

Kucich, Greg. "Cockney Chivalry: Hunt, Keats and the Aesthetics of Excess." In *Leigh Hunt: Life, Poetics, Politics*, edited by Nicholas Roe, 118–133. London: Routledge, 2003.

———. "Leigh Hunt and Romantic Spenserianism." *Keats-Shelley Journal* 37 (1988): 110–135.

———. "'The wit in the dungeon': Leigh Hunt and the Insolent Politics of Cockney Coteries." *European Romantic Review* 10, nos. 1–4 (1999): 242–253.

Labbe, Jacqueline. *Romantic Visualities: Landscape, Gender and Romanticism*. New York: Palgrave Macmillan, 1998.

Lawrence, C. H. *Medieval Monasticism: Forms of Religious Life in Western Europe in the Middle Ages*. 2nd ed. London: Longman, 1989.

Le Faye, Deirdre. *A Chronology of Jane Austen and Her Family, 1600–2000*. 2nd ed. Cambridge: Cambridge University Press, 2013.

———. *Jane Austen: A Family Record*. 2nd ed. Cambridge: Cambridge University Press, 2004.

LeGette, Casie. "The Lyric Speaker Goes to Gaol: British Poetry and Radical Prisoners, 1820–1845." *Nineteenth-Century Literature* 67, no. 1 (2012): 1–28.

Lévy, Ellen. "The Philosophical Gothic of *St Leon*." *Caliban* 33 (1996): 51–62.

Lloyd, Thomas. "Impositions and Abuses in the Management of the Jail of Newgate; Pointed Out and Exposed, in a Letter Addressed to the Late Grand Juries of the City of London and County of Middlesex." In *Newgate in Revolution: An Anthology of Radical Prison Literature in the Age of Revolution*, edited by Michael T. Davis, Iain McCalman, and Christina Parolin, 67–80. London: Continuum, 2005.

Lofft, Capel. "Prefatory Address." In *Thoughts on the Construction and Polity of Prisons, with Hints for their Improvement*, by John Jebb, iii–xi. Bury St Edmund's, UK: J. Rackham, 1785.

Malthus, Thomas. *An Essay on the Principle of Population*. Edited by Geoffrey Gilbert. Oxford: Oxford University Press, 1993.

Manogue, Ralph A. "The Plight of James Ridgway, London Bookseller and Publisher, and the Newgate Radicals, 1792–1797." *The Wordsworth Circle* 27, no. 3 (1996): 158–166.

Marshall, Peter. *William Godwin: Philosopher, Novelist, Revolutionary*. Oakland, CA: PM Press, 2017.

Marshall, William H. *The Structure of Byron's Major Poems*. Philadelphia: University of Pennsylvania Press, 1962.

Mays, J. C. C., ed. *Poetical Works II: Poems (Variorum Text)*, by Samuel Taylor Coleridge. No. 16 of *The Collected Works of Samuel Taylor Coleridge*, edited by Kathleen Coburn and Bart Winer. Princeton, NJ: Princeton University Press, 2001.

McCalman, Iain. "Newgate in Revolution: Radical Enthusiasm and Romantic Counterculture." *Eighteenth-Century Life* 22, no. 1 (1998): 95–110.

McConville, Seán. *A History of English Prison Administration*. London: Routledge, 1981.

McGann, Jerome. *Fiery Dust: Byron's Poetic Development*. Chicago: University of Chicago Press, 1968.

———, ed. *Lord Byron: The Complete Poetical Works*. Vol. 4. Oxford: Clarendon Press, 1986.

———. *The Romantic Ideology: A Critical Investigation*. Chicago: University of Chicago Press, 1983.

McGowen, Randall. "'He Beareth the Sword in Vain': Religion and the Criminal Law in Eighteenth-Century England." *Eighteenth-Century Studies* 21, no. 2 (1987–1988): 192–211.

———. "The Problem of Punishment in Eighteenth-Century England." In *Penal Practice and Culture, 1500–1900: Punishing the English*, edited by Simon Deveraux and Paul Griffiths, 210–231. Basingstoke, UK: Palgrave Macmillan, 2004.

———. "The Well-Ordered Prison: England, 1780–1865." In *The Oxford History of the Prison: The Practice of Punishment in Western Society*, edited by Norval Morris and David J. Rothman, 71–99. Oxford: Oxford University Press, 1998.

McLynn, Frank. *Crime and Punishment in Eighteenth-Century England*. Oxford: Routledge, 1989.

Mee, Jon. "Treason, Seditious Libel, and Literature in the Romantic Period." In *Oxford Handbook Topics in Literature*. Online ed. Oxford: Oxford Academic, 2016. http://doi.org/10.1093/oxfordhb/9780199935338.013.113.

Mellor, Anne Kostelanetz. "Were Women Writers 'Romantics'?" *Modern Language Quarterly* 62, no. 4 (2001): 395–405.

Middleton Murray, John. *Studies in Keats*. New York: Haskell, 1972.

Milton, John. *A Mask Presented at Ludlow Castle, 1634 . . . Honorable Privy Council*. In *John Milton, Complete Poems and Major Prose*, edited by Merritt Y. Hughes, 86–114. Indianapolis: Hackett, 2003.

———. *Paradise Lost*. In *John Milton, Complete Poems and Major Prose*, edited by Merritt Y. Hughes, 173–469. Indianapolis: Hackett, 2003.

Minor, Mark. "Clare, Byron, and the Bible: Additional Evidence from the Asylum Manuscripts." *Bulletin of Research in the Humanities* 85, no. 1 (1982): 104–126.

Mizukoshi, Ayumi. *Keats, Hunt and the Aesthetics of Pleasure*. Basingstoke, UK: Palgrave Macmillan, 2001.

Mooneyham White, Laura. *Jane Austen's Anglicanism*. Burlington, VT: Ashgate, 2011.

Morris, Norval, and David J. Rothman, eds. *The Oxford History of the Prison: The Practice of Punishment in Western Society*. Oxford: Oxford University Press, 1998.

Morrison, Robert, and Michael Eberle-Sinatra. Introduction to *Periodical Essays, 1805–14*, edited by Greg Kucich and Jeffrey N. Cox, xi–xix. Vol. 1 of *The Selected Writings of Leigh Hunt*, edited by Robert Morrison and Michael Eberle-Sinatra. London: Pickering and Chatto, 2003.

Mücke, Dorothea von. "'To Love a Murderer'—Fantasy, Sexuality, and the Political Novel: The Case of *Caleb Williams*." In *Cultural Institutions of the Novel*, edited by Deidre Lynch and William B. Warner, 306–334. Durham, NC: Duke University Press, 1996.

Murphy, Michael. "John Thelwall, Coleridge, and *The Ancient Mariner*." *Romanticism* 8, no. 1 (2002): 62–74.

Myers, Mary Anne. "Keats and the Hands of Petrarch and Laura." *Keats-Shelley Journal* 62 (2013): 99–113.

Neild, James. *State of the Prisons in England, Scotland, and Wales . . . to Explain and Improve the Condition of Prisoners in General*. London: John Nichols and Son, 1812.

Newey, Vincent. "Byron's 'Prisoner of Chillon': The Poetry of Being and the Poetry of Belief." *Keats-Shelley Memorial Bulletin, Rome* 35 (1984): 54–70.

Newlyn, Lucy. *Coleridge, Wordsworth, and the Language of Allusion*. Oxford: Clarendon Press, 1986.

Nicolazzo, Sal. *Vagrant Figures: Law, Literature, and the Origins of the Police*. New Haven, CT: Yale University Press, 2020.

O'Neill, Michael. "'Even now while I write': Leigh Hunt and Romantic Spontaneity." In *Leigh Hunt: Life, Poetics, Politics*, edited by Nicholas Roe, 135–155. London: Routledge, 2003.

———. "Poetry of the Romantic Period: Coleridge and Keats." In *A Companion to Romance: From Classical to Contemporary*, edited by Corinne Saunders, 205–220. Malden, MA: Blackwell Press, 2007.

Park, Julie. "The Poetics of Enclosure in *Sense and Sensibility*." *Studies in Eighteenth-Century Culture* 42 (2013): 237–269.

Parker, Reeve. *Coleridge's Meditative Art*. Ithaca, NY: Cornell University Press, 1975.

Parolin, Christina. *Radical Spaces: Venues of Popular Politics in London, 1790-c. 1845*. Acton, Australia: ANU Press, 2010.

Paul, Lissa. *Eliza Fenwick: Early Modern Feminist*. Newark: University of Delaware Press, 2019.

Pearce, Lynn. "John Clare's 'Child Harold': A Polyphonic Reading." *Criticism* 31, no. 2 (1989): 139–157.

Perkins, David. *The Quest for Permanence: The Symbolism of Wordsworth, Shelley, and Keats*. Cambridge, MA: Harvard University Press, 1959.

Petrarch. *The Canzoniere*, or *Rerum bulgarium fragmenta*. Translated and edited by Mark Musa. Bloomington: Indiana University Press, 1996.

Philips, David. "'A Just Measure of Crime, Authority, Hunters and Blue Locusts': The 'Revisionist' Social History of Crime and the Law in Britain, 1780–1850." In *Social Control and the State*, edited by Stanley Cohen and Andrew Scull, 50–74. New York: St. Martin's Press, 1983.

Phillips, Philip Edward, ed. *Prison Narratives from Boethius to Zana*. New York: Palgrave Macmillan, 2014.

Pickering, Danby, ed. *The Statutes at Large, from Magna Charta to the End of the Eleventh Parliament of Great Britain, Anno 1761, Continued*. Vol. 32. London: Charles Bathurst, 1778.

Porter, Roy. "'All madness for writing': John Clare and the Asylum." In *John Clare in Context*, edited by Hugh Haughton, Adam Phillips, and Geoffrey Summerfield, 259–278. Cambridge: Cambridge University Press, 1994.

Pratt, Lynda. "Interaction, Reorientation, and Discontent in the Coleridge-Southey Circle, 1797: Two New Letters by Robert Southey." *Notes and Queries* 47, no. 3 (2000): 314–321.

Radzinowicz, Leon. *The Movement for Reform*. Vol. 1 of *A History of English Criminal Law and Its Administration from 1750*. 1948. Reprint. London: Stevens and Sons, 1969.

Raiger, Michael. "The Poetics of Liberation in Imaginative Power: Coleridge's 'This Lime Tree Bower My Prison.'" *European Romantic Review* 3, no. 1 (1992): 65–78.

Robinson, Jeffrey C. *The Current of Romantic Passion*. Madison: University of Wisconsin Press, 1991.

Roe, Nicholas. *Fiery Heart: The First Life of Leigh Hunt*. London: Pimlico, 2005.

———. "Leigh Hunt: Some Early Matters." In *Leigh Hunt: Life, Poetics, Politics*, 19–31. London: Routledge, 2003.

———. Preface to *Fiery Heart: The First Life of Leigh Hunt*, xiii–xvi. London: Pimlico, 2005.

Rose, Richard, ed. "Appendix A: Prisoner of War Hulks at Portsmouth." In *The Floating Prison: The Remarkable Account of Nine Years' Captivity on the British Prison Hulks during the Napoleonic Wars, 1806 to 1814*, by Louis Garneray, 232–233. London: Conway Maritime Press, 2003.

Roth, Norman. *Conversos, Inquisition, and the Expulsion of the Jews from Spain*. Madison: University of Wisconsin Press, 2002.

Rousseau, Jean-Jacques. *The Confessions, and Correspondence, Including the Letters to Malesherbes*. Translated by Christopher Kelly. Edited by Christopher Kelly, Roger D. Masters, and Peter G. Stillman. Vol. 5 of *The Collected Writings of Rousseau*, edited by Christopher Kelly, Roger D. Masters, and Peter G. Stillman. Hanover, NH: University Press of New England, 1995.

Russell, Gillian, and Clara Tuite, eds. *Romantic Sociability: Social Networks and Literary Culture in Britain, 1770–1840*. Cambridge: Cambridge University Press, 2002.

Rutherford, Andrew. *Byron: A Critical Study*. Stanford, CA: Stanford University Press, 1961.

Rzepka, Charles J. "Thoughts in Prison/Imprisoned Thoughts: William Dodd's Forgotten Poem and the Incarceration Trope of Coleridge's 'This Lime-Tree Bower My Prison.'" *Romantic Circles*, October 2010. https://romantic-circles.org/editions/prison/HTML/poetryEEd.28intro.html.

Sales, Roger. *John Clare: A Literary Life*. New York: Palgrave, 2002.
Scheffler, Judith. "Romantic Women Writing on Imprisonment and Prison Reform." *The Wordsworth Circle* 19, no. 2 (1988): 99–103.
Scheuermann, Mona. "The Study of Mind: The Later Novels of William Godwin." *Forum for Modern Language Studies* 19, no. 1 (1983): 16–30.
Schwan, Anne. *Convict Voices: Women, Class, and Writing about Prison in Nineteenth-Century England*. Durham, NH: University of New Hampshire Press, 2014.
Scourfield, J. H. D. "Consolation." In *The Oxford Classical Dictionary*, revised 3rd ed., edited by Simon Hornblower and Antony Spawforth, 378. Oxford: Oxford University Press, 2003.
Seffers, Tracy Prior. "'A Bowery Nook Will Be Elysium': The Image of the Bower in the Poetry of John Keats." PhD diss., The College of William and Mary, 1993.
Semple, Janet. *Bentham's Prison: A Study of the Panopticon Penitentiary*. Oxford: Clarendon Press, 1993.
Shakespeare, William. *King Lear*. In *The Riverside Shakespeare*, edited by G. Blakemore Evans et al., 2nd ed., 1297–1354. Boston: Houghton Mifflin, 1997.
Shanafelt, Carrie D. *Uncommon Sense: Jeremy Bentham, Queer Aesthetics, and the Politics of Taste*. Charlottesville: University of Virginia Press, 2022.
Sharpe, J. A. *Crime in Early Modern England, 1550–1750*. London: Longman, 1984.
Sheehan, W. J. "Finding Solace in Eighteenth-Century Newgate." In *Crime in England, 1550–1800*, edited by J. S. Cockburn, 229–245. London: Methuen, 1977.
Short, Clarice. "The Composition of Hunt's 'The Story of Rimini.'" *Keats-Shelley Journal* 21/22 (1972/1973): 207–218.
Sidney, Philip. *The Old Arcadia*. Edited by Catherine Duncan-Jones. Oxford: Oxford University Press, 2008.
Slethaug, Gordon E. "Patterns of Imagery in 'The Prisoner of Chillon.'" *Queen's Quarterly* 78 (1971): 449–455.
Snodgrass, Mary Ellen. *Encyclopedia of Gothic Literature: The Essential Guide to the Lives and Works of Gothic Writers*. New York: Facts on File, 2005.
Southey, Robert. *The Collected Letters of Robert Southey*. Edited by Lynda Pratt, Tim Fulford, Ian Packer, Nicholas Roe, Susan J. Wolfson, and Duncan Wu. *Romantic Circles*, March 2009. https://romantic-circles.org/editions/southey_letters.
Stabler, Jane. "Leigh Hunt's Aesthetics of Intimacy." In *Leigh Hunt: Life, Poetics, Politics*, edited by Nicholas Roe, 95–117. London: Routledge, 2003.
Stafford, Fiona J. *The Last of the Race: The Growth of a Myth from Milton to Darwin*. Oxford: Clarendon Press, 1994.
St. Clair, William. *The Godwins and the Shelleys: The Biography of a Family*. Baltimore: Johns Hopkins University Press, 1989.
Stewart, David. *Romantic Magazines and Metropolitan Literary Culture*. New York: Palgrave Macmillan, 2011.
Stockdale, Eric. *A Study of Bedford Prison, 1660–1877*. London: Phillimore, 1977.
Storey, Edward. *A Right to Song: The Life of John Clare*. London: Methuen, 1982.
Storey, Mark. *John Clare: The Critical Heritage*. New York: Routledge, 1996.
———, ed. *The Letters of John Clare*. Oxford: Clarendon Press, 1985.
———. *The Poetry of John Clare: A Critical Introduction*. London: Macmillan, 1974.
Stuart, Daniel. "The Abuse of Prisons." In *Essays on His Times*, edited by David Erdman, vol. 2, 109–110. No. 3 of *The Collected Works of Samuel Taylor Coleridge*, edited by Kathleen Coburn and Bart Winer. Princeton, NJ: Princeton University Press, 2001.
Thismiames. "Penitentiary House." *Examiner*, no. 131, July 1, 1810, 407–408. *British Newspaper Archive*, http://www.britishnewspaperarchive.co.uk.
Thompson, James. *Leigh Hunt*. Boston: G. K. Hall & Co., 1977.
Thompson, Judith. "An Autumnal Blast, a Killing Frost: Coleridge's Poetic Conversation with John Thelwall." *Studies in Romanticism* 36, no. 3 (1997): 427–456.

Throness, Laurie. *A Protestant Purgatory: Theological Origins of the Penitentiary Act, 1779.* Aldershot, UK: Ashgate, 2008.

Tibble, J. W., and Anne Tibble. *John Clare: A Life.* 1932. Revised ed. London: Michael Joseph, 1972.

Todd, Janet, and Antje Blank. Introduction to *Persuasion*, by Jane Austen, xxi–lxxxii. Cambridge: Cambridge University Press, 2006.

Trenck, Frederick Freiherr von der. *The Strange Adventures of Frederick Baron Trenck.* Edited by Philip Murray. New York: Frederick A. Stokes, 1927.

Trilling, Lionel. "*Mansfield Park.*" In *The Moral Obligation to Be Intelligent: Selected Essays*, edited by Leon Wieseltier, 292–310. Evanston, IL: Northwestern University Press, 2000.

Tysdahl, B. J. *William Godwin as Novelist.* London: Althone Press, 1981.

Ulmer, William A. "The Rhetorical Occasion of 'This Lime-Tree Bower My Prison.'" *Romanticism* 13, no. 1 (2007): 15–27.

Van Ghent, Dorothy. "Keats's Myth of the Hero." *Keats-Shelley Journal* 3 (1954): 7–25.

Vendler, Helen. *The Odes of John Keats.* Cambridge, MA: Belknap Press, 1983.

Wade, Stephen. *Jane Austen's Aunt behind Bars: Writers and Their Criminal Relatives and Associates, 1700–1900.* London: Thames Rivers Press, 2013.

Ward, Aileen. "Romantic Castles and Real Prisons: Wordsworth, Blake, and Revolution." *The Wordsworth Circle* 30, no. 1 (1999): 3–15.

Watt, Ian. *The Rise of the Novel: Studies in Defoe, Richardson and Fielding.* Berkeley: University of California Press, 1957.

Webb, Sidney, and Beatrice Webb. *English Prisons under Local Government.* 1922. Reprint. Hamden, CT: Archon Books, 1963.

Webb, Timothy. "After Horsemonger Lane: Leigh Hunt's London Letters to Byron (1815–1816)." *Romanticism* 16, no. 3 (2010): 233–266.

———. "Stories of Rimini: Leigh Hunt, Byron and the Fate of Francesca." In *Dante in the Nineteenth Century: Reception, Canonicity, Popularization*, edited by Nick Havely, 31–53. Bern, Switzerland: Peter Lang, 2011.

West, Tessa. *The Curious Mr Howard, Legendary Prison Reformer.* Hook, UK: Waterside Press, 2011.

Weston, Rowland. "Politics, Passion and the 'Puritan Temper': Godwin's Critique of Enlightened Modernity." *Studies in Romanticism* 41, no. 3 (2002): 445–470.

Wheeler, K. M. *The Creative Mind in Coleridge's Poetry.* Cambridge, MA: Harvard University Press, 1981.

Whiting, J. R. S. *Prison Reform in Gloucestershire, 1776–1820: A Study of the Work of Sir George Onesiphorus Paul, Bart.* London: Phillimore, 1975.

Wilson, David. "Millbank, The Panopticon and Their Victorian Audiences." *The Howard Journal* 41, no. 4 (2002): 364–381.

Wiltshire, John. Introduction to *Mansfield Park*, by Jane Austen, xxv–lxxxiii. Cambridge: Cambridge University Press, 2005.

Wolfson, Susan J. *Reading John Keats.* Cambridge: Cambridge University Press, 2015.

Woolf, Virginia. *The Diary of Virginia Woolf.* Edited by Anne Olivier Bell and Andrew McNellie. 1st Harvest ed. Vol. 2, *1920–1924.* Orlando: Harcourt, Brace, 1980.

Wordsworth, William. "Lines Written a Few Miles above Tintern Abbey, on Revisiting the Banks of the Wye during a Tour, July 13, 1798." In *Lyrical Ballads, and Other Poems, 1797–1800*, edited by James Butler and Karen Green, 116–120. Ithaca, NY: Cornell University Press, 1992.

———. "Preface to *Lyrical Ballads*, 1800." In *Lyrical Ballads, and Other Poems, 1797–1800*, edited by James Butler and Karen Green, 741–765. Ithaca, NY: Cornell University Press, 1992.

Wunder, Jennifer N. *Keats, Hermeticism, and the Secret Societies.* London: Routledge, 2008.

Zim, Rivkah. *The Consolations of Writing: Literary Strategies of Resistance from Boethius to Primo Levi.* Princeton, NJ: Princeton University Press, 2014.

Zimmermann, Johann Georg. *On Solitude. Or the Effects of Occasional Retirement on the Mind, the Heart, General Society, in Exile, in Old Age, and on the Bed of Death. In Which the Question is Considered Whether It is Easier to Live Virtuously in Society, or in Solitude.* London: Vernor and Hood; J. Cuthell; J. Walker; Lackington, Allen and Co.; J. Nunn, Ogilvy and Son; Darton and Harvey; W. Otridge and Son; R. Lea, 1798.

INDEX

ABOUT THE AUTHOR

JONAS COPE is an associate professor of English at the California State University, Sacramento. He has published books, articles, and reviews on a variety of topics related to British Romantic literature and culture, including Landon studies, Shelley studies, Clare studies, Irish Romanticism, affect theory, and women and Romanticism. His work appears in such journals as *Studies in Romanticism*, *Romanticism*, the *Keats-Shelley Journal*, and *Studies in English Literature, 1500–1900.*